24 (9-92) 0

GOING BACK TO BISBEE

GOING BACK
❖ ❖ TO BISBEE

RICHARD SHELTON

THE UNIVERSITY OF ARIZONA

PRESS   TUCSON & LONDON

The University of Arizona Press
Copyright © 1992
Arizona Board of Regents
All Rights Reserved
⊗ This book is printed on acid-free, archival-quality paper.
Manufactured in the United States of America.

97 96 95 94 93 92 6 5 4 3 2 1

LIBRARY OF CONGRESS CATALOGING-IN-PUBLICATION DATA
Shelton, Richard, 1933–
    Going back to Bisbee / Richard Shelton.
        p.   cm.
    Includes bibliographical references.
    ISBN 0-8165-1302-3 (CL : acid-free, archival-quality paper) —
ISBN 0-8165-1289-2 (PBK : acid-free, archival-quality paper)
        1. Arizona—Description and travel—1981–   2. Arizona—History,
Local.   3. Natural history—Arizona.   4. Desert ecology—Arizona.
5. Shelton, Richard, 1933–   —Journeys—Arizona.   6. Bisbee (Ariz.)
I. Title.
F815.S54   1992   91-41131
979.1—dc20   CIP

British Library Cataloguing-in-Publication Data
A catalogue record for this book is available from the British Library.

The Western States Book Awards are a project of the Western States
Arts Federation. The awards are supported by "Corporate Founder"
The Xerox Foundation, Crane Duplicating Service, and the Witter
Bynner Foundation for Poetry. Additional funding is provided by
the National Endowment for the Arts Literature Program.

For Lois *Who Got the Hell Out*

and for Ida *Who Stayed*

❖ ❖ ACKNOWLEDGMENTS

I want to acknowledge Oso, Sadie, and the late Chauncey Heffalump (Big, Bigger, and Clydesdale) without whose help I would have finished this book much sooner than I did.

My thanks to two editors: Greg McNamee and Joanne O'Hare. Greg first suggested that I should write a nonfiction book, and when I had done it, Joanne told me how much of it I shouldn't have written.

Tom Miller and Lois Olsrud kindly found information I needed; Gary Nabhan encouraged me to steal from his published work on ethnobotany; and Robert Houston was and is an inexhaustible source of information and funny stories about Bisbee. My special thanks to them, and to Ann Zwinger for reading a portion of this book in manuscript and for her steady encouragement and friendship.

For their hospitality and help, I thank the staff of the Bureau of Land Management at their Fairbank headquarters for the San Pedro Riparian Conservation Area, especially Eric Campbell, John Herron, and most especially Mike Hoffman, who braved the mesquite *bosques* on my behalf and has scars to prove it.

Of the citizens of today's Bisbee to whom I owe a debt of gratitude, I can mention only a few. My thanks to: Tom Vaughan of the Bisbee Mining and Historical Museum; David Eppele of Arizona Cactus and Succulent Research; Don Fry of the Bisbee Convention Center; Dick Bakken, Bisbee poet; Lee Adcock, Bisbee stonemason, ambulance driver and healer of smashed fingers; and Bill Taylor, my colleague at Lowell School who recently gave me a nostalgic tour of the building.

And to Ida Power, the Queen of Bisbee, who has been both my subject and inspiration, no acknowledgment of my debt is sufficient.

My wife, Lois, read, proofread, and criticized the book chapter by chapter and by some magical process, with the help of Me Linda Johnson, Ila Abernathy, and Chris Johnson and his staff, all of the University of Arizona, translated my typed script onto computer disks. Her help has been so great and constant with this book that thanks seem hardly sufficient, and I hope she will also accept responsibility for any errors the book contains. If not, I will.

Author's Note: Both Molly Bendixon and Byrd Granger died while this book was in production.

GOING BACK TO BISBEE

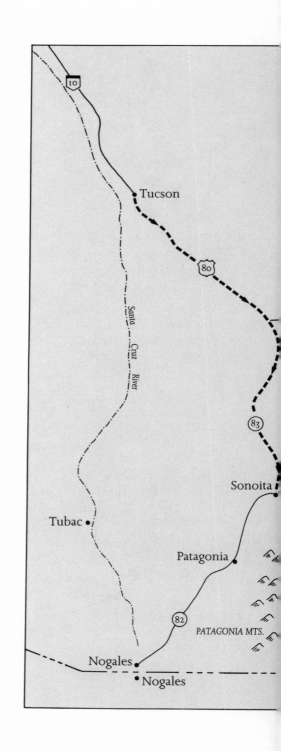

Map of Southeastern Arizona

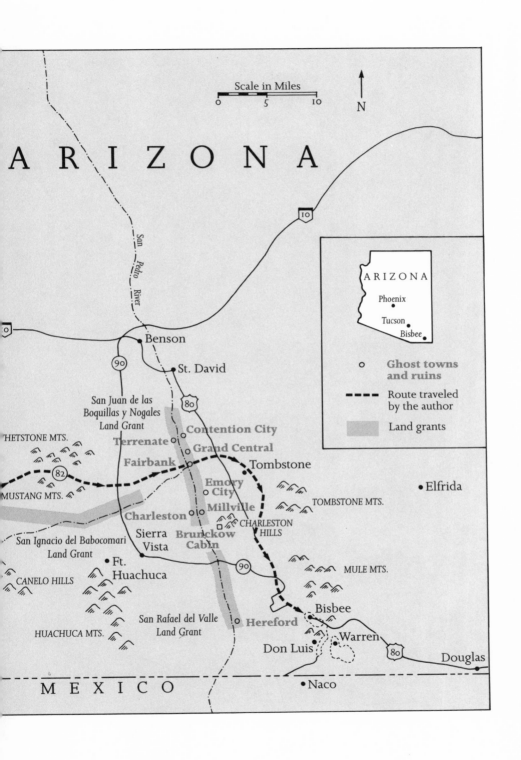

Scale in Miles

0   5   10

N

ARIZONA

San Pedro River

ARIZONA

Phoenix •

Tucson •

Bisbee •

○ **Ghost towns and ruins**

- - - Route traveled by the author

Land grants

● Benson

● St. David

San Juan de las
Boquillas y Nogales
Land Grant

WHETSTONE MTS.

○ Terrenate   ○ **Contention City**

Grand Central

Fairbank   ○ Tombstone

82   **Emory City**   ● Elfrida

MUSTANG MTS.   ○ **Millville**   TOMBSTONE MTS.

Charleston ○   □ CHARLESTON HILLS

San Ignacio del Babocomari
Land Grant

Sierra   **Brunckow Cabin**
Vista

● Ft.
Huachuca   MULE MTS.

CANELO HILLS

90   ● Bisbee

HUACHUCA MTS.   San Rafael del Valle
Land Grant   ○ **Hereford**   **Warren**

Don Luis   80   Douglas

M E X I C O   ● Naco

It is July 20, 1989, early afternoon, monsoon season in the Sonoran Desert, and I am going back to Bisbee. As I drive east out of Tucson, the temperature is 106 degrees and the humidity must be in the forties. Huge white thunderheads are building up in the south, drawing moisture from the Gulf of Mexico, but they don't look very promising yet. Too white and too far apart. Between them the sky is cerulean under a fierce sun. The heat doesn't seem to have anything to do with the sun. It comes up from the ground and just hangs there, almost solid. Perhaps the clouds mean a storm later in the afternoon, or perhaps they will just drift north like idle promises. No blue-black horizon yet. No thunder. But the breeze is from the southeast, what there is of it, and a monsoon can move in quickly at this time of year, especially late in the afternoon.

The desert could certainly use a storm right now to cool things off and lower the humidity. I am reminded of what somebody said about a fundamentalist fire-and-brimstone preacher. "It's not the heat so much as the humility." I've been on the road only a few minutes and already my backside is melting into the car seat. The sane part of me says "Stop! Roll up the windows and turn on the air conditioner!" The insane, masochistic part of me answers "No! You will be leaving the desert floor soon, climbing out of this furnace and into the rangeland where it will be cooler. Don't be a pantywaist." I engage in these dialogues with myself about the air conditioner quite often. They have as much to do with the history of the van I am driving as they do with my own warped point of view.

The van bug bit me a few years ago when Rosalie Sorrels, the folk singer from Idaho, came to visit us, driving her elderly van which she had named Mabel Dodge. Rosalie and Mabel Dodge had been batting around the country doing concerts. In fact, Rosalie had been batting around the country so much that she was known as "The Travelin' Lady" from the title of one of her best known songs. The romantic notion of a home on wheels attracted me at once. Why couldn't I get a van and bat around the country doing whatever it is I do, and I wasn't exactly sure what that was, but the idea felt good. So my wife and I started looking for a used van. I didn't want any furniture or fancy trappings, just room to stretch out in. With a sleeping bag and an ice chest I would be fine.

And soon, on one of her trips to West Texas to visit her family, my wife found the almost-perfect van. She called me from Ft. Worth.

"Happy birthday. I bought you a van."

"Great! Wonderful! What color is it?"

"It's the color of your eyes." My wife can be a little romantic herself sometimes, especially when she has just driven a hard bargain.

"Good lord! I don't want a red, white and blue van."

"No, it's blue all over, inside and out."

It was a 1978 Dodge with one previous owner and a considerable number of miles on its odometer. It had front seats and a bench across the back and was otherwise devoid of furniture. But it was gloriously, decadently carpeted—floor, walls, and ceiling—with a deep shag, light blue carpet. Sleeping in it, I was soon to find out, was like sleeping in a blue womb. Otherwise its personality was masculine. I named it Blue Boy.

Other than a Rickenbacker owned by my grandparents, which was an elegant antique when I was a child, Blue Boy is the only automobile for which I have ever felt genuine affection, and we have had many adventures together from Canada to the tip of Baja California and from the Atlantic to the Pacific. Blue Boy is badly faded now, like my eyes, from years of Arizona sun, and he has a gash near the rear where my wife backed him into a paloverde outside our garage. (When asked how it happened, she said, "God moved a tree," and she sticks to that story.) He is a little loose in the joints and has many rattles as the result of some of the worst roads on the North American Continent, but he continues to purr along like the perfect traveling machine he is.

But Blue Boy had one peculiarity which was linked to the fact that he had lived all his previous life in West Texas, although I didn't make that connection until years later. His motor ran cool enough, even with the air conditioner on, until the outside temperature rose above one hundred degrees. Then he began to overheat when the air conditioner was on. From the depths of my ignorance of automobile mechanics, I assumed that Blue Boy's engine was not powerful enough to take on the added burden of the air conditioner at such high temperatures, and I simply got used to driving without the air conditioner most of the time, and always when the outside temperature was very high. I took a certain macho pride in being able to "tough it out," as my father used to say, and had a tendency to sneer at the occupants of other vehicles as they rolled down the highway all sealed up in their air-conditioned capsules.

This went on for several years until last summer when we took a trip from Tucson to the West Coast, during which my wife wept, complained, and threatened to faint nearly all the way to Los Angeles. She flew home and announced that she was never going anywhere in Blue Boy again in the summer. My wife is resolute. When she makes up her mind, she makes up her mind; and when she issues an ultimatum, there is no getting around it.

The situation called for drastic action. So I decided to take Blue Boy to a mechanic to see if anything could be done about his peculiarity. The upshot was that my diagnosis had been wrong. Blue Boy's engine was quite powerful enough—how could I have doubted? But his radiator was all clogged up, and his circulatory system couldn't cool the engine properly. His radiator was clogged because his previous owner had put West Texas water in it, and West Texas water is loaded with minerals and alkali and God knows what, causing deposits to build up to the point that the radiator was functioning at less than half its normal capacity. I gave Blue Boy a new radiator and his peculiarity disappeared. Now he can go up the steepest hill in the Southwest in August and never overheat.

But I am a creature of habit and stubborn in my own way. I have driven for so many years in the desert without an air conditioner that I still rarely use it unless I have passengers—one passenger in particular. I have the notion that in order to see the landscape properly one must experience the temperature as well. I agree with one of my dogs who keeps telling me, "What good is it to travel if you don't slow down enough to smell the country?" But right now, as my van pulls away from the sunset and my bottom slowly melts into the driver's seat, I would like to see and smell and feel a good slap-dash Southern Arizona monsoon storm. I think Blue Boy would enjoy it too.

I love the Sonoran monsoons when they finally arrive. They are usually brief, violent, and incredibly dramatic, with enough thunder, lightning, and hard-driven rain to make life exciting, even precarious. After the clouds build up into great white cathedrals, as they are trying to do now but without much success, the desert turns suddenly dark and still. The light is dim, green, and eerie. Everything seems to be holding its breath, waiting. The air becomes languid, palpable with humidity. Low thunder begins to roll around in the distance, almost comforting after the unnatural silence. Then somebody up there starts flipping light switches. Enormous panels of sheet lightning go on behind the clouds, hold for a few seconds, then go off. The effect is totally theatrical, as if some wizard lighting technician were playing bravura pieces on the control board offstage, never quite repeating the same brilliant display twice.

Then all notions of theatricality are destroyed and things get serious. The entertainment is over, but the show has just begun. And if you are in it, that is, if you are out in it and cannot get out of it, you will never forget it. Suddenly there is a wrenching, shrieking explosion as a lightning bolt connects with the ground nearby. It sizzles, pops, and sputters. The air smells strange, pungent with ozone. Another bolt strikes, and another. The desert has become an exploding mine field. Thunder breaks directly overhead, so loud and close you can almost see it, as if a huge chasm had opened in the clouds. The vibration makes you duck and nearly knocks you off your feet. Reverberations rattle away in the distance. More bolts of lightning strike—to the left, to the right, straight ahead. The temperature is plummeting. It can drop more than thirty degrees in a few minutes. In the flashes of lightning you see paloverde and ocotillo lashing in the wind, which seems to come from all directions at once. Cottontails huddle at the base of a greasewood, ears down, noses twitching, black eyes huge and shining with terror. A young javelina, the peccary or wild boar of the Sonoran Desert, panics, breaks from shelter, and runs wildly down the arroyo, snorting at every step. The sharp crack of thunder, the spluttering pop of lightning, and the screaming of the wind are reaching unbearable levels. The world has gone mad.

Almost imperceptibly under all this, then growing louder, another sound like the tattoo of a million tiny drums rises to a crescendo. Rain. But "rain" is not the right word. Rain is what comes to the Sonoran Desert in the spring, if we are lucky. It is gentle and civilized. But this is neither gentle nor civilized—it is brutal. Huge drops in tight formation strike the earth with such velocity that they often bounce four feet in the air. Thunder and lightning continue, but now the dominant element of the storm is water, which seems to be almost solid, not so much falling in drops as poured from some vast container and driven by the fury of the wind. Water is everywhere. There seems to be no air left to breathe. And it is cold, the cold plunge after the steam bath. It comes down much faster than the earth can absorb it and runs in sheets over the desert pavement, the thin layer of small stones and gravel which holds the earth in place and without which the desert soil would quickly be carried away.

Within a half hour after the first real clap of thunder, the storm is usually over, leaving the desert bedraggled but the air soft and aromatic with the smell of wet greasewood. The danger, however, is not over so quickly. Flash floods can race down arroyos and across roads with a bore like that of the sea rushing into a narrow inlet at high tide. The floods reach their peak after the storm is over and often inundate low-lying areas far downstream. Midwesterners quote the old saw: "If you don't like the weather, just wait a minute." But we could change that to a more sinister desert version: "If the lightning doesn't get you, wait for the flood."

Both lightning and flood do get some of us every year. Prominent signs—DO NOT ENTER WHEN FLOODED—are posted where arroyos cross roads, but some people choose to ignore them, and often they drown. The water crossing a road might look shallow, but the current can be extremely strong. Many years ago a friend who was on his way to our house for dinner in his vw Bug entered a seemingly shallow arroyo after a brief summer storm. He discovered that his vehicle had a watertight bottom. It carried him on a fast half-mile boat trip down a twisting, roaring arroyo before it bumped, like the basket carrying Moses, into a safe harbor. By that time the Bug was a wreck and so was our friend. One of the first things I remember seeing when I arrived in Tucson in the late fifties was a pickup truck stranded in about eight feet of water in a downtown railroad underpass. Three people were on its roof, screaming for help. Before they could be rescued, one of them was swept into the current and drowned.

According to Southwestern tradition and folklore, the *chubascos*, or monsoon storms, are supposed to begin two days after Summer Solstice, on June 24, or San Juan's Day. But they are usually late and some years seem to have great difficulty getting it all together, teasing for weeks and then finally materializing in late July, as they have this year. But how fitting that they should be associated with San Juan's Day, which isn't the day of St. John the Apostle, but of Señor Juan, John the Baptist himself, who said, "I baptize you with water." And he didn't mean he was going to sprinkle a little on. He went into the desert and lived on locusts and honey, but we associate him with rivers and with wrath, a fierce and dramatic wrath. I never witness a chubasco without thinking of him, of his cleansing fury and his promise for the future. And when I see a bona fide member of the "generation of vipers" beginning to crawl with all haste toward higher ground as a storm approaches, I chuckle to myself and say, "A wise move, Mr. Pharisee. A very wise move. Señor Juan wants to baptize you good."

Since few desert creatures like to swim, although a remarkable number of them can if they have to, most of them head for high ground before a summer storm. We live in the Tucson Mountains. Our house sits on the saddle of a low hill with an arroyo on either side. It did not occur to us when we built the house many years ago that the hill on which we built undoubtedly served as a place of refuge when the arroyos became torrential rivers. And so, without knowing it, we built a shelter for more than ourselves. It seems as though desert creatures must have a universal communication network. When a storm is approaching, I think they must drop all predatory inclinations. I can imagine the spiders telling the toads who tell the lizards who tell the snakes who tell the rats who tell the squirrels who tell the rabbits, *"Arriba! Arriba! Vamos a la casa."*

And they come. Walking, running, hopping, and crawling, they come. Spiders of all denominations, shiny or shaggy, large or small. Iridescent beetles. Toads the size of salad plates. The little banner-tailed kangaroo rat and the big rock squirrel, whose front end is gray while his rear end is brown. And many kinds of snakes, mostly harmless, but some dragging their little noisemakers behind them. Some stay only until the storm is over, but others move in for more extended periods. In their attempts to stay in the house or in the courtyard just outside the kitchen door, some are incredibly, pathetically persistent. None more so than the tarantula.

I have a considerable affection for tarantulas. They are the victims not only of our aversion to spiders, but of a very bad press which portrays them as quite different creatures than they are. The mythic, and I'm afraid still predominant, view of tarantulas seems to have originated in Southern Italy, in the seaport of Taranto, whose citizens, between the fifteenth and the seventeenth centuries, were visited with repeated epidemics of a strange disease that created frenzy. This came to be known as tarantism and was thought to result from the bite of a tarantula. From this comes the name of a somewhat frenzied folk dance, the tarantella. Evidently the spider was named after the town, the disease was named after the spider, and the dance was named after the disease. But at the bottom of all this, the spider was innocent. I don't think we know what really caused tarantism. Perhaps it was just a particularly potent wine in the stomachs of some volatile Italians with a natural tendency for body language. At any rate, the tarantula took the rap and has henceforth been thought to be a sinister, even deadly, creature.

But the tarantula is not significantly dangerous to humans. It almost never bites, even when tormented; and if it does, its bite is no more potent than the sting of a bee. It is true that the sexual practices of the female tarantula will not hold up to the close scrutiny of a moralist, but as far as I'm concerned, sexual practices are inexplicable throughout the entire phyllogenetic scale, and let those without sin get out their stones. Tarantulas are somewhat large and hairy, to be sure, but less so than many of the creatures we choose as pets. In fact, tarantulas make excellent pets if they are given the full run of the house in order to find sufficient food.

So I have a considerable fondness for tarantulas, but my wife does not share this feeling. While she allows some varieties of large spiders to remain in the house and even refers to them as my "friends," she draws the line at tarantulas. I have explained to her that tarantulas are quiet, well-behaved house guests who pay for their lodging by eating flies and small insects. I have told her that they eat ticks, which are troublesome to our dogs, although I am not absolutely sure this is true. I have even hinted that a few tarantulas around the house would have a tendency to cut down on the number of other long-staying guests, including relatives. When she said she was afraid of stepping on a tarantula while she was barefooted, I told her that the possibility was very remote because they usually climb up the walls. This did not seem to comfort her very much. My wife is resolute. No tarantulas!

Consequently, when a tarantula lumbers in, lifting one leg at a time and lowering it with great care and deliberation, I am expected to put it out. But tarantulas are also resolute, and persistent. I have put the same tarantula out as many as five times in one evening, each time placing it farther from the house. And each time it would laboriously turn itself around and head back for the open door from which it had just been ejected, like a stray dog who has adopted a new home and will not be discouraged. On its third or fourth entry, it will even begin to take on some of the mannerisms of a stray dog unsure of welcome—tentative, cringing a little, trying to be inconspicuous. But a tarantula crossing the kitchen floor with its slow, stately, inexorable walk has difficulty being inconspicuous, and my wife notices it every time. Several times I have managed to keep one hidden for a day or two, but eventually it grows bold and strikes out across the floor or up a wall, and as soon as my wife sees it, expulsion is inevitable.

Tarantulas probably come in the house to avoid summer storms, but they are also attracted to light. I once thought that this was because light attracts some of the small insects on which they feed, but perhaps they are attracted to light for its own sake or for some reason we do not understand. Edmund C. Jaeger in his book *Desert Wildlife* tells about camping in the Sonoran Desert with two companions and being visited by a "number of tarantulas, which seemed to be attracted by the firelight. They rapidly approached the fire, then suddenly about-faced when they felt the heat. Time and again they returned, only to repeat the withdrawal." Jaeger also mentions their astonishing longevity, which has been documented. Some female tarantulas live for twenty-five years.

There is another persistent creature who makes its appearance in large numbers at our house during the monsoon season, either coming inside or congregating in the small courtyard just outside the kitchen door, where I have seen as many as nine of them at a time. I call it Bufo, short for *Bufo alvarious*, the Colorado River toad. But I can manage very little affection for Bufo, partly because it is ugly by just about any standard one wants to apply, and partly because it is dangerous to our dogs, of which we always have several, usually several more than we should have. On the scale of natural beauty, I would have to place Bufo somewhere near the bottom as compared to other desert creatures. It presents an aesthetic problem I cannot overcome. Bufo is large, often seven inches long and almost as wide, olive-gray to nearly black-brown, with an amazing assortment of lumps, bumps, and wart-like protuberances all over its head and body. I am sure it would have these on its neck if it had a neck, but it doesn't seem to have one. Some of these lumps and bumps are glands. Others seem to be—and I hesitate to use the words—purely decorative. But Bufo's skin is not the real aesthetic problem for me. The problem is the casual relationship between Bufo's skin and everything it contains. The toad moves with a queasy, sloshing, rolling, jiggling motion, like a rubber bag only partly filled with some viscous fluid. When Bufo hops, and it can hurl this entire, loosely organized arrangement through the air with great force and cover more than three feet in a single hop, it lands with a loud, sickening plop, and everything sloshes around for a while before settling into repose. None of this seems to bother Bufo, who wears an expression of absolute equanimity, if not stolidity; but it is a real aesthetic problem for me.

Another thing which probably affects my judgment is that Bufo's skin is covered with a slimy substance whose chemical makeup closely relates it to cobra venom. This helps protect the toad from predators, such as coyotes, but it also has a devastating effect on any domestic dog foolish enough to lick or bite Bufo. The dog immediately has a seizure, which in some cases can be fatal, and goes down head-first, splay-legged, gasping for breath. Evidently the toxin paralyzes the dog's respiratory system. The remedy is to wash the dog's mouth out with water, being careful not to drown the dog by letting water run down its throat.

We once had a Doberman who could never resist grabbing a Colorado River toad whenever she encountered one. She was unable to make a connection between the toad and the terrible things that happened to her immediately afterward. But our present three dogs, Big, Bigger, and Clydesdale, have sense enough to leave Bufo alone, in spite of the fact that only two of them were desert-raised. The third is probably just too lazy to be bothered, or else, like me, he has an aesthetic reservation about Bufo.

When I left the dogs about a half hour ago, they had all gone into an extended pout. They are pessimists. When they see me putting clothes into the van in preparation for a trip, they assume it is going to be a long one and do their dying-swan routine, which includes tragic looks from piteously drooping, glistening eyes. When this fails to impede my preparations, they go into a pout. They turn away and stare, fixedly, at the wall, uttering long, dejected sighs. One of them can sigh in such a way that it sounds exactly like a wrenching sob. The others encourage her to longer and deeper sobs. "Let him have it, Sadie. Break his heart."

Nevertheless, I and my stony heart got into Blue Boy and drove away. I am going back to Bisbee, and it feels good in spite of the heat and humidity. No storm yet, and I haven't turned on the air conditioner. I am only a few miles from the intersection of Highway 83, which will take me south and up into the grasslands where it will be cooler. I am driving over a fairly level alluvial plain, the desert floor, which stretches up from the Santa Cruz River. The river is dry now, as usual, but waiting to be transformed into a real hell-raiser if the storm materializes.

The basin I am driving through is almost completely surrounded by mountains. Behind me and on the other side of the river is the jagged, toothy outline of the Tucson Mountains, in the foothills of which is the house where three dogs are probably still pouting. The Tucsons are older than most of the large mountain ranges in the vicinity, and not as high, worn down to a kind of runic grandeur. Their foothills, which were almost untouched desert twenty-five years ago, have become the suburbs of sprawling Tucson's west side. In spite of this, their higher peaks, protected from development by a county slope ordinance as well as Saguaro National Monument West and Tucson Mountain Park, are full of mystery and the play of shadows.

Because of their starkness and their science-fiction shapes, I think of the Tucsons as "the mountains of the moon." When a winter storm comes over them from the west, they are dramatic in the way the Alps are dramatic, but on a much smaller scale of course. Clouds and mist swirl and billow around their peaks, and their deeply eroded canyons become places of mystery. Once every few years they are even covered with snow, a brief but glorious transformation that usually lasts until about noon the following day. And in spite of their stark contours, their surfaces are pelagic, almost shaggy when seen in the slanting light of late afternoon, covered with a heavy growth of desert plants that includes thick stands of saguaros, a sizable part of the last significant saguaro forest left in the world.

I have wandered through the Tucson Mountains at all times of the day and night, have climbed many of their peaks and followed their arroyos for miles, and yet they remain a mystery to me. Some presence is there, some numen which I am aware of but cannot describe nor come to grips with. It is powerful, wonderful, and I fear it is dying. I have tried to write about the Tucsons and that presence many times, and have always failed. Years ago, when I did not know them as well as I do now, I wrote,

> you could get here from anywhere
> but once you are here
> there are many places you can never go

That is from a failed poem called "The Upper *Bajadas*," a technical term identifying a kind of landscape that includes the foothills and talus slopes of the Tucson Mountains. I am fascinated with the term because it seems to be contradictory—upper lowlands, although *bajada* actually means "slope"—and includes words from both English and Spanish, suggesting two elements of the complex mix of cultures now living in this area. And somehow, for some reason I do not entirely understand, I have continued to live in the upper *bajadas* for more than a quarter of a century, which is no time at all in terms of the life of the mountains, but it is the entire lifespan of a very lucky tarantula, and it is a long time for me.

Range after range of mountains as far as I can see and much farther. To my left, making up the entire northern horizon, is an enormous mass, dark blue now in the shadow of the thunderheads. It is actually three ranges of mountains extending from almost due north of Tucson to a point far to the southeast, the Catalinas, Tanque Verdes, and Rincons. The Catalinas are the most spectacular in terms of height and bulk. They are young, vital, awesome mountains. Their steep, treeless sides suggest nothing of what is above and beyond. It is hard to believe, as I drive across the oven of the desert floor, that up there about forty miles away is a large subalpine forest of pines and firs and a ski resort where the high temperature today is in the upper sixties.

Directly south of me are the Santa Ritas, which are much larger and more formidable than they appear to be from here. They too have a heavy growth of timber on their upper elevations and were the source of much mineral wealth in Spanish Colonial times, causing Tubac, on the Santa Cruz River just west of the Santa Ritas, to become the earliest center of colonial culture in this area. In 1752 the first non-native woman to set foot on what is now Arizona soil arrived in Tubac. Nobody seems to know who she was, but she was undoubtedly Spanish, probably creole—of pure Spanish descent but born in New Spain, now Mexico. I doubt that any contemporary women envy her her small niche in history. Her life, by our standards, must have been hell.

Range after range of mountains. To the east the Whetstones, and south of them the Huachucas. Farther east the Dragoons and the magnificent Chiricahuas where a couple of months ago I and one of the dogs climbed Silver Peak to an elevation of 7,975 feet. Fortunately it was the smallest of the large dogs—the largest weighs more than I do—because he collapsed near the top of the mountain and I had to carry him most of the way down. When we got to Cave Creek, I dumped him in, for which he has never forgiven me, but it cooled him down and probably saved his life. As my less-than-courageous dog found out just before he tried to crawl under my sleeping bag while I was in it, the Chiricahuas have a considerable population of black bears, wildcats, and javelinas. The mountains are also attracting a large population of campers and tourists, nearly all of whom seem to be frantically searching for the same reclusive and very beautiful bird, the coppery-tailed trogon. Someone should start a rumor that the coppery-tailed trogon is a myth invented by the Bureau of Tourism, that there is no coppery-tailed trogon. It might save an entire mountain range from destruction at the hands and feet of hordes of binocular-carrying faddists.

This is pure basin and range country—mountain ranges of all sizes which once had deep and extensive valleys between them. But through the process of erosion, the valleys have filled in and leveled off to become vast basins that we refer to in a general way as the desert floor. A glance at the map shows Interstate 10, on which I am driving, twisting across Southern Arizona like a huge snake crawling from the New Mexico border to Phoenix. A closer look at the map shows why it takes such an indirect route. Range upon range of mountains, between which it must twist, trying to stay on low and fairly level ground. These ranges extend generally north and south or northwest and southeast, so that a road from east to west is doomed to encounter them broadside and must constantly maneuver around and between them. The section of freeway on which I am driving is heading straight southeast on its way to Lordsburg, New Mexico, considerably to the north.

I am moving down the length of a broad, relatively flat corridor bordered on both sides by extensive mountain ranges. From here it is difficult to tell where one range ends and another begins. Distances in the desert are tricky, where visibility is often more than sixty miles and mountain ranges thirty miles apart appear to be flat, tissue-paper collages with one range pasted directly on the range behind it. Human depth perception cannot deal with such distances accurately, especially in the brilliant light and usually dry air. Perhaps that is why many travelers along this road hardly notice the mountains at all. They will say it is "just flat desert. Nothing much to see." The mountains look less solid and real than the thunderheads above them and appear to be painted on the sky in colors ranging from the most delicate pastels to the darkest purple. At the moment, the lower slopes of the Santa Ritas are a soft yellow-green, fuzzy with vegetation.

This stretch of the desert floor is also much greener than usual, shockingly green in contrast with what it looked like a few weeks ago before the rains came. This area must have had several good soakers recently. The predominant growth here is greasewood, a sea of grease-wood with an occasional stand of jumping cholla or ocotillo and once in a great while a stunted mesquite. Most of the year this stretch has a faded, desiccated look, suggesting either severe overgrazing or the presence of caliche close to the surface. Probably both in this case.

Even at its most verdant, greasewood is not a lush plant, but it is the most commonly found plant in the Sonoran Desert and often seems to be able to grow where almost nothing else will. It is delicate and lacy, with bare, silvery-gray stems and bright metallic-green leaves. Along here it averages about three-and-a-half feet tall but can grow to be a very tall plant if it gets more water. When I first moved into the desert, I watered the greasewood near the house from time to time. Within two years I had a fifteen-foot-high jungle. At the moment, the foliage of the greasewood has distinct glints and undertones of yellow, indicating that many of the plants are in bloom, but the tiny yellow blossoms, each with five petals twisted like the blades of a fan, are too inconspicuous to be seen clearly from a distance.

The saguaro has come to be the plant which is most often used to symbolize the Sonoran Desert, and as much as I admire these giants, each with its individual style and personality, they are not nearly as widespread and typical of this desert as is the humble greasewood. Nor is the saguaro, except for its size, any more surprising. The unassuming greasewood is a truly amazing plant. It is an evergreen which often displays buds, blossoms and fruit on the same plant at the same time. The fruit is a small, furry, silver-white globe that can quietly stick to fur or fabric and hitchhike for miles. As a greasewood matures, it sends up concentric circles of new shoots from the same root. Eventually the central and original part of the plant dies and disintegrates while the peripheral "clones" continue to grow. Some of these individual plant colonies, shaped like doughnuts with the original portion in the center long since dead, are more than sixty-five feet across. The botanist Frank Vasek recently radiocarbon-dated one of these colonies in the desert of Southern California at 9,400 years old, making it the oldest living plant known to man, and bumping the bristlecone pine from that prestigious position.

And in another way, greasewood is the signature plant of the Sonoran Desert. Its leaves are resinous, slightly sticky to the touch, although not unpleasantly so. This substance, called lac, gives the Sonoran Desert its distinctive smell, especially after a rain. Each desert in the United States has a distinctive smell, and that smell is usually caused by a specific plant. I always associate the Great Basin Desert with the bracing odor of sage. And everybody who has known the Sonoran Desert associates it with the smell of greasewood after a rain, a slightly medicinal but exhilarating smell.

Those who have lived in the Sonoran Desert for any period of time never forget that smell, and no matter how far away they go, many of them can never get over it. I meet them when I am doing poetry readings in many different parts of the country, when I am reading poems about the desert. They approach me after the readings and softly speak the magic words like a litany: "desert," "greasewood," "saguaro," "rain." Sometimes they have tears in their eyes as they tell me where they once lived in the desert and how they can never get it out of their minds. Each time I realize that I am in the presence of a kindred spirit and that we who love the desert speak a language whose significance others cannot entirely understand. And each time I am thankful that I, too, am not an exile, that the circumstances of life have not forced me to leave the desert.

Most botanists would probably raise at least one eyebrow at my use of the name greasewood to identify the plant which is technically known as *Larrea tridenta*, claiming that it should be called creosote bush to distinguish it from two other desert plants—one found in the Mojave and one in the Great Basin—called greasewood. But I stick to my guns and call it greasewood, as most of us who live in the Tucson area do. We prefer this name probably because of our proximity to the native Tohono O'odham people (previously called Papago), who refer to the plant as greasewood rather than creosote bush and rely on its medicinal properties for a wide range of ailments. In fact, in O'odham folklore, greasewood was the first thing that grew, and from its resin, or lac, Earth Maker formed the mountains. When the lac dried, the mountains stiffened and remained in place. There's probably a principle in that which could be used as a symbol of the basic difference between the Anglo and the Native American points of view. I would have a tendency to think that the plant was created from the mountains, but the O'odham believe the mountains were created from the plant.

The whole greasewood vs. creosote controversy reminds me of the subject of popular taxonomy and the way things get their names. This is the science of what-you-call-it, and I think of it as an absolute science because it often seems to make absolutely no sense. In the case of the greasewood and creosote problem, what you call it depends not only on where you are, but on who you are. People interested in or baffled by this science often ask me such questions as: "Does the jumping cactus really jump?" I have several answers to this question depending on what mood I'm in. Sometimes I say, "Only when your back is turned." At other times I answer with another question. "Does the weeping willow really weep?" And although they seem contradictory, there is a sense in which both these answers suggest the truth. That's the way it is with the science of what-you-call-it.

The popular, as opposed to the scientific, names for plants and animals are often based on figurative language, the language of impression and comparison, the language of poetry. These names are descriptive, concrete, highly compressed, and usually require some kind of imaginative leap. I am not a linguist, but it seems to me that the more "primitive" a language is by our standards, the more it relies on such names.

At the moment, looking south and back a little to the west, I can see clouds hanging in delicate long streamers like veils. The streamers do not reach the ground, and the clouds are moving steadily northwestward. It is a common phenomenon in the desert—rain which is falling in a localized area but evaporating before it reaches the ground. The name which comes into my mind is *walking rain*, an expression translated from the language of a Native American culture. It is descriptive, concrete, accurate in a metaphorical sense, and so highly compressed as to require a slight leap of the imagination. It is also beautiful. Somewhere rain is falling but never comes to rest on the earth, while at the same time it is moving. *Walking rain*.

The name jumping cholla, the official, nonscientific name found in all the respectable books, was arrived at in the same way and is based upon close observation of the plant's structure and resultant behavior. The jumping cholla is one of the great beauties of desert vegetation, and it is a true devil. Its trunk is a tube of intricately woven wooden mesh, very strong and very light, often found transformed into ugly lamps in curio shops. Above the cholla's trunk it produces soft, fleshy green segments, each connected to the one before it by means of a delicate joint, and each covered with barbed spines. When you brush against the plant, even ever so lightly, the spines pierce flesh and the barbs hold them in place. As you pull back or move away, the joint neatly disconnects and the entire fleshy segment remains embedded in its victim—in this case, you. Only the slightest contact is required. These large green spiny monsters seem to jump on you and hang on.

But this is only the beginning. The subtle lengths to which this plant will go in order to do you bodily harm are truly insidious and diabolical. If you should step on one of the fleshy segments which has already fallen on the ground, and they often cover the ground around a plant in great profusion, you will squash it, exposing its slimy, slick inner pulp. Its spines will often attach the segment lightly to the sole of your shoe. As you take the next step and your foot comes up behind you, the upward thrust of your foot will cause the spines to dislodge, and the lubrication of the slimy inner pulp will aid the segment in sliding easily over the sole of your shoe. The entire segment will fly up behind you, or jump up behind you, and impale you in the back of the lower leg, penetrating even heavy trousers.

When this happens, if you don't have a comb with you, you can be in considerable trouble. If you try to dislodge the segment with your hand, you will find that your hand is immediately attached to the back of your leg by means of the cholla segment, leaving you bent over in an awkward position while you slowly fry in the sun. The thing to do, while you still have at least one hand free to do it with, is to slide a comb between your flesh and the cholla segment and lift it away with one quick, hideously painful jerk. And it's a good idea to do this as quickly as possible because the cholla still has one more card to play in its diabolical game. Poison. It is the only cactus whose spines are coated with a slightly toxic substance which can cause severe festering and has been known to cripple horses when the spines are not removed soon enough.

And yet the jumping cholla is a beautiful thing, especially when seen as I am seeing them now, from a safe distance. Even more so when seen in the moonlight. They are about the height of a person, and moonlight turns the long pale spines which cover their tops to platinum blond. They look like many statuesque 1930s starlets standing out there waiting to be discovered. But drive on, drive on! To touch that glamorous creature even once is to know pain and learn the cruelty of a truly ruthless beauty.

About twenty miles out of Tucson I swing south off the freeway and onto Highway 83, which will take me up into the rangeland. I haven't turned on the air conditioner, and suddenly the heat seems unbearable, probably because of my reduced speed and because I know it will be a little cooler soon. The storm clouds seem to be stalled just above the southern horizon. *"Ven, Chubasco!"* I chant. *"Ven, ven, Chubasco!"* There is no immediate response.

I always talk to things more than I do to people. I talk to stones, plants, animals and even the weather, but I have a superstitious belief that when I address the natural things of this region, I must use Spanish. Their experience with Spanish goes back to the sixteenth century, while they have heard English for only about 150 years. I have a feeling that it takes the natural things of the world a long time to get used to a new language. And since I don't know any Pima or Apache, I try to use Spanish. But my Spanish is dreadful. I not only speak it very poorly, I hear it even worse. If I can ask the right question, I can't understand the answer. And to be asked a question in Spanish which requires more than a *si* or *no* is a nightmare from which I cringe. It's much easier to speak Spanish to things which cannot or do not reply. Also, the plants and animals are less critical. They do not correct my mistakes. And I'm sure the stones and mountains have heard much garbled and ungrammatical Spanish since one spring day in 1540 when the twenty-nine-year-old Francisco Vázquez de Coronado and his ill-fated band struggled down the valley of the San Pedro River past the point at which I will be crossing it in less than an hour.

I still blush when I remember one of my classic blunders in Spanish. Although it was only one of many, it stands out in my mind. I had just arrived in Cuernavaca after a three-day train and bus ride from Nogales. I was exhausted and sick. The taxi driver deposited me and my luggage in front of the house where I had rented a room from a Mexican family. My landlady-to-be, a truly gracious person, came out to the sidewalk to meet me and escort me in. Looking at my haggard face, she asked in Spanish, "Are you tired?" The word is *cansado*.

But I confused it with *casado* (married), and in my impeccable Spanish replied, "Yes, I have been tired for fifteen years and I have a twelve-year-old son." Her eyes opened wider for a moment, but she merely nodded, patted me on the shoulder with compassion, and led me into the house to rest after my long ordeal.

Historically, however, it seems fitting for me to speak in Spanish to the things which make up this landscape, no matter how bad my Spanish is, since the landscape was part of New Spain until 1821, when Mexico gained its independence, and then part of Mexico until 1854 as a result of the Gadsden Treaty, although the United States did not take possession of it until 1856. This 27,305 square miles of what is now Southern Arizona, plus 2,365 square miles of what is now New Mexico, cost the United States ten million dollars. It was not, as is generally believed, purchased from the Mexican people or from any duly constituted Mexican Government. It was privately and secretly sold by the one-legged dictator, Antonio López de Santa Anna, who had already played a leading role in Mexico's loss of another chunk of real estate now known as Texas.

Santa Anna became dictator of Mexico four different times before that infant country was forty years old. In his day, he was thought of by many of his fellow citizens as Mexico's savior. Most contemporary historians, looking back, see him as its nemesis, one of the darkest of the dark angels who ministered to that bleeding young republic. He must have been a fairly good general, at least he could raise an army when almost nobody else could, but he was treacherous, unscrupulous, vain, and childlike. He billed himself the "Napoleon of the West," and needed much money to maintain his army and his style. As a dictator, he had chosen the title "His Most Serene Highness," which was indicative of his style. He lived in gilded, rococo luxury, and loved parties and huge celebrations, especially when they were in his honor. And his sale of a large part of what was left of Mexico in order to make ends meet was not the most shameful transaction he engaged in. He also sold the natives of Yucatán as slaves to Cuban plantation owners at twenty-five pesos each.

When we look back on Santa Anna and the Gadsden Purchase, the recent outrage of the United States Government, upon discovering—lo and behold—that the Dictator of Panama was selling drugs, seems strident and exaggerated. For Latin American dictators, such things have often been a matter of style. And for us, it seems to be a matter of whether or not we want what they happen to be selling at the moment. When it was the land through which I am now driving, we did.

The United States Government wanted a southern railroad route to the fabled land of California. California had just fallen, like a ripe avocado, into the hands of the United States in 1848, the same year large chunks of gold were found lying around in its rivers and streams. So we bought the strip of desert land from His Most Serene Highness, or "Old Santy Anny" as the Texans called him, who had found himself temporarily short of cash and was eager to sell.

But when President Pierce paid Santa Anna his ten million dollars—seven immediately and the balance upon completion of the border survey—a big page in history's book flipped over for this land which is now part of Southern Arizona. And although that page has subsequently become a palimpsest of notations, forgotten dates, and appointments with destiny, it is the page we still live on if we live in Arizona south of the Gila. Whatever our backgrounds, our foregrounds are shaped by the rip-roaring, boom-or-bust American Era, which arrived with the Gadsden Purchase and is still going strong all around us. What Faulkner said about the Deep South is true here as well: "The past is not dead; it is not even past."

The American Era arrived in Tucson, a one-story adobe town of about six hundred people, in the spring of 1856 when a detachment of United States Dragoons marched into town while the Mexican troops marched out. Even that quiet transition included a foretaste of what was to come. The newcomers just couldn't wait. Some of the Gringo residents, one of whom was later to become a judge in the Territory of Arizona, tied several mesquite poles together and hoisted an American flag over Miles' store, with loud cheers, while the Mexican troops were filing past on their way out of town. It was an insult. An ugly incident ensued. Fortunately, nobody started shooting. In that respect the incident was unusual.

The civilian Mexican population was quiet and polite. Some packed up and moved south across the newly established border. Many of the older residents stayed. They had already lived under two governments, although on the ragged frontier of both, and they would wait and see if this one would be different. Certainly neither of the others had done much for them in their frontier isolation, danger, and poverty. Nobody had consulted them about whether or not they wanted to become part of the American Era. And nobody had asked the mountains or desert basins or plants or animals about it. But not since the mid-tertiary age, vaguely twenty million years earlier, had the landscape known such sudden and dramatic changes as it was about to undergo. And nobody had asked the native Pimas or Tohono O'odham or Apaches if they wanted to enter the new era, which would bring their cultures to the brink of annihilation and sometimes beyond. The Americans, the restless changers and movers, had come. In less than 150 years we have changed everything in the region except the weather, and during this, the hottest summer on record in Southern Arizona, we are beginning to wonder if we haven't changed that too.

As I drive through the heat toward the low hills which skirt the Santa Rita Mountains, much of what I see reminds me of how thoroughly we have changed this landscape. Layer upon layer of our discarded history lies everywhere around me, more obvious than the aluminum cans and broken glass along the road. I am a product of the American Era, of that dream of the endless frontier, of that push toward new lands to use up for my purposes, of that greed. And I am going back to Bisbee, where I will look down into a gigantic crater, an inverted mountain of empty space which was, seventy-five years ago, a real mountain. I will not be shocked. Along the way, I will see no antelope where once they were everywhere, and I will not be shocked. I will drive through valleys where grass once grew shoulder-high and where now only the ubiquitous greasewood is able to find a foothold in what is left of the soil, and I will not be shocked. I am a product of the American Era. It is my heritage.

And I am going back to Bisbee, not really knowing why. Perhaps it is because two years of my life were left there, put behind me, and now I have reached an age at which I cannot afford to forget even two years out of those allotted me. Perhaps I am looking for the spirit of a mountain I never knew, a mountain which became a crater on whose edge I lived for two years, happily, while the landscape and even the earth around me was being destroyed. Or perhaps it is just nostalgia. I was happy there, while the destruction went on twenty-four hours a day, and now I want to go back.

We are starting to climb. Blue Boy feels it, and I feel a wave of something like euphoria. Sunflowers and brilliant white prickle poppies flaunt themselves beside the road. The storm is beginning to build more rapidly now, and I want to feel cold water on my face. Maybe I am suddenly happy just because I am going somewhere, anywhere. I have put down roots in the last thirty years, but I am still the child of those who kept moving, always westward. Did they ever look back? The record of the birthplaces of my mother, father, aunts and uncles reads like a trail map from the Mississippi River to Oregon. Once, when I asked my mother where one of her younger brothers was born, she said, "In a wagon. I think it was somewhere in Arkansas." I am the child of those who were born along the road, and it was a long, long road.

Blue Boy was raised in West Texas, so he likes flat country best. He's no mountain goat when it comes to climbing hills, but he's had plenty of experience since he came to Arizona. He's slow but steady. He puts his head down and takes the incline at his own speed. At first all the jackrabbits—the Datsuns and Hondas—pass him. Then, as the hill gets steeper, they begin to falter, but he keeps on at the same dogged pace. If it's a long hill, by the time we are near the summit he is steadily passing most of them. And when we start downhill, I can't hold him in. Even in low gear he tends to run away, careening around curves, tires squealing. I don't always enjoy the downhill part as much as he does. His center of gravity is a little too high for me to feel secure, although I appreciate the view from up here. Sometimes, when he leans at an extreme angle around a downhill curve, I have the sickening sensation that all four of his wheels are not entirely in contact with the road. Going downhill he reminds me of a horse, a big rawboned sorrel I had when I was a kid. As soon as we turned toward home, he would break into a wild gallop no matter how hard I tried to slow him down, and all I could do was grab the saddle horn and remember to duck low as we sailed through the barn door, which was just low enough to knock me off. It wasn't an act of aggression. At that moment he had his mind on something else.

Just now Blue Boy is starting a steady, winding climb. Not too steep, but enough to make him lean into it. We aren't into real rangeland yet, but these low hills, rising toward the Santa Ritas, are cattle country. The sea of greasewood is giving way to more varied, widely spaced vegetation. Ocotillo, yucca, and prickly pear are most obvious, each plant standing out smartly with plenty of space around it, guarding its territory. The ground is rocky and eroded, with here and there a pastel tint of green—new grass just coming up after the recent rains and not yet discovered by the cattle. It won't last long. There isn't a building in sight, and sight is a long way, but I can see a cattle pond near a dirt road, and I know there are a few ranch houses scattered miles apart off to the left, tucked away in the clefts of the low-lying Empire Mountains.

I should enjoy this stretch of the road, especially now when it is greener than usual. The view is expansive, and the shapes of the hills are intrinsically pleasing, like curves of the female body in repose. The growth is varied and dramatic. Soft greens, soft browns, soft grays, with here and there a burst of sunflowers or a prickle poppy waving brilliant white handkerchiefs. But all of a sudden this stretch of the road begins to get on my nerves. Bad memories. These low, rolling hills depress me, and the past isn't past enough as I drive through them.

There must be millions of people who live in the East who would look at this landscape and consider it paradise, who would give anything they have to live on one of these sprawling cattle ranches. The easygoing pace, the magnificent vistas, the hard, honest work close to nature. Haven't most of us dreamed of it at one time or another? Isn't this one of the dreams that drove our grandparents and great-grandparents across the plains and over the mountains, suffering and dying as they came west, always west. Unlimited sun and space. Land, and the opportunity to work on it, to be one's own boss. Air not breathed by anyone else. Some of the lucky ones, the tough ones, or the unscrupulous ones secured that dream and created a way of life that was to become the dominant idyllic symbol of American culture, translated through literature and film to all the world. And in spite of the fact that we know the translation was generally romantic and inaccurate, it is also somehow comforting to know that somebody, sometime, somewhere really did live on those cattle ranches in a manner even remotely similar to the one portrayed in books and films. With the addition of a few more gadgets and technology, somebody still does. Right over there on the other side of that low hill.

I don't know exactly how many acres of this particular kind of country it takes to support one cow, but I know the ranches have to be very big in order to support a sizable herd. When I hear ranchers talking about hundreds of thousands of acres in a single spread, my mind goes blank. I cannot envision it. Years ago when I spent some happy weekends riding horseback on one of the larger ranches in Southern Arizona, I could never really fathom how big it was. I knew it was so big that the horses were kept mostly for pleasure because the cowboys had to use jeeps and walkie-talkies just to stay in touch. I knew I could ride north thirty miles from the ranch house and I would still be on the ranch, but I could never come to grips with all that land actually being part of a single piece of property.

And with the exception of the enormous land grants made by the Spanish kings and later the Mexican government, many of which were ultimately disallowed and split up by the United States government, it is difficult to figure out exactly how these huge ranches got that way. The Homestead Act of 1862 said that the maximum number of acres of public land allowed to a homesteader was 160, or 320 for a man and wife. Even if a homesteader had a wife and ten grown children, not an unusual size for a family in 1862, they could jointly obtain only 1,920 acres, small potatoes as compared with many of the cattle ranches in Arizona, then or now. And although some exceptions were made, the magic figure of 160 acres was never changed until President Franklin Roosevelt withdrew what was left of the public domain from homestead entry in 1934.

The Homestead Act of 1862 was a foolish, catch-all piece of legislation. It was part of the Jeffersonian plan to insure a nation made up of small, independent farmers; but in the West it didn't. East of the hundredth meridian, where there was rich soil and abundant rainfall, 160 acres was plenty of land to support a family, often more than one family could work. But in the West, especially in the Southwest, with little rainfall, no irrigation, and alkaline soil, 160 acres wasn't nearly enough land for one family to survive on. And the major loophole in the Homestead Act was that it did not regulate transference of deeds and consequently could not prevent land speculation.

Yankee ingenuity in its most flagrant forms circumvented the Homestead Act and its corollaries—the Desert Land Act and the Timber and Stone Act. Homesteaders often built bird houses on their land so they could swear that the land had been improved. Or they dumped a barrel of water on it and paid a witness to swear that the land had been irrigated. Some claimed many 160-acre parcels under different names and using false identification papers. Historians have estimated that about 95 percent of the final proofs of land improvement under the Desert Land Act were fraudulent. But such fraudulent acquisition of public land represented a relatively small portion of the total land available. Enterprising land speculators acquired whole empires by obtaining, for a song, deeds to homesteaders' land, Spanish and Mexican land grants, and railroad land, often for European investors.

Many of the Mexicans who had settled in what is now Southern Arizona before the Gadsden Purchase, who did not speak or read English and did not understand Anglo ways of doing business, lost their land to Anglo homesteaders or speculators. Some were simply driven off their land at the point of a gun and fled south into Mexico, leaving no legal record of ownership. And the Southwest was won, for some homesteaders at least. The dream became a reality. But dreams which require such desperate methods to achieve often have a tendency to turn into nightmares somewhere down the road. One of them did, recently and right down that dirt road which cuts off from the highway and over the hill to a comfortable ranch house on a ranch which is not very large by local standards.

I know a young man who was raised in that ranch house. His name is Chad. He is well built and handsome, with a thick mane of dark, curly hair. Chad married the daughter of one of our neighbors in the Tucson Mountains. I attended their wedding. They settled on Chad's father's ranch and had a baby. It was all part of the Southwestern American dream—a beautiful young couple and their beautiful child on a ranch in a magnificent landscape. But Chad's father had had a long-standing land dispute with a neighboring rancher. I don't know how much land was disputed or why, but one day Chad's father took his gun to his neighbor's ranch and killed the rancher. Then he killed himself with the same gun. Then I lost track of Chad for a few years, although he continued to live on the ranch and work it. But he wasn't living there the last time I saw him. He was in the state prison. When the Southwestern version of the American dream starts to turn back on itself, there is no end of troubles.

Safford is a small farming community on the Gila River in the southeastern part of the state. It must have been sometime in 1981 that I went to the state prison there to visit a creative writing class. I didn't know Chad was there and didn't recognize him at first. Somehow, you don't expect to run into part of the American dream in a state prison. In 1980 Chad had been tried for unlawful imprisonment, kidnapping, and aggravated assault. Because he had a very good lawyer and the case was tried in Tucson, Chad was found guilty only of aggravated assault, but that crime carried a mandatory five-year sentence because it involved the use of a deadly weapon which was, of course, a gun.

During the trial, Chad admitted that he had detained a twenty-year-old Mexican man at gunpoint, padlocked a chain around his neck, chained him to a toilet, and left him for a day and a night without food or water. The Mexican's name was Manuel, and he was an illegal alien whom Chad had employed to work on the ranch for seven dollars a week. Chad believed that Manuel had stolen three thousand dollars worth of tools from the ranch, although Manuel had denied it. Somebody else later admitted to having taken the tools from Chad to settle an outstanding debt. At the trial, Chad said he had chosen to place the chain around Manuel's neck because "it looked like the most comfortable place." He also said, "I liked Manuel. I liked him for a long time. He was a friend of mine."

Rural farm workers and cattle hands in Mexico are called *campesinos*, which translates, literally, peasants. Thousands of campesinos come across the border in search of work each year, and they are often employed by Southern Arizona ranchers. I have seen groups of them many times, tramping resolutely down some dirt road, carrying little but a plastic jug of water, the one thing essential to survival in this country. Often I have given them rides, being careful not to ask them questions that would give me unwanted information about their status, since it is against the law to transport an illegal alien. But they usually speak little English, and my Spanish is so wretched that it isn't difficult to avoid finding out what I don't want to know. Blue Boy is commodious, and if people are willing to sit on the floor and scrunch up a little, he can carry a good many. I have sometimes wondered, idly, what I would do if I were caught near the border transporting a van load of illegal aliens, but it doesn't bear dwelling on.

The employment of illegal campesinos on ranches in Southern Arizona is traditional and has been a common practice as long as there have been American ranches in Southern Arizona. Recently the federal government has taken fairly drastic steps to try to stop this practice, but my feeling is that the government is trying to bail out the ocean with a tea cup. The attitudes of many Arizona ranchers toward these ragged campesinos is strangely ambivalent. They want to employ them, since the campesinos are experienced and will work for little pay, but at the same time the ranchers accuse the campesinos of slaughtering their cattle and stealing from their ranches.

In Chad's case, the fact that he assumed his tools had been stolen by an illegal alien, rather than by one of his Anglo acquaintances, is significant and fairly typical. And the particular nature of his treatment of Manuel is also significant. Some of the ranchers don't seem to feel that the aliens are quite human. They seem to think of them as varmints, almost like coyotes, which most ranchers routinely exterminate. For every case like Chad's that was reported by "an anonymous tip" to the United States Border Patrol, there are undoubtedly many which are not reported. And legal records would suggest that until quite recently even reported cases were not usually prosecuted.

Chad's case did not receive very much publicity. I had not heard about it before I encountered him in the prison. But one similar case received so much publicity that it monopolized the front pages of Arizona newspapers, off and on, for years. Seldom has the dirty laundry of the Southwestern American dream been so thoroughly exposed for all to see. Legally, it was a complex proceeding, and much of its complexity arose from the attitudes of the people of Southern Arizona, quite a few of whom, before it was over, sat on one or the other of its three juries.

The original defendants were George Hanigan, a wealthy, politically active rancher, and his two sons, Tom and Pat. All three were accused of detaining, robbing, and torturing three campesinos on the Hanigan ranch. The ranch extends on both sides of Highway 80 between Bisbee and Douglas, but closer to Douglas, where the highway parallels the Mexican border about two miles away. Before the first trial, however, the father died. The two young sons—Tom was under twenty and Pat was in his very early twenties—stood trial three times, and each time with a different result.

The first was an Arizona Superior Court trial in Bisbee in 1977, at the conclusion of which both defendants were acquitted. The federal government then stepped in, basing its case on an interstate commerce act which it claimed had been violated when the three victims were detained and not allowed to pursue employment. The first federal trial took place in Tucson in 1980 and resulted in a hung jury. The second federal trial, necessitated by the hung jury of the preceding one, was held in Phoenix in 1981. Obviously, each subsequent trial was being moved farther and farther away from the cattle ranch area in the southeastern corner of the state in order to obtain an unbiased jury. Bisbee is less than 25 miles away from the Hanigan ranch, Tucson is about 120 miles away, and Phoenix is about 240 miles away. It is noteworthy, I think, that Phoenix is north of the Gila River and well beyond the land included in the Gadsden Purchase. It is surrounded by farming and industrial areas and has a distinctly different style and outlook from the predominantly ranching-mining communities farther south. In the federal trial held in Phoenix, Tom was acquitted, but Pat was found guilty and sentenced to four years in prison.

The next year, while Pat was serving his sentence in a Pennsylvania federal prison, Tom was tried in Tucson for possession of five hundred pounds of marijuana, which had been found in the Hanigan barn. He was acquitted. Apparently Tom's trial for possession had no connection with the preceding legal actions, but it does suggest another thread in the tangled social fabric of life on the great ranches along the Mexican border.

Perhaps I shouldn't be depressed when I see those low hills on my left that remind me of Chad and the last time we met. Perhaps I should see in all this some progress being made toward respect for the human body and the human spirit. Chad's arrest came after the Hanigan case had received so much publicity. Without that publicity, the "anonymous tip" which resulted in Chad's arrest might never have been made. Without that publicity, whoever called the Border Patrol might not have had the courage to do so. Perhaps there is a force at work in recent years here in Southern Arizona that will make ranchers think twice before they torture or kill an illegal alien. Chad's lawyer admitted as much when he said his client felt that the trial came as a result of "Hispanic pressures." But in his closing statement to the jury, Chad's lawyer also said, "If the so-called victim was not a Mexican alien and this had not happened in the Southwest, this trial never would have happened." That means, I guess, that if you live in Lansing, Michigan, and you take your employee hostage at gunpoint, put a chain around his neck, chain him to a toilet and leave him there for twenty-four hours you will not be prosecuted. I don't know. I've never been to Lansing, Michigan. I'm sure the people there have problems of their own, but I doubt that they have this one.

Nobody knows how many unmarked graves are hidden in all those thousands of miles of the Southwestern American dream along the border. And nobody knows how many cases of murder, torture, or rape have gone unreported or unprosecuted in this beautiful country through which I am driving. The bones of dead bodies are soon scattered by coyotes in this country, and nothing is left to record what happened.

So I am depressed on this stretch of the road through lovely, undulating hills somewhere between grassland and desert. I keep thinking about the sparrows and wondering if God's eye is really on them. Maybe it's like the Messenger says about the sparrows in MacLeish's play J.B.: "Hardly ever see one dead." And a girl asks, "What happens to them?" The Messenger replies, "They get over it . . . over being there."

And I guess that's how I'll get over it, too, by getting over the next hill, and the next and the next.

drive, he sd, for
christ's sake, look
out where yr going.
   —Robert Creeley

A nd I do. And as I top the crest of the next low hill, a miracle lifts me out of my bad mood. It is a commonplace miracle, but a miracle nonetheless—a Parry's agave with a stalk fourteen feet high, like a huge candelabrum holding, at symmetrical intervals, what looks like shallow bowls about half a foot across and filled with frothy pink ice cream. Later, when the thousands of tiny blossoms in each bowl open more fully, they will shade from burnt orange at the top to ever more delicate yellow at the rim of the pale green bowl. No color coordinator could bring together a series of colors and tones so perfect. No wonder Parry's agave was called a century plant in the mistaken belief that it blooms only once in a hundred years. Each time I see one in bloom, it is the first time, the only time, and I think, "My God! What have I ever done to deserve this?"

My reaction to the sight of other desert plants, even to the mighty saguaro, is seldom this strong. I have lived in a saguaro forest for almost thirty years and have come, probably, to take those giants for granted. I think of them with affection as comic gods of the desert, gods whose comedy can be quickly turned into tragedy by disease or man's casual brutality. But this short-lived symmetrical wonder, with its dramatic silhouette and delicate colors, which stands as if it were offering bowls of delicious food to the sun—I could never take this for granted.

If I had to choose the seven plant-wonders of the desert region, Parry's agave would be one of them. Many other desert plants are more exotic or more spectacular when in bloom, but none is so dramatic while at the same time so delicately beautiful and none is more aesthetically right, at least not to my taste. Agaves are members of the amaryllis family, which includes daffodils and jonquils. Perhaps this accounts for the subtle but magnificent range of colors in their blossom clusters. I remember, many years ago, being struck speechless when I saw a field of wild jonquils in bloom.

Agave comes from a Greek word meaning noble or admirable, and the plant is well named. When in bloom it has majestic dignity. And it is admirable in many ways. It has provided humans with food, fabric, fiber, soap, medicine, an important tool, and a weapon. It has also provided us with a range of potent alcoholic drinks, including pulque, tequila, and mescal, which can temporarily ease our troubles. The ghastly looking thing at the bottom of a bottle of mescal is not a worm, as it is often called, but a pickled grub, the larval form of a moth for which the agave is the host plant. And it is true that good manners south of the border require the person who is served the last shot out of the mescal bottle to eat the grub as well. When the mescal bottle is three-fourths empty, it is a good plan to find some pressing excuse to leave the party, especially if you can still walk.

Each agave blooms only once, then dies. It takes between seven and twenty years for a Parry's to bloom, and I doubt that anyone can predict accurately which will be the big year for a given plant. About twelve years is probably an average lifespan. In the spring of its final year the plant suddenly begins to send up a central stalk, often as big around as a hefty man's lower leg, and the stalk puts out small alternating side branches. The stalks grow so fast that they seem to have appeared overnight. Some have been clocked at the rate of eighteen inches, straight up, a day. They are usually ramrod straight and harden into a woody material that is tough, light, and resilient. Both prehistoric and historic native people of this area used them as lances.

The leaves of the Parry's agave are flat, grayish-green swords that form a beautiful but wicked rosette from the center of which the stalk will ultimately grow. They stand at graduated angles. Each is between one and two feet long, has sharp serrated edges, and ends in a sharp tip like a large needle. In fact, they were traditionally used as needles. If removed properly, the needle comes attached to its own long strand of tough fiber which serves as thread. The needles will even sew through leather without difficulty. We prize the agave as a landscape plant in the Tucson area, but woe to the gardener who must work with it. One careless gesture can drive the tip of an agave leaf completely through his or her hand, leaving a stigmata for life. In captivity, when given water, these plants grow to be more than five feet tall before the central stalk appears, formidable guests on the patio unless it is a very large patio. But in its uncultivated state it prefers slightly higher elevations than the lower sections of Tucson, at about 2,390 feet, can provide. It thrives at between 4,000 and 5,000 feet. This is the first Parry's I have seen since leaving town, but I will see them in increasing numbers for the next few miles as I gain elevation.

I am also beginning to see the smaller and more spartan cousins of Parry's agave, the lechugilla. Its leaves are narrower, stiffer, and more sharply serrated, like bread knives. In this area, lechugillas usually grow singly and are widely spaced. But in parts of the Chihuahuan Desert they grow in dense stands that cover large stretches of terrain. A horse or person on foot who attempts to cut through these stands will usually wind up with badly lacerated legs. The leaves can also slash the tires of off-road vehicles, which is another reason I think this relative of the agave is well named with the Greek word meaning admirable. The lechugilla also sends up a single stalk when it blooms, usually no more than seven or eight feet high, and very slender. The stalk has no side branches but is covered with tiny blossoms which turn it, as the blossoms open, from pale yellow-green to mauve to gold. In full bloom it reminds me of a single stalk of a delphinium—taller than I am and bright gold. After the lechugilla blooms and dies, its central spike turns to the color of ripe wheat and often remains standing for several seasons, dry and stiffly erect, with a marvelous kind of grace and audacity.

In my personal system of taxonomy, I classify both Parry's agave and lechugilla among "things-that-stick-straight-up." This is not an expression from some Native American culture. I got it from my students at the University of Arizona. Many of my students, especially the graduate students, have had no experience with the Southwestern landscape and have never before seen a desert. I sometimes take groups of them into the desert on brief outings. I enjoy listening to them later when they try to describe what they saw. Some of their attempts to describe the desert have resulted in astonishing feats of description from which I learned a great deal, at least a great deal about the students, if not about the desert. One, whose response was fairly typical, said, "There were lots of bushes all tangled up and some cactus things. There were some little trees and some other things that stuck straight up. It was a disheveled mess and it scared me."

While not a model of scientific precision, such a description is full of information. It verifies my suspicion that many people expect all deserts to be sand, sand, and more sand. When faced with the lush and varied growth that characterizes the Sonoran, they are confused and surprised and can suffer from sensory-overload. The description also tells me that if one cannot identify the native plants in a particular landscape—and almost any name will do—the plants tend to blur into one another and become a confused and confusing mass of vegetation, or bushes. In other words, if you can't name it, you can't really see it. In this lies the magic of names and naming. To name a thing is to give it a second creation, a creation by the viewer. God created the plants and creatures, but they were not part of Adam's world until Adam named them. Then he could see each one of them clearly, deal with it, and have some power over it, if only the power to run when he saw it coming. And ultimately, what I am trying to teach my students is the power of names, a form of word magic which was practiced, in its most obvious form, by primitive peoples. I think all poets believe in word magic. Maybe that's what distinguishes them from novelists.

In spite of all this, my student's description tells me that some arid-land plants are so distinctive and visually arresting they can be somewhat distinguished from others even though the viewer does not have a name with which to identify them. And so we have things-that-stick-straight-up, which is one of the major categories in my personal system of taxonomy. This category includes Parry's agave and the lechugilla when they are blooming, as well as the saguaro all the time, unless, of course, it has fallen down. When I want to be particularly scientific and impressive, I refer to the saguaro as either Serious Giant (*Cerreus giganteus*) or Public Library Giant (*Carnegiea gigantea*), since both names are used by specialists to identify it.

I am eclectic about where I get the names of things. If all else fails, I simply make up a name. I invented the name Engelman dingleberry

(*Dingleberrius engelmannii*), and that name is well on its way to becoming the accepted one for a relatively rare desert plant. At least my students accepted it. From a poet friend I learned to call the prickly pear "ping-pong-paddle cactus," unless it happens to be cow tongue or beaver tail, which is a closely related cactus with elongated pads. From the Spanish I have picked up the names for many desert plants. The yucca I am seeing along the highway now, for instance, I call "Spanish bayonet." When it bloomed in May and early June, I referred to it as "our Lord's candle." In this way my personal system adds a further refinement to the more scientific system. What you call it, according to my system, depends not only on who you are and where you are, but on when you see it. And when you see it is important in the desert, whose plants often pay little attention to the conventional four seasons.

The ocotillo, which is scattered over these low hills, is a good case in point for the effectiveness of my system. It is the most prominent Sonoran plant in my category things-that-stick-up-at-an-angle, and it sometimes grows in stands so thick as to be impenetrable. But the ocotillo appears to be several different plants depending on when you see it. At the moment, it is rich and green and luxuriant because of the recent rains; but two months ago, when it bloomed, it resembled nothing but thorny bunches of dead sticks, each ending in a clump of vivid red blossoms. In that phase it could be called "blood-tipped spear," from the Spanish.

To say that the ocotillo is a strange plant means very little, since the desert world in which it lives is filled with plants that are considered bizarre by genteel plant-lovers. But the ocotillo is truly strange, even by desert standards, and it comes from a strange and still somewhat mysterious family, the *Fouquieria*. The most bizarre member of the family, a cousin of the ocotillo, although there is little family resemblance, is the Boojum tree, named after a dreaded creature in Lewis Carroll's *The Hunting of the Snark*.

Beware of the day,
If your Snark be a Boojum! For then
You will softly and suddenly vanish away,
And never be met with again!

I need not be afraid of meeting a Boojum here. They grow only in the Vizcaíno region of the Sonoran Desert, about halfway down the peninsula of Baja California, and in a small area along the eastern edge of the Gulf of California. I think the Boojum would defy even my students' powers of description, but it is definitely one of the things-that-stick-straight-up. It looks like a gray and hairy upside-down rutabaga and can be thirty feet tall. Even at its tallest, it is a fat, complacent-looking creature with a pin head. Some think that the Boojum has not been studied very thoroughly by botanists because it grows only in areas that are difficult to get to, but I believe that it is still mysterious because no one dares to examine it too closely for fear the examiner "will softly and suddenly vanish away." I remember the weird feeling I got from standing in a forest of Boojums in Baja California, as if I had stumbled onto the set of a surrealistic science-fiction movie. I would not have been much surprised if they had suddenly begun to jabber in an unintelligible Martian dialect.

The ocotillo is not as strange looking as the Boojum, by any means, but it does look like something one might encounter at the bottom of the sea, and its long arms undulate in the wind as if in an ocean current. The arms or branches of the ocotillo are usually between nine and fifteen feet long, and each grows independently from a central stump barely protruding from the ground. A mature plant produces between forty and seventy-five branches. In the spring, when the tip of each branch is covered with a large clump of orange-red blossoms, the weight of the blossoms has a tendency to bend the tops of the branches down in graceful arcs.

Each branch has long curved thorns at brief intervals, which is probably why some people think of the ocotillo as a cactus. But its thorns are thorns, not needles. They are sharp but not barbed, as many cactus spines are, and they do not detach themselves when they encounter a victim. They are more like the claws of an animal, which can rake and tear. And because the ocotillo moves so much, waving its long arms in the slightest breeze, it seems animal-like. The branches are flexible and can be bent down almost to the ground without breaking, but they snap back into place with great force, which is probably why the ocotillo is sometimes called "coachwhip." Those who bend a branch down to examine or smell the blossoms often find that when they let go, the backlash rakes deep furrows in their flesh. The most gruesome thing I know about the ocotillo is that its branches were used by the Penitentes, a religious sect in the Sangre de Cristo Mountains in New Mexico, to flagellate themselves and one another. Sometimes the Penitentes replaced the blossoms at the end of each branch with small, sharp pieces of tin.

I have read that deer find the blossoms of the ocotillo a great delicacy and will leap onto the plant and force its branches down in order to reach the blossoms. I have never seen a deer do this and am a little skeptical, considering the damage the deer would probably sustain. On the other hand, I have seen javelinas chomping happily on pads of the prickly pear, in spite of the hideous damage the spines must surely do to their mouths and lips. Perhaps nature has equipped these creatures with some unknown way to avoid such damage. If so, I would very much like to learn the secret. I have never been injured by an animal in the desert and have been bitten by only one snake—it was in my own kitchen and completely my own fault—but I have been attacked and injured by thousands of plants.

In fact, I sometimes have difficulty making a clear distinction in my mind between plants and animate creatures of the desert. They often have striking similarities. The thorns on the branch of a mature ocotillo, for instance, have almost the exact curve, color, and size as the beak of a curved-bill thrasher, one of the most common and aggressive birds of both the Sonoran and Chihuahuan deserts. The form evolved for two different purposes, but is almost identical in both cases. A plant with a thorn like the beak of a bird, and a bird with a beak like the thorn of a plant—I wonder what Lewis Carroll would have made of that?

Other things about the ocotillo suggest that it would be at home in Alice's Wonderland. It changes its appearance so drastically and rapidly that sometimes it is almost unrecognizable from one week to the next. During much of the time its arms are leafless and sere, a dead-looking gray, and its claws are prominent. But after a rain, even a brief rain, it puts out tight clusters of lush green leaves, each about an inch-and-a-half long, which entirely cover the length of each branch. The leaves hide the thorns and turn the slender dead-looking sticks into plump, sinuous columns of green. It is suddenly beautiful. This can happen at any time of year, although it happens most frequently in early spring and during the monsoon season in late summer, like right now. Within forty-eight hours after a rain, the branches are well covered, and the transformation is complete in three days. As soon as the ground dries, the leaves change colors with the same rapidity, turning a vivid pinkish yellow or gold. Then they fall off, and the dry sticks reappear. Even in one of the drier years, this transformation was recorded five times between February and August. It is as dramatic as the changing appearance of the maple during different seasons in New England, but the ocotillo goes through these changes rapidly, again and again during the year, seeming to compress summer, fall, and winter into three weeks, and spring often lasts only one day.

It is a complex juggling act. The plant needs green cells to carry on photosynthesis, so it puts out leaves; but it also needs to conserve water, so it quickly drops the leaves when moisture is not available, thereby cutting down on evaporation, which occurs most rapidly in leaves. The branches are coated with a semi-transparent waxy substance that inhibits evaporation, but even without the leaves ocotillos are capable of carrying on a low level of photosynthesis because each branch is striped longitudinally with pale green bark. This ability to manage photosynthesis through the trunk or branches is, of course, the hallmark of cacti, but it is also fairly common in several other kinds of arid-land plants, especially the paloverde, a tree with a green trunk and branches, whose name means "green stick" in Spanish.

The ocotillo has been a significant element in desert architecture almost as far back as there was any desert architecture. Both prehistoric and modern peoples have used it in their jacal structures, houses whose walls were formed by sticking branches upright in the earth and covering or daubing them with clay. Its branches are also used as a standard roofing material for the ramadas built by the Tohono O'odham and other native peoples. Such structures, with their ocotillo roofs, provide shade in some of the desert gardens of the homes in the Tucson area today. But to me, the most fascinating of its architectural uses is the living fence, still commonly seen in the rural Southwest on both sides of the border. Individual branches are cut to whatever length is desired and simply stuck in the ground in a row. When woven together with a couple of strands of rawhide, or, in more recent times, wire, they form a wickedly impenetrable fence, often used for corrals. If one wants a drab, gray fence, they are left alone. If one wants a lush, green fence, they are watered and quickly put out leaves. The cut branches will never produce new plants, but they will live and put out leaves whenever the soil is sufficiently damp. Such a fence will outlast a picket fence exposed to the dry air and sun of the Southwest, and it will paint itself bright green at irregular intervals.

The ocotillo is green and inviting now, but as soon as the rainy season is over it will quickly revert to tall clusters of dry, thorny sticks. Thinking about it, I chuckle, remembering a young man who came to the university from Brazil to learn English. He was a handsome devil, but not a very good student of languages. In fact, he managed to master only two expressions in English, but with those and his charm he was able to make friends and get along quite nicely, especially with women. The two expressions, either of which could be inflected as a question or a statement, were: "Is beautiful" and "Is not beautiful." That's the way it is with the ocotillo. It is either beautiful or it is not beautiful, and everything depends on when you see it.

When I first saw it, it was not beautiful. I didn't know what it was, and it depressed me. That was in November of 1956, and I was miserable as only the young can be miserable. It was about forty-five miles southeast of here and a little higher, where ocotillos grow in dense stands at the base of the Huachuca Mountains, which rose up to the west like a huge wall. To the north, slightly farther away, were more mountains. To the east, across the sweep of a great valley, was an enormous palisade of mountains. And the southern horizon was cut off by something ugly and menacing, thousands of things that stuck up at strange angles, blocking all passage like a tangle of barbed wire fifteen feet high. I didn't know it then, but is was a thick stand of ocotillos in their most unattractive phase. I felt that I was being held prisoner, surrounded by mountains with the only escape route blocked by some hideous barricade. Actually, I was a prisoner in a sense, but not a prisoner of the mountains and ocotillos. I was trapped by the United States Army, and I was projecting my inner frustration onto the landscape, as we all do sometimes. The landscape was new to me, and threatening.

I had been drafted immediately after four years of undergraduate school and sent to boot camp in central Texas, where my prolonged adolescence came to a sudden, painful end. I think our cycle of training was more brutal than most boot camps, even in those days, since it resulted in many serious injuries to the men and a congressional investigation. I was lucky to complete it with the loss of only two wisdom teeth and my illusions about mankind's basic goodness. At the conclusion of boot camp, when we were given our future assignments, I don't recall anyone complaining. There was no war on at the moment, and we all knew that wherever we were to be sent, it had to be better than where we were.

But my assignment and that of a few other men in the group did produce a few laughs. We were to be sent to a Signal Corps facility to be trained as "ultra-high frequency radio operators." That sounded sophisticated and impressive. But none of us had ever heard of the place, and we couldn't pronounce its name. The sergeant, who couldn't pronounce its name either, told us that it was an overseas assignment but that we would not get overseas' pay. He also told us that it was called Ft. Hootchy-kootchy, but the nearest unmarried women were seventy-five miles away and they were all Mexican whores. This, a reference to the red-light district in Nogales, on the Mexican border, was quite inaccurate, since there were four square blocks of brothels in Naco, also on the Mexican border but only about thirty miles away. But none of this mattered to me. I felt that whatever part of me had survived boot camp could survive anything, and I was getting out of hell.

So they put the dozen or so of us on a train headed vaguely west, toward Ft. Hootchy-kootchy. The pullman car we were in was repeatedly shunted onto sidings, where it was left standing for hours, once all night, but we were in no hurry. We played poker while our car sat on sidings or while Texas and New Mexico rolled past the windows. Finally, about 2:00 A.M. of the third night, we arrived somewhere— nobody knew exactly where. We were awakened and told to get our gear and get off the train, which by this time was a freight train with the exception of the car we were in.

When we stumbled off the train, it was very dark, with no moon, and the stars were brighter than I had ever remembered seeing them before. After the train pulled out, there were no other lights anywhere.

We stood in the dirt beside the railroad tracks, dazed by darkness and still half asleep. When we realized that we were totally alone, somebody found a flashlight in his duffel bag. By shining it around, we could make out a barbed-wire fence along the tracks, and beyond it a rickety cattle chute and a small herd of cows, who turned their white faces and big, luminous eyes toward us as if we had just dropped from the sky. There was a dirt road that crossed the railroad tracks, and near it the ruins of what had once been a large, pretentious two-story house, but totally deserted and with all its doors and windows broken out. The country seemed to be fairly flat, but we couldn't really tell with just the stars and a flashlight.

The night was cool but not cold. We stood around and discussed the situation. The general consensus was that we had been let off the train at the wrong place, and I hoped it was true. But I had a sinking feeling it wasn't, especially when I remembered the sergeant's evil laugh when he had given me my assignment. We didn't know how long it would be before another train came along or whether it would stop for us. The tracks didn't look as if they were often used, and the road didn't look much used at all. But there wasn't anything we could do about it until dawn, so some of us lay down on the ground with our heads on our duffel bags and tried to go back to sleep.

About an hour later, somebody saw a pair of lights, far in the distance, coming toward us. It turned out to be an ancient military bus with a sleepy young driver. He told us he was sorry to be so late, but he hadn't been sure when the train would come through since it was a freight and didn't operate on a regular schedule. When we asked him where in the hell we were, he told us we were at Hereford, Arizona, the railroad drop-off for Ft. Huachuca (Wa-CHU-kah). That wasn't too much help, but at least we learned how to pronounce the name of our destination. The hootchy-kootchy jokes had begun to wear a little thin. When we asked the driver why there wasn't a depot at Hereford, he said there wasn't anything at Hereford but a chute for loading cattle and an old abandoned house. So we had seen all of Hereford with one flashlight.

Today there is even less to see, since the ruins of the old house have been torn down. Hereford is just one of many names on the map of Southern Arizona for which there is no town, not even a ghost town.

It has a past, a history, but today it exists only as a geographical idea, a place where something used to be. And even its name is misleading. I thought for years that it was named after a certain kind of cow, but it wasn't. Like the town of Bisbee where I am now heading, it was named after a lawyer. We don't seem to name towns after lawyers much anymore, and I don't know if that says something about today's lawyers or about the people who name towns.

But Hereford and Bisbee share some history and are linked by more than the fact that they were both named after lawyers. In the late 1870s Colonel William Herring, a New York mine promoter who had come west, developed the Neptune Mine just southeast of the infant Copper Queen Mine in the Mule Mountains. (In those years every man of wealth and property was given the honorary title "Colonel." It had nothing to do with military service.) The mining camp in the Mule Mountains had, as yet, no name, but in 1880 its residents officially named it Bisbee after the San Francisco lawyer DeWitt Bisbee, a member of the firm that had helped secure financial backing for the Copper Queen Mine. The ore in the Neptune was rich, but the Copper Queen Mine controlled the only source of water in the Mule Mountains with sufficient volume to cool a refinery. So Colonel Herring constructed a road fifteen miles westward to the San Pedro River, purchased six hundred acres of the San Rafael Land Grant, and built a smelter on the east bank of the river. On the west bank he laid out a town for the smelter workers and named it Hereford, after his friend Benjamin J. Hereford, a Tucson lawyer who later served a term in the upper house of the Arizona Territorial Legislature.

Colonel Herring built the headquarters of the Neptune Mine and an elaborate home for his family, called "The Castle," near the Bisbee mining camp in the Mule Mountains. But the ore in the Neptune Mine soon gave out, and Herring had spent most of his investors' money on improvements. The mine closed, and in 1882 all the Neptune property in the Mule Mountains was sold at sheriff's auction. The smelter on the San Pedro burned down, and Hereford was abandoned. But it wasn't the end for Colonel Herring. Having failed as a mining entrepreneur, he became a lawyer and politician like his friend Hereford and was appointed attorney general to the Territory of Arizona in 1891.

Hereford was deserted from 1882 until 1892 when William Greene established a cattle ranch there. Greene was later to become a multi-millionaire and a legend in the Southwest and beyond. His empire would include copper mines and cattle ranches on both sides of the border, and he would ride through it in his private railroad car accompanied by governors and friends who controlled the financial pulse of America. When he spoke, Wall Street would not only listen, it would come to attention and salute. But in 1892 he was just a rancher with about three hundred head of cattle, and he was to encounter the greatest tragedy of his life at Hereford on the San Pedro River.

For several years Greene feuded with a neighboring rancher, a man who was already a legend in his own time—Jim Burnett. Both Greene and Burnett were transplanted New Yorkers, and both had made remarkable adjustments to their Western environment. In addition to his cattle ranch on the San Pedro, Burnett owned a livery stable and a butcher shop in nearby Charleston, and he was a Justice of the Peace who administered rough, two-gun justice. Nor was he, evidently, too fastidious about how he obtained his cattle, although the major dispute with Greene seemed to be about water. Burnett was unpopular. Wearing so many hats, he had made many enemies in one capacity or another. Greene was well liked. He was generous and had a way with people that was to serve him well in later years when labor disputes turned his mines into armed camps.

In 1897, on June 24, San Juan's Day, that day we associate with water, somebody blew up the dam that impounded a large quantity of water on the Greene ranch. As a result, Greene's nine-year-old daughter Ella and her little friend and neighbor Katie Corcoran were drowned. Greene was sure that Burnett had blown up the dam, and he was probably right. On July 1 he encountered Burnett by accident outside a livery stable in Tombstone. Newspaper accounts later said that Burnett was armed, but eyewitnesses said he wasn't. Greene shot Burnett once. Burnett staggered into the side door of the livery stable, through the office, and out the front door, where he fell in the street. Greene came around the building, found Burnett lying in the street, and shot him a second time, killing him. Later, while in the nominal custody of the sheriff of Tombstone, who was his good friend, Greene said in an interview, " 'Vengeance is mine, I will repay,' saith the Lord." In December he was tried for second degree murder in the courthouse at Tombstone. The jury deliberated less than ten minutes and acquitted him.

When Greene settled at Hereford, he thought the land was available for homesteading. Later, after the death of his daughter and her friend, he found out that his cattle ranch was part of the San Rafael Grant and was legally owned by the Camou family. He was a squatter. He vacated, but years later, when he had become a copper king and cattle baron on both sides of the border, he bought the tract of land at Hereford. Perhaps it was just a good investment. Or perhaps it was because of Ella and her friend, who had drowned in the San Pedro River, which was normally no more than a foot deep.

At the site of old Hereford, Greene built a mansion to be used as ranch headquarters and his residence when he was there. It was one of several similar mansions he built at his various ranches and mines on both sides of the border in Arizona and Sonora, Mexico. It was still there, although in ruins, when I arrived in the night at Hereford. At the time, it meant nothing to me. Just a big old house with all its windows busted out. Now it is gone, like the town of Hereford, which was gone when it was built. I miss it. Whenever I cross the river at Hereford, I have a strange, uneasy feeling, as if I were floating off into the future in a balloon with nothing to anchor me to the past and no way to come down.

Hereford still appears on the map, and my assumption about how it got its name was logical, but wrong. The only Herefords who ever lived there were the four-legged kind, and they still do. They stared at our little military contingent when we arrived and again when the bus took us away toward something we hoped would pass for beds. I managed to stay awake during the bus ride out of Hereford, but only because the dirt road was so bad and the bus had long since given up any claims to shock absorbers.

After about eight miles which seemed like fifty, we encountered a paved road and turned north onto it. About ten miles down that road we came to an intersection and turned west. At the intersection was a small country schoolhouse, the first sign of civilization I had noticed. A couple of miles farther down that road we drove through the small community of Fry, Arizona, which ended abruptly at the main gate of Ft. Huachuca. There wasn't much of Fry to see on the main drag, which seemed to be the only paved road it could boast of—a block of storefront buildings, a motel, a gas station, and several bars. There were a couple of large two-story buildings, one a frame building in military style that proved to be a noncommissioned officers' club, and the other a stucco building very near the entrance of the fort, which I later found out had been donated to the community by the boxer Joe Louis when he was stationed at Ft. Huachuca during World War II. It was a recreation center for the soldiers. I often wondered how broadly the term "recreation" was defined in those days during the war when Fry was called "Hook" by the soldiers because of all the hookers who flocked to it. But whatever it had been, the building was merely a recreation center during my stay at Ft. Huachuca.

Actually, when I arrived in 1956, Fry was not the town's official name. It had been named Fry in 1937 in honor of an early settler, but the year before I arrived the citizens had decided that Fry, Arizona, was not a name calculated to attract tourists or anyone else. They had changed it to the more poetic Sierra Vista, although the new name had not yet caught on and the town was still called Fry.

After we entered the fort's main gate, we drove for what seemed like a long time without seeing much of anything. The country was rolling grassland, and the short, dry grass showed blond and tawny in the headlights as the road dipped and curved. Finally, we pulled up in front of a very large two-story frame building, which was unmistakably a military barracks but not like any barracks I had ever seen. It had a dignity and style that suggested much earlier times, with deep verandas at both levels across the front and back. It was built on a gentle slope so that it had only about a foot of foundation at one end, but at the other end the foundation of dark basaltic stone was tall enough to form a kind of above-ground basement under the first floor. The building was totally unadorned, but in spite of its general austerity and military paint job, something about it made me think of a simple but gracious Southern mansion. My idea of military architecture was based on the ugly salt boxes the military constructed throughout the West during World War II, but this building had generous lines and dimensions and an imposing, if utilitarian, look about it, as if it contained ample space for some military version of gracious living.

We went inside and found a clerk who issued us mattresses and bedding and directed us downstairs to a barracks room in the above-ground basement portion of the building. We spread our mattresses on the bunks, and some of us simply fell on them, too tired to make up our beds or take off our clothes.

When I woke up, the room was bright and most of the other men were still asleep. I could hear, far off, a drill sergeant shouting orders, and I could smell—but it couldn't be—horse manure? The smell wasn't very strong but it was the smell of horse manure. This brought me wide awake. Something was wrong. In my mind I quickly reviewed my assignment. "Signal Corps . . . Ultra-high frequency radio operator." No mention of horses or cavalry. So I got up and went outside to investigate. What I saw was so unexpected that I climbed the outside staircase to the second floor veranda to get a better view. It was my first daytime look at a nineteenth-century Wild West cavalry post twelve miles from the Mexican border.

The building on whose veranda I was standing was one of several very similar ones that marched in a symmetrical line down a great slope to the east. In front of them was a large quadrangle of parade ground with a very tall flagpole on the far side and a Victorian gazebo bandstand at the west end. Across the parade ground, in another line as inevitable as the slope of the hill itself, were about a dozen old houses, most of which were almost exactly the same. Each had screened sleeping porches across the first story, three large dormer windows across the second, and a tall chimney rising from each side wall. The houses were shaded with enormous cottonwoods whose leaves were brilliant gold. It was magnificent. I decided it was a movie set and went in search of breakfast.

When I arrived in 1956, Ft. Huachuca had been a Signal Corps facility for less than two years, but it had been a cavalry post for more than five decades. The building in which I spent my first night was built in 1883, part of the oldest section of the fort. The room I slept in must have been used as a stable at one time, probably before the foundation was closed in to make a room. I woke up that morning smelling history and thought it was just horse manure. The horses and men who had ridden them were long since dead, but the look and smell of the place had not changed very much. The cavalrymen had to keep their horses as nearby as possible to prevent them from being stolen by the

Apaches, who were the reason the fort had been established in the first place. The soldiers at Ft. Huachuca would have been particularly sensitive about the need to keep their horses away from the Apaches because of what had happened at Camp Wallen, about eight miles to the north.

Camp Wallen, which lasted only from 1866 to 1869, was one embarrassment after another to the military. It was manned by Troop A, First Cavalry, but the Apaches stole all their horses, leaving Troop A afoot, an awkward situation for the cavalry. It was probably also humiliating when Troop A was replaced by Company G of the Thirty-second Infantry, who had walked all the way from the west coast. But the worst was yet to come. The army discovered that it had accidentally established Camp Wallen on private land, part of the San Ignacio del Babocomari land grant. This must have been even more embarrassing to the military than the same kind of mistake was to Colonel Greene at Hereford, twenty-five years later. By the time Greene made his mistake, the country along the border was "settling up," but in 1866 the great majority of the land was still public, and one had to look rather diligently to find any that wasn't. So Camp Wallen folded its tents and disappeared, leaving the Apaches unopposed in the area.

Since 1849, immigrants from the settled parts of the United States had been streaming overland to California. Some were land-hungry and some were gold-hungry, some were in search of a dream and some were running away from a dream gone sour, but they came in increasing numbers and by several routes. The most southerly overland route, the route often taken by settlers from the South, split in several different trails as it crossed what is now Southeastern Arizona, but all the trails led through hundreds of miles of land controlled by the Apaches. The southern route was a trade-off. Travelers avoided the high mountain passes and snow of the northerly routes, but they got, instead, the Apaches. For many the southern route proved to be a fatal choice.

The most heavily traveled of the divergent southern routes snaked through Southeastern Arizona roughly parallel to present Interstate 10, avoiding the largest of the mountain ranges. The trail was fairly level, but it went through dreaded Apache Pass north of the Chiricahua Mountains, probably the most dangerous passage of the entire journey. Fort Bowie was established nearby in 1862 to protect the travelers from the Apaches, but not always with much success. During one period in the late 1870s it was all the cavalry could do to hold the fort, while the Apaches stole all its cattle and raided all its supply wagons. Partly to avoid Apache Pass, many immigrants chose an alternative trail even farther south, which dipped into Mexico near the line that now divides Arizona from New Mexico and reentered the United States by way of either the San Pedro or Santa Cruz valleys, then leading north to Tucson.

During the Civil War, protective troops were withdrawn from Southern Arizona to fight elsewhere. The Apaches were quick to take advantage of this military vacuum. At the conclusion of the war, the government cut military funds severely, and subsequent cavalry posts in the Southwest were widely scattered, understaffed, and inadequately funded. But there were other reasons why the Apache Wars dragged on into the last decade of the nineteenth century.

The Apache warriors were among the greatest horsemen ever to ride on the North American Continent, along with the Navajos to the north and the Comanches to the east. An Apache war party could travel seventy miles a day for many days while a cavalry unit usually did well to average thirty miles a day. The Apache warriors were usually better mounted than the United States Cavalry, since they had their pick of all the horses in the area, including the horses of the cavalrymen, like those at Camp Wallen. In many cases the Apache warriors were also better armed than the cavalry. While the rifles of the cavalrymen were often old and outmoded, the Apaches were, in many cases, armed with the most recent model rifles, often new. And it is no mystery how they got them. Some were stolen or taken from dead victims, but the majority of their rifles, along with great quantities of ammunition, were brought west over the Santa Fe Trail, sold to gun runners in New Mexico and Arizona, and then traded to the Apaches. It was a lucrative business, and as long as the Apaches were in the field, the government was never able to stop it. Thousands of United States citizens, both military and civilian, were killed by rifles sold to the Apaches by other United States citizens. If the scenario has a familiar ring, it is because of its similarity to today's traffic in illegal drugs, much of which takes place in exactly the same area. As long as a product is in sufficient demand, no matter how dangerous or damaging it is to others, somebody will come forward to sell it.

It wasn't merely the climate or the lack of water that inhibited settlement in Arizona south of the Gila River. Many ranchers and miners proved they could handle those problems. But they could not survive in the land of the Apaches. At the end of the Civil War, the entire non-Indian population of Arizona had dwindled to less than six hundred, and most of those were huddled in Tucson, virtual prisoners of the Apaches, afraid to go outside the town even to tend their fields. Tubac had been abandoned, as had most of the ranches and mines in the area.

William Tecumseh Sherman, commanding general of the United States Army, strongly recommended that all the non-Indian population be ordered out of the Arizona Territory. Thirty years earlier, before he had become a famous Civil War general, he had said, "We fought one war with Mexico to take the Southwest . . . we should fight another war to make them take it back." And it wasn't even clear that Mexico wanted it back. The Mexican government complained repeatedly to the United States about Apache depredations on their side of the border. The Apaches constantly swept southward across the border, raided the ranches and towns in Mexico's northern frontier, sometimes penetrating several hundred miles into Mexico, and then quickly withdrew to their mountain retreats in Southern Arizona. They were deadly, incredibly swift, and almost invisible.

General Sherman's recommendations, however, which were sound from both a military and a humane standpoint, did not prevail. To shut off the Arizona Territory would have blocked the southern thrust of westward expansion by the United States. It would have isolated much of Southern California from the rest of the country, and then there was the matter of the proposed railroad line which had been the main impetus for the Gadsden Purchase. Was that ten million dollars simply to be thrown to the wind because of some recalcitrant redskins in some Godforsaken mountains with unpronounceable names? Of course not!

So the government slowly established cavalry posts at key points in Southern Arizona to protect the immigrants and settlers, mostly ranchers and miners, and to try to keep the Apaches from crossing the Mexican border. The government also inaugurated a reservation system in Arizona for the Apaches. The system never worked for several reasons. One was that the Indian agents sent to manage the reservations were often corrupt and victimized the Apaches. Another was that some of the Apaches got into the habit of using the reservation as a home base from which to carry on their raids and to which they could return for protection when pursued. Clever, those Apaches. And cruel, terribly cruel. The history of the Apache Wars is one long story of the United States government finding out just how clever they were, and almost always a little too late.

In the San Pedro and Santa Cruz valleys through which the immigrant wagons on the most southerly overland route to California rolled, and into which a few daring miners and ranchers had ventured even after the debacle of Camp Wallen in 1869, the situation was deplorable. And so, in March of 1877, the army ordered a Civil War veteran with a wonderful name and proven ability, Captain Samuel Marmaduke Whitside, to take a detachment consisting of two companies of the Sixth Cavalry, one from Ft. Lowell near Tucson and one from Ft. Grant in the Pinaleño Mountains, and to establish a military camp on the east side of the Huachuca Mountains, which lie between the valleys of the San Pedro and Santa Cruz. The task assigned to Captain Whitside was complex and difficult. His men were to protect the settlers and miners in the area, protect the wagon trains of the immigrants, keep an eye on Cochise's stronghold in the Dragoon Mountains to the east, patrol the Mexican border, and apprehend any renegade Apaches who might decide to leave their reservation at San Carlos, north of Ft. Bowie, before they could get into Mexico.

But first Captain Whitside and his detachment had to find a place to establish the camp, a place which was somewhat protected from the Apaches, which provided a view of the San Pedro Valley, which was close to the Mexican border, and which had a good supply of water, wood, and grass—assuming the men were able to keep their horses. After inspecting the area, Captain Whitside located the camp toward the northern end of the Huachuca range in a canyon about eight miles from where Camp Wallen had had its brief, troubled existence.

At first the camp consisted of nothing but tents, but soon the men were able to take enough time out from chasing Apaches to construct a few simple adobe buildings, which proved unable to stand up to the weather. The Huachuca Mountains had been called Thunder Mountains by the Apaches. They seemed to attract storms. During the camp's second monsoon season most of the adobe structures washed away or collapsed, and those that remained had leaking roofs or none at all. Captain Whitside, who was not a man generally given to complaint, described the situation in a letter: "Conditions are very trying and discouraging. . . . We have labored constantly getting out materials and erecting buildings, all of which are now washed away or rendered uninhabitable."

And although the history books say that Camp Huachuca was established in March 1877, it was not called that for the first year of its existence, at least not by the people living in the area, including the itinerate miners who hung around the camp for protection. It was known as Camp Detachment. I don't think the term was used in an absolute sense, but it was certainly fitting. During the camp's first few years, nearly everything about it was, or was rapidly becoming, detached—even its buildings.

When I was stationed at Ft. Huachuca from 1956 to 1958, it still had a strong aura of detachment. It was a remote military island surrounded by many miles of sparsely inhabited mountains, rangeland, and desert, not on the beaten path to anywhere, and basically inaccessible by public transportation. It was cut off on the south by the Mexican border and on the north by the lack of a paved road to Tucson. Even its hospital was a series of detachments, a row of temporary one-story barracks buildings connected to one another by wooden walkways, like wagons that nobody had formed into a circle. Our son was born in that strange affair in 1958, and we had no complaints about the finished product. But about fourteen years later, he complained to me that he wished he had been born in some regular town like everybody else. When he filled out his place-of-birth on a form, somebody had found the name amusing, and at fourteen he was sensitive about such things. Well, my only Son, it could have been worse. If the fort had retained its original name, it would have been: "Place of Birth—Camp Detachment."

Ft. Huachuca is the only one of the many nineteenth-century cavalry posts in Arizona to survive as a military installation. It outlived them all, but its life has been tenuous at times. During its first year the men of the camp nearly precipitated a second war with Mexico while pursuing their border patrol duties, evidently with great enthusiasm. When a group of Mexican bandits raided north of the border, men from Camp Huachuca chased them deep into Mexico and killed them. Mexico reacted with a strong show of force to this violation of its territory, but such violations were to occur many times in later years.

The army elevated the camp to permanent status, making it a fort in 1882, and immediately began building large barracks buildings and spacious officers' quarters. I slept in one of those barracks buildings the night I arrived—or, more accurately, under it. Most of the construction work on those buildings was done by the soldiers, who complained that they had to work as lumberjacks, carpenters, bricklayers, and everything except the job for which they had enlisted.

Even so, over the next fourteen years the cavalrymen at Ft. Huachuca saw plenty of action chasing bandits and Apaches, including Geronimo and his followers. It was a Ft. Huachuca officer, Capt. Henry W. Lawton, who pursued Geronimo and his band of warriors for months through the mountains and deserts of Mexico and brought them back for the last time in 1886. The final capture of Geronimo is generally considered to mark the end of the Apache Wars, but for the men of Ft. Huachuca it was not the end of problems with Apaches, which included the outbreak of the Apache Kid in 1889 and some sporadic battles in 1896. Considering that the Apaches had begun harassing the Southwestern Spanish missions in the late 1600s, that they had repeatedly caused the evacuation and destruction of such communities as Tubac, that on May Day in 1782 they had attacked and almost overcome the walled Presidio of Tucson, that they had controlled Southern Arizona during the Civil War, and that they were still being chased around the area in 1896, one has to admit that they were persistent. Their threat to the non-native population of Arizona lasted about two hundred years, and they had been a threat to the more sedentary native tribes for a long time before that.

In 1898 the first of the legendary Buffalo Soldiers arrived at Ft. Huachuca, members of the Ninth and Tenth Cavalry Regiments. The United States Army was a segregated institution. From then until after the end of World War II, Ft. Huachuca was to be an installation for black troops, usually but not always commanded by white officers. The Apache Wars were over, but problems along the border were just getting underway. With the outbreak of the Mexican Revolution in 1910, and the long period of political turmoil which followed, Ft. Huachuca became one of the hottest spots, militarily speaking, in the country.

During the three-way struggle for power between Venustiano Carranza, Pancho Villa, and Emiliano Zapata, which tore Mexico apart in a prolonged civil war that Mexican history books euphemistically call "the Revolution," the United States Government, under President Wilson, supported Carranza. When Carranza won, Pancho Villa returned to his native Chihuahua and began to take vengeance on the United States. In January 1916 his troops stopped a train in Chihuahua and shot sixteen United States engineers who were on board. Soon afterward, Villa raided Columbus, New Mexico, killed sixteen more United States citizens and burned the town. He chose Columbus because two businessmen there had accepted his thirty thousand dollars in payment for weapons and supplies but had never delivered the merchandise. Other Mexican bandits and local leaders were raiding towns on both sides of the border. The borderland was at war, whether war had been declared or not. At the same time, the United States was being steadily drawn into a European war with Germany, and anti-German feelings were running high. Most of the fractured Mexican government was pro-German. During these explosive times, some sheriffs along the border were shooting Mexican nationals almost on sight.

On March 9, 1916, President Wilson ordered General John (Black Jack) Pershing to enter Mexico and capture Villa, dead or alive. On two hours' notice the Tenth Cavalry left Ft. Huachuca and joined General Pershing's troops in Texas. They chased Villa's army through much of Chihuahua but were never able to destroy it completely. Villa escaped to become a Mexican national hero, but the hero who led the Tenth Cavalry in a pistol charge during the most definitive battle was Lt. Col. Charles Young, the first black officer ever to command a United States military installation. The installation was Ft. Huachuca.

During World War I, the Buffalo Soldiers remained at Ft. Huachuca to guard the border against German saboteurs and Mexican bandits. In the wartime hysteria which had risen to unprecedented heights along the border, bandits were saboteurs and saboteurs were bandits. The tension was not eased when bandits actually invaded Nogales, Arizona, in August of 1918, only to be driven back across the border by the Buffalo Soldiers. Fortunately, the distrust and hysteria felt along the border at this time were not repeated during World War II, when Mexico, under more stable leadership, allied itself solidly with the United States.

After World War I, the government considered abandoning Ft. Huachuca. In 1924 the commanding officer was ordered to estimate the entire value of the fort so it could be put on the market. His estimate was $325,000, but the fort was not sold.

At the beginning of World War II, Ft. Huachuca became a training base for black infantrymen who fought in France, Italy, and the Pacific. In preparation for this massive training effort, which at its peak involved more than thirty thousand soldiers and civilians, the fort was expanded on a huge, if not a grand, scale. The army put up five hundred new one- and two-story barracks and office buildings in the typical World War II military style—double ugly. But the new construction was decentralized into several widely scattered clusters of buildings making the fort less vulnerable to attacks from the air. It was in one of those clusters, after several years and two wars, that I lived and worked. They had none of the charm or dignity of the old, original part of the fort.

But one result of the decentralization was that the Old Fort, that part which dated back to the 1880s, was left almost exactly as it had been, as it still is. When I was stationed there, however, that fact was not particularly high on my list of things to be thankful for. I had no car, the decentralized areas were distant from one another, and bus service between them was almost nonexistent. I wore out several pairs of ill-fitting army shoes trudging from one area to another. With the exception of the food, which is usually the soldier's number one complaint, I think we complained most about the way the fort was designed.

I had not been at Ft. Huachuca very long when I received a visit from Mr. and Mrs. H. B. Bruce, an imposing couple who were soon to become my in-laws, and still are. I did not yet know the Bruces very well, although I knew that H.B. was a highly successful engineer whose construction company built large dams. He had been one of the major contractors involved in building the largest dam in Idaho, my home state, and that's how I met his daughter. The Bruces arrived at Ft. Huachuca in their big Buick, and I was given time off from my duties to show them around. I drove them from one decentralized area to another, complaining all the way about how inconveniently the fort was laid out. I said it must have been designed by an idiot with no concern for the people who would have to live there. During my tirade, H.B. looked a little strange and cleared his throat several times, but I paid no attention. Finally he said, "If I remember right . . . ahem . . . must have been early '42 . . . affiliated with the Army Corps of Engineers then . . . I was called in on that . . . ahem . . . job . . . member of a team. Seems to me like one of the things we did was lay out this . . . ahem . . . installation." He spoke quietly, without any sign of irritation, and he was telling the truth. He was one of the "idiots" who had designed the expansion of Ft. Huachuca as a wartime training base.

Knowing him as I do now, I am sure there must have been a twinkle in his eye when he spoke, but I was too embarrassed to notice. Nor did I know that I was dealing with one of the sweetest human beings it would ever be my good fortune to meet, a man far too patient and forgiving to resent the foolish statements of a very foolish young man. Soon afterward, I married his daughter in his home, and he has never treated me with anything but kindness, never once alluding to my big, stupid mouth. But when his daughter moved to Ft. Huachuca to join me the following summer, she brought with her the shiny new Chevy he had given us, and I did not have to walk from one area to another after that.

At the end of World War II, the future of Ft. Huachuca did not look promising. Border patrol duties had been taken over by state and federal agencies, and there was no longer any need to train large numbers of soldiers for combat. It was obvious that the government didn't quite know what to do with the installation, stuck off out there in the middle of nowhere as it was. It was deactivated in 1947 and stood largely deserted until 1949, when the military transferred it to the State of Arizona to be used by the National Guard and as a game preserve. A large herd of buffaloes was turned loose on its grassy hills. I wonder if there was any irony in that act. I can imagine a group of politicians sitting around in Washington trying to decide what to do with Ft. Huachuca, and one of them says, "Well, if the Buffalo Soldiers were stationed there for such a long time, it must be a good place for buffaloes." I don't know what became of the buffaloes. They had disappeared before I arrived, as had much of the wartime construction.

More than one hundred of the wooden buildings erected at the outset of the war were sold and hauled away on trailers. This had more of an impact on the landscape of Southern Arizona than did the buffaloes. This afternoon, just as I was leaving Tucson, I passed a group of houses near the freeway which had the unmistakable military look that no amount of landscaping or junked cars in the yard can hide. Those wooden barracks buildings and houses were scattered all over the southern part of the state. It is not unusual to come across a church which, in spite of the steeple perched incongruously on its roof, still looks like a barracks.

The Air Force reclaimed the fort at the beginning of the Korean War, and for one month it was an air base without airmen. It was deactivated again in 1953 and reactivated by the Signal Corps as the army's Electronic Proving Ground in 1954. The Electronic Proving Ground was just getting underway when I arrived in 1956. It was a highly sophisticated operation in the least sophisticated of settings. Much of the top-level, hush-hush work was done by civilian scientists and engineers who lived about thirty miles away on the southern slopes of the Mule Mountains near Bisbee. What little housing there was available in Fry, or Sierra Vista, was mostly temporary or semitemporary. The whole community had a dusty, forlorn, temporary look. It was tied to the fort, and the fort had boomed and busted so many times since the early forties that few people were willing to put down roots in the town, or even make major investments in a place whose future was so questionable. Nothing about it that I could see suggested that it was soon to become the fastest-growing community in Arizona.

I think most of the draftees, like me, had the impression that the army had sent us there because it didn't know what else to do with us, and it wasn't quite sure what to do with us after we got there. We saw large hangarlike buildings that were off-limits to nearly everybody, and we were never officially informed what they were used for. The grapevine had it that the Electronic Proving Ground was trying to develop a drone, a small, unmanned aircraft directed by remote control. I caught a glimpse of one only once, and it was a short, fat, mean-looking apparatus, all black. We thought of it as something out of science fiction and could only surmise what it might be used for. Some said reconnaissance. Others said bombs. Others said atomic bombs.

When I first arrived, I went through several weeks of training to learn to operate an ultra-high-frequency radio, but I never learned to operate it effectively, and I don't remember that anybody else did either. The damned thing was inoperable. It was a heavy, cumbersome German affair that came in several very large metal boxes and had a separate antenna like a thirty-foot metal umbrella. The antenna always fell down or blew over, but it didn't matter because we could never get the radio on the right frequency anyway. I think the whole thing was Germany's retaliation against the United States for winning World War II. It was designed for use in combat, but it was the last thing I would have wanted to be anywhere near in a combat situation, except perhaps a mine field. It was too heavy to move quickly, and the antenna was impossible to hide, especially from the air. No matter how we tried to camouflage the antenna, it always looked like exactly what it was, a sore thumb sticking up on the landscape.

After I finished my training with "the monster," as we called the ultra-high-frequency radio, somebody checked my records and discovered that I was one of those weird anomalies, a draftee with a college education. It was assumed, on no greater evidence than this, that I could read and write, and I was sent to the battalion personnel office to be trained to replace the career sergeant who had been running that office. He was getting out of the army in order to fulfill his lifelong dream—to become a farmer.

The job was a little awkward at first. There were several career men in the office who naturally resented being told what to do by a draftee, but I had been given sufficient rank as a specialist something-or-other to do it, and I did the best I could. I had to spend much of my time on the telephone, which was probably the most dangerous duty I ever pulled at Ft. Huachuca, at least during the monsoon season. Once, during a summer storm, a man in the office who had been on the phone when lightning struck the telephone pole outside, was thrown about twenty-five feet across the room. He weighed around 250 pounds, and I was a skinny guy. After that, I tried to use the phone as little as possible during the rainy season.

In 1967, the Strategic Communications Command took over Ft. Huachuca. STRATCOM directs telecommunications for the army and Department of Defense. If you need to send a message to a planet or star, I suppose Ft. Huachuca could help you do it. The post has been greatly expanded, with housing, recreational facilities, and a large, permanent hospital. A fine paved road heads straight north to Tucson. The fort is now the home of one of the army's ultra-high-tech operations, but the old section has been left much as it was. The fine old houses are still used as officers' quarters. The barracks built in 1883 are now used as offices, but they look much the same from the outside. I sniffed around one of them recently but could detect no lingering smell of horse manure.

Not long ago the fort designed a balloon to detect illegal drugs being smuggled across the border. It looks like a small blimp. I have no idea how it works, but I hope it works better than the Signal Corps' ultra-high-frequency whizbang, although I haven't noticed any dramatic decrease in illegal drug activity lately. But in a sense, when that balloon went up, Ft. Huachuca had come full circle. The Apaches aren't raiding in Southern Arizona these days, but Fort Huachuca is, once again, patrolling the border.

During my unwilling stay at Fort Huachuca, I must have been bitten by some kind of bug. After awhile the landscape no longer depressed me. Instead of feeling like a prisoner, I came to love the great, sweeping vistas, the space, the colors. I determined that I wanted to spend the rest of my life in Southern Arizona, and here I still am, getting over the next hill, and the next and the next, looking up toward the mountains.

3

T
he clouds are developing dark centers now. It begins to look
promising for a storm. And the temperature seems to have
dropped a degree or two. The country gets greener and
greener, positively lush by desert standards. The road here curves
through low hills, following, and slightly above, a wash that runs between the Empire Mountains, just to the east, and the northern thrust
of the Santa Ritas, to the west and south. This must be the upper
reaches of Pantano Wash, a twisting ribbon of bright sand and stone
ledges, dropping down to the desert floor where it passes under the
freeway I have just turned off of and heads northwest toward Tucson.
It is usually dry, but today, because of recent rains at higher elevations,
it is running a thin sheet of water several feet across, often dividing into
rivulets which leave small islands of sand and gravel between them.

The water looks inviting. Just as I'm considering whether or not to
stop and go down for a cooling wade, I see a coyote who must have
had the same idea. He—I assume it is a male because of its size—is
standing on one of the little islands of sand, looking intently downstream. He seems oblivious to the highway and traffic just above him.
He is magnificent, one of the subspecies I call big blondes, although I
don't know its technical name. In the bright sun his coat glows golden-
amber, exactly the color I suspect many women try to duplicate at
the hairdressers, but seldom with total success. The amber, which is
most prominent around his head and hindquarters, shades into lighter
buff on his belly, with darker, almost black striations on his shoulders,

back, and tail. He looks healthy and well fed, ears up, tail down, in an alert but casual posture, totally elegant.

There are at least nineteen subspecies of *Canis latrans*, and this has got to be one of the most beautiful. Since coyotes are noted for their ability to adapt to new habitats, this may be a subspecies which originated at a higher elevation where water and food are more plentiful, a subspecies that has spread or been driven to the edge of the lower desert, into the upper bajadas. The most commonly encountered coyote in the lower Sonoran Desert is the subspecies *Mearnsi*, which is much smaller and scrawnier, surviving as it does in spite of little water, extremely high temperatures, and a more limited food supply. It is also paler, grayer, and has little of the vivid coloring of this glamorous creature in the wash.

The Navajo name for coyote translates "God's dog," and they give the coyote a place of prominence above that of the wolf, referring to the wolf as a big coyote, rather than the other way around. But the coyote's name comes to us from the Aztec *coyotl*. The Aztecs associated the coyote's name and character with several gods and goddesses, including *Heuheucoyotle*, the mischief maker, and *Coyolxauhqui*, the moon goddess. Early Anglo settlers called the coyote a prairie wolf, but the Aztec name prevailed.

The relationship between humans and canines, both domesticated and nondomesticated, is fascinating to me. I do not understand how the person who truly loves a dog, loves it enough sometimes to risk his or her life for it, can exterminate coyotes, the dog's cousin, in hideous and sadistic ways. The war against coyotes in the Southwest has been monumental and has gone on since the earliest settlers arrived. In many respects, here and elsewhere, it represents a kind of ethnic vendetta that has nothing to do with economics. Something very basic in humans resents the coyote, just as something very basic in humans domesticated certain canines at an early stage in our groping toward civilization and our own humanity. We love and cherish our dogs because they respond with loyalty and affection, and because they obey us. But the coyote, so much like the dog in appearance and even behavior, has refused to accept us as masters, has spurned us, and we can never forgive it.

I have lived with large dogs most of my life. Some of my earliest memories involve a large German Shepherd who would have fought to the death to protect my older brother and me, although we didn't always treat him as well as we should have. And I have lived in close proximity to coyotes for the last thirty years, have observed them enough to be able to distinguish between them and have come to have a strong admiration for them. But not one of them has ever shown me any deference, and only a couple of them have ever shown that they trusted me, even a little and for a few minutes. Coyotes generally avoid us and make us feel insignificant in the natural scheme of things. Dogs make us feel loved and can break our hearts.

Large dogs seem to run in some families like a tendency toward insanity runs in some families. Or perhaps a penchant for large dogs is a form of insanity. My wife and I consider any dog who weighs less than 70 pounds a runt. And there are some advantages to having large dogs. If you should trip over one of them in the dark, as I have done, the dog will cushion your fall. On the other hand, our Great Pyrenees once knocked me unconscious while being playful. He weighs 165 pounds. I think of our dogs as house-horses and don't expect anyone except another large-dog lover to be understanding about the condition our house is in.

My first real awareness of coyotes came about because of one of our large dogs, an oversized male Samoyed who had a brief but harrowing love affair with a big blonde coyote, a female version of the one down in the wash, who is very much aware that I have stopped the van and am watching him, although he is ignoring me.

The dog's name was Shushu, which we were told was the Navajo word for bear, although we didn't name him and called him Shushy, rhyming with bushy. A friend found Shushy wandering in a distracted state along the highway near Tucson, where he was struck by a car but not seriously injured. She took him home, but all her attempts to find his owner failed, so she named him Shushu. Then, because she already had a male dog who was jealous, she gave him to us.

After getting to know him, we realized that Shushy had been a show dog, if not a movie star, and we surmised that he had been stolen in Southern California and was being transported east for sale when he escaped from his dognappers. He was the best-trained dog we have ever had, primarily because we had nothing to do with his training. He never walked anywhere—he pranced. Strangers on the street would throw their arms around him without asking if he were gentle. One look at his grinning face was enough. Each of the long white hairs of his outer coat was tipped with silver. He glistened in the daylight and glowed in the dark. He could do all manner of tricks and loved to entertain. He could learn a new trick in ten minutes and never forget it. He mimicked human facial expressions with an audacity that was astonishing, and sometimes hilarious, especially after I taught him to wrinkle his nose as if he smelled something unpleasant. He was also a terrible ham. Once, in a shopping mall, we encountered a professional clown who was entertaining a large group of children. Shushy loved children, and he picked up on the idea at once. He stood up on his hind legs and began to dance in circles. The children immediately deserted the clown and gathered around Shushy, laughing and applauding. The poor clown stood at a distance, alone, dejected, and thoroughly upstaged.

Shushy and I often took long hikes in the desert. I had heard that there were packs of feral dogs in the Tucson Mountains, but I had never seen any and believed such stories were local folklore, like reports of flying saucers. According to the stories, abandoned or runaway dogs turned wild in the desert and roamed in packs that could be dangerous. But one evening Shushy and I were walking down a desert road, which had been cut over the brow of a hill so as to leave a bank about four feet high beside it, when suddenly I heard what sounded like horses galloping toward us. As I turned in the direction of the sound, two very large dogs, a German Shepherd and a Boxer, leaped from the bank and landed almost on top of us. Both were in terrible condition and must have been living off the land for some time. The Shepherd went for Shushy and the Boxer hurled himself at my throat. I was carrying Shushy's heavy chain leash. Using it like a whip, I struck the Boxer across the face as hard as I could, catching him in mid-leap. Shushy was totally occupied with the other dog in a wild melee. Acting out of pure panic, I continued to lash the Boxer with the leash until it ran off into the desert, yelping. By then, Shushy had the Shepherd down with a death grip on its neck. When I pulled Shushy off the Shepherd, it too fled, bleeding badly. The whole encounter probably lasted no more than two minutes, and when it was over and my adrenalin began to subside, my first thought was of rabies.

In the desert counties of Southern Arizona, we take the activities of the rabies control units of the County Health Departments very seriously. I sometimes make fun of the pretentious building at the edge of Tucson which houses the Pima County Rabies Control Center—it looks like a cross between a fake Moorish palace and the Taj Mahal—but I never make fun of the work done by the people there. And although they have made significant progress toward controlling the spread of rabies among wild and domestic animals in the desert in the last twenty years, the disease is still a continuing problem. It is generally believed that bats spread the disease to rodents and larger mammals, who then infect domestic dogs. I remember years in the early sixties when rabies reached epidemic proportions and it was foolhardy to take one's dogs into the desert at all.

After our encounter with the two feral dogs, as I began to get my wits together, I realized that neither Shushy nor I was in any real danger of being infected. He had had his rabies shots, and neither dog had actually broken my skin. So we were safe, and I learned to pay more attention to local folklore. I also learned that my pampered, movie-star companion was as tough as he was beautiful.

But I had not yet learned anything about the habits of coyotes, and it was a coyote who would prove to be the one menace Shushy could not handle. And what a beautiful menace she was, the big blonde coyote who began to hang around our house, even during the day, sitting beside the driveway and retreating only when we approached. I thought she had come to mate with Shushy, and congratulated her on her good taste. Later, when I found out more about the behavior of coyotes, I realized that she had probably already mated with him and was waiting for him to accompany her, help her dig a den in which to raise their pups, and help her later to feed and protect them, as any good male coyote would do. And as Shushy ultimately tried to do, not because he had the instincts of a coyote, but because he was a husky. Huskies are the only breed of domestic dogs whose males have a tendency to take responsibility for their offspring. All other male domestic dogs are merely lotharios, but a male husky, possibly because huskies are so closely related to the wolf, will sometimes attempt to assist his mate in the rearing of pups. The big blonde must have sensed that this handsome hunk of dog had all the right instincts to make him a fit companion and helpmeet.

Female coyotes seem to choose their mates, rather than being chosen. In most other matters they are subservient to the males, but in affairs of the heart, they seem to be dominant, and a female coyote will drive away any other female who tempts the male on whom she has fixed her attention. The pair-bond is extremely strong and is, in some observed cases at least, formed long before the pair mates. Once they have mated, the pair becomes the nucleus of an extended family unit whose primary function is the protection, feeding, and training of the pair's offspring. Coyotes are superb parents. It has not been scientifically determined that they mate for life, but many veteran coyote-watchers believe they do and have documented instances in which the pair-bond lasted several years during which the same couple raised several litters.

So it might not have been exactly the call of the wild Shushy heard; it might well have been the call of domesticity. At any rate, he ran off with her into the desert. But while his husky lineage made him willing to enter into such an arrangement, for a while at least, he was only a domestic dog, and a pampered one at that. And we did not know what was going on. We thought he would be back in an hour or two, when his immediate needs were satisfied, tired but happy. But he did not come back. We began to search for him, driving down desert roads and beating our way from ridge to ridge. We searched until dark. The next day we started again, this time carrying a photograph of him, canvassing every house in the sparsely settled area. Toward evening of that day we knocked on the door of a house where a woman recognized the photograph. She had seen Shushy—he wasn't exactly inconspicuous—running with several coyotes. She gave us a general direction in which to pursue the search, and renewed our hopes. But by sunset of the fourth day we were heartsick, trying to convince ourselves to give up, knowing he could not have survived so long in the desert without water. There had been no rain in months.

We turned the car around and started slowly for home, straining to see in the growing darkness. Then we saw a patch of something white lying just off the road. It was Shushy, and he was almost dead, but he was able to lift his head a little and give us a ghastly version of his irresistible grin. It looked as if he had been trying to make it home, but had collapsed several miles short of his goal. We tried to give him water, but he was too weak to drink. He had several bad wounds from fighting, probably with male coyotes. His mouth, lips, and tongue were impaled with cactus spines. I lifted him into the car and broke every speed limit getting to the animal hospital, where they immediately began pumping liquids into him intravenously. The vet told us he was suffering from dehydration, malnutrition, and a raging fever caused by infection. But he survived, and after a prolonged stay in the hospital, recovered completely. The vet said it was probably his color that ultimately saved him. His silver-white coat had reflected more of the sun's rays than a darker dog's would have, retarding the dehydration which would otherwise have killed him before we were able to find him. And as it was, he could not have lasted more than a few hours.

Shushy never again showed any inclination to run off with a coyote. I guess, as far as he was concerned, one grand affair was enough for a lifetime—almost too much. Nor did I ever see any suspiciously light-colored young coyotes in that part of the desert, although I kept on the lookout for them. They probably did not survive. It is unlikely that coyote pups will survive in the wild when their mother has no mate to help her feed and protect them.

Coyotes seldom mate with domestic dogs. When they do, the off-spring are called coy-dogs. But nature has provided a set of mechanisms that prevents Canis latrans from being mongrelized by inter-breeding with domestic dogs. Once the first generation of coy-dogs is produced, they cannot breed with coyotes, but only with domestic dogs or with other coy-dogs. The coyote male is sterile for at least eight months of the year, and the female is sterile at least ten months of the year. Both come into season in the winter, or very early spring, de-pending on the climate in which they live, and breed at no other time. The coyote's gestation period is about sixty-three days, and combined with their limited period of fertility, this assures that the puppies will be born at the time of year when they have the best possible chance of survival.

But both male and female coy-dogs come into season in the fall. Even if two coy-dogs were to breed with one another, it is not likely that their young would survive in the wild. The pups would be born at the worst time of year, in terms of weather, and the male coy-dog would not help his mate feed and protect the pups, since he inherits the domestic dog's instincts, or lack of them, in regard to paternal duties. Even if the male coy-dog is part husky, these instincts are slight as compared to the fierce paternalism of the male coyote.

Documented cases indicate that the mother coyote has more help with her litter than even her mate is able to provide. The mating pair seems to be the dominant male and female members of an extended family, which often includes several younger, subservient males and females, who help feed and babysit the pups. These "aunts" and "uncles" bring food to the mother and pups, either in its natural state or by regurgitating what they have already eaten. They also help dig new dens in which to hide the pups in the event of danger to the currently used den. In one documented case, an "aunt" moved all five pups to a new den, carrying each one in her mouth a considerable distance to a safer location, while an "uncle" went to find the parents, who were away hunting, and lead them to the new den. The subservient members of the family also corral the growing pups when they wander away from the den and bring them toys—small bones, sticks, or bits of hide—to keep the pups occupied.

Parenting is in coyotes' blood whether they are parents or not. Members of the extended family show marked affection for one another and for the pups. And although the "aunts" sometimes fawn on the dominant father, he does not breed with them. Nor do the "aunts" and "uncles" breed with one another, at least not during the time of their apprenticeship in the family. All energy seems to be directed toward the pups' survival.

Coyote pups, like all canine pups, alternate periods of feeding and sleep with periods of wild play. They often play at the mouth of the den, watched over by one of the adults in the family. The adults are almost totally indulgent. As long as the pups are not in danger, they are allowed to romp and chew on everything, including their parents and baby-sitters. This probably explains why the adults bring them toys to play with, diversions intended to keep the little devils, quite literally, out of the adults' hair. When a nursing pup bites its mother's teat, she sometimes yips with pain but does not usually chastise the offender. If the pup persists, she gets up and moves away.

As the pups grow, the adults take turns teaching them to hunt. One of the babysitters will often lure the pups to a good hunting site by regurgitating small amounts of food along the way. The pups begin by learning to catch grasshoppers and then graduate to mice and other small rodents. Coyotes are eclectic and extremely adaptable in matters of diet, and this is undoubtedly one of the reasons they have survived in spite of our fierce efforts during the past two hundred years to drive them into extinction. Their diet varies widely depending on the season and where they happen to live; and their habitat now extends over more than three-fourths of the United States, including Southeastern Alaska, as well as large portions of Canada and Mexico. They seem to prefer fresh meat and sweet fruit, but in a pinch they will eat juniper berries, carrion, and even grass. In parts of Southern California they eat mostly dates, when such delicacies are available. In the deserts of the Southwest, they generally subsist on grasshoppers and other insects, rodents of all kinds, lizards, snakes, and rabbits. They also fish when water is available. From streams and pools they snatch up fish, frogs, tadpoles, fairy shrimp, and other small aquatic creatures.

That may be what the big blond in the wash was doing when I spotted him. It is unlikely that he would catch much in such an intermittent stream, but there are probably plenty of spadefoot toad tadpoles in the shallow pools along the arroyo this time of year. And probably plenty of Colorado River toads, although they would be more likely to put in an appearance at night. I don't know for sure if coyotes leave noxious Bufo alone, although I would be willing to bet they do. Even most domestic dogs have enough sense to steer clear of old Bufo, and the coyote strikes me as generally more intelligent than most domestic dogs.

Coyotes can also outrun domestic dogs. They are the fastest runners among *canids*. They can cruise at twenty-five to thirty miles an hour and have been clocked at forty miles an hour for short distances. I once had an astonishing exhibition of their speed—astonishing not only because they were so fast, but because they were having such a good time showing off just how fast they were.

One evening in the fall, about fifteen years ago, I was walking with two of our dogs down a dirt road not far from the house. The dogs were a female Doberman and a male Great Dane, both young and both very fast runners. The road led along a low hill, about halfway between an arroyo and the top of the hill. Suddenly the dogs took off after something, and I turned to see two coyotes leisurely crossing the road behind us, heading down toward the arroyo. With the dogs in pursuit, the coyotes picked up speed, running in a large half-circle, which eventually brought them back to the road in front of me. They crossed the road and ran in another large half-circle across the side of the hill and back to where I had first seen them cross the road.

From my vantage point on the road, I could see that the coyotes were running in a circle about a quarter of a mile across. The dogs chased the coyotes around that circular course, crossing the road in front of me and then behind me, three times before I was able to intercept the dogs and put them on leashes. The coyotes would let the dogs gain on them a little, and then put on a burst of speed and leave the dogs behind. Once, when they had a considerable lead on the dogs, they stopped for a few seconds and one of them actually sat down, waiting for the dogs to catch up. I was too far away to hear the coyotes laughing, but I could see them grinning, and they had to be aware that I was watching the entire performance. When I finally stopped the exhausted dogs, the coyotes loped up to the top of the hill, looking nonchalant. The dogs were winded, baffled, and furiously frustrated. They had been so intent on the pursuit that it had not occurred to them to cut across the circle and eliminate much of the distance. I have to admit that those were not the two most intelligent dogs we have ever had, but compared to the coyotes, their stupidity was exceeded only by their lack of speed. We three were not a particularly proud group as we turned and plodded toward home, watched by the victors on the hill.

And the big blond in the arroyo is watching me now, aware that I have stopped the van to inspect him. I am close enough that I haven't attempted to use my field glasses, but foolishly I start to open the van door. The coyote gives me one last look over his shoulder and starts to trot smartly downstream, the direction in which he was looking when I first saw him. As he disappears, I think of two lines from the poet Basho:

Another thing
that will never be my friend.

It's a rare treat to see one of these big tawny creatures in the lower desert, or even at this slightly higher elevation. But seeing smaller coyotes in the desert, and even in the suburbs of Tucson, is not as uncommon as many people believe. Hardly a week goes by that I don't see at least one, and often near the house. From time to time I look up and see one getting a drink from the birdbath about twenty-five feet from the glass door of my study. And we hear them yipping and barking at night, sometimes sounding as if they are very close to the house, although it's hard to tell just how far away they are, especially when they howl. Some people believe that coyotes have the ability to throw their voices, like ventriloquists, but I doubt it. They are capable of vocal effects that would make a coloratura soprano envious, but I think their reputation as ventriloquists is caused by the fact that the desert mountains, whose surfaces are mostly stone, act as sounding boards and throw sounds at unexpected angles. I have noticed the same effect with human voices in the desert mountains.

The coyote we most often see in the lower desert is of the subspecies *Mearnsi*, named after Dr. Edgar Mearns. Its lighter shades are very nearly those of the surface of the ground, and its darker shades are about the color of greasewood branches, making it almost impossible to see at a distance unless it moves. And it certainly can hold still. When stalking prey, such as a mouse or squirrel, coyotes go into a "point" like a hunting dog. They have been observed to hold the "point," without any discernible movement, for more than fifteen minutes. When danger is near, they can move with incredible stealth and silence, taking advantage of every bit of cover the desert offers, but at other times they seem to be wildly reckless.

The Mearnsi is usually very thin and looks frail and undernourished.

I always marvel at the delicacy of its lower legs, which resemble thin little sticks, knowing the speed and stamina those tiny legs are capable of and the distances they travel. Coyotes often come into the suburbs of Tucson, presumably in search of food or water. An adult has a range of more than twenty-one square miles, and if that range happens to be a long, fairly narrow area, the coyote could live forty miles out of town and still visit the suburbs on a daily basis.

And the desert has provided a fine set of hidden thoroughfares which make it possible for coyotes to come into Tucson with little danger of being seen—the arroyos, or dry washes, that wind down out of the mountains toward the Santa Cruz River, which is also usually dry. I see coyote tracks in the sandy bottoms of the arroyos constantly, especially after a rain when the sand is damp and the impressions are easier to identify. They always seem to have a destination in mind, and their tracks, unlike those of a domestic dog, usually make an arrow-straight pattern, deviating neither to the left nor to the right. Some of them prefer a more direct route to town, and it is not unusual to see one trotting down a dirt road or beside a highway. I once saw a Mearnsi crossing the parking lot of Tucson's International Airport in an absolutely straight line. It seemed oblivious to the traffic and low-flying jets, as if it had somewhere to get to and saw no reason to go around the parking lot when it could cut across.

There is a female Mearnsi who hangs around the parking lot of the state prison near Tucson where I teach a creative writing workshop. I usually see her just after sunset, or a few hours after dark. The fact that the parking lot is lighted at night does not seem to bother her, and as long as I stay in the van and make no sudden movements, she will come quite close. She is a scrounger and a sad-looking waif. This spring I saw her with a companion who was slightly larger, probably a male. She had a potato chip bag in her mouth, and she carried it to the edge of the parking lot where, together, they worried it open and licked out the crumbs with great relish. I wondered if she had a litter somewhere in the open desert that surrounds the prison.

With her sadly undernourished appearance and her potato chip bag, she hardly resembled the creature described in a huge body of literature which has grown up around the coyote, creating a coyote mystique that persists today. Channeled through Native American myth and folklore, Coyote tales, which form the bulk of material in print concerning the coyote, are delightful. They portray the coyote as a supernatural trickster and shape-changer—intelligent, wily, and untrustworthy. But they are fiction, and highly fanciful fiction, often parables which have more to say about human behavior than the behavior of coyotes. The Apaches, at least in earlier times, believed that when someone behaved badly, in a particularly tricky or insidious way, he or she was under the irresistible influence of the coyote, was "doing coyote." It was a wonderful justification for bad behavior, much like our own "temporary insanity"; and like our own excuse, it seemed most often to pop up in conjunction with large quantities of alcohol.

Viewed in a general way, the Coyote tales do have some connections with the real habits of coyotes, tenuous though those connections may be. The tales often associate coyotes with ravens and badgers. Primitive peoples must have noticed that coyotes sometimes feed on dead animals side-by-side with ravens, although coyotes will kill and eat other birds when they can catch them. And in a sense, ravens also serve as babysitters for coyote pups. When ravens give a certain call, which is their signal for danger, coyote pups scurry into their den and remain perfectly still for a long time. The association with badgers probably came about because coyotes sometimes raise their young in abandoned badger dens. And like badgers, coyotes are skilled and formidable diggers. When digging a den in the side of a bank or hill, they often work in pairs, one extending the tunnel while the other scoops out the loose dirt at the entrance.

Compared to this large and fascinating body of material concerning the mythical coyote, there is relatively little in print about the habits and behavior of the real coyote in the wild, little material based on close observation and documentation, and most of that is quite recent. There seems to be more factual information available to us concerning the wolf, which is a curious fact, since most of us will never have the opportunity to see a wolf in its natural habitat. Perhaps this suggests that we become seriously interested in wild creatures only when they are about to become extinct. It's a sobering thought.

Some Tucsonans tell me that they never see coyotes. I think these people must live in the downtown area and never leave it. And they probably don't have any friends or relatives to visit in prison, or they might see the hungry lady who hangs around the prison parking lot. Some of them have probably never seen a prison either, although there are four big prisons just four miles off the freeway southeast of town. "We always build our prisons out of town," I once wrote in a poem, "so we won't have to look at them." It might have been more accurate to say that we don't see what we don't want to see, whether it is as massive as a prison or as small as the smallest coyote.

I imagine that people who never see prisons and never see coyotes would be equally terrified to encounter either a prison inmate or a coyote, although the chances of their being harmed by a healthy coyote are nonexistent. Many people have been seriously injured, and some killed, by traps and poison devices set out for coyotes, but there is no documented evidence of a healthy coyote in the wild ever attacking or biting a human. Rabid coyotes have been known to attack humans, and a coyote in a trap or cage will defend itself when approached, but a healthy coyote in the wild will avoid contact with humans. They are not dangerous.

It is not because coyotes are dangerous to humans that they have been slaughtered by every means available. We have poisoned them, trapped them, and shot them from airplanes. We have given them bait laced with broken glass and strychnine. We have destroyed their dens with dynamite and developed a poison device that explodes when triggered. We have employed metal drills which bore through the ground and impale the coyote cubs in their dens. And our tax dollars have paid for this, are still paying for it every day. The Department of Agriculture spends close to thirty million dollars annually to kill coyotes, mostly on the rangelands of the West. That fact fills me with rage, a sick frustration.

For years after the Department of Agriculture knew that the most common poison being used to kill coyotes, a poison called "1080," was seriously dangerous to humans and was also killing the American eagle and other endangered species of wildlife, it persisted in using the poison on public lands and employed a large staff to exterminate coyotes with the poison. At the same time, it employed another staff to create slick and misleading propaganda to cover up what the other staff was doing.

One can only wonder why. I suppose this is done for the same reason that the government currently permits insane people to buy, over the counter, AK-47s and other rapid-fire weapons designed for military combat, people who then open fire on groups of children in schoolyards. The government responds to pressure, to the strong, organized pressure of vested interest groups who are protecting their commercial interests regardless of the damage that results to others. The vested interest group which insists that coyotes must be exterminated by whatever means is made up of sheep and cattle growers throughout the West and Midwest. For decades this unified group, always well-financed and highly vocal, has been able to control most state and national legislators elected from their areas. Consequently, state and national government agencies have become agencies for the extermination of both the wolf and coyote, although they have had far greater success with the wolf. And the taxpayer, whether or not in agreement with this policy, must pay for it.

What is particularly grotesque is that the government's policy of extermination is based largely on ignorance. Data concerning the amount of damage coyotes do to sheep and cattle have been scanty, often undocumented and unverified, sometimes spurious, and almost always so colored by emotional exaggeration as to be the result of something close to hysteria. It is true that coyotes sometimes kill sheep and, more rarely, cattle; but nobody knows to what extent or under what circumstances, and not until very recently has the situation been presented in any kind of rational perspective. The two things most destructive to the natural environment of the West have been the sheep and the cow. They have destroyed the natural habitat of rabbits, rodents, reptiles, and insects on which the coyote normally subsists. In view of all this, the loss of a few sheep and cows seems a small price for the sheep and cattle growers to pay. But they have never, and probably never will, see the situation in that light.

Earlier this summer, while hiking in a remote area of Utah, I came upon the body of a poisoned coyote. The preceding summer, in the same general area, I stumbled upon an enormous flock of sheep—I estimated more than one thousand—being herded very quickly to higher ground by a group of men on horseback. I was in the Wasatch National Forest. It occurred to me that such a large flock of sheep in a national forest might not be legal, but I had no way of knowing. If the behavior of the shepherds was any indication, my suspicions were correct. They were hostile and obviously unhappy to be seen doing what they were doing, and they were moving the sheep faster than was good for the sheep. I was a little frightened by the way the men acted and glad that I had two companions a short distance down the trail. A lone hiker can disappear too easily in that remote and rugged area.

The destruction of coyotes in the Southwest has had its bad effects even in the suburbs of Tucson. It is one thing to talk about upsetting the balance of nature but another thing to have to live with the results. In the Tucson Mountains, we suffer from a lack of coyotes. Without enough coyotes to keep their populations under control, jackrabbits, cottontails, and particularly rodents have become a problem. Much of the Sonoran Desert now has a superabundance of two kinds of jackrabbits, and both are large. The antelope jack is more than twenty-six inches from stem to stern and stands very high on its long hind legs. It has enormous ears which help regulate its body temperature and seem out of all proportion to the rest of it. We call it a "Jackelope" and tell tourists it is a cross between a rabbit and an antelope. I am afraid they sometimes believe us. The other jackrabbit, the black-tailed jack, is really a hare, since its young are born covered with fur and with their eyes open. Both jacks are similar in appearance, but the "Jackelope" can be distinguished quite easily because of its incredible ears.

When jackrabbits converge in large numbers at night, the effect is so eerie as to be almost frightening. I first saw such a convergence about twelve years ago, shortly after one of the prisons was built in the desert southeast of town. The warden had decided to put in an extensive lawn in front of the entrance. Since he had an almost unlimited labor pool, he spared no effort to do it right. The land was carefully leveled and cultivated. The grass seed was planted and fertilized, and young grass quickly sprouted. That week, when I drove into the prison parking lot just after dark, what I saw belonged in a Hitchcock film. The area that had been so carefully planted was covered with hundreds of jackrabbits. It was almost solid jackrabbits. As my headlights swept across it, the rabbits sat up perfectly still with their huge ears erect—a field of frozen "Jackelopes" in the moonlight. Their eyes glowed amber and unblinking. It looked like a field of bizarre statuary in the garden of a madman. After a minute or so they resumed their munching, and by morning the prison lawn was a bare, dusty field.

The desert cottontail, which has also increased to alarming numbers in Southern Arizona, is smaller and camouflaged a light buff-brown, almost the same color as the desert pavement in many places. The amazing thing about the cottontail is that it can climb low trees and shrubs and often does when pursued by coyotes or roadrunners. I once found a whole litter of young cottontails about four feet up in the branches of a paloverde. The cottontail has shiny black shoe-button eyes, which give it the expression of a sly child about to raid the cookie jar. No matter how old they are, they always look like children in some way; and no matter how angry they sometimes make me, I always wind up laughing at them. Once, when I was setting out ice plant on a terraced area next to the house, two young cottontails sat a few yards away, watching me and anticipating a feast. As soon as I finished, they ate all the ice plant. Then, for the rest of the afternoon they sat nearby, waiting for me to plant more. How can I stay angry at such an ingenuous creature, although I have tried repeatedly to grow a small plot of vegetables, only to have the young plants disappear, almost before my eyes.

But the rabbits, even the oversized "Jackelopes," are only a slight problem as compared to the rodents—one rodent in particular. This is the rock squirrel, the largest squirrel in the Sonoran Desert. The mature rock squirrel is more than twenty inches long, with a magnificent bushy tail and a voracious appetite. Like the coyote, it will eat almost anything. But it is extremely beautiful and graceful, mottled gray in front and tan-brown in the rear.

When my wife sees a rock squirrel near the house, her eyes narrow, her mouth becomes a hard line, and her chin trembles. Fear and rage play over her face, and her hands make convulsive movements. "Where is Henry?" she moans. "Why did he leave us? We were good to him. Go find him! Why did you let him go?" Henry is a six-foot bull snake, often called a gopher snake; and my wife is the woman who, before she was married, refused to go on picnics because there might be ants.

I try to calm her. "If the squirrels move in again," I say, "Henry will come back."

"How do you know?" she says, but with some hope in her voice. "How will Henry know when we need him?"

"Henry will know," I answer with complete conviction, "because Henry knows everything."

She nods, somewhat reassured. It might be stretching the truth to say that my wife loves Henry, especially since she hardly saw him and did not get acquainted with him as I did. Henry, who is gallant to the core, seemed to sense that my wife might be frightened by his formidable size and stayed out of sight as much as possible when she was around. But it can truly be said that she came to value his presence, and all because of the rock squirrels. We had an infestation of rock squirrels. It was a siege that turned into all-out war, and we lost every battle. Had it not been for Henry, we would probably have lost the war.

I never knew exactly why the rock squirrels chose us. Perhaps it was because we had a compost heap which provided them with food, or perhaps it was because I fed the birds and the birdseed attracted them. But we were chosen, and to be so chosen is to enter into daily torment and frustration sufficient to try one's sanity.

We had always had a good many rock squirrels in the general area of the house, playing on the front terrace or in the fenced-in area behind the house or cavorting on one of my stone walls. We thought they were cute. The dogs sometimes chased them but could never catch them. We noticed the entrances to several burrows at some distance from the house but paid no attention. Then the entrance to a burrow appeared in the fenced-in area, and another just off the back patio. We began to see more and more squirrels and could often hear one running across the roof. Then one day when my wife was taking a bath, somebody or something began pounding on the underside of the bathtub with what sounded like a stone. My wife spends a great deal of time in the bathtub, reading. It's her way of relaxing and combating the dryness of the desert—a long warm bath in the winter and a long cool bath in the summer. But something was under the bathtub, banging away, and it continued to bang away for the better part of two years. It was disconcerting, but it was only the beginning.

The house is built on a concrete foundation several feet thick. I had watched the workmen pour that foundation, and I knew it was impregnable. Then I remembered—Lord help us!—the bathtub had been "sunk." It is customary in houses with concrete foundations, or slabs, to omit the foundation directly under the bathtub in case the bathtub should someday leak. Our bathtub rested directly on the ground, or at least it had been resting directly on the ground, but now something was under it. I began to investigate. I tore out a section of the wall in the closet adjacent to the bathroom and discovered that the squirrels had excavated a large burrow under the bathtub, where they were raising their young. Evidently they had tunneled completely under the foundation slab and had come up where the bathtub was "sunk." It was an ingeniously devised fortress. I could see part of it but could not reach it. I also discovered that they had tunneled up beside the pipes leading to the bathtub, which gave them access to several of the interior walls. The young squirrels under the bathtub were playful, and the noise we had heard was caused by their romping around among the stones. Sometimes they would scratch on the bottom of the bathtub.

These were not the only noises we heard. Rock squirrels, when in distress, make a high-pitched, repeated sound somewhere between a whistle and a scream. It is very loud and sounds something like a back-up signal on a truck, but it is more piercing. Squirrels often continue to make this unnerving sound, with brief pauses, for over an hour. *Beep! Beep! Beep!* We had heard this sound coming from under the bathtub. Now we began to hear it in the walls of the kitchen. I remembered that squirrels usually have more than one entrance and exit to their burrows. I had several times noticed one of them scamper up onto the roof and disappear. I checked the roof. They had eaten away most of the tin shield on top of one of the soil pipes that vented the plumbing in the kitchen and bathroom. So they had at least two entrances to all the interior walls in that section of the house.

My wife and I discussed the situation. It was, in fact, about all we discussed for a long time. She was willing to resort to poison. I refused for three reasons: One was a matter of principle. One was that the poisoned squirrels would be dangerous to anything that fed on their bodies, possibly even the dogs. The other reason was that if the squirrels died under the bathtub or in the walls, the stench would be so great we would probably have to move out of the house.

But I was willing to fight the squirrels in other ways. First, I tried to flood their burrows from the outside. I put the hose down one of their tunnels as far as I could, and let it run full blast. After an hour the tunnel showed no sign of filling up. They must have had miles of tunnels around and under the house. Then I plugged the entrances to the tunnels with concrete. They dug new ones. Then I resorted to noxious substances, hoping to drive them out of the walls. Into the tunnel I had exposed by tearing out the wall in the closet, I placed a whole series of noxious substances, starting with moth balls. No effect. I tried Clorox, various insecticides, disinfectants, and even ammonia. The house began to smell like a cross between a laundry and a recently disinfected public restroom.

The result of all this was that the squirrels began to retaliate. First, they ate the wiring in my truck. As winter came on, several of them had taken to spending the night under the hood of my pickup. Not only did they begin to eat the wiring under the hood of the truck, but from there they had access to the ashtray. Each night they would fill the ashtray with whatever they wanted to store—paloverde or mesquite seeds, peanuts or whatever—and push the ashtray back into the cab until it fell to the floor, scattering debris everywhere. Each morning, before I started the motor, I would bang on the hood of the truck and squirrels would fly in all directions. Then I would have to clean the cab before starting out. Once, when I stopped for a light after having driven almost to town, about five miles, a squirrel jumped from under the fender and ran off down the street. It must have been riding on one of the supports just under the fender.

As I increased my efforts to run them out, the squirrels increased their retaliation. One evening when I was cooking dinner, bits of metal began to drop from the hood above the kitchen range into the food I was cooking. From the space within the interior wall of the kitchen, the squirrels had got into the fan in the hood above the range and were chewing on the metal filter behind it. A few days later, neither the light above the sink nor the electric range would work. I called an electrician. The exterior walls of the house are adobe brick, but much of the wiring runs in a wooden channel between the top of the exterior walls and the roof. The electrician and I tore off several of the wooden panels under the eaves and discovered that the squirrels had eaten through the wiring. The electrician repaired the wiring, but I knew that we were now in danger of an electrical fire if the squirrels persisted in tampering with the wires. I also realized that, bit by bit, I was tearing down the house.

What I did not realize was that by this time the squirrels had chewed their way into the metal ductwork that leads from the heating-cooling system to all parts of the house. One evening when we were sitting in the living room, we heard the sound of gnawing, and a squirrel burst through the wooden louver that covers the openings to the ductwork near the ceiling, flew in a great arc across the room, and landed almost in my lap. I did not think the squirrel had intended to attack me, but I was unnerved. The idea of poison was becoming less and less offensive. Still, I resisted. Surely I could outsmart a pack of squirrels, I thought, but I was running out of ideas. My wife, by this time, had passed through several phases, including hysteria, and had settled into a stony silence alternating with periods of the jitters. She was afraid to take a bath, afraid to cook, and surrounded by the noise of the enemy running through the walls, shrieking their shrill war cry.

But during the second summer of our ordeal, when all else had failed, Henry arrived. I was building a stone wall around our back patio. To work with stones and mortar during the dry part of the summer in Southern Arizona is tricky business. The mortar must dry slowly or it will weaken and crumble, and yet the heat and dry air suck all the moisture out of it almost as soon as it is applied. The solution is to cover each section of the wall as soon as it is completed with tarps, burlap bags, old towels or any kind of fabric, and keep the fabric soaked with water, cooling the mortar by evaporation and keeping it moist. It's wet work. You have to stop a couple of times an hour and spray the wall with a hose.

One afternoon I was squatted down working on the wall when I caught a slight movement out of the corner of my eye. There was Henry, all six feet of him, right beside me—the biggest snake I had ever seen except for a python I once saw in the San Diego Zoo. I fell back and scrambled away, but he meant me no harm. He had come to get a drink. He got his drink from a puddle on the patio floor and decided to stay. He stretched out full-length on the cool, damp bricks of the patio floor in the shade of the wall. I watched him, and he ignored me, but I was afraid to get close enough to him to resume my work.

After a few minutes, two of the dogs came out of the house where they had been sleeping during the heat of the day. When they saw Henry, they barked ferociously and ran toward him. Henry simply raised his head about a foot off the ground, opened his mouth—displaying a truly impressive set of fangs—and hissed at them. If threatened, bull snakes usually hiss before they attack. If that doesn't work, they lunge with incredible force and speed, grip the threatening creature with their teeth, and coil quickly around its body, often strangling it within seconds. In this case, as soon as Henry hissed, the dogs fell all over one another in their haste to retreat, and they never again threatened him. I shut the dogs in the house, and Henry settled down for a nap. Slowly, and being careful not to make any sudden movements, I eased back to where I had been working. Henry ignored me. He stayed about an hour during that first visit, while I worked on the wall. Then he turned away, as if bored, and slid back across the patio, just beyond which was a large opening to one of the squirrel tunnels. Henry examined the opening, smelled it with his tongue, put his head into it and slowly, slowly disappeared. In a flash, like a revelation from heaven, I knew that our savior had come.

Henry stayed the rest of the summer and through the following summer. The rock squirrels disappeared. I know he ate some of them, and the others, I suppose, decided to move elsewhere. I saw Henry most often that first summer. Every few days I would look up and there he would be, either getting a drink or just stopping by for a visit. I got into the habit of talking to him. He was a very good listener. If one of the dogs approached, he would hiss at it and drive it away. It sounds ridiculous, but I got the impression that he was protecting me from the dogs. If I wasn't working on the wall, he would sometimes come into the kitchen through the sliding glass door, which was always left open, and get a drink out of the dogs' water bucket. As far as I know, he never ventured farther into the house than the kitchen.

I could tell by looking at his face that he was a very wise creature. His head was slender, with a somewhat blunt nose. His eyes were dark, brooding, and set well back. He did not have the protuberances over his eyes that give the rattlesnake such a sinister appearance. His head was mostly cream colored, which seemed to be his base color all over, but from the neck back he was marked with an intricate pattern of dark brown squares, triangles, and rectangles. He was dry and his scales were sharp to the touch. At his thickest point, I could not stretch my two hands around him. I have never known a living creature, human or nonhuman, with as much dignity as Henry had. He moved with absolute grace, never showing any sign of fear or uncertainty. He always arrived as if his arrival were inevitable, and he departed the same way.

In addition to ridding us of the rock squirrels, Henry performed an important service for me, personally. One afternoon while I was working on the wall and he was drowsing nearby, I looked up to see a little Harris antelope squirrel teetering toward me across the patio, as if drunk. It took me a few seconds to realize what I was seeing. Only in the national parks where Harris squirrels are accustomed to being fed by tourists will they approach a human, but not in the Tucson Mountains. And the poor little thing was walking so strangely and looked so ill. Ill! Of course—it was rabid. I was sitting on the floor of the patio, and by this time the squirrel was less than two feet from my hand. In a panic I fumbled around for a stone or something to kill it with. Suddenly there was a movement like water flowing in a stream, and the squirrel's hind legs and tail were disappearing into Henry's capacious mouth. I was relieved and then frightened again. What would happen to Henry? I rushed to the phone and called Rabies Control. They assured me that Henry could not be infected by rabies since he was a cold-blooded creature. So Henry had saved me again. He looked rather pleased with himself as he stretched out to continue his nap. The little antelope squirrel made no perceptible bulge in his sleek body, although I had seen him with bulges before, and each was about the size of a rock squirrel. Of course I never mentioned the bulges to Henry. It seemed somehow indelicate of me even to notice them.

We didn't see Henry all winter. He was probably sleeping under the bathtub or in one of the squirrel tunnels. But in the spring he reappeared, and presented us with a gift. He hooked his skin on one of the stones in the backyard and crawled out of it. When we straightened it out and let it dry in the sun, it was a chitinous, translucent veil, beautifully marked with a pattern of darker and lighter scales. We measured it and, sure enough, Henry was over six feet long.

That summer we went to the state of Washington for about a month, where our son and his family lived and where I was teaching at a writing conference. We left the house and dogs in the care of a young couple we had known for several years. One morning, in Port Townsend, Washington, I got a frantic call from Tucson. "There's a huge snake coiled around the dogs' water bucket in the kitchen. Is he a friend of yours, or is he just passing through?" I had forgotten to tell them about Henry. I assured them that I considered him a very good friend and that he would not stay in the kitchen long after he had satisfied his thirst. It's remarkable to watch a snake drink from a container. One sees no movement of the mouth or throat muscles, but the water level in the container drops rapidly, as if being sucked up through a large straw.

Henry did not show up the next spring—evidently his food supply was exhausted—and I have never seen him since, although my wife has. As she was driving home one day she saw him crossing the road just up the hill from the house. When he had rid us of our menace, he went off to help somebody else who needed him. But we know he isn't very far away, making the world safe for Democracy, or at least a more pleasant place to live in; and if we ever need him, he will return. *If some terrified neighbor doesn't kill him.* The thought makes me grind my teeth. White knuckles on the steering wheel. *Think about something else!*

4

I am about twelve miles beyond the place where I stopped to watch the coyote. *Some rancher will probably kill him, too. Think about something else!* The clouds are a little darker, but still no certainty of rain. Maybe they are just going to tease today. I am beginning to see the first junipers, which means that I must be reaching about 4,000 feet, getting into real rangeland. Coming up on the right is a rest stop, typical of rest stops on secondary highways in Arizona—a concrete picnic table with an ocotillo-roofed ramada over it and a trash can. That's all. But I need to rest, so I'll stop and go behind a juniper. Junipers are excellent trees to go behind when one needs to rest, since their foliage forms a dense screen all year long. The screen extends all the way to the ground in case the resting person happens to be a woman but is more than tall enough to screen a man who is standing.

There are two kinds of junipers dotting the hillsides at this elevation, one-seed junipers and alligator junipers. I prefer the alligator, although it isn't as thick and lush as the one-seed, but it's more interesting, often twisted into gnarled shapes. Its bark resembles the skin of an alligator, deeply furrowed into squarish plates. The combination of its gnarled shape and furrowed skin often makes the alligator juniper look ancient, although an individual plant might be relatively young. Both kinds of junipers have blue-gray berries, which are actually a form of cone, much prized by deer and other wildlife, although they taste exceedingly bitter to me. One of the most curious things I know about junipers is that native peoples in the Southwest used their bark as a form of diapers. They shredded the bark and put it in the bottom of their cradleboard. Then, once in a while, they removed the baby and dumped out the cradleboard. This was the prehistoric version of disposable diapers.

As I get back in the van, I can see some of Davidson Canyon to the south and east, although it's difficult to tell exactly which it is in the jumble of hills and eroded side canyons in that direction. Davidson runs between the Santa Ritas and the Empire Mountains, and down toward the desert floor from which I have come. It doesn't figure into recorded history until the coming of the American Era with the Gadsden Purchase, and its most notable history since then has been bloody, especially in the 1860s and 1870s when the road ran through it. It wasn't so much a place to live in as a place to get through, if you were lucky. Davidson was named after an Indian agent who was killed by the Apaches. These junipers must have made excellent cover for the Apaches, but Apaches didn't need much cover. Sometimes they seemed to come up out of the ground.

Between 1867 and 1873, Ft. Crittendon was just a few miles south and west of here, but it couldn't protect travelers through Davidson Canyon. Cpl. Joe Black had the job of carrying the mail from Ft. Crittendon to Tucson, through the canyon, and he always made the run at night. The Apaches almost never attacked at night. But once, on August 27, 1872, he decided to make the trip during the day, accompanied by Lt. Reid Stewart and a group of soldiers on their way to Tucson. Black and Stewart were in a buckboard that got somewhat ahead of the marching soldiers. The Apaches attacked the buckboard. Stewart was the lucky one. He was shot through the head, and whatever they did to him afterward, he couldn't have known about. But Black, while still living, was tied to a dead tree, probably a juniper, and the Apaches set fire to the tree. He was still screaming when the party of soldiers arrived, but it was too late. His burned body contained more than one hundred wounds made by lances, knives, and firebrands. Similar stories could be told about dozens of canyons in this area. Because this one involved the military, it was recorded, but many of them involving settlers were not.

Today, these hills are beautiful, quiet and idyllic, touched with a hint of green, nothing behind the junipers but an occasional cow or tourist, and the roadside is covered with wildflowers. Some people say that spring follows summer in Southern Arizona, which simply means that we have two seasons of wildflowers—one in early spring and another during and after the monsoon rains in late summer. The second crop often blooms right through until November or December, depending on the altitude and weather.

Just off the edge of the road, the ground is covered with brilliant patches of purple mat, a low creeper that grows from a central point and spreads in all directions, forming a showy "mat" of tiny, cerise-purple blossoms. Although its name in Greek, *nama*, is a reference to springtime, purple mat blooms almost anytime after a rain. During the dry seasons it is spindly and bare and looks half dead, but that is a common pattern with arid land plants.

White horsenettle is also in full bloom beside the road. It's an interesting example of the science of what-you-call-it, since it is neither white nor a nettle. I don't know how it got that name. It, too, blooms purple, but a deep purple. Saturnine, I would say, rather than royal. It's strange that saturnine should pop into my head, because an archaic meaning of that word referred to lead poisoning. I wonder if the presence of the plant indicates a high concentration of lead in the ground. Farfetched, but possible. It's more likely that the plant made me think of that word because it reminds me of deadly nightshade and is in the same family, a group of plants which often have narcotic qualities, although the potato is in the same family. The Latin name signifies "quieting" or "sleep inducing." Native Americans used the crushed berries of the horsenettle to curdle milk when they were making cheese, and settlers used them as remedies for sore throats and toothaches. Most of the horsenettle along here is about two feet high and not as dramatic as the mat, since its blossoms don't form a solid mass. But the individual plant is elegant and graceful, if somewhat insidious looking. Everything about it droops, including its stems, which are covered with silver hairlike prickles, and its leaves, which are long, narrow, and bluish-gray. Each blossom is a five-pointed star about an inch across with a bright yellow cone in the center. The blossoms have the rich look of crumpled purple leather.

Just past the rest stop a dirt road winds off to the right and a sign says "Rosemont Canyon." The road looks interesting, but I resist the temptation to turn down it. The highway climbs steeply, and all at once I have an expansive view of Empire Gulch, which runs roughly east and west, coming out of the Santa Ritas. The juniper gives way to oaks—shrub oaks, canyon live oaks, and Mexican blue oaks. They nestle up the draws, and their soft round contours produce a feeling of peace and spaciousness. In this country, oaks grow singly or in small groves but are not tall enough nor so closely spaced as to obscure the view, which is seventy miles on a clear day.

As I drop down into the broad basin of Empire Gulch, I see a road sign—GREATERVILLE/MADERA CANYON—and a narrow, paved road winding off to the west. I've been to Madera Canyon many times, always coming in from the other side of the Santa Ritas, but I've never been to Greaterville, although I've read about it. According to the road map, it's only four miles down that road. "Why not?" I say to Blue Boy. "It's a little cooler up here. Let's be tourists." Blue Boy turns down the road, and we're off for Greaterville.

The country is magnificent—rolling, green hills with generous stands of oak. We pass a ranch on the left, then another with a sign over the entrance—OAKDALE RANCH. Accurately named. Then we pass through an extensive spread with many outbuildings and corrals. Up on the hill to the left is a large water tank with THURBER painted across it in letters large enough to be read from miles away, as if Thurber is the name of a town, but I know it isn't. I've seen the Thurber Ranch indicated on the topographical map, and this must be it, although I can't tell where it ends or begins. It looks old, sleepy, and idyllic, spread out on both sides of the road with oaks scattered everywhere. Everything seems to have stopped, to be resting during the heat of the day. There is no one in sight, not even a cow.

The grass, in places, is knee-deep. They have had some good rains here in the past few weeks. Along the road are bright stands of sunflowers and individual prickle poppies, actually prickly poppies, but I've always called them prickle poppies. Another of those gorgeous, poisonous plants. Fortunately, cattle leave it alone, since every part of the prickle poppy is poisonous to some extent, including its blossom. But what a beautiful blossom, about three inches across, with big, floppy petals of glowing white and a clump of bright yellow stamens in the center. Each plant is three to four feet tall, and its foliage is unimpressive, but the blossom makes up for that. The leaves are long, pale green, deeply lobed, and covered with silver prickles. The whole thing looks like a tall thistle, but it's really a poppy, and a handsome one. The blossoms have a crumpled texture and wave in the breeze like dazzling white handkerchiefs. The prickle poppy usually indicates overgrazing, but I don't see how that can be the case here, since the grass is so deep. But the poppies are along the edge of the road, so I guess they don't indicate much of anything, except how beautiful they are.

Just past Thurber Ranch the road forks and abruptly ceases to be paved. A road sign indicates that the right fork goes to Madera Canyon, fourteen miles away. That road looks well graded. Madera Canyon is a great spot for camping and picnicking. It has oaks, big sycamores, a noisy little stream, and far too many people. The road sign also indicates that the road to the left goes to Melendrez Pass, five miles away. The road looks rough, rocky, and washed out in places, but Greaterville is that way and not more than a mile or two. I should get out my topographic map, but it's too much trouble. So I go to the left, down a steep hill and past a road sign that says NO OUTLET. I have faith in Blue Boy. If he can get in, he can get out; and if he can't get in, he won't need to get out. But the road proves to be truly terrible, partly because of recent rains and partly because it never was much of a road. At the bottom of the hill it twists through a wash that is almost impassable and turns up a draw coming in from the west. Where the road crosses the wash, another little road comes in from the left, and beside it is a mailbox with URQUIDES and under that PALLANES painted on its side. Next to it is a large sign. NO TRESPASSING. Down the little side road I can see an enormous cottonwood and the roof of a house. So Greaterville must be farther up the road I am on. It can't be far.

Blue Boy gets through the wash with some difficulty, and we start to climb and wind. A sign says ENTERING PRIVATE LAND. The road climbs and dips, again and again, following a sizable gulch on the left. At one point, while going down sharply, the road becomes so rutted and rocky that it's like a set of steps. I have to let Blue Boy down one wheel at a time. He lurches, creaks, and rattles piteously. Vehicles raised on the plains never get used to this kind of country. But Blue Boy has had plenty of experience. He once brought my wife and me through the Patagonia Mountains, a few miles south of here, on an abandoned logging road I don't even like to think about. Although he complains, I know he will make a gallant effort. I remind him that I recently bought him a new set of shoes at great expense. That settles him down a little. We climb and drop, climb and drop, following the gulch. No Greaterville.

I have given up on Greaterville when I see rusty metal equipment off to the left—several tanks and a broken-down chute which climbs part way up the side of the hill. Maybe this is a suburb of greater downtown Greaterville. Around the next bend, an abandoned and impassable road cuts sharply down the side of the hill and joins the road I am on. A barely legible sign says MORNING STAR RESEARCH PROJECT. I remember having seen "Morning Star Mine" on the topographic map, but I can't remember where it was in relation to Greaterville. Judging by the road that leads to it, the Morning Star Mine must be abandoned. But over the next rise the road widens and I come to a mining camp.

On the ridge to my left is a house trailer, a huge, rusty tank, and a metal chute leading out of the tank and down a gully about one hundred feet. Nearby, a very noisy bulldozer is tearing hell out of the side of the hill. To my right, down in the dry wash, a man is doing something with plastic buckets. The place doesn't look friendly, and the noise of the bulldozer is distracting. I keep going for about another mile until the road becomes almost impassable. Obviously, I have missed Greaterville. When all else fails, read the map. So I stop and dig out the topographic map from a tangle of books, maps, boots, and a sleeping bag in the back of the van. Sure enough, I am at least three miles past Greaterville on a road that winds through Ophir Gulch, climbs over Melendrez Pass and dead-ends at something identified as a Radio Facility. I must not be too far from the pass. Greaterville is down the side road where I saw the mailbox and the huge cottonwood. Beyond the NO TRESPASSING sign. It must be a downright unfriendly town. And well hidden.

Turning Blue Boy around on this poor excuse for a road is tricky. We jockey back and forth between a steep bank on one side and a sheer drop on the other and finally get ourselves headed down toward the mine. When we get there, the bulldozer has ceased operations and the place is very quiet. This time I stop and get out of the van. There's nobody in sight up on the hill by the equipment, so I go to the edge of the bank below which the man is still doing something with his plastic buckets.

"Is this the Morning Star Mine?"

"No, that's down there. This is the Grey Beard Mine."

I stifle the impulse to ask him if he's Grey Beard, and the thought almost makes me laugh. Instead, I slide down the bank and introduce myself. He's wearing rubber boots, overalls, a plaid shirt, and a straw hat that surely belonged to Huckleberry Finn. In fact, he looks exactly as I would imagine Huck to look, at about age twenty-five. He has wildly curly brown hair to his shoulders, snappy blue eyes, and a grin that would charm the berries off the bush. He's young, cheerful, and clean-shaven. Nothing about him fits the name of the mine.

"Are you the owner?"

"No, I'm the caretaker." He sticks out a hand, still muddy although he gives it a quick wipe on his overalls first. "Steve Hampton, one of America's homeless." He throws back his head with a laugh that makes me feel good all over. He seems willing, almost eager, to stop working and chat.

"Are you panning for gold?" I ask, looking dubiously at the three plastic buckets at his feet.

"Yep," he says. "Actually, I'm classifying, but it amounts to the same thing."

"I thought they used those big metal pans."

"Well, they do when they have running water, but we don't have any water here. It has to be hauled in. Never was any water here. That's why there's still some gold left."

It doesn't take much urging to get Steve to show me how classifying works. He shovels sand and gravel from the bed of the wash into one of the plastic buckets until it is full. He then transfers one shovelful into the second bucket, which is almost full of dirty water. The second bucket has a plastic unit fitted into it which extends about one-fourth of the way down and acts as a sieve. The bottom of this unit is covered with holes, three-eighths of an inch in diameter. In this unit Steve stirs the sand and gravel while it is submerged in water in the bucket. He stirs and stirs. Then he removes the sieve unit and dumps its contents on the ground. Then he carefully pours the water from the second bucket into the third bucket, which is used to store the water, and into which the sieve unit will be placed for the next batch. In the bottom of the second bucket he finds a grain of gold. Grains of gold are heavier than sand and gravel, and small enough to sink through the holes in the bottom of the classifier.

I'm fascinated, and Steve seems to enjoy answering questions. Any excuse to straighten up is probably good enough. It's stoop labor, and the strain on his back must be intense.

"How much do you get in a day?"

"Oh, on a good day I get about seventeen dollars worth. I get maybe 10 grains out of two bucketsful of sand. It takes 480 grains of gold to make an ounce."

"What's an ounce of gold worth?"

"It varies from day to day, but right now it's about four hundred dollars." I do some quick calculations. At five grains a bucket, he needs to process more than four buckets to make seventeen dollars.

"How long does it take you to do a bucket?"

"About an hour."

So for more than four hours of backbreaking work he is making seventeen dollars a day. And now it's his turn to ask a question.

"Hey, Professor, what department are you in at the University?"

"English." He looks disappointed. He must have expected geology or at least history or anthropology. As a university department, English just doesn't cut much ice with gold miners.

"I go down to the University a lot," Steve says. "Maybe I'll look you up sometime."

"Are you taking classes?" I ask.

"No. I just go down there to find girls." He straightens up, arches his back, and gives another of his wonderful laughs.

Laughing, I would guess, helps to relieve the tension on his back. Must remember that the next time I'm building a stone wall. And he's a smart young man. Prefers educated women. I'm sure a good many of the young women at the University would find him exotic and very interesting. It isn't every day they meet a genuine gold miner. And he doesn't have to tell them that his mining equipment consists of a shovel and three plastic buckets.

"They were still finding big nuggets up here as late as the 1930s,"

Steve says. "Couple of guys found some almost as big as hen eggs in 1935. But somebody killed both of them and stole the nuggets. They never did find out who did it."

"I guess people will do almost anything for gold," I say. "Did you know this area was called Renegades' Route in the late 1800s?"

"No," he says. "I guess that's why I like it here. I've always been a kind of renegade."

Suddenly I hear thunder to the south. Not too loud, but ominous. I've been so engrossed in talking to Steve I forgot all about the weather. I look up and see that the clouds now cover more than half the sky and are noticeably darker and more threatening. Holy chubasco! I feel like a fool. Standing in the middle of a wash in the Santa Rita Mountains during the monsoon season with a storm ready to break at any minute and with at least three miles of a god-awful dirt road and several more washes between me and any semblance of a pavement. I thank Steve for his time, wish him luck, and scramble up the bank. As Blue Boy and I start down the mountain, Steve waves, and I wave back. Then he bends over his buckets again, handsome young gold miner, renegade, and "one of America's homeless." I chuckle, and Blue Boy and I get our tails down the mountain as fast as we can.

On the way, I see the small, battered sign I missed while going up. MINING OPERATION. NOT RESPONSIBLE FOR LOSS DUE TO FIRE, THEFT OR PERSONAL INJURY DUE TO ACCIDENT. 2 SQ. MILE AREA. GREY BEARD MINING CO. I wonder how much of the two square miles Steve will process with his three plastic buckets at one hour per bucket. The next barely legible sign says FOREST LAND—NO PAN-NING. And I didn't even bring my pan. It makes me think of a joke I never tire of. A man was going through customs inspection at the airport. "Do you have any pornography?" the inspector asks. "Pornography!" the man replies. "I didn't even bring my pornograph."

With a lurching jolt I arrive at the place where the last wash twists across the road, and I see the other side of the mailbox. GREATER-VILLE ARIZONA. So Greaterville is one of those towns that exists only if one approaches it from the west. If one approaches it from the east, it is URQUIDES/PALLANES. I turn into the road beside the mailbox, deciding to have a quick look in spite of the NO TRESPASSING sign.

There are two low buildings near the big cottonwood. The larger one is occupied; the smaller one is probably not, and in ruins. The area is littered with junk, including old bedsteads, tools, and building materials. A beautiful calico guard-cat is on duty in the yard in front of the occupied house. Just past the houses, the road is blocked with a log, probably one of the branches from the cottonwood. As I am turning around, a young Hispanic woman comes out of the house and stands in the yard, eyeing the van with considerable disapproval. I know what she's thinking, and I know what she will say. "Can't you read the sign?"

I have my story ready in case she approaches the van. I'm a professor from the University of Arizona and I'm doing research. My story, like most stories, is true only if approached from the right direction. I am a professor from the University, but if I'm doing research, I don't know what I'm researching. I don't know what I'm looking for, or why. And I don't know if I'll recognize it when I find it, if I find it. I have a crazy notion that whatever it is, it's in Bisbee, something I lost there or left there, and if I find it, I will be able to see all my past and future from a reasonable perspective, the perspective of the inevitable. Faced with the young woman on the other side of the rickety fence, I know that my story is so full of holes I can't even tell it with any degree of conviction. And besides, I don't look like a professor from the University. I look like a poor, dumb, lost tourist. But the woman just stands in her front yard without approaching the van, and I'm already moving on, having seen all that is left of lesser and greater Greaterville.

Greaterville was one of those tough little mining communities that sprang up all over Southern Arizona in the 1870s. Some of them had more interesting names, like Total Wreck a few miles to the northeast, or Contention City on the San Pedro River, or Tombstone, which I will soon be passing through. Greaterville wasn't as tough as some of them because it was too small and didn't have a large enough Anglo population. But there were enough Anglo drifters, gunmen, and outlaws to create a problem for everybody. Southern Arizona seemed to attract half the violent punks from the frontier communities of the Midwest and Texas. More than enough. This stretch of country, between Tucson and the Mexican border, was called Renegades' Route because it was used so frequently by outlaws, either looking for something to rob or fleeing back across the border. Between the outlaws who drifted through and the Apaches who raided frequently, it's a wonder the people of Greaterville got any mining done at all.

But they did. In the 1870s a miner at Greaterville could produce about ten dollars a day in placer gold. Placer gold is gold deposited in gravel or sand, as distinguished from the other kind, which is more conveniently packaged in veins. Ten dollars a day doesn't seem like very much, but in the 1870s it was a considerable amount of money. Augmented by a little cattle ranching and a few plots of corn, beans, and chiles, it supported the town. But the same problem that affects the Grey Beard Mine today and causes Steve to use three plastic buckets rather than the traditional big, shallow pan, limited the output of the mines around Greaterville—lack of water. All water had to be hauled in canvas or goatskin bags on the backs of mules from Gardner Canyon, four miles south of here. By 1881 the gold had pretty well played out, although obviously there is still some in the area. But Greaterville hung on as a kind of quasi-ghost town. It had a post office until 1946. The wooden buildings must have been gradually torn down for firewood, and the adobe ones were either bulldozed or just melted away in the monsoons.

One important part of Greaterville is still intact, and I catch a glimpse of it up on the hill as I'm driving out. The graveyard. Now that I'm safely past the NO TRESPASSING sign and the rain is still holding off, I decide to stop and go up and have a look at it. It's a fairly typical, small-community Hispanic graveyard, but what I notice first is its setting, on the brow of a steep hill facing south and west. The view is superlative. To the south I can see miles and miles of blue hills and valleys, well into Mexico, and to the west are the rugged Santa Ritas and Mt. Wrightson at 9,432 feet. With the dark clouds and occasional flashes of lightning in the south, the view is like something out of a movie.

Now that I think of it, most of the old graveyards in this part of the country were located on hills, and most of them provide wonderful views, views that would turn modern developers green with envy, which is their favorite color, the color of money. I can think of many such windswept graveyards, always on hills with a view, but my favorite is Black Oak Cemetery, about thirty miles due south of here. Black Oak has been used by the Anglo ranching families in that area since there were Anglo ranching families in that area. It seems to get very little in the way of maintenance, but it is beautiful. It is situated on the brow of one of the Canelo Hills. The view is to the southeast and goes on forever. The growth has been left as it was—mostly large manzanitas with their glowing, dark red wood, and many oaks and junipers. Some of the headstones are natural boulders with the names of the dead either carved into them or attached to them in wrought iron. To an easterner accustomed to cemeteries with manicured lawns, rose gardens, and cypress trees, Black Oak might seem barbaric, but I love that place.

The graveyard at Ft. Huachuca is also very old and is situated in an oak grove on a slightly elevated slope of one of the Huachuca Mountains. It too commands a view to the southeast. As one would expect of a military graveyard in current use, it is much more tailored and immaculate than most of the older civilian graveyards. But each marker tells its story, even the ones that say "Unknown." When I first saw the graveyard at Ft. Huachuca, I was puzzled by the large number of graves marked "Unknown." Later, I found out the reason. Many victims of the Apaches were so badly mutilated that they could not be identified.

But why did the early settlers in this country, both the Hispanics and the Anglos, usually locate their graveyards on hills facing views that are magnificent? Did they feel that the dead would enjoy the view? Did they want to put their dead as close to heaven as possible, regardless of the ultimate destination of the deceased? Or did they, somehow, associate death with the sublime? I don't know. The cynic might say it was because that particular piece of land couldn't be put to any other use, but that is not true in this country. These hills would have been as good for grazing as most of the land around them. Whatever their reasons for locating their graveyards on hills with magnificent views, we don't seem to follow the practice today. Our developers build subdivisions on the tops of hills and increase the price of each house according to the view it commands. And the dead make way for the living. I know this is inevitable. I know it is the way the world works, but as Edna St. Vincent Millay said in one of her more lucid moments, "I know. But I do not approve. And I am not resigned."

The graveyard at Greaterville, with its view of Mexico in the distance, is not large. About half the size of a city block. It is fenced in and basically unlandscaped. Many of the markers are small wooden crosses from which all paint and lettering have long since disappeared. The wooden crosses themselves are splintered and ragged with age. Other markers are mortar or stone, and some are fairly elaborate. Somebody, long ago, planted a short row of junipers across one section of the graveyard. Otherwise it is dirt, wild grasses, and weeds. Many of the graves are decorated with bright plastic flowers.

To Anglos, these small Hispanic graveyards often have an extremely dreary appearance. It has something to do with the bare, unkempt ground in contrast with the garish plastic flowers. Even in the desert, we expect our graveyards, like our golf courses, to be covered with well-clipped lawns, water or no water. And ideas of good taste, as well as funerary customs, vary greatly from culture to culture. Having told myself all that, I am still a little taken aback to see an automobile steering wheel impaled on one of the more elaborate stone crosses. It is a fancy steering wheel from, I would guess, a 1950s model car. Both cross and steering wheel are lavishly bestowed with plastic flowers. The inscription on the cross reads: "Joquin R. Mendoza, May 26, 1902—June 10, 1955." Why the steering wheel is part of the grave marker is anybody's guess. My guess would be that Joquin either loved his car very much or he had a serious accident in it, or both. I wonder what became of the car. Maybe they buried him in it. I have a momentary vision of Joquin heading for eternity in a '52 Chevy convertible without a steering wheel, his hair blowing in the wind.

I want to stay longer and check the dates on other headstones, but the thunder and lightning are getting portentous. Blue Boy and I have almost a mile to go before we encounter a paved road, and several more miles before we get back on Highway 83, heading south toward Sonoita. A flash flood anywhere between here and the highway could be a serious problem, so we move out smartly, or as smartly as the road will permit. Except for the thunder, everything is very still, waiting for the storm. The sky is taking on a decidedly green tinge, and the atmosphere is electric. I have the feeling that I'm driving under water, although not a drop has fallen yet. When we get to where the road is paved, Blue Boy and I race with the storm.

Highway 83 is a welcome sight and still no rain. I turn south and head for Sonoita, remembering that this highway has been rebuilt and rerouted in recent years so the floodwaters flow under it through culverts rather than across it. But the old road was more interesting. It snaked up and around the low hills, past the ruins of a couple of small ranch houses and an abandoned one-room schoolhouse. I pass a small sign—ENTERING SANTA CRUZ COUNTY—and I'm in the County of the Holy Cross, Arizona's smallest county, which extends sixty miles along the Mexican Border and thirty miles northward. Small by Arizona standards, Santa Cruz County still gives me the impression that it's enormous, unlimited, stretching on forever.

I suppose any county that contained the magnificent San Rafael Valley would seem that way. It's a breathtaking sweep of tawny rangeland which lies almost directly south of here between the Canelo (Cinnamon) Hills and the Patagonia Mountains. It was one of Col. William C. Green's cattle empires, where he built the largest of his mansions. That ranch, although somewhat restricted, is still functioning, and the "ranch house" is still inhabited by his descendants. The Santa Cruz River, from which the county gets its name, rises in the San Rafael Valley and heads due south into Mexico, where it quickly makes a U-turn around a mountain and heads north, back into the United States and on to Tucson. It is one of Arizona's intermittent rivers nowadays, flowing only after a rain, but until the severe overgrazing of surrounding lands, which came with the American Era after the Gadsden Purchase, and especially after the Civil War, it flowed year-round and to a point a few miles north of Tucson, where it died in the desert.

When the Santa Cruz River comes back into the United States heading north, it forms the beautiful Santa Cruz Valley, and between that valley and the San Rafael lie the Patagonia Mountains, which attracted Europeans to this area in the first place. The Patagonia Mountains contained fairly extensive deposits of silver, and some gold, and these deposits were known to the native Pimas, who were mining them in a primitive fashion before the Spanish entered this far northern frontier of New Spain in the seventeenth century. The Spanish developed the mines, using native Piman slave labor, and mined them to whatever extent the raiding Apaches would permit. A considerable amount of silver from the Patagonia Mountains found its way into the outstretched hands of the Spanish Empire, but that empire was growing ever more senile and ineffectual, losing its colonies abroad as it lost its wars at home.

After the Gadsden Purchase, American mining engineers, backed with capital from the eastern part of the country and from Europe, developed those mines still further, hampered by frequent Apache attacks. Tubac, on the Santa Cruz River, flourished as a center of wealth and culture, although it had to be abandoned to the Apaches several times and stood in ruins during the Civil War. After the war the mines were revived and so was Tubac, at least to the extent that the Apaches would permit, and the mines were worked for the next forty years until the ore gave out. Only a few ruins of that late flourishing of mining activity in the Patagonia Mountains remain, ghost towns in the final stages of decay, but their names remain on the map: Washington Camp, Duquesne, Mowry, Harshaw, the signatures of ghosts who wrote their names in silver. The ghosts attract a few tourists, but since the Civil War the county has supported itself with cattle ranching, cattle ranching, and more cattle ranching. Lately, however, judging by the looks of things around Sonoita, real estate development has been a major part of the economic picture in Santa Cruz County.

From here, it's a fairly straight shot and just a few miles to Sonoita, through what was once some of the richest rangeland on the continent. The entire eastern horizon is mountains, and I have a sweeping view, especially dramatic in this weird light, of the country drained by Cienega Creek, which flows to the north when it flows at all. Due east are the Whetstone Mountains, just south of them the fantastically shaped Mustangs, and still farther south the Huachucas, with Miller Peak rising to 9,449 feet.

Just as I'm slowing down for the approach to Sonoita, a sudden explosion of thunder directly above Blue Boy makes me duck. There are a few large, tentative drops of rain on the windshield, and then the sky opens in a deluge. Rain is not so much falling as slamming down and leaping back up from the hot pavement in front of me. Blue Boy's roof has turned into a metal drum. With the windshield wipers on high, I can barely see the taillights of the car a few feet in front of me as I approach the intersection of Highways 83 and 82, the center of Sonoita.

The buildings along the highway are a blur, but I know there are two gas station–groceries, a bar, a large steak house, and several real estate offices. Half the people in Santa Cruz County seem to be real estate agents. I suppose it's no wonder. You wouldn't say that Sonoita has become fashionable, but the land around it certainly has. Several of the large ranches nearby, like the Crown C a few miles down Highway 82 to the west, have been put on the market and "developed" in the last fifteen or twenty years. The Crown C was divided into large parcels of land, from forty to about eighty acres each, with heavy restrictions concerning where houses could be built, utilities, and so forth, but not all developers in the area have been so conscientious about trying to preserve the natural beauty of the land. I never cease to be amazed at the way people in real estate use language. Land in its natural state is called "undeveloped," which sounds like a euphemism to describe a woman with small breasts. After the land is destroyed, it is called "developed" land, and its destroyer is called its "developer."

Almost everybody has pulled off the highway now. This thunderstorm can't last too long. In a few minutes it will either stop or turn into a steady but less violent rain. Very carefully, I turn onto Highway 82 heading east, and try to see through the wall of water to find the Cactus Flower Cafe, about a quarter of a mile down on the north side. I've got to get off the road until this lets up, and I might as well have a late lunch. I worked up an appetite with all that panning for gold. There's the cafe, totally surrounded with cars. Everybody else on the road is seeking shelter, too. There's nowhere to park near the building, so I will have to make a dash for it. I take the plunge, run like hell, and am drenched before I reach the porch, but it feels great. The temperature has dropped at least twenty-five degrees, maybe more. "*Muchas gracias, Chubasco,*" I say, and go in.

The Cactus Flower Cafe is small and unpretentious. It serves good country food, including several Mexican dishes, at reasonable prices, and the waitresses are always cheerful. I've stopped here five or six times in as many years. Today it's fairly crowded with locals and people on the road. There's a film crew seated in the little dining room on the left, seven or eight of them, including an actress and actor. I nearly have to crawl over them to get to the washroom. The actress is very blond and willowy, but it's hard to tell what her face looks like under the makeup, which has run down in places, probably from the heat. The actor is young, rawboned, and good-looking in a stereotypical, square-jawed sort of way. Either his makeup gives his eyes an unnatural brightness, or he's been taking funny pills.

When I come out of the washroom and find a small table by the window, a waitress goes by with her arms full of food and calls, "Be right with you." Business is booming today, especially for midafternoon. When the waitress comes back to take my order she says, "Honey, you're soaked. Ain't this some storm? You must have left your slicker in the wagon."

"Cloudy in the west and it looks like rain," I half-sing, half-say, and she jumps in on the next line with a husky contralto, "And the damned old slicker's in the wagon again." Then we both laugh.

"I didn't think anybody still knew that song," she says.

"I was raised on it, along with a lot of others I can't sing in mixed company."

"Honey, I know a few of those," she grins, and we both laugh again.

"What are they filming?" I ask, nodding toward the group in the dining room.

"Oh, some commercial," she says. "I think it's for a car or something. They sure picked the weather for it. Somebody is always filming around here. I keep waiting for Hollywood to discover me, but I think I've waited too long—maybe twenty-five years too long."

I like the Cactus Flower Cafe. It's a big improvement over Greaterville. I order a Mexican combination plate. Rain is running down the window in sheets. I can't see even across the highway, but there are no buildings on that side of the road to see anyway, just thirty miles of grassland and another range of mountains. I notice a man sitting at the counter a few feet away. He's short and slight, but wiry, and probably in his late thirties, with dark hair and a weathered face. Probably some Hispanic blood back a few generations. Cowboy boots, jeans, and straw hat. Pale hands and a pair of leather gloves sticking out of his hip pocket. "Local cowboy," I say to myself. What drew my attention to him is the fact that he's so bowlegged I don't see how he can walk. He must have walked in; I don't see any horse in here, although there's a large photograph of a beautiful palomino on the wall above the counter. I make a mental note to pay attention when the cowboy leaves, just to see how he manages.

Sonoita is not one of the oldest towns in the area. It looks like a crossroads community, but it owes its beginnings to a railroad, although no railroad goes through it now and there is no depot. The story of that railroad could serve as a recipe for the development, in every sense of that word, of the entire southern part of the state after the Civil War: one part ruthless greed, one part romantic dream, one part chicanery, one part courage, and years of pick-and-shovel work under a hot sun by crews of men who usually slept at night on the ground beside the railroad bed they were constructing.

It was the Atchison, Topeka, and Santa Fe, which has come to signify the romance of the rails and Harvey Houses for hungry travelers. Like rivers in Mexico, it had a tendency to operate under different names depending on which part of the country it was going through, but its goal was always the same—to reach the Pacific. And thereby hangs a railroad tale in which little Sonoita was only a whistle stop on the wrong road to glory. It began in 1859 in Topeka, Kansas, when Cyrus K. Holliday was bitten by the railroad bug and became a railroad promoter, a job that was to furnish him with hard work for the rest of his life.

Topeka, which young Holliday had helped to establish, was fine; but what it needed was a railroad to connect it with the rest of the country. So Holliday began to promote a railroad. This meant getting wealthy people to subscribe large sums of money in return for stock, and getting the government to allocate large quantities of land that could be sold to provide an income for the as yet unborn railroad. In those days shortline railroads were springing up all over Kansas. The government was generous with land grants, and the farmers needed to get their products to market.

One of the thirteen members of the railroad corporation that Holliday founded in Topeka in 1860 was S. C. Pomeroy, an agent for the New England Emigrant Aid Society, which channeled newly arrived immigrants to Kansas in return for their votes at election time. As the Civil War became inevitable, the Republican Party rushed Kansas into statehood, partly to increase the party's strength in Congress. Pomeroy was one of the two Republican United States senators elected to represent the new and bleeding state, and he quickly became the Republican political boss in Kansas. As such, he was able to do Holliday and the fledgling railroad no end of good. In fact, Senator Pomeroy, who served as president of the railroad for a spell, was so typical of the crooked, greedy politicians of the post–Civil War era that Mark Twain used him as a model for his nefarious Senator Dilworthy in *The Gilded Age*.

With Senator Pomeroy's help, the Atchison and Topeka, which was for years called "the jerkwater railroad," was able to obtain a land grant from the United States Congress consisting of alternate sections on both sides of the railroad right-of-way and was also able to convince several Kansas counties to float bonds to finance the railroad. But all this was not enough to build on a scale Holliday dreamed of. Again Senator Pomeroy rose to the occasion, not unlike many politicians of his day and our own, and in 1863 he saved the jerkwater railroad. He simply convinced the Commissioner of Indian Affairs to sell the Atchison and Topeka almost 340,000 acres of the Potawatomie Indian Reservation, one of the most fertile, valuable, and beautiful areas in the State of Kansas, with ample water, heavy forests, and valuable coal deposits, and all for one dollar an acre. Then he convinced Congress to ratify the deal.

Such deals were not uncommon during the period, although this one was even more flagrant than most. It was based on the old semantics game, the fine art of what-you-call-it, the belief that a rose by any other name has no odor. Indian reservation lands, when originally set aside by the United States government, were sacrosanct and could not be sold, but the individual states had found a way to get around this by classifying large portions of them as "reserve" rather than "reservation" lands. Reserve lands could be sold. Later, Senator Pomeroy, who had his fingers in many lucrative pies, was charged with bribery and denied a third term in the United States Senate, but by then he was so rich he didn't need a third term.

But Holliday dreamed of a transcontinental railroad to the Pacific, and his dream drove the corporation for the next century. Now a well-financed and ruthlessly competitive operation, the Atchison and Topeka frantically laid tracks westward across Kansas and into Colorado where it fought competitors for every mountain pass in a series of battles that came to be known as "the Rio Grande Wars." By buying a half interest in the financially troubled Atlantic and Pacific, it was able to extend its tracks across New Mexico and become the Atchison, Topeka, and Santa Fe. Then it built rapidly on across the Arizona Territory and arrived in 1880 at the California border, at a Colorado River crossing called Needles. Here it was effectively stopped by its major competitor, C. P. Huntington, whose two railroads, the Central Pacific and the Southern Pacific, controlled all railway access to California.

By 1880 the jerkwater railroad had come a long way from Topeka, and it had become the longest railroad in the world. Still it had no access to the Pacific and its shipping trade. Smarting from having been outmaneuvered by Huntington, its president and board of directors decided they would just have to find some other way to get to the Pacific. They would have to go through Mexico, whose long-time dictator Porfirio Díaz was eager to accommodate foreign business interests if such accommodation brought large sums of money to his government. But there was only one Mexican port on the Gulf of California within striking distance, and it was Guaymas, about three hundred miles due south of the Arizona border community of Nogales. It was a long shot, but it seemed to be the only shot the Atchison, Topeka, and Santa Fe had.

At the beginning of the 1880s, Guaymas was a tiny, sleepy fishing village on a good bay with not much else to recommend it except devastating heat. Like Mazatlán and San Blas to the south, it was a tropical pesthole. Typhoid, cholera, and malaria epidemics were fearsome, and although dysentery didn't bother the adult natives much, it could be fatal to visitors. Commercial ships did not generally put in at these ports during the summer months, and if they did, the passengers and crews were usually not allowed to go ashore.

But Guaymas it was because Guaymas it had to be if the Atchison, Topeka and Santa Fe was going to extend its rails to a Pacific shipping port. The company sent its highest ranking engineer, W. R. Morley, dashing hero of "the Rio Grande Wars," to Guaymas to look it over and do some surveying. Morley seems to have been a born promoter himself, and he, too, dreamed on a large scale. He realized that in order to attract shipping away from the already developed California ports and get the ships to put in at Guaymas, something drastic had to be done about Guaymas; and he had an amazingly simple solution based on historical precedent. Just take the huge state of Sonora away from Mexico and attach it to the United States. The history of Texas provided a blazing example of how it could be accomplished.

First, gringo settlers would have to be attracted to Guaymas, and Porfirio Díaz was not opposed to this. So ballyhoo Guaymas. Play up the mineral wealth in the area. Advertise Guaymas as a tropical paradise, a resort with limitless commercial potential, *the San Francisco of the Gulf of California*. Then, Morley wrote in a letter to the president of the railroad: "This would bring Adventurers, who will persistently work for, and finally succeed in obtaining another 'Texas' from the Territory of Old Mexico."

I don't know how seriously this proposal to steal the State of Sonora from Mexico was taken by the top brass of the Atchison, Topeka, and Santa Fe. They could not, of course, have made such plans public or Díaz would have thrown them out of Mexico, lock, stock and caboose. But they did build the railroad, more than three hundred miles of parallel tracks to a dream that never materialized, a possibility on the horizon doomed from the start by climate and geography.

As the survey party worked northeast from the border at Nogales, surveying the line which would connect the Mexican part of the railroad with the existing track at Benson, Arizona, they found that the country had already been overgrazed, and they suffered from a lack of grass for their horses and a lack of water. However, at one point they found a rich valley with a creek that ran southwest. The valley was full of corn, which the settlers sold to them for eight cents a pound. The creek would have been Sonoita Creek, not far from Sonoita, whose name comes from a Tohono O'odham word that means "place where corn will grow." Early settlers said that corn grew as well here as in the lush Missouri River bottoms and that the whole Sonoita Valley was full of golden corn. But the valley was almost totally uninhabited between 1861 and 1876 because of the Apaches. The present town grew up when the railroad was built through here in 1882.

Both the railroad and most of the corn are gone now, but the town remains and has grown in the last twenty years. The cost of the surrounding real estate, which is being chopped up for the contemporary American dream, a few acres of rangeland with some oaks or mesquites, has gone sky high. Sonoita, with its huge fake barn on the highway, its ice cream parlor, Chuchina Rustica Delicatessen, and Equees Art Gallery, is trying desperately to become fashionable. And it almost succeeds at certain times of the year when there is a rodeo or quarter horse show. The crossroads and rodeo grounds are mobbed then. But the rest of the time the community has a deserted look, although the little, unpretentious Cactus Flower Cafe never seems to want for customers. Sonoita is a cow town and a horse town, although it took a railroad to make it any kind of town at all. Now, many of the people in the surrounding community, and many who have invested in it from a distance, have discovered that they have something more than cows and horses to sell, and they seem to be selling it as fast as they can—the surrounding rangeland with its magnificent view and clean air.

When the demand for something is great enough, somebody will always come forward to sell it, no matter what it is, and there will always be promoters. The need to develop and destroy is in our blood, part of our heritage. It got off the boat at Plymouth Rock, crossed the prairies on horseback, financed railroads with land set aside for Indian reservations, tore down mountains, and brought the light to those who were in a dark and undeveloped state. If they didn't choose to see the light, it mostly killed them, one way or the other.

But the ballyhoo didn't work for Guaymas, and the huge State of Sonora is still firmly attached to Mexico. Guaymas has never become a great tourist attraction or retirement community, although it has grown some, mostly because of its fishing and fish-processing industries. Most of the diseases, except dysentery for the tourists, have been brought under control by modern medicine. It is still hot and somewhat sleepy, but it wakes up once each spring when it is inundated with students from the University of Arizona on spring break, often drunk and disorderly. The students bring in a little cash along with the mayhem and return to Tucson with hangovers and sometimes a good case of the trots. I doubt that they or the Mexican natives are aware that Guaymas was once briefly scheduled to become the San Francisco of the Gulf of California.

The railroad still runs through Guaymas, now part of the Mexican Central that comes up from Mexico City through Guadalajara. North of Mazatlán it isn't too heavily used, and it ends at Nogales. The tracks of the old New Mexico and Arizona line have been torn up from Nogales to at least Sonoita, maybe farther, but the railroad bed is still there in many places. I think the tracks would have been just across the highway, which I can see now because the rain has let up some. I can also see the bowlegged cowboy pulling out of the parking lot in a small but bright, new pickup. Dammit! I missed his exit. But I've finished my lunch and it's time to roll, rain or no rain. It should be stopping soon. At least it probably would down on the desert floor, but this close to the Huachucas, old Thunder Mountains, one never knows.

I make a dash for the van and we head east with windshield wipers going full blast. It is blessedly cool. Even through the rain the rangeland basins between mountain ranges are magnificent. The Whetstone Mountains are to the north of me now, and to the south, like a smaller extension of the Whetstones, are the Mustangs. For years I thought that the Mustangs got their name because of their wildly dramatic, arched shapes, like the curves of a mustang trying to throw a rider, head and tail down, back up, and shooting straight up into the sky. But the books say that settlers, probably Mexican, had abandoned horses in this area, probably because of the Apaches, and the result was large herds of wild horses, or mustangs. Hang the books. I like my theory better. Farther south I can just make out the Huachucas with their summits enveloped in dark clouds. They and the storm completely block off the southern horizon. Suddenly I remember that the valley I am passing through, between the Whetstones and the Mustangs, is called Rain Valley. I have the window partway down so I can feel, smell, and taste Rain Valley. Lovely. It's beautifully green now, but I have been through here when it was sere and suffering from lack of water. Usually it is tawny gold, like rolling wheat fields after the harvest.

I remember once, many years ago when I was stationed at Ft. Huachuca, I was driving this road, Highway 82, in the opposite direction headed for Nogales when I barely missed colliding with an airplane. As I came over the summit of one of the rises, a small plane was coming toward me down the highway, taking off. The pilot managed to get the plane off the ground somehow, as I braked frantically, but its wheels passed no more than a foot above the roof of the car. A surprise like that and you don't even have to cross the border to suffer from the Mexican two-step, the Tijuana trots, Montezuma's revenge, or whatever you prefer to call it. How many times have I stood in front of the counter of a *pharmacía* somewhere in Mexico with distress written all over my face while the clerk was reaching for a bottle of pills even before I could say the magic word Lomotil? "*Por favor*, Lomotil! For God's sake Lomotil, hurry *pronto!*" However many words disappear from my Spanish vocabulary, I will never forget that one. But there aren't any planes taking off from Highway 82 today, probably because of the rain.

5

The storm seems to be over, although the sky to the south is still a mass of dark clouds. White cumuli are dispersing northward. Their shadows, like huge dark ships, sail over the rangeland. The temperature is beginning to climb after the rain, but it's still cool compared to what I left behind on the desert floor. I wonder if it rained in Tucson. Probably not. These summer storms are highly localized, and this one seemed to be of the Huachuca Mountain variety; I don't think it extended very far to the north. Everything is wildly green and fresh after the rain, and the air smells of greasewood. As I drive on through Rain Valley, I can see well into Mexico. I must be about thirty miles from the border.

And there's the sign ENTERING COCHISE COUNTY. Cochise forms a square in the southeastern corner of the state, the most neatly symmetrical county in Arizona. The line I have just crossed runs straight north and south for its entire length with only a tiny jog so small as not even to be recorded on most maps. Cochise split off from Pima County in 1881, and Tombstone accepted the dubious honor of being its county seat. After the discovery of a fabulous lode of silver in the Tombstone Mountains in 1877, Tombstone had rapidly become the largest town in the Territory of Arizona. For awhile it was larger than San Francisco. But the miners hit water in the mines at the five-hundred-foot level, and it was necessary to pump like hell in order to do any mining at all. A fire in 1886 destroyed the pumps. Five years later the town was nearly dead. It had a resurgence in 1901 when new pumps were installed, but they failed in 1909, and that was about the end of it. Twenty years later, the year the stock market crashed, Tombstone was almost a ghost town. County officials moved the county seat about twenty-five miles southeast to Bisbee, which was still a viable mining community, although it too was soon to fall on hard times. Bisbee has been the county seat since then, but now that the mines at Bisbee are no longer operating, the county itself is the largest employer in the town.

Each county in Arizona—each county in every state I suppose— has a different kind of reputation. Cochise County has a reputation for being tough, plain mean-and-ornery tough. Cowboys and miners, shoot-em-ups and bordellos. That reputation was established in the 1880s, and although the major mines are all shut down in the county and the cowboys don't wear six-shooters anymore, at least not in town, the reputation lingers. Part of it is pure hype to attract tourists, but part of it, I think, is still justified. Cochise has always been very much aware that it is a Mexican-border county. For many years that border was little more than a line on a map; no fence, no official ports of entry, and no border patrol except the cavalry at Ft. Huachuca. It was easy-come, easy-go. When the law got after an outlaw on one side of the border, whichever side that happened to be, he could simply cross to the other.

Tombstone has come back, almost from the dead, as a highly successful tourist attraction that bills itself as THE TOWN TOO TOUGH TO DIE. But Bisbee, which is almost on the Mexican border, was probably a rougher and tougher town, and it has been tougher for a much longer period. As late as 1917, labor problems and massive vigilante activity brought Bisbee bad national publicity it did not want. And even from 1958 to 1960, when I lived in Bisbee, it had its violent moments, mostly connected with labor unrest and strikes at the mine. Today Cochise is still very much aware that it is a border county with a potential for violence. Its two ports of entry to Mexico, Naco and Agua Prieta, once famous for their brothels, are now famous as points of contact with huge, well-organized drug smuggling operations which reach deep into Mexico and beyond. And the people involved with drug smuggling these days can be about as tough as you can get.

In contrast to all this, Cochise County still has plenty of space for people to move around in without stepping on one another's toes.

Sweeping rangelands so vast as to lose themselves in blue distances. Sulphur Springs Valley, on the other side of Bisbee, is one of the state's largest and least populated rangeland basins. And the county has mountains, the most magnificent range of mountains in all of Southern Arizona, the Chiricahuas, lying roughly north and south like a huge wall parallel to the eastern border of the state. And Cochise has a river, a real river, not one of those temporary affairs with water in it maybe twice or three times a year like the Santa Cruz. The San Pedro River runs north out of Mexico, like the Santa Cruz, but unlike the Santa Cruz, which dies in the desert, the San Pedro usually keeps going and empties into the Gila. There is no highway running along the San Pedro from the border northward, but its valley was Coronado's highway in 1540. He brought horses and cows into the area, and he was in search of a precious metal—gold. In a sense, those three things, horses, cows and valuable metals, mostly silver and copper, have made Cochise what it is today—and destroyed much of what it once was.

In 1956 I knew a very old man in Fry, which had just changed its name to Sierra Vista, who told me that when he came to the area at the age of seven, the grass in the San Pedro Valley was taller than he was. It now grows in little clumps here and there, about ankle high, and in many extensive areas there isn't any at all. The topsoil is gone. And at Bisbee there was a mountain, one of the Mule Mountains called Sacramento. In old photographs of the town it forms the most prominent feature of the eastern horizon. Now it is a hole called Sacramento Pit. We can move mountains by means of modern technology, but we haven't learned how to put them back together again, and we haven't learned to make grass grow where there is no soil to grow it in.

I am entering the San Pedro River Valley over a low crest between the Whetstone Mountains to the north and the Mustangs to the south. Actually they are both part of the same range of mountains, but they wound up with different names. The earliest Hispanic ranchers called the entire range the Mestinjes, or mustangs, because of the band of wild horses that roamed through them. As early as 1694, Father Kino found that the Pimas in this area had caught, broken, and were riding mustangs. Later, settlers discovered novaculite, a mineral used as a whetstone, in the northern section of the range, which gradually came to be known as the Whetstone Mountains, while the southern section retained the name Mustangs.

As I come over the crest, I get my first unobstructed view across the enormous panorama of the San Pedro River Valley. The palisades of the Dragoon Mountains form the skyline to the northwest, and up there somewhere is Cochise's Stronghold, from which he and his band of Chiricahua Apaches dominated the valley and surrounding areas so effectively and for so long that the whole county was eventually named after him. South of the Dragoons and closer to the river, nearly out in the middle of the valley floor, are the Tombstone Mountains, actually just hills. Tombstone is on their northeastern slope, and I can't see it from here. Still closer to the river is a series of small, well-defined conical hills, the Charleston Hills, like isolated pyramids, which show their volcanic origins by their distinctive shapes. Behind the Tombstone Mountains and a little to the south are the Mule Mountains, with Bisbee perched on the sides of two canyons on their far slopes. South of the Mule Mountains, mirage after blue mirage of mountain ranges stretches deep into Mexico. Most of the southern horizon farther west is taken up by the looming Huachucas, magnificent this time of day in their purple robes which flow down into the valley. Ft. Huachuca and sprawling Sierra Vista are barely visible on their eastern slopes, about ten miles south of here.

And invisible from here, but running right through the middle of all this in a meandering line from south to north, is the San Pedro River. Southwestern rivers have a way of hiding themselves and the vegetation that borders them, even in the middle of a fairly flat river basin. They have eroded their beds deeply, leaving a series of low mesas like steps on either side. Even the tops of tall cottonwoods along their banks are below the level of the surrounding terrain and usually cannot be seen from a distance of more than a mile or two. But I will see the river soon, and when I do, I will see it from above, from the edge of one of the mesas. It will be a ribbon of the most brilliant green winding through a dry land.

As I come down the slope between the Whetstones and the Mustangs, I begin to see signs of civilization—litter, junked cars, and a few scattered houses and trailers. Then an intersection with a blinking yellow light for caution, an understatement, because a wild stream of traffic is hurtling up Highway 90 from the south, not even slowing down where it crosses Highway 82. In 1956, when I was stationed at Ft. Huachuca, Highway 90 ended here. Now it cuts straight through to Interstate 10 and carries the commuter traffic between Sierra Vista/Ft. Huachuca and Tucson. These drivers are going home, and it's obvious that they aren't going to let anything get in their way. I have to wait a long time to find an opening in the traffic through which Blue Boy and I can dash. Getting across Highway 90 at this time of day is the most dangerous part of my trip to Bisbee. Once across, I decide to stop at Mustang Corners, a gas station and convenience market on the northeast corner of the intersection, and get something cold to drink.

When I was at Ft. Huachuca, in order to get to Tucson, which is about forty-two miles west and considerably north of Ft. Huachuca, we had to go east. We came to this point, where Highway 90 ended, and turned due east, taking Highway 82 for about seventeen miles toward Tombstone, then north to Benson, and then back west toward Tucson. It was a long, roundabout way to go, but there was no shorter way to get to Tucson on a paved road. Before I left Ft. Huachuca, somebody cut a road straight south from the Tucson-Benson highway, connecting with Highway 90 here. The new road shortened the drive by about forty miles and made it possible for a few hardy souls to commute from Tucson to their work at Ft. Huachuca, which employed many civilians. But the commuters paid dearly. As I recall, they came on a bus, an old, beat-up bus, since nobody wanted to trust a car to that new road, and I doubt that most cars could have made it. The new road was an ungraveled cut which forded washes, plunged up steep slopes of jagged stone, and was impassable in the rainy season. It was about twenty miles long and took about an hour to navigate. The commuters called it "Hell Road," and when they got off the bus they looked as if they had been through hell. Now Hell Road is an extension of Highway 90. At the rate these cars are whizzing past, it must take them about twelve minutes to get over old Hell Road. Ah, progress. But don't get in its way at rush hour.

There is no highway sign announcing it on Highway 82, but I am in greater downtown Whetstone, not one of the area's noteworthy contributions to recent urban development. The signs announcing it are on Highway 90 only, but the town extends, in its haphazard, discontinuous way, from a little south of the Mustang Corners intersection to considerably north of it. Fortunately, since I will be continuing on Highway 82, I will see little of Whetstone, but I have seen it before, one of the ugliest little communities in Arizona. As the architectural historian Reyner Banham said about Las Vegas, "It will never make noble ruins." It seems to be a scattering of buildings and trailers with no central focus to hold them together, as if they had dropped from the sky and remained wherever they happened to land. The most distinctive of the buildings is a boxlike church which, in spite of its white paint and attached steeple, looks amazingly like a barracks building from Ft. Huachuca, which it was.

The whole community looks raw and yet worn out, young and yet beat down. That must be what most frontier towns in this area looked like when they were young. Dreary, hopeless, and prematurely old. And if old photographs are to be trusted, that's what most of the young people in those frontier communities looked like, too. Young men and women, less that twenty years old as this raw community is, stare out of old daguerreotypes from under their beat-up broadbrimmed hats with a look of defiant hopelessness, of lost youth never to be found again. They had seen the elephant. It was a popular phrase used by those who headed into the fabulous West in their covered wagons. They were "going to see the elephant." The young people in those old photographs, often standing in front of a one-room adobe house in a land without enough water, had seen the elephant, had touched it, and it had kicked and stomped them a few times. They were worn out on arrival, and they got more worn out the longer they stayed, worn out by the heat, the wind that blew from March until July, the lack of water, the grinding work, the merciless sun, the obdurate earth. They were haggard and young. They didn't have to be beautiful or noble to suffer, but if they were, the Southwestern frontier could destroy both qualities quickly.

Between here and Ft. Huachuca, near the point where Babocomari Creek crosses Highway 90, is another small community of fairly recent origin, another satellite of the military installation, but this one is a little older and has a more established and less dreary look. It is Huachuca City, and as I recall, it was there at least in embryo when I arrived at Ft. Huachuca. I was told that it was a black community, providing housing for the families of black trainees during World War II. It was still largely a black community in 1956 when I arrived. It was then a small cluster of houses and trailers on the east side of the highway near the north gate to the fort. It has grown considerably and now sports a short strip of uncontrolled commercial growth on both sides of the highway. It seems to have entered the mainstream, for better or for worse.

There are still several miles of open country between here and Huachuca City. The rangeland is dotted with mesquite and large stands of yucca. Even where the development has destroyed most other native plants, the yucca remains in many places, probably left undisturbed because it is so dramatically beautiful when in bloom. I can see hundreds of plants from here, on both sides of the highway, although it is too late in the season for them to be in bloom. When they bloom, it gives this stretch of road a kind of glory, in spite of everything.

It's difficult to sort out the yuccas because there are many species and the same variety often goes by several different names. I recently found, in two different but quite authoritative plant books, the identical photograph of a yucca. In one book it was identified as a blue yucca and in the other as a banana yucca. It isn't blue, and I can't figure out what it has in common with a banana, but both books are correct in their fashion. It is also correct to refer to that particular yucca, as many people in this area do, as the Candle of the Lord. It grows in this region, but it is not the big, dramatic kind I can see down Highway 90.

Those are the yucca *elata*, also called the Arizona yucca or the soap-tree yucca, or God knows what else. But I prefer yucca *elata* because when I see them in bloom, they make me feel elated. The *elata* is tall, sometimes about fifteen feet, but often shorter than that. It starts as a large, symmetrical ball of pale green spikes close to the ground, which grows upward each year as a stalk develops beneath it. The stalk is covered with a shag of dead leaves from previous years' growth. Yuccas are members of the lily family, and when the yucca *elata* blooms in April, May, or sometimes as late as June, depending upon the weather and the elevation, its blossoms are creamy white and have a texture and color similar to that of the traditional Easter lily. A slender, woody stem, or sometimes two or three, grows rapidly from the center of each ball of spikes and produces a huge clump of blossoms, which is shaped something like a pyramid and two or three feet tall. The individual blossoms are bell-shaped and up to two inches long. There must be hundreds of them on each stalk. The *elata* often grows in stands covering several acres. A stand in bloom creates an unforgettable field of showy white. They are dazzling, especially in the moonlight.

I will always associate yucca blossoms with the stretch of Highway 90 I am looking at now and with a house we lived in for about a year in Sierra Vista. It was a modest house, but I had been living in the barracks for many months, and it seemed like a palace to me. My wife was not so enthusiastic about the house, but it had a bathtub and a television set, the two items without which she cannot survive. At any rate, we were lucky to get it. Housing in Sierra Vista was at a premium, and there was no married housing on base for draftees. Draftees, I guess, were not supposed to be married, or even worse, to get married after they were drafted, as I did. But when an officer whom I had met was being sent overseas, he let us rent his house while he was gone. We were living there when our son was born and for about five months afterward.

I have a strongly developed nesting sense. I can't just live in a house; I have to make it a home, give it some kind of personality. My wife is more concerned with the utilitarian, like hot water and electricity, but I want a house to be beautiful. I decided that what we needed was flowers, lots of flowers. I had noticed a stand of yucca in bloom out along Highway 90, and they were very beautiful, so a friend and I drove out there and cut several of the woody stems with their luscious creamy white clusters of blossoms. I put them in a tall vase on the floor in the living room and was enormously pleased with the effect. They were about four feet tall and very dramatic. The odor was a little sweet, but not unpleasant.

Next morning when we got up, the living room was full of bugs. Bugs of all descriptions—shiny little black bugs, big gray spiders, beetles of several varieties, and moths. And the odor of the flowers was so strongly sweet that it was nauseating. I did not know that yucca blossoms open at night, nor that hundreds of small creatures spend their days safely ensconced in the blossoms and emerge at night when the blossoms open. But I found out. It was our first, but not our last, experience with yucca at close quarters. Some people, like me, require more than one lesson to learn anything.

My next enlightening experience with a yucca came the following December. By then I had finished my stint with Uncle Sam and had taken a job teaching English in the seventh and eighth grades at Lowell School in Bisbee. As Christmas approached, that first year in Bisbee, we were living in a tiny apartment. Most of our living room was taken up by a fifty-year-old grand piano that had been our first major purchase as a married couple. Not a baby grand, a grand grand. Our son was about nine months old. Naturally I wanted to get a Christmas tree, but the standard variety, a little pine, didn't seem right. I wanted something indigenous, something Southwestern. My wife's face took on the pensive, worried look it always gets when I become particularly creative in domestic ways. Come to think of it, she gets that look when I am being creative in any way at all. For her, my creativity can mean only one thing—trouble. Often big trouble.

She had already suffered through my painting phase and was living with the results. When we moved into the apartment a few months earlier, we couldn't afford paintings for the walls, so I had decided to paint my own. I had no training, but like most dabblers, I believed that I could make up for in originality what I lacked in skill. The results were quite astonishing. I painted on poster board or plywood, using mostly house paint, thereby saving what I would otherwise have had to spend on canvases and oils. In order to give the paintings texture—I was into texture—I sometimes mixed the paint with sand or soap powder. I found that different kinds of laundry detergent created different effects. But when I used laundry detergent, I had to leave the painting outside for several days because the detergent produced bubbles which would later burst and splatter house paint in all directions. But the burst bubbles left behind a wonderful, I might even say unique, texture on the surface of the painting. My paintings were all abstract, of course, because I could not draw or produce a likeness of anything. But they were bright. Early on I had discovered that I could achieve wonders with the judicious use of silver and gold metallic spray paint.

Creativity is a very strange thing. The enjoyment one gets from it seems to have no relationship to the quality of the finished product. I keep telling my students that, but it's a hard lesson to learn. They feel that because they enjoyed writing a poem so much, it must be an extremely good poem. That was the way I felt about my paintings. I don't remember ever enjoying myself more than I did when I was painting. I painted all that fall and into the winter, rushing home from school each afternoon in order to paint in the backyard as long as there was light. I fashioned a makeshift easel and accumulated a large collection of cans of house paint. I went through a black period, a green period, and finally a gold period. With a large piece of poster board, a can of gold spray paint and some soap powder, I was happy as a clam. And when I was sure each painting was dry and that no more bubbles would burst from it unexpectedly, I would take it inside and hang it on one of the walls of the apartment.

My wife seemed to like the paintings. With one exception, my wife has always been singularly uncritical of my creative products. That exception occurred when I took up cooking with the same gusto I had taken up painting. I suppose I could say that she is singularly uncritical of my creative products as long as she doesn't have to eat them. Anyway, she praised my paintings and didn't seem to mind having them on the walls of the apartment. I imagine that in the back of her mind she thought I could be doing something worse, like huge metal sculptures or creative surgery.

Friends and neighbors who came into the apartment were quite astonished at my paintings. I remember one elderly neighbor who was so astonished he couldn't carry on a conversation. He could only stare in open-mouthed amazement at the largest of the paintings, which hung in the living room. But in matters of art, Bisbee was a very conservative town in those days, and not at all the arty place it has become since the mines shut down and hundreds of artists arrived. I guess I was, in a sense, one of the unknown pioneers of the art movement which now flourishes there, and I have recently seen some paintings in one of the Bisbee galleries that reminded me a little of the work I did in the late 1950s. But I never tried to sell any of my paintings. Now, when I see some of the things offered in the Bisbee galleries, and at high prices, I think perhaps I should have. Evidently there is somebody, somewhere, who will buy almost anything.

When the time came for us to leave Bisbee, I decided to leave the paintings behind. They had been painted for the particular rooms in our apartment and probably wouldn't suit another place. I figured that when we got settled in Tucson, I could always paint more. None of our friends had expressed a strong desire to have the paintings, and they weren't exactly the kind of thing one gave to the Salvation Army, so I decided to throw them away. After I had loaded a little rented two-wheel trailer with all our worldly possessions except the piano, which had already been put in storage, I took the paintings down and put them with the trash in the alley. As we were pulling out, my wife and I turned back for one last look and saw, in the alley, one of the neighbors whom we had never met. She had taken all the paintings out of the trash and was lugging them home. So perhaps they are still in existence somewhere, astonishing the world.

But as our first Christmas in Bisbee approached, my creative energies naturally turned to the selection and decoration of a Christmas tree, our first family Christmas tree. I chose a yucca *elata*. There is a part of this plant that makes a handsome, small Christmas tree. The fruit of the yucca consists of a three-celled cylindrical capsule full of tiny black seeds. In the fall, these capsules dry and split open, scattering the seeds. But the open pods remain in place, like stiff flowers. Many people in the Southwest cut the dry stem where it emerges from the evergreen ball of spines, stick it upright in a pot of sand, decorate it to their tastes, and with a minimum of expense and effort they have a Southwestern Christmas tree. But I was not content with anything so simple. I wanted to be more creative. So I chose the other part, the wrong part. I chose the large green rosette of spikes.

I drove out to the bajada east of the Mule Mountains and found a likely specimen—about four feet high and almost as broad, bright green and perfectly symmetrical, like a huge green porcupine with erect quills. It was young and had not yet developed a stalk, so it grew directly on the ground. My plan was to dig it up in such a way that I could plant it in the yard later. But I knew almost nothing about yuccas.

First of all, the damned thing, which later came to be known as "the monster," fought back. The end of each stiff leaf was needle-sharp. I was soon bloody from repeated jabs and stabs. And I didn't understand how yuccas survive in an arid climate. I had assumed that their root system was shallow and broad, like the root system of cacti, making it possible for them to take advantage of surface water quickly, and also making them relatively easy to transplant. But I was wrong. Yuccas have long taproots which go down very deep and permit them access to moisture far below the surface. By the time I realized this, I had done so much damage to the plant and the plant had done so much damage to me that I decided just to hack it out and forget about the transplanting part of the plan. I hated to kill a desert plant, but I wanted a Christmas tree, and if ever a plant deserved to die, that vicious monster did.

I don't remember how I got it into the trunk of the car and out again when I got home, but I did. When one's creative juices are flowing, anything is possible. I put it in a washtub, which was the only thing I could find large enough to hold it, and draped the washtub creatively with a sheet. By moving all the furniture in the living room except the piano, I was able to get the yucca into one corner. The spiny monster took up about all the available space in the small room and then some, but I figured it was only for a short time. Then I decorated it with large gold balls and added a few touches of gold spray paint—it was during my gold period. After I had lit it with a spotlight rigged from the ceiling, the effect was stunning. Dangerous, but stunning. Then I cleaned up the blood spots on the floor and rearranged the creatively draped sheet to hide the blood spots on it. During all this creative activity my wife stood around with our son clutched in her arms in an attitude that I thought was somewhat more protective than was necessary. She didn't complain, but she had that worried look.

After that Christmas, we never had to tell our son not to touch the Christmas tree. He lurched into it once, while he was toddling around the house, and never went near it again. Nor did he go near any other Christmas tree for several years. And the neighbors, who could see it through the window, all green and gold and lit by a spotlight, began to drop in to find out what it was. They were almost as astonished by it as they were by my paintings. They said it was beautiful, but I noticed they always backed out the door when they left, usually shaking their heads as if they had water in their ears.

And the monster left us its own Christmas present, actually two presents. Soon after I had got it installed in the washtub in the corner, two lizards crawled out of it. They were western whiptails, quite harmless and very handsome, with a mosaic pattern of dark spots on buff, and long gray tails. They took up residence in the apartment for the rest of the winter, usually staying up on the ceiling beams. I told my wife that they ate flies and were therefore excellent houseguests, and she seemed to accept them.

One day early in the spring, however, I noticed a long lizard tail hanging out of our son's mouth. I pulled it out, but it was only a tail. He said, simply, "Izzard gone." He had eaten one of them, and we never found the other one, so we assumed he ate it too. We watched him closely, but he never showed any ill effects from his diet of raw lizards. We consulted Dr. Spock, but even his excellent book had no suggestions that covered that specific circumstance. Somehow we all survived my creative endeavors. Our son is now thirty and has two children of his own. I'll bet neither of them will ever have the chance to eat a raw lizard.

I didn't learn a thing from all this except not to choose a yucca as a Christmas tree. In subsequent years I chose other indigenous plants. As Christmas trees they were all disasters, but some of them were very beautiful. I tried never to use a living plant unless it was growing in a pot, but dead plants in the desert often have a stark beauty that is intriguing. I've used paloverdes, chollas, and saguaro skeletons. One of the paloverdes fell over and scratched the finish on the piano pretty severely, and I still have scars from some of the chollas, but the saguaros were unqualified successes in aesthetic terms, although we had a tendency to poke holes in the ceiling getting them in place.

Our son, during his years as a teenager, was always enthusiastic about our desert Christmas trees and helped me put them up, but I notice, now that he has a family of his own, he and his wife invariably have the most traditional kind of Christmas tree, a pine with little lights and a star on top. I wonder why that is? I must have failed him in some way. We always fail our children in some ways, but if we are lucky they forgive us; and our grandchildren, who don't realize that we are largely responsible for their parents' problems, love us without reservation. It's not a bad system if you survive enough Christmases and enough Christmas trees.

None of our subsequent Christmas trees was ever as spectacular as that first yucca, the monster; and if I had known more about desert plants, I would never have tried to use such a dangerous thing for a

Christmas tree. If I had known about the yucca's root system, I would not have planned to transplant it. And if I had known about the yucca's reproductive process, I would have stood before it in awe, because the yucca's reproductive process is even more astonishing than my paintings. I don't know if its process is unique, but it is at least very close to being unique. It involves a moth, a little silver-gray but very smart moth called the pronuba.

While the blossoms of the yucca attract many insects, all that glorious display is designed for only one creature, the little pronuba. What is possibly unique is the fact that the pronuba does not pollinate the yucca by accident or in the process of gathering food. It pollinates the yucca deliberately and receives no immediate benefit to itself. It is dangerous to attribute conscious purpose to a moth, but the pronuba seems to know what it is doing and why it is doing it. It seems to know that if it doesn't pollinate that particular plant, the yucca will produce no fruit, and if the yucca does not produce fruit, the pronuba's offspring will have nothing to eat, since the larva of the pronuba eats only the fruit of the yucca.

When the yucca blossoms open at night, the female pronuba gathers a ball of pollen from the anthers of one flower, a ball usually bigger than her head. Carrying her ball of pollen, she then goes to a different flower, inserts her egg tube into its pistil, and deposits several eggs. Then comes the astonishing part. She climbs to the top of the pistil, to the stigma, and deposits the ball of sticky pollen she has already gathered from a different flower. Then she rubs the pollen well in by moving her head back and forth across it. The pronuba is the only insect which can pollinate the yucca because it seems to be the only insect that knows how. Without the pronuba's help, the yucca would bloom but bear no fruit, and consequently no seeds. No more pronubas means no more yuccas. When I cut the yucca blossoms for a bouquet, I interrupted one of the most amazing processes known to the worlds of botany and entomology, a process in which an insect deliberately gathers pollen from one flower and deliberately pollinates another. And it all takes place right down there along Highway 90 between used-car lots and hamburger stands every spring.

If I went down there and examined the yucca now, I would find that it is heavy with fruit at this time of year. And if I tore open the fruit,

I would find in each pod one or more larvae of the pronuba moth. Later, the larvae will bore their way out, leaving one small hole in each pod. The yucca will have sacrificed a few seeds, out of the hundreds it produces, to the larvae of the moth in return for the moth's services, without which it would bear no seeds at all.

But I don't go down there. I get back in the van and head east toward the San Pedro River. From here, one wouldn't know there is a river anywhere in the area, but I am now in the San Pedro River Valley. Long before I can see the river, I am getting a little excited, although it's not as if I haven't seen it before. Running water is something for a Southwesterner to get excited about. It's scarce, it's cool, it's wet, and it creates an oasis of shade, a green retreat from the sun and desiccation of the surrounding country. And yet we Southwesterners, with a lot of help from the United States government, have been notoriously cruel to our rivers, probably more destructive of rivers than have the people in any other part of the country. We who need them most. It's one more irony in the bundle of contradictions which form the character of the Southwesterner, whether native-born or transplanted, like me.

Not one drop of the mighty Colorado, of which we are so fiercely proud, ever makes it to the sea; and what was possibly the most stunningly beautiful riparian area in the state, Glen Canyon, now lies drowned at the bottom of Lake Powell, which leaves the dirty rings of an immense bathtub on the surrounding landscape. In a poem I once referred to the Colorado as the "saddest of all the poor damned rivers of the West." That was several years ago. It's even sadder now. When we cross the Gila on the freeway between Tucson and Phoenix, we wouldn't know we were crossing a river if it weren't for the highway sign. Not only is the water gone, but the lush growth which once fringed the river is also gone, and with it the wildlife. Things might change for the Gila, and rather suddenly, although it would cost many lives. Coolidge Dam, which impounds its water, has just been declared the most dangerous dam in the United States, so dangerous that it is under around-the-clock surveillance in order to give the people downstream as much warning as possible if it should suddenly wash out.

The San Pedro is small, but it is still something to get excited about. It's the longest stretch of undammed river in Arizona, a state which has destroyed 95 percent of its riparian environments, 95 percent of the cool, green oases running through a hot and arid land. The San Pedro provides the largest of the riparian areas left in the state. So I get excited just approaching the river. I have waded in it, sat in it, played in it, and even tried to swim in it, although it isn't exactly a swimming kind of river. Most of the year there isn't enough water. Sometimes, during dry spells, it disappears entirely in places.

Even so, it is beautiful. I like to pretend that it looks much as it did when Coronado rode along its banks in 1540, or when the first Mexican ranchers settled along it in the early 1830s only to be driven out by the Apaches, or when the earliest Anglo settlers arrived after the Gadsden Purchase. I like to pretend that it still looks the same, but it doesn't. The river I will see today is a different river. It has a different personality and flows through a different kind of riparian area. The San Pedro has very nearly died and become another ghost river, like the Santa Cruz, but recently it has been rescued. Nobody knows yet if the rescue came in time to save it. If the first Anglos who settled in the area could see it today, they would not recognize it as the same river.

Except after a considerable rain, the river today is so small that most easterners would probably call it a creek, or "crick," depending on where they came from, and even that would be generous. But our scale is different. In Southern Arizona we have a tendency to call anything that ever had a steady flow of water a river. Most of the year the San Pedro today is little more than ankle-deep, and at times I have been able to jump across it without getting my feet wet. It runs fast and usually confines itself to a single narrow channel, sometimes splitting into two or three little rivulets, depending on the terrain. It meanders through a broad and relatively flat riverbed, which is anywhere from one hundred yards to more than a mile wide, and often has steep vertical banks caused by erosion, suggesting an earlier river.

When the first Anglo settlers arrived, the San Pedro in this area was a broad, slow, sluggish river, much given to sloughs, swamps, and marshes. In general, it filled much of the area which now constitutes the fairly flat land between its steeply eroded banks. It often presented a serious problem for those attempting to cross it, although by the time they got this far the early settlers had become experts at how to get themselves, their wagons, and their livestock across a river. In addition to the enormous cottonwoods and the thick mesquite bosques which today line its banks, its riparian area included many marshlike plants—willows, reeds, and grasses. During the rainy season, it was generally impassable.

There are several reasons for the dramatic changes in the river, and the transformation took place in an amazingly short period of time as compared to those ongoing changes that naturally take place in a riparian landscape. Beaver, who lived along the river in great numbers, played an appreciable part in making it the kind of river it was. Beavers built dams across the inlets and creeks which flowed into the river, and sometimes across the river itself. These slowed the river's flow, helped to prevent it from eroding its banks, and encouraged it to spread out into marshy areas.

The mass destruction of the beavers on the San Pedro came rather late as compared to the destruction of the beavers on many other Western rivers. The period of the mountain men, the period of the most extensive trapping of beavers on many Western rivers, was roughly 1824 to 1846, and the San Pedro was not spared, but it was probably not as extensively trapped as were many other rivers. For one thing, it was illegal for mountain men to operate in Mexico, and when they were caught doing so, the penalties were severe. There was also the problem of the Apaches, no small problem even for the rugged mountain men, some of whom trapped in the area anyway and took their lumps. They were generally furtive about it and naturally kept few records, so it is hard to tell just how many of them did trap on the San Pedro. James Ohio Pattie was probably the first Anglo to trap on the San Pedro, in 1824, but he stayed only a short time. Others followed, possibly including the equally famous Pauline Weaver. But the activities of the mountain men on the San Pedro did not last long enough to exterminate the beaver population on the river.

After 1877, miners began to arrive in the Tombstone area in droves. Some of their favorite pastimes, when not looking for rich veins of silver or digging ore out of the ground, were shooting or trapping beavers and blowing up beaver dams. It was the end for the beavers on the San Pedro, but only the beginning of rapid changes that would affect the river, whose flow had been slowed down and partly controlled by the beaver dams.

Then came the Anglo ranchers. Not including the sheep, of which there were a great many, the number of cattle in the Arizona Territory rose from 35,000 in 1880 to more than 720,000 by 1891. The majority of these cattle were in the drainage basins of the Santa Cruz and San Pedro rivers. A severe three-year drought followed, during which cattle died by the thousands, but not before they had eaten every available morsel of grass on the rangeland. When the hard rains came again in 1893, there were not enough living grass roots to hold the soil. It came off in sheets and ran down the washes. Down Sonoita Creek west into the Santa Cruz, and down Babocomari Creek east into the San Pedro, then down the San Pedro into the Gila, down the Gila into the Colorado, and down the Colorado into the Gulf of California, where it helped create an extensive delta.

The banks of the San Pedro eroded rapidly and deeply, constricting its channel and causing it to run more rapidly, creating still more erosion. Settlers began to drain the marshes and swamps. Cottonwoods, walnuts, and other tall growth which could put down very deep roots began to replace the low, marshy growth that had had a tendency to impede the flow of the river and keep erosion at a minimum. The denuded rangelands increased quick runoff, making the river more and more intermittent and subject to flash flooding.

As ranchers and settlers drilled deep wells to tap the groundwater, and as population centers grew, the demand on groundwater began to affect the flow of nearby rivers. Today, the most serious threat to the San Pedro consists of groundwater demands made by wells in and around burgeoning Sierra Vista. And so the San Pedro is dying, but it is still very beautiful.

We in the Southwest don't seem to love our rivers very much or to get to know them well. Some people maintain that the only way to get to know a river in the Southwest is to float down it on a rubber raft. I've rafted through Marble Canyon and Grand Canyon on the Colorado, and through Gray and Desolation canyons on the Green, but I didn't really get to know either river. I learned about river time, how it doesn't exist, how only the water moves, carrying you with it through a still landscape, and how you come to accept movement as a substitute for time. I learned a little about canyons, about geology, about the excitement and treachery of rapids, and about lovely little beaches with a ribbon of bright stars above each of them at night. I had wonderful times and brought back many stories, but I didn't really get to know either river.

I suppose Mark Twain got to know the Mississippi when he was working as a river pilot, but rivers of the Southwest do not lend themselves to that kind of intimacy. Only the extreme lower section of the Colorado, of all the rivers in Arizona, ever proved to be even semi-feasible as a waterway for transportation, and only for about thirty years in the mid-1800s. That dangerous and limited enterprise in Southwestern water transportation was maintained off and on and with the loss of many steamboats because, as a San Francisco reporter who had made the trip said, "The land travel is far worse."

It has seldom been pointed out, probably because it's so obvious, that while many of the river valleys of Arizona and of the desert Southwest have been used extensively as highways, the rivers themselves, with the brief exception of the lower Colorado, have never been used as waterways for general transportation. They are not suitable for navigation as are the rivers of the East, the Northwest, and the Mississippi River drainage. They are either too shallow or too swift and brutal, too filled with rapids or too fickle about which channel they choose to follow. Many of them are intermittent—they flood or they dry up. Explorers and settlers as well as trappers and soldiers followed the valleys of the Gila, the Santa Cruz, and the San Pedro, but they were never able to float down the rivers for any great distance; and the Colorado forms a barrier to land transportation which, even today, adds hundreds of miles to what would otherwise be a relatively short trip. All of this has, of course, had important implications in regard to the exploration and settlement of the Southwest as compared to the exploration and settlement of other parts of the country. But it might also be one of the reasons that Arizonans, and Southwesterners in general, have never gotten to know and to love their rivers.

Another way to get to know and love a river is to live on its banks for a long time. But this option proved more expensive than most Southwesterners could afford, although many tried. Even small Southwestern rivers had the ability to turn suddenly into liquid bulldozers that swept whole communities away. Easterners had their troubles with flooding rivers, too, but not unless a dam collapsed did an Eastern river flood with the speed and lack of warning that a river in the Southwest often did.

Living near a river in Southern Arizona brought other problems as well. The first settlement of United States citizens on the San Pedro is a good example. It was St. David, about thirteen miles downstream from the point where I will soon be crossing the river. St. David was established by a group of Mormons who left their previous settlement on the Salt River in 1877. They built on the river, which fanned out into marshes nearby. The first year was dreadful for that hardy group of Mormon farmers. Nearly all of them came down with malaria, and several died. At one point, there was no one well enough to give adequate care to the dying. They knew there was some connection between malaria and standing, stagnant water, but the mosquito had not yet been identified as the carrier of the disease. It was generally thought that malaria was caused by some sort of effluvium or vapor which rose from low, swampy places, especially at night. During one summer, many Mormon settlers in the area fled to the Huachuca Mountains to avoid the disease, but eventually the St. David community moved their town more than a mile back from the river, where it stands today.

Things went better in the new location, and there was less sickness. In 1885 the McRae Brothers dug for and found an artesian well, whose pure water was a blessing to everybody. In 1887 an earthquake damaged much of St. David and flattened the pride of the community, its adobe schoolhouse. But the earthquake also proved beneficial to the little community. It disturbed the earth sufficiently to allow many more artesian wells to seep or spring up, and they have been providing water ever since. In 1916 one of the Mormon leaders reported that there were two hundred artesian wells in the San Pedro Valley. Today, St. David is one of the greenest and most productive places in Southern Arizona, thanks to its good Mormon farmers, the San Pedro River, and an earthquake.

That earthquake of 1887 has been given credit for changes in the area which it probably doesn't deserve. There is a story, probably of the Mrs.-O'Leary's-cow variety, that before the earthquake of 1887 the Santa Cruz was a permanent and sizable river, not the dry bed it is today. It is said that the earthquake disturbed a mountain just across the border in Mexico near where the Santa Cruz has its source, and the result was a major change in the river. Whether or not it is true, the story is interesting and involves an act of God for which humans need take no responsibility. Handy things, those acts of God.

Next to the Apaches, malaria seemed to be the most severe tribulation of the early settlers in this area, since they usually built their homesteads near the rivers. Early Mormon settlements on the Little Colorado and the upper Gila had to be abandoned because of "chills and fever." Malaria also decimated the cavalry posts and hampered military efforts to control the Apaches. Fort Goodwin on the upper Gila had to be abandoned, and Camp Grant, at the juncture of the San Pedro and Aravaipa Creek, was moved into the Pinaleño Mountains farther east. Ironically, the mining towns, those sin cities of the late 1800s, did not suffer as much from the scourge of malaria, which devastated the God-fearing Mormon communities. The mining camps were located where the ore was, on high ground at some distance from the rivers. It was probably some consolation to members of the more righteous communities, however, to see that God did not entirely spare the sin cities, like Tombstone and Bisbee, from his wrath. The mining towns, which consisted mostly of hastily constructed wooden buildings huddled together, had a tendency to burn down . . . repeatedly.

In narrow riparian areas like the San Pedro's channel, the restrictions of elevation on plants seem to be somewhat relaxed. Many plants normally found on the desert floor seem to thrive here alongside others normally found at slightly higher elevations. Desert broom and sycamores, prickly pears and walnut trees, chollas and ash, desert willows and junipers. And there are runaway imports like the tamarisk, which is a native of Asia and southeastern Europe but was deliberately introduced at the turn of the century and has made itself very much at home. The lower growth is lush to the point of being rank in places, but the dominant growth along most stretches of the river is the cottonwood. On warm autumn afternoons when the cotton from the cottonwood and the tiny parachutes of desert broom seeds drift through the air and the sun slants through the foliage, everything turns gold and magical, and time seems to be a remote and unimportant abstraction. The river talks to its stones very low. The cottonwood leaves whisper a little, and even the calls of birds seem to be muted and quiet.

Perhaps there are good reasons why many Southwesterners have never fallen in love with any of their rivers. Perhaps the rivers have been difficult to love, erratic and unpredictable as they are, unsuitable for transportation and associated with disease. But I don't know how anyone could spend an October or November afternoon on the bank of the San Pedro without falling in love with the river.

The gracefully leaning mesquites, which grow very large along the San Pedro, are reason enough to love such places. They are natives of deep arroyos and river bottoms, but they have spread onto the rangeland and desert floor. The mesquite is the coyote of the Southwestern plant world. No matter what is done to eradicate it, it seems to survive and increase its range. And like the coyote, it is intensely clever. The Southwesterners who have been trying to exterminate the coyote for the past one hundred years are the same ones who have been trying to eradicate the mesquite during that period, and with about the same degree of success. Ranchers hate the mesquite because it has come up from the river and creek bottoms and invaded the rangeland, although ranchers are responsible for its having done so. They believe it is a threat to the rangeland just as the coyote is a threat to cattle. Since the deterioration of the rangeland and the spread of mesquite have taken place simultaneously, the notion that the mesquite is responsible for the deterioration of the rangeland has fixed itself firmly in the minds of many ranchers. But both have been caused by the same thing—the cow. It's difficult for ranchers to blame the cow for anything.

Several local people have told me, with absolute assurance, that mesquite is not indigenous to Southern Arizona, that it came from Texas and was brought into this area by longhorn cattle during the great cattle drives of the late 1860s and the 1870s. I can't pass judgment on the story about the earthquake and the Santa Cruz River, but this one is an out-and-out Mrs.-O'Leary's-cow story, except it involves more cows. When such myths take hold, they are harder to drive out than coyotes or mesquite. I'm sure I have swallowed my share of such stories, and have probably spread a few, especially family stories that are usually part myth anyway; but this one is preposterous.

The prehistoric Hohokam people who lived along the Santa Cruz and San Pedro rivers at least as early as 300 B.C. used mesquite poles to support the roofs of their pit houses. Mesquite is a very hard, dense wood which holds up well to the ravages of time and weather. Since it is so durable, it has often survived in prehistoric ruins and provided specialists, using tree-ring or carbon dating techniques, a means of dating the ruins. Either mesquite was growing in this area in prehistoric times, or the Hohokam went all the way to Texas to get their wood, which would have been difficult because they never discovered the wheel.

But mesquite has spread from the deep arroyos and river bottoms up onto the rangeland in historic times, and cows and horses have helped make that spread possible. Only recently have we begun to understand why and how. Cows and horses will eat mesquite pods, or beans as we call them, in large quantities when they are available. Recent studies have compared the germinating ability of mesquite seeds in pods that have passed through the digestive system of a cow or horse with the same ability of those seeds in pods that have merely fallen to the ground. Twice as many of the seeds that have passed through the digestive system of a cow will germinate, and three times as many will germinate if they have passed through the digestive system of a horse. Evidently the digestive juices of the cow or horse kill the insects— the leaf-footed bugs, beetles, and weevils—which normally destroy the mesquite seed's ability to germinate. And also, the cow or horse deposits the mesquite seeds packaged in fertilizer.

Largely because of cows and horses, the mesquite has been freed from its river bottom and arroyo prisons and has spread across the land, much to the chagrin of the ranchers. Coronado, who first brought cows and horses into this area, struck the first blow for the emancipation of the mesquite. Father Kino, the Jesuit who first taught the Pima and Sobáipuri natives to raise cattle in the late seventeenth century, was a great leader in the ensuing struggle for freedom. But the real heroes, those who opened the floodgates, so to speak, allowing millions of mesquite to leap out of their lowland prisons and spread over the wide open country, were the ranchers of the 1880s who brought in thousands and thousands of head of cattle, not only to spread the mesquite, but to eat up all the grass so the mesquite would have less competition for water and nutrients. How frustrating it must be for ranchers to realize, if they realize, that every cow they graze on the land is a soldier fighting for the mesquite they are trying to destroy.

And what would the early ranchers have done without mesquite? They built their corrals of mesquite, made their furniture from mesquite, cooked their food with mesquite, and heated their homes with mesquite. When they had to fence the rangeland, they used durable mesquite fence posts. In a region where trees of any kind are scarce, some of the ranchers probably wouldn't have survived without mesquite. Yet their efforts to destroy the mesquite have been nothing short of heroic, and they have had a lot of help.

It's fascinating, in a gruesome kind of way, how the history of the ranchers' attempts to exterminate the coyote has paralleled so closely the history of their attempts to stamp out the mesquite. In both cases the struggle began with fairly crude and localized techniques and, as the ranchers grew increasingly desperate and enlisted scientific experts, usually government experts, turned into ever more sophisticated and widespread methods of destruction. The war against mesquites began with cutting and burning, and progressed to chaining and pouring diesel oil around the stumps of cut mesquites. But the mesquites resprouted. Then the ranchers called in government experts and got serious. Poison. For many years ranchers and government experts have waged chemical warfare on the rangelands of Southern Arizona with all the horrible results and side effects that that term suggests— damage to other plants, wildlife, livestock, and even humans. They have used herbicides singly and in combinations. They have experimented with toxins whose effects are not entirely understood. They have used some of the same chemicals which were used as defoliants in Vietnam. And they have failed. The mesquite is too resilient.

During this long history of attempts by ranchers to destroy the mesquite, others have joined the fray for their own reasons. The many mines which came into being in this area in the late 1870s and 1880s, and their attendant boomtowns, used mesquite at an awesome rate. Stamp mills that processed silver, and there were several of them on the edges of the San Pedro, especially in the Tombstone area, required a cord of wood to process ten tons of ore. The mines also used mesquite to fuel their steam hoists and water pumps. The families in the mining camps and towns used mesquite for cooking and heating. Most of the groves or bosques of mesquite along the creeks and rivers in this area were probably leveled at that time.

There are also contemporary threats to the mesquite, and they grow worse daily. Mesquite wood is prized as fuel because it is long-burning and gives off intense heat, and also because it is aromatic and gives meat cooked over it a wonderful, smoky flavor. There must be hundreds of restaurants in Arizona alone that specialize in mesquite-broiled steaks. And just across the border in northern Sonora, an old industry has been revived on a large, commercial scale. Members of the *ejidos*, or collective farms, are processing mesquite into charcoal for export. Charcoal makers, unlike woodcutters, do not leave the smaller trees. They take everything. Thousands of acres of mesquite bosques in Sonora have been destroyed in very recent years.

In spite of the destruction, somehow, nature has provided the mesquite with the means to survive, at least for a while longer, just as she has provided the coyote with the means to survive. The coyote's strong parenting instinct is undoubtedly one of the reasons, and the coyote has spread its range, lessening the chances of total extermination. Mesquites make use of the digestive systems of cows and horses to insure a higher percentage of survival for their offspring, not the most glamorous method, but effective. And the mesquite has also spread to a much larger range, which insures that, although they are killed out in one area, they will survive in another.

But even mesquite, as clever and resilient as it is, has limits beyond which it cannot go, and in many places those limits have been reached. Mesquites have very long taproots, making it possible for them to tap underground aquifers at considerable depth and survive even prolonged droughts. There seems to be little consensus on just how long the mesquite's taproot is. Various authorities have given figures ranging up to 164 feet. But no matter how long the mesquite's taproot may be, there is a limit beyond which it cannot reach. There are places in Southern Arizona where one can see large groves of dead mesquite covering many acres and indicating that the water table in the area has dropped below a level the trees' roots can reach. As Southern Arizona farmers continue to pump groundwater for agriculture, and as cities like Tucson, which for many years depended on wells for its total water supply, continue to pump, the level of the aquifers continues to drop. This depletion of the underground aquifers, which is occurring at a terrifying rate, could put an end to the ranchers' problems with the mesquite in a matter of years. It could, in fact, put an end to a great many things, and mean that human life could no longer survive in the arid Southwest except on a most marginal basis.

Before the coming of the Anglos, that's the only way human life ever did survive in this desert—marginally. One of the staples which permitted its survival was the mesquite bean. The Pimas and other natives of the area ate them in many forms—raw, ground into a kind of mush, or cooked in little cakes. Whole tribes survived on mesquite beans when there was little else. In times of drought when the corn and squash failed, those long mesquite taproots insured that the trees would bear and the people would survive. When mesquite beans are young and tender, they are delicious raw—sweet and tasty. But I once made the mistake of eating too many of them when they were, evidently, too young and tender. The effect was violent—as if I had eaten too many green apples. An eighteenth-century missionary to the Pimas, Fray Pedro Font, complained that eating too much *pechita*, or ground mesquite pods, caused the natives to produce a bad odor. I don't know about that, but I know what happens if you eat too many of the pods when they are green.

Mesquites are thorny creatures. The thorns are not noticeable, but they are brutally sharp. Mesquite thickets can be impenetrable, except to cows. That is probably one of the reasons why ranchers hate mesquite so violently. Cows, with their tough hide, can wedge themselves into a mesquite thicket, and no amount of yelling or cussing will get them out. The cowhand or rancher must dismount and go in after them. Then the mesquite takes its sweet revenge for all the horrible things humans have done to it.

Right now I'm not looking for mesquite. I can see plenty of it scattered over the rangeland on both sides of the road. What I'm looking for, and with considerable anticipation, is cottonwoods, a meandering line of bright green which rises out of the river bottom and is tall enough to be seen from a distance. It will be the same ribbon of green that those who crossed this part of the continent in wagon trains looked for day after hot, dusty day, until one of the scouts would come galloping back to the wagons, hell-bent for leather, shouting, "River! River dead ahead." Then the pace would quicken. As soon as the animals smelled water, they were hard to hold back. Miles before anybody in the wagon train could see it, they all knew it was there. Gaunt women from the hills of Arkansas smiled for the first time in many days, in spite of the pain it brought to their cracked lips. Boys ran ahead, whooping, while their mothers screamed warnings about rattlesnakes and quicksand, warnings the boys paid no attention to as they threw themselves into the cooling, cleansing water.

And suddenly, there it is, below, and almost blinding in the late afternoon sun with a bank of dark clouds on the horizon behind it. I have seen tropical rain forests, but I don't think I have ever seen a green as green as a grove of summer cottonwoods along a river in a dry land. Beneath them, the river is neither as swollen nor as muddy as I had expected it to be this time of year. It is just muddy enough to look amber-gold in the slanting sunlight. But no matter how much rangeland soil it is carrying down to the Gila, I've got to get in it.

I park just before the bridge and get in the back of the van to put on my swimming trunks, not that I will be swimming, but I intend to wade and will probably fall down negotiating the slippery rocks in the riverbed. I put on my trunks and a pair of old tennis shoes, lock the van, and scramble down a steep bank which is already almost dry after the shower of less than an hour ago. Partway down the bank I must crawl through a rickety barbed wire fence. Crawling through a barbed wire fence must be like riding a bicycle—once you learn how, you never forget. Or maybe it's one of those abilities one can acquire only during a childhood spent on a farm or ranch in the West. I spent only part of my childhood on a farm, but even during that period I must have crawled through several thousand barbed wire fences, and still, in my present state of advanced senility, I can do it with ease.

I never thought about it at the time, but for a boy growing up on a farm in the West, barbed wire fences represent something like rites of passage. Maybe this is true for girls, too, but I don't know about that. A boy learns about himself and his process of maturing by the way he gets through barbed wire fences.

When he's very little, he simply crawls under the bottom strand on his belly. When he is a little older, he tries to slip between the bottom strand and the next strand. This means he is no longer a baby. Later, when he's nearly grown, he goes between the second strand from the bottom and the next strand above it, being very careful to hold the strand between his legs down as far as possible, because he has become aware that the parts of his anatomy which are in close proximity to the vicious barbs on the second strand are somehow more vulnerable and valuable than anything which might come in contact with the third strand above his back. A coward lies down and crawls under the bottom strand like a snake or a baby, but it takes some degree of courage to put one leg between two strands of barbed wire, bend over parallel to the strands, ease your body through, and then bring the other leg through behind you. In school, when the biology teacher explains the difference between dorsal and ventral surfaces, a farm boy catches on right away. It's no great problem if a barb happens to come in contact with his dorsal surface while he is getting through a fence, but he must take great care to protect the precious ventral portions of himself.

The whole process is made infinitely more hazardous if the barbed wire fence happens also to be an electric fence, as many of them were where I was growing up. Once, when I took hold of a hot wire on a fence while I was standing in water, I could not let go. My older brother, who had got me into the mess in the first place, had to run a quarter of a mile back to the barn to shut off the juice. We learned to be very careful. Faced with an electric fence, many of us chose discretion and slithered under it on our bellies with our hips as close to the earth as we could get them.

The fence I have just eased through is so flimsy as to be only a slight deterrent to anything or anybody. My major concern in getting through it was that I wouldn't accidentally break the whole thing down. I hope it isn't the barrier which is supposed to be keeping the cows out of the river bottom. No self-respecting cow would pay the slightest attention to it.

The river has a single, fairly broad channel here, about twenty-five feet across and almost knee-deep. The cool water on my hot feet is exhilarating. As I wade in, I can see that there is more water than there was when I was here in the spring. Then, it was only slightly more than ankle-deep. I wade upstream under the bridge and around a bend. I haven't managed to fall down yet, so I pick a spot with a soft, sandy bottom, lower my tail to the surface, and fall backward with a great, satisfying splash. The shock of cold water takes my breath, but in seconds I'm comfortable, sitting in the San Pedro River and listening to the birds.

I never seem to have my field glasses with me when I need them, which pretty well proves that I'm no bird watcher. Bird watchers have a tendency to be too single-minded for me. Sometimes I think that in their anxiety to add one more bird to their life list, they miss everything else. They stalk birds with a quiet frenzy which bothers me a little. And if I were a truly dedicated bird watcher, I would probably go crazy along the upper San Pedro River where 315 species of birds have been identified. As it is, I can just enjoy myself, sitting in the middle of the river and not worrying about keeping my field glasses dry.

I think I can hear about 300 of those species from where I am. Many of them are old friends I know from the Tucson Mountains—the cardinal and its pale Mexican cousin, the pyrrhouloxia, the curved-bill thrasher with its wicked red eye, the lovely Gambel's quail. I can hear at least two kinds of doves with their soft, drowsy murmurs which are exactly the right accompaniment for late afternoon relaxation. One is the white-winged dove and the other I'm not sure about, probably an Inca dove.

Somewhere behind me a cactus wren is quarreling with the world. There are canyon wrens here, too, but I think they are more common over in the canyons of the Huachuca Mountains on the west side of the valley. I'm always startled by the differences in personality between those two closely related wrens. Although the canyon wren is a little smaller, they are similar in shape, but that's where the similarity ends. The canyon wren is shy and coquettish with one of the sweetest, most seductive voices found in the Southwest. I usually see canyon wrens along streams in the mountains, and their voices remind me of the gurgle of water over stones, as if they had learned to imitate that sound but with a broader range. It's delicious, like the echo of a song rather than a song itself, or like the sound of a cello coming from a distant cave. On the other hand, the cactus wren is incorrigible, brash, tendentious, assertive, and has one of the ugliest voices in the bird kingdom. It's more of a harsh squawk than a song, and once it gets started, there is no stopping it. It reminds me of the yapping of a small, ferocious dog.

Suddenly something very black, shiny, and streamlined, like an obsidian arrowhead, flits above me across the river, giving off flashes of white each time it spreads its wings. I'm lucky today. It's a male phainopepla, the silky flycatcher. Phainopeplas are actually tropical birds who usually subsist on mistletoe berries but catch bugs on the wing when berries are not available. I can see two huge clumps of mistletoe in a nearby paloverde, so there are probably plenty of phainopeplas in the area. They are one of the most elegant birds I have ever seen— slim, with long, graceful tails and a crest. They are small, only about seven inches long, but they have an upright posture which gives them great dignity when perched. They seem to hold their heads higher than most other birds, and they dress with such good taste and so formally. The female wears a soft gray, but the male wears solid black with a sheen like silk. When he flies, he shows white wing patches, his only decoration.

Phainopeplas are much too well bred to be intrusive, and usually stay out of sight, especially the females, but I have had the good fortune to see one of the males on a fairly regular basis in the Tucson Mountains. He and his mate have a nest in a thicket near where I walk the dogs, and if we walk early in the morning, he almost always puts in an appearance, and sometimes he sings. Because Phainopeplas sing so seldom, many bird books ignore their song and record only their call, which is nondescript. I don't know about the female, but the male can certainly sing if he wants to. It's a short song, but magnificent, an arpeggio of descending notes like drops of crystal. It's startling to hear such a song in the desert, where birds generally have more strident voices. It's worth getting up early for. But I have learned to listen closely the first time, because he would never do anything so vulgar as give an encore. I listen now, hoping this one will sing, but he doesn't. Wrong time of day, I suppose. At least the cactus wren has stopped its vitriolic yapping.

There are scores of water birds and shore birds along the San Pedro, exotic to me because I live in the desert whose river is dry most of the time. Last spring I saw a great blue heron just a few miles upriver, and once a snowy egret. I wouldn't know a semipalmated sandpiper from a palmated one, but the sandpipers are here, along with kingfishers, terns, gulls, ducks, geese, and snipe.

I always wonder about the people who named birds. Did they have a perverse and subtle sense of humor, or did they not have any sense of humor at all? I suspect that they didn't have any sense of humor at all, and those people are often the funniest. In their attempts to be precise, they have created the preposterous, and have stretched the language well beyond limits of the creative. The names are often misleading. Like the flammulated owl. Poor thing, how did it get that way? It's only an owl with reddish markings on the face, but it sounds as if it were on fire. How bitter is the least bittern? Surely the white-faced ibis is an Egyptian statue and the Virginia rail is some kind of fence. The northern shoveler must be a snowplow and the whimbrel is, I think, an eighteenth-century vehicle pulled by a horse. Isn't the water pipet the little gadget inside the faucet on the sink? I know the Nashville warbler is Hank Williams, but I'm not sure who the yellow-rumped warbler is. And they all live along the San Pedro River, pretending they are birds.

For some people, this kind of linguistic madness is infectious. I can't resist it. It leads me to the old Engleman dingleberry game, but the game is more fun with the names of birds, since the names of birds are intrinsically more insane and suggestive than the names of plants. When I am walking through the desert with a curious visitor from some other part of the country, especially a visitor who knows even less about birds than I do, I am overcome by the temptation to play the Engleman dingleberry game and see how long I can get away with it. It requires a poker face and a tone of complete assurance. And it's an incremental game. Each name must be slightly more preposterous than the last.

Usually the first bird we see, or more often hear, is a cactus wren. When the visitor asks what it is, I say it's a hepatic virago. If I can get away with that, the sky's the limit. The next bird I am asked about, I identify as a semi-precious plover. Then I watch the visitor's face carefully to see how I'm doing. I can see some indecision, a dialogue going on inside the visitor's head.

"Is he pulling my leg? What if he isn't? I mustn't expose my ignorance. But if he's pulling my leg . . . no, I guess he isn't. He lives here, and I guess he would know. But it sounds a little strange. Lots of birds have strange names, though."

Then the clever visitor usually asks a probing question, but a question which would be appropriate whether I am kidding or not, a question which covers both possibilities. Like, "Just how precious is a semi-precious plover?"

I reply in an offhand way, but with complete seriousness, "Oh, they're fairly common here, but this is almost the northern limit of their range. They're very rare north of Phoenix."

The visitor looks satisfied. Score 2 for the offensive team, which is me. Then I usually throw in a real name or two as sucker's bait, maybe a white-winged dove or a white-rumped shrike. Sooner or later we see a curve-billed thrasher, very common in the Sonoran Desert. When asked, I identify it as a red-eyed vertigo. And anybody can see that it has orange-red, wild looking eyes. So far so good. Move up to the next level. If we see a hawk, buzzard, or raven—anything soaring, large, or formidable looking—I say it is a greater American regret. The game is usually over right there. But if it isn't, I'm prepared to go on to the rosy-breasted pushover and the extra-marital lark. I've never gotten anyone to accept either of these, but who knows? Maybe someday. And I'm getting better at it with practice, learning the exact tone of casual authority with which to present my contributions to the art of naming birds. I don't think serious bird watchers would approve of it, but the game has given me hours of pleasure. Not so much pleasure, though, as sitting in the San Pedro River on a hot afternoon, listening to the birds and letting fatigue soak out of my body.

6

Go, said the bird, for the leaves were full

   of children,

Hidden excitedly, containing laughter.

Go, go, go, said the bird: human kind

Cannot bear very much reality.

Time past and time future

What might have been and what has been

Point to one end, which is always present.

           —T. S. Eliot

I t is a picnic beside the river. I am with two women and two children. One of the women is my wife and the little boy is my son. The other child is a little girl about four years old. Suddenly a huge red bull plunges out of the underbrush, enraged. He charges at us. We scatter, but the little girl falls. The bull is running straight at her, his long horns dipping down toward the screaming child on the ground. I pick her up and run. The bull is inches behind us. I can hear him snorting and panting as he runs. There is a barbed wire fence in front of us, but I cannot make it. The bull is too close. I throw the child as far as I can. The picture freezes. The child is in the air, sailing over the fence. Her mouth is a round O screaming. Her hair is flying out behind her. I am falling . . . .

I wake up lying in the grass on the bank of the San Pedro. I must have been asleep for only a few minutes, and it was the dream again, the dream I haven't had for a long time, but I know why I had it this time. The river brought it back to me. It happened on this river, upstream just a few miles and more than thirty years ago. Nothing ever happens next in the dream. And it was so long ago I can't remember what really happened next, but we all survived. I suppose the little girl, who was the daughter of a friend, fell into the underbrush on the other side of the fence and was scratched up but not badly hurt. I suppose I rolled out of the path of the bull and somehow got through the fence. But I can't remember any of that part, although I could find the spot on the river where it occurred. I suppose the bull went away eventually and we picked up the remnants of our picnic and went home to Bisbee, where I was a young schoolteacher, a young father, a young scout master . . . where I was young.

Why have I come here this time? I have been here before, many times before. Or was that another life, another dream of afternoon light on a golden river? Were there afternoons in that life? Was there a river? Nothing important ever seemed to happen then, and yet everything that happened was important. Have I been on this river so many times that they all become one time, and is it the past or the present? Some vague tone, some hidden music in the leaves, some slight ruffling of the surface of the water disturbs me. Why am I going back to Bisbee? There is something I need to find out, but I don't know what it is. Some part of the past for which there is no dream, no photograph, no memory. But where is it? Or is it gone beyond recapturing, used up, torn down, destroyed. There must be some way in, some way out, but I can't find it.

Maybe I don't have to go back to Bisbee at all. No real reason I can think of. Why not just stay here, sleep in the van tonight, and play in the river all day tomorrow? No food! But I could drive into Tombstone and get some. I think about it and like the idea.

But what about Bisbee? When I got up this morning, I felt an impulse so strong as to be undeniable. I had to go back to Bisbee. There was no real reason—impulses don't come equipped with reasons. I just knew that I had to go back to Bisbee, if only to spend one night. Now that I'm sitting here beside the river in dappled light and enjoying the cool breeze from the water, the impulse is fading.

You only go around once. Stay here! Be lazy and enjoy it! Whatever it is you need to find in Bisbee, it will wait. You probably won't find it anyway. Bisbee makes you feel young because you were young when you lived there. It's vanity. Some kind of syndrome or something that attacks men in middle age. Next thing you know you will be chasing young women down the halls of the university. Forget it! Foolishness. It's peaceful here. Stay here by the river.

Then I remember the phone calls I made this morning. When I decided to go to Bisbee, I called the Copper Queen Hotel and made a reservation. No big deal. I can call from Tombstone and cancel it. But the other phone call? I can't cancel that. I called Ida Power and asked her to have dinner with me. It was, somehow, part of the impulse. I can't cancel out on Ida, and I can't stand her up. She's too beautiful, too important to me, too important to everybody. God would strike me dead.

But I can stay here a little while longer. I don't wear a watch, but judging by the slant of the sun and the shadows, I can stay here a little longer and enjoy the cool, golden river under its canopy of cottonwoods. And as beautiful as it is, this isn't my favorite spot on the river. That's upstream a few miles, a place of ghosts and pure magic, where the bottom of the river is covered with long, undulating water plants and where I saw the great blue heron last May.

I came here in May to see a miracle—a real, genuine, bona fide miracle—and I did. But it's funny about modern miracles. First, they seem to be much harder to come by than miracles were at an earlier period; and second, they are not accompanied by angels or flashes of lightning. That kind of miracle seems to have died out about the time the Renaissance began, although there have been a few sporadic examples from time to time. Modern miracles usually come about slowly and are the results of years of strenuous effort, downright hard work, on the part of many people. But they are miracles nonetheless because they depend on faith. Somebody has to believe that it can be done. That somebody's faith inspires others to believe. And after fifteen or twenty years of hard work—Whammo! A miracle. And we can't expect modern miracles to be either permanent or absolute.

What I came here to see last May was the salvation of the San Pedro River, a river which had been doomed as surely as anything or anyone can be doomed. It lay directly in the path of progress, the worst place in the modern world for anything to be—a sure ticket to speedy destruction. And that destruction had been coming for a long time.

It began with two large Mexican land grants made to members of the prominent and illustrious Elías family between 1827 and 1833. Each was about three miles wide but very long, following the river on both sides for about seventeen miles. It occurs to me now that I'm sitting in almost the exact center of the more northerly of the two, the San Juan de las Boquillas y Nogales. I wonder why they named it after St. John when it was on St. Peter's river, but that is just one more of those connections between John the Baptist and water, connections which seem to pop up frequently in a dry land where human life has been, until recent times, quite literally marginal—existing only on the margins of streams. Surely old Señor San Juan knew about the meaning of rivers that run through a desert, how they have special power and a special place in history.

I think this grant had the best name of any land grant in what is now Arizona. The name loses much of the beauty of its Spanish sound in translation, but it's not too shabby in English. St. John of the Little Mouths and Walnuts. The name is, at the same time, accurate and imagistic, descriptive and evocative—in short, poetry. *Boquillas* refers to the many little streams which enter the river along here, mostly from Babocomari Creek, and walnut trees have always grown along this stretch of the river. The name of the more southerly grant, which extended all the way to where Hereford used to be but isn't anymore, was also beautiful—The San Rafael del Valle.

Members of the Elías family ran cattle on their land for a few years until the Apaches made life too difficult for them to remain. The Apaches had developed a taste for beef and had already, in pursuit of it and horses, killed several male members of the Elías family on nearby land grants. The family had nothing further to do with their land in the San Pedro Valley until after the Gadsden Purchase, when it became part of the United States, and gringo land speculators, each with his carpetbag, came calling. Then they sold for a song and probably for many reasons. The titles to their lands would be tied up in a foreign court for years and might never be granted to them anyway. Immigrants from the United States were notoriously land-hungry and had been known to take land away from the native owners by force. And while the land speculators were willing to gamble that the Apaches would soon be brought under control, the Elías family had had a great deal more experience with Apaches and knew how long they had controlled the area, raiding and killing. So the Elías family sold.

The San Juan de las Boquillas went through the hands of two speculators fairly quickly and wound up as the property of George Hearst, the California newspaper magnate who dabbled on a large scale in both mines and ranch land in the Southwest, and who served for many years as a California senator. George Hearst was the raw material of legend, but one story about him is so persistent that I think it must be true. When Hearst was visiting in the dusty little frontier town of Tucson, a scorpion stung him, as the story goes, on his "private parts." The story goes on to say that the scorpion dropped dead immediately. I do not know if this was before or after George Hearst fathered his even more famous son, William Randolph Hearst, to whom George willed half of the San Juan de las Boquillas land. The other half went to his widow. The land on the San Pedro was only a tiny fraction of the Southwestern holdings of William Randolph Hearst. At one time he owned seven million acres of the Mexican State of Chihuahua.

In 1901, the Hearst family sold the grant on the San Pedro to the Boquillas Land and Cattle Company, which was headquartered in Bakersfield, California, and soon the land was pretty much ruined by overgrazing, as most of it still is today. Shortly after the turn of the century the sacaton grass was gone, mesquite covered much of the rangeland, and deep channels had been cut by erosion.

The nature of the soil in the upper San Pedro River Valley makes it particularly susceptible to erosion. It is a light clay, made up of very fine particles of igneous and metamorphic rock. When it is dry, it is pale gray and has almost the consistency of talcum powder. Now that it has almost no grass to cover it and hold it in place, the wind blows it as a gray dust which covers everything. When I place my hand, palm down and ever-so-gently on the dry ground, my palm is covered with the finest gray powder. But it washes away quickly and easily when I place my hand in the river. It washes away quickly and easily when the summer monsoons come, as well. It is extremely fragile.

I can see the sheer walls of the river channel from here. In many places they are about twenty feet high and have been formed in quite recent times. Back from the river, the runoff channels are deep, narrow slits rather than the fairly shallow washes usually found lower down on the desert floor. A single hard rain can cut a channel more than a foot deep, which deepens and broadens with later rains into an impassable chasm with unstable walls. The land just back from the river, both north and south of here for many miles, is veined with such chasms. A cow falling into such a chasm can easily break its leg or neck, and the driver of a pickup that plunges in might never be heard of again.

The San Rafael del Valle grant found its way into the hands of the

Boquillas Land and Cattle Company, too, but ten years later and by a quite different route. The Rafael Elías branch of the family, to whom it was originally granted, lost it through a mortgage to the Camou family of Hermosillo, who sold it to the fabulous and famous Colonel William C. Greene, whose heirs sold it to the Boquillas Land and Cattle Company. In 1912, the cattle company joined the Rafael and the San Juan grants and formed a single spread, the Boquillas Ranch. Legal ownership of the ranch has floated, as one giant company merged with or was swallowed by another. In 1967, the Kern County Land and Cattle Company, an enormous California corporation, held the title to the Boquillas Ranch when it merged with Tenneco Realty Development Corporation, taking most of the land along the upper San Pedro River with it. The writing was on the wall and it said BULLDOZERS.

The next step would have been development. It seemed inevitable. During the preceding twenty-five years Sierra Vista, on the west slope of the San Pedro Valley, had been growing faster than anyone could have thought possible, reaching out for land and water like an octopus. To the north and west, one huge ranch after another in the Sonoita area had been sold to developers and chopped into homesites, often to build one-season homes for winter visitors.

But there are such things as modern miracles, and I'm sitting here beside the San Pedro River looking at one. It's all around me, in the dappled shade of the cottonwoods and the songs of the birds. The water gurgling over smooth river stones says, "Miracle, miracle, miracle," and a bullfrog just upstream answers in a *basso profundo*, "Beautiful! Beautiful!" The San Pedro is not a major river, but it's the only undammed one we have left, and no one will come here now with bulldozers and destroy it and the land along it. The beaver and trout are gone, but no one will drive out the hundreds of other creatures who remain, for whom this is home. That's a major miracle in a day when miracles are hard to come by.

The miracle involved the efforts of hundreds of people in many environmentalist groups, in some cases for about fifteen years. Their efforts were generally led and coordinated by the Sierra Club and the Nature Conservancy. Part of what they achieved was the redistribution of public lands, which doesn't sound very exciting, but it saved the San Pedro River and the land adjacent to it. The Bureau of Land Management agreed to swap land in its possession near Phoenix, land with little natural resource value, for land along the San Pedro, including all the Boquillas Ranch. The San Pedro land, 43,371 acres appraised at 26.5 million dollars, was sold to an intermediary, Arizona White Tank Associates, by Tenneco Realty Development Association. The BLM then swapped its land near Phoenix for the San Pedro land in March of 1986. The BLM already owned some land along the San Pedro, and it added more through land exchanges with farmers and ranchers.

Then the Arizona Congressional Delegation introduced legislation in the United States Congress to establish the San Pedro Riparian National Conservation Area, to be made up of the land the BLM had already obtained. At this point the forces of greed felt threatened, and the fight was on. Two Western senators, Malcolm Wallop of Wyoming and James McClure of Idaho, successfully blocked the bill for three years. Both said they feared that maintaining the river at its current level would take water away from surrounding ranchers. Both are ranchers. Finally, after much struggle, language was included in a piece of omnibus legislation, the Arizona-Idaho Conservation Act, which made the San Pedro Conservation Area possible, and which was approved by the Senate in October 1988. It designated 56,431 acres along the San Pedro River as the San Pedro Riparian National Conservation Area.

During dedication ceremonies on May 6, 1989, there was the usual plaque as well as the usual rhetoric from several speakers. Phrases like "biological gold from desert dross" and "this grand biological drama before you" were thrown around with considerable abandon, but everybody knew what the speakers meant anyway. The man chosen to give the main speech is not prone to fancy rhetoric. It was Stewart Udall. He said, "Thanks to the work of conservationists and the BLM, folks can take their children and grandchildren hiking here and nobody can say, 'Get off my land, you're trespassing,' because you own it. We own it."

And yet . . . and yet the river and its riparian area are not entirely out of danger, just as no modern miracle is ever absolute or permanent. The major threat to the river is groundwater pumping for domestic use, mostly in the Sierra Vista area. The BLM has already bought up and retired as many wells as possible in order to favor the flow of the river, but continued groundwater pumping still poses a threat to the life of the river itself. And of course, if the water disappears, so will the riparian area and everything it supports.

But there is hope now where there was none before, and the river has found many friends, some of whom have formed a volunteer group based in Sierra Vista that calls itself "Friends of the San Pedro River" and includes about 150 members. And now the river and its riparian area are in the hands of BLM professionals whose job it is to protect them.

Perhaps I am overly optimistic. I know that the BLM has a disastrous record in terms of stewardship of public lands, largely because it is subject to the political pressures and vagaries of the Department of the Interior and particularly the secretary of the interior. But, on the other hand, I feel good about the situation in this case. The BLM seems to be making the right moves. Surely, with the Nature Conservancy, the Sierra Club, and other environmental groups so deeply involved and alert, the BLM will not play fast and loose with this poor little dying river that has been placed under its protection. *But what about the other rivers? What about the Colorado and Glen Canyon Dam?* It's unthinkable that the BLM could violate this trust. But it has happened before. *Think about something else. Don't ruin your afternoon.*

The BLM Headquarters for the San Pedro Riparian Area is just across the river in the old ghost town of Fairbank, where its staff operates out of a big double-wide trailer and some of them live in other trailers scattered through a mesquite bosque. At their invitation I came up here for a tour last May, after the dedication ceremony but before the northern half of the Conservation Area had been opened to the public. I met and talked to Eric Campbell, the head honcho, and John Herron, the BLM historian, but I spent most of the time with Mike Hoffman, who was in charge of recreational activities, but that term seems to have been defined rather broadly because Mike was in charge of me. He is young, knowledgeable, and charming. He gave me a two-day tour which was glorious. We tore our clothes up crawling through mesquite thickets in search of ruins and hit it off as if we had known each other for years. I had the feeling that Mike was more than happy to get out of the office for a couple of days and ramble around.

Mike and I started out from Fairbank in an official government pickup with four-wheel drive, serviceable, and to judge by its rattles, very experienced. Some of the roads Mike found were purely historical. They might have existed once, long ago, but they had since given up all claims to any connection with transportation. Often they were ghost roads leading to ghost towns, and both were hard to find. In some places the roads had eroded into chasms, and in others the mesquite was doing its best to make them impassable.

None of the country we explored the first day was open to the public, but nearly every time we arrived at a remote spot where I felt sure nobody had been in a very long time, we found fresh beer cans or shotgun shells or some sign that humans had been there recently, leaving a trail of debris behind them. The BLM was working on plans to open that part of the Conservation Area to the public while still preserving the landscape and its ruins. But during the two days I spent there, I began to wonder if such contradictory goals were not impossible, given the truly vicious habits of much of the American public. In spite of the fact that the area was posted with large signs and fenced, several times we saw the three-wheel tracks of all-terrain vehicles, and twice we saw where barbed wire fences had been cut and left lying on the ground in order to admit an ATV to a wash or to the riverbed itself.

We picked up the shotgun shells and beer cans and threw them into the pickup, and I suppose the philosophical way to look at it was to view the debris as representing the latest layer of human civilization in a giant layer cake—the San Pedro Riparian Area. There are few areas in the Southwest that display so many layers of cultural history so distinctly, largely because both prehistoric and historic cultures lived, of necessity, near the river, and because the area has not been "developed" by means of the bulldozer.

Murray Springs, beside the river south of here, undoubtedly represents the bottom or oldest layer in the cultural layer cake, where anthropologists from the University of Arizona have unearthed remnants of a people they call Clovis Culture, whom they believe to be between thirteen thousand and eleven thousand years old, making Murray Springs one of the oldest sites of human occupation ever discovered on the North American continent. At the same location, anthropologists have also discovered the remains of many extinct animals such as the mammoth, North American horse and camel, bison, lion, and the Dire wolf.

From the anthropologist's point of view, Murray Springs is one of the most valuable pieces of real estate in the world because it will yield further knowledge about stone-age man, especially as technology advances and makes it possible to analyze and interpret findings more effectively. It's the job of the BLM to protect and preserve the site for future study. I imagine it makes them a little nervous to have that kind of responsibility, especially since one happy child with a pair of wire cutters and an ATV could destroy much of the site and any hope of gaining future knowledge from it.

I didn't see any artifacts of the Clovis Culture while Mike and I were exploring the river area, but I stumbled onto a relic of the next layer of human culture quite by accident, or I should say I crawled onto it. Mike and I were working our way through a mesquite thicket looking for the ruins of a ghost town with the intriguing name, Contention City. Mike had wisely opted to go around a particularly dense area of spiny mesquite, but I got down on my hands and knees and started crawling through. (I've always argued that if we got out of our automobiles and slowed down to a walk, we would find a whole new and fascinating world out there. But it hadn't occurred to me that by slowing down even more, to a crawl, we would find yet another still more fascinating world.) Because I was watching the ground to see where to put my hands down, I found an exquisite shard of Hohokam pottery, and I think I was more thrilled than if I had found a Clovis Culture spear point.

Of all the prehistoric natives of this continent, the Hohokam are the people I know and care the most about. I devoted a large segment of a documentary film to them years ago, and later wrote a long narrative poem called Hohokam, which was published as a separate book. I found that it's difficult to bring prehistoric people to life in a poem or story, since we have only artifacts and conjecture to go on, and we don't really know what they were like. The main character in my narrative poem turned into a Jewish mother, but I figured that even the ancient Hohokam had a few Jewish mothers, since all other cultures seem to be well supplied with them. I meant it as a tribute. I remember once hearing my son say to one of his friends, "My father is a Jewish mother, and that's the best kind to have." Actually, while I was writing that long poem, I fell in love with the main character and couldn't bear to kill her off, as the story line seemed to require. So she gets very old before it's over and finally walks off into prehistory. No one who has read the poem has ever complained to me about the Jewish-mother quality of the main character, but then I suppose not many people have read it. The book is not exactly a best seller, even as books of poetry go these days, and they don't go far.

While I was doing research on the Hohokam, I discovered the one anthropological principle to which there is no exception—no two anthropologists agree on anything. Faced with this, I looked around and found the anthropologist I most admired as a person. Then I accepted whatever he wrote or told me. His name is Emil Haury, and I believe he knows more about the Hohokam than anybody. He's also a kind, gentle, generous person. Emil believes that the Hohokam came to what is now Southern Arizona from somewhere farther south in Mexico between 600 and 100 B.C., and that they came with their culture already largely developed. They were a sedentary people who lived along the San Pedro, Santa Cruz, Gila, and Salt rivers, raising corn, beans, and squash in terraced plots. They also grew cotton and wove it into cloth. They were masters of irrigation in a dry land and constructed hundreds of miles of irrigation canals. Although they did not possess the wheel nor use fertilizer for their crops, their civilization survived here against all odds for about fifteen hundred years, a good deal longer than ours has.

Anthropologists give several possible reasons for their slow decline and rather sudden disappearance in the fifteenth century. One is that the soil might have become sterile from an accumulation of salts caused by irrigation. Or perhaps they were pressured and harassed by a warlike people moving in from the Northeast, a people who were later to be known as the Apaches, but there is no evidence of violence in connection with their departure. Perhaps, ultimately, their technology failed them. As the riverbanks eroded, the level of the river would have been much lower than the level of the fields beside it. Perhaps they could no longer channel the water up and onto their crops. Emil Haury, with a disarming but gentle grin, suggests another possibility. "Perhaps it was the will of the gods. We do not know."

What we do know is that the Hohokam were here, living in pit houses near the river for all those years, and it isn't unusual to encounter some evidence of their presence, like the beautiful pottery shard, red-on-buff with one complete section of the circular maze pattern so often found on Hohokam pots. I called Mike into the thicket to see it, and when he asked me how old I thought it was, I did some rapid and probably inaccurate calculation based on my scanty knowledge of the various periods of the Hohokam and the accompanying styles of pottery.

"You mean," Mike said when I had come up with a tentative answer, "that piece of pottery might be nine hundred years old?" I agreed, thinking that it predated by at least five hundred years anything that could have been left here by a European, including the members of Coronado's not-so-merry band. I wondered if someday, after we have vanished perhaps as mysteriously as the Hohokam did, somebody from a different culture might be crawling through a thicket in this valley and might find a remnant of our culture and say, "Ah-hah! Late Coors period—end of the twentieth century."

So on we went, gathering artifacts of our own culture and throwing them into the pickup while looking for signs of earlier cultures. While we could find only small pottery shards from the Hohokam cultural layer, the first Europeans to live in the valley left an artifact bigger than a city block, and it represented a whole era of bloodshed, a long struggle for existence between different cultures.

When Europeans first came to the area to stay, at the end of the seventeenth century, the river valley was inhabited by a peaceful tribe of sedentary Pimas, possibly descendants of the Hohokam. They were the Sobáipuris, but they were not living in peace because they were constantly being raided by the Apaches, who would return after each raid to their almost impregnable retreats in the Dragoon Mountains. The Sobáipuris had fought a defensive war for years, and they had proven their bravery, but they could never stop the Apaches from swooping down upon them, robbing, killing, and taking captives. The Sobáipuris were delighted when the first Spanish soldiers arrived, hoping these tall, godlike creatures with their magic guns and horses would help protect them from the Apaches. And the Spanish soldiers tried to overcome the Apaches, but time and again they failed. Finally, the government of New Spain decided that the only way to protect the Sobáipuris was to move them out of harm's way. In the

1760s the government of New Spain moved the Sobáipuris westward into the Santa Cruz Valley, but this proved futile in the long run since the Apaches later overran and controlled that valley to such an extent that the remaining Sobáipuris were forced to flee to the walled Presidio of Tucson.

Then, for a few years, the Apaches had things pretty much their own way in the San Pedro Valley, which they used as a highway leading southward into the populated frontier regions of New Spain, which they raided with impunity. At the times of their greatest raiding activity and for many years the Apaches effectively stopped further non-native settlement on the northern frontier of Spain's largest colony. In response to them, the Spanish government decided in the 1770s to reorganize its defensive perimeter along the northern border of New Spain by establishing a great arc of presidios through what is now Northern Sonora and Southern Arizona, and they located one of these huge forts, named Santa Cruz de Terrenate, beside the San Pedro River about three miles north of where I'm sitting now.

Mike and I got there over a series of roads that I thought were bad until I saw the roads we took to get out, roads on which we could have used five-wheel drive if we had had it. The adobe ruins of Santa Cruz de Terrenate are extensive but not high. They outline many structures within the outer surrounding wall, including a chapel, a bastion at one corner where cannons were probably mounted, some barracks, and the house of the commander. Charles Di Peso excavated Terrenate in the early 1950s under the auspices of the National Geographic Society, but he did not backfill the site, and the adobe walls have continued to erode rapidly since his excavation. Pot hunters and people who like to tear up ruins just for the hell of it have also vandalized the site.

But it is still extremely impressive, located on a high escarpment on the west side of the river and facing east toward the Dragoon Mountains with a steep drop, almost a cliff, directly in front of it and an arroyo to act as a dry moat behind it. The valley narrows sharply at that point and would have provided an excellent place for the Apaches to ambush anyone traveling through it. The builders had planned an installation to help protect travelers along the San Pedro going to or from the Gila River, which connected with the trail to Spain's remote but important settlement of Santa Fe. And it might have worked if the soldiers at Terrenate, along with the Spanish settlers and native Pima allies who joined them, had been able to get the fort fully built. But the Apaches could see what the plan was, and they knew they must not permit the Spaniards to complete the fort. It was a race and the soldiers and their allies lost. The Apaches had not yet obtained firearms, but they must have thrown everything else they had at the intruders.

The Spaniards and their allies began the construction of Terrenate in 1775 and abandoned it, unfinished, four years later. During that time they lost two captains and more than eighty soldiers to the Apaches, and this does not include the large number of settlers and Pima natives undoubtedly killed.

One of the first things I noticed at Terrenate was the stone footing that runs all the way around it to support the outer adobe wall. That wall was to be the main defense for soldiers and civilians. They had brought in two oxen to haul the stones up from the river, but the Apaches killed and ate the oxen. Then, I would guess, the Spaniards made the Pimas haul stones. In places along the footing I could see the ruins of the adobe wall, sometimes as much as two feet high. The outer protective wall of a presidio was ordinarily about fifteen feet high. I asked Mike if he knew how high they had managed to build the outer wall before the fort was abandoned, and he said that scholars believe it was no more than four feet tall. At that rate, they were losing more than twenty soldiers for every foot in height they were able to build the wall, not counting casualties among the settlers and Pimas. Yes, I thought, the Apaches understood the importance of that outer wall.

Just building the outer wall exposed the soldiers and settlers to great danger, but there were some drawbacks in the setting of the Presidio as well. Its location would have placed it in a highly defensible situation once it was completed and everybody was in it, but it was never completed and not everybody could stay in it. There was no spring or well inside the Presidio. Somebody had to go to the river for water. The river was broad in those days, but it was still more than a quarter of a mile away across open country. The fields where they grew corn, beans, and chiles were off to the north on flat land down by the river. Too far away. Anybody working those fields, even with a weapon in one hand, was a sitting duck. The closest pasturage for the horses was also too far away from the fort, and nothing attracted Apaches more than horses. Each soldier at a presidio was supposed to be assigned six horses and a mule, but I'm sure the apaches cut that number down very quickly. They could also pick off the soldiers assigned to guard the herd.

The Apaches didn't have time to play a waiting game and pick off the soldiers and settlers one by one, and they knew it. They had to drive the Spaniards out before that outer wall was completed, or at least high enough to provide significant protection. Repeatedly, they engaged the entire command in battle right at the front gate. They killed the first commander, Francisco Tobar, and more than half the garrison a short distance from the wall in a fierce battle in 1776. Then they killed the second commander, Francisco Ygnacio de Trespalacios, in much the same way. When orders came for the Presidio to be abandoned, its third and only surviving commander, José Antonio de Vildósola, financed the evacuation of the soldiers and their families with his own funds. Few gifts were ever so quickly accepted. Santa Cruz de Terrenate meant "the holy terrestrial cross," but it must have meant hell to those soldiers, and to the settlers who were foolhardy enough to join them.

I stood on the parade ground of Santa Cruz de Terrenate last May and looked across the riverbed at the dazzling pink and blue facade of the Dragoon Mountains, once home of the Apaches. They were huge, like a wall across the horizon, and they looked very near in the dry air. It was like looking up into a citadel which loomed above me, and for a moment I felt trapped, as I'm sure the Spaniards must have felt. Then, as we wandered around the Presidio, Mike and I were surprised to see that the river below was dry at that point. Somewhere between there and Fairbank, about three miles upstream as the crow flies, it had gone underground after several hot months without rain. *How to keep a dying river alive!* I thought desperately, frantically. And no answer came to me. Then I noticed, in the river's dry, sandy bed, the three deep and distinct tracks of an ATV. I shuddered, involuntarily, much as the Spaniards and their native allies at Terrenate must have shuddered when they looked down and saw the tracks of Apache horses along the river. "In the San Pedro Valley," I said to Mike, "it's just one damned thing after another."

It was late afternoon of our first day exploring along the river. Mike and I were tired, dusty, and thoroughly scratched up from our encounters with the guardian mesquites that were doing their best to hide and protect the ruins along the river from intruders like us. Mike's fancy BLM uniform was torn in several places, and the crown of my straw cowboy hat was flapping in the breeze. But we had become friends, and I didn't want the day to end on that sour note: a dry riverbed and a set of fresh ATV tracks.

So while Mike navigated the pickup back to Fairbank over purely imaginary roads, I told him the story of the Battle of the Bulls, which I had first heard about many years earlier from the famous folklorist Byrd Granger. There is a monument to the Battle of the Bulls up the river a few miles from Fairbank, and Mike had seen it, but he didn't know much about the battle itself. I guess the battle isn't very well known, but it should be. It was the only battle of the Mexican-American War fought in what is now the State of Arizona, and it was the best kind of battle to have if you have to have a battle—nobody got killed.

After the Spanish forces abandoned Santa Cruz de Terrenate, the Apaches dominated the San Pedro Valley without much opposition. In 1821, Mexico gained its independence from Spain, and the valley became the property of Mexico rather than Spain, but I doubt that anybody in the frontier valley paid much attention. Actually, there wasn't much of anybody in the valley except a great many wild cattle which were the descendants of cattle left behind by the Elías family when they abandoned their two land-grant ranches years earlier. Bands of Apache passed through the valley on their way to raid settlers to the south, but otherwise things in the old San Pedro River Valley were remarkably quiet.

In the United States, in 1846, President Polk had managed to get Congress to declare war on Mexico, using Texas as a pretext. What Polk really wanted was the Mexican territory of California, and as soon as war was declared, he sent Gen. Stephen W. Kearny and his Army of the West overland, headed for California as fast as possible. Just as Kearny was beginning to move his army west, another huge group was straggling westward. It was the Children of Israel, the Mormon immigrants, thousands and thousands of them, sick, exhausted, and often starving, but led by one of the greatest leaders the United States has ever produced, the prophet Brigham Young. They were fleeing from hideous persecution in Illinois and Missouri and heading for the Promised Land, although none of them, including Brigham Young, as yet knew where the Promised Land was. Believers would say that Brigham was expecting divine guidance as he went along, dragging the Children of Israel with him. Others might say that he was flying by the seat of his pants.

How the Children of Israel got mixed up with the Army of the West, which was made up largely of their hated persecutors from Missouri, is a long, unbelievable story that could have happened only in real life because it was much too bizarre for fiction. But Brigham saw a way to get some of the Saints westward toward the Promised Land, wherever that was, at the expense of the United States Government while, at the same time, using their army salaries to help their families make the exodus. President Polk, fearing that the Mormons would turn upon their persecutors and begin a rebellion against the United States that would severely hamper him in the prosecution of his war with Mexico, allowed some of the Saints to join the Army of the West, thus insuring that the Mormons would remain loyal.

The fact that the Prophet convinced the Saints to do it is probably the most unbelievable element of the entire story. But this was not your garden variety prophet. This was Brigham Young. First he prayed and exhorted. It didn't work. The men would not volunteer to desert their families in order to fight for their enemy. The Prophet cajoled, enticed, and pointed out the benefits of his plan. Only a few men volunteered. Then the Prophet showed the stuff that had made him a prophet in the first place. He called down the wrath of God on the stiff-necked and disobedient Children of Israel. He threatened hell with all its tortures. He became a flaming sword to bar the path of his people, as they fled from bondage, unless they obeyed him. He said that if the men would not volunteer, he would accept the women, and if he could not get enough women to volunteer, he would draft the aged and infirm. He didn't give a damn whether the war was justified or not. The Children of Israel would volunteer to fight on the side of their enemy, and they would do it NOW!

More than five hundred men volunteered. They included the best Israel had, but Israel had been under siege for a long time. Many of them were undernourished and ill. Some were grandfathers. They had no notion of military discipline, feared and hated the other soldiers in Kearny's army more than they did the enemy, and didn't know why the war was being fought or exactly where. They left their families, often sick and suffering, in the worst possible straits. But they volunteered, and most of them marched to California, complaining at almost every step of the way. They were called The Mormon Battalion.

Brigham Young gave them his blessing and promised that none of them would be killed in battle. None were, but some died of distance and disease. They walked south from Winter Quarters, which the Mormons had established near the present city of Council Bluffs, Iowa, to Ft. Leavenworth on the eastern border of Kansas, where they were mustered in on August 1, 1846. There was little time for military drill or training at Ft. Leavenworth. Then they marched—if their disorganized, straggling method of locomotion could be called marching—down the trail to Santa Fe, accompanied by rumors, miracles, and much exhortation from their religious leaders. Those too frail, sick, or old to continue were sent from Santa Fe to Pueblo, Colorado, to join an advance party of Israel and spend the winter. The others, more than 350 of them under the able command of Phillip St. George Cooke, marched south down the Rio Grande, cut across the mountains to the San Pedro, and traveled north on the San Pedro.

Kearny's army was plagued with supply problems from the beginning. Much of the time The Mormon Battalion marched on half-rations or less, and most of the men were convinced that the Battalion doctor was trying to poison them. They also suffered from a galling divided loyalty. Should they obey the religious leaders among them who could help them save their souls, or the military leaders they resented, who might be able to get their bodies through to California? They prayed and sang hymns and exhorted one another. Sometimes at night they had impromptu dances around the campfire, with half of them wearing arm bands to signify that they were taking the place of the female partners. And they made it through.

Many of them kept journals full of complaints, miracles, accounts of prayer meetings and who preached at them, and the worst spelling imaginable. In their orthographic originality they followed the example of their Prophet, whose letters indicate that he made up spelling as he went along, perhaps, as in other matters, awaiting Divine Inspiration. A typical letter to one of his wives begins, "Having a fue mineuts I atempt to wright a fue lines to you." But when the Battalion got to the San Pedro and had their one and only battle, their journals fairly blossom with good cheer and enthusiasm. Many of them were expert shots. They had developed skill while trying to defend their homes from the mobs in Missouri and Illinois. They weren't too keen on shooting Mexicans, whom they would have preferred to convert from their heathen and idolatrous religion, but when attacked by rampaging bulls, they could exercise their skill with gusto. The herd they encountered was all bulls, evidently, as they surmised, because the Apaches had killed all the cows. That was also probably why the bulls were in such a bad mood.

The battle took place in a narrow part of the San Pedro channel with fairly steep hills on both sides. Several of the men were hunting, while the rest of the Battalion was marching down the river. Two wounded bulls charged the marching men, running over Sgt. Albert Smith and breaking several of his ribs. The men shot those two bulls, put Sergeant Smith in a wagon, and moved out. When they stopped and went down to the edge of the river to water the mules, however, they were attacked by two more bulls. These upset a wagon and gored one of the mules "till his entrails hung out, which soon died." They also threw Private Amos Cox into the air and gored him severely in the groin. Private Cox survived, but complained that the wound caused him pain for the rest of his life. The men pursued these two bulls, who were joined by a much larger group of bulls and a wild melee broke out, with officers yelling contradictory orders, men climbing whatever they could find in the way of trees, and some holding their ground and shooting. Even after all these bulls were killed or routed and the Battalion had resumed its march, one more bull came dashing out of the brush, attacked a wagon from the rear and upset it, knocking down a mule.

That was the end of it, but most of the men who kept journals commented on how hard the bulls were to kill, and that they could "run off with half a dozen balls in them unless they were shot in the heart." The men killed about twenty bulls and wounded perhaps twice that many. Later, they had a good dinner of somewhat tough beef. They had marched fifteen miles that day.

Like other major historical battles, this one has been celebrated in song. Each of the five companies of the Battalion included two official musicians, and they composed song lyrics almost on the spot whenever something unusual happened. Most often, the lyrics were sung by the men to hymn tunes or popular tunes of the day. Although the battle had to wait 114 years to get a proper monument, it got its song almost immediately—nineteen stanzas of unremitting iambic quatrameter written by Levi W. Hancock, one of the two official musicians for Company E. Knowing that Mr. Hancock is in heaven and cannot be offended, I have to admit that his poem is about as bad, if not worse, than anything I have ever read, and I am allowing for the fact that the period was not one of the high-water marks of American poetry.

The poem is a narrative which tells, blow by blow, the events of the battle. It begins:

Under command of Colonel Cook
When passing down San Pedro's brook,
Where cane-grass, growing rank and high,
Was waving as the breeze pass'd by:

and gets worse. It's nadir is probably reached in stanza nine:

A bull at one man made a pass,
Who hid himself amid the grass,
And breathless lay until the brute
Pass'd him and took another shoot.

The song ends, as such songs usually do, with a reference to the magnitude of the day's victory:

And when the fearful fight was o'er
And sound of muskets heard no more,
At least a score of bulls were found,
And two mules dead upon the ground.

There must have been some Apache scouts lurking about in the underbrush the night the Battalion sang this song around the campfires. Apaches knew everything that was going on in the valley in those days, and they must have followed the Battalion's progress with great interest. I wonder what they thought when the Children of Israel belted out this song, all nineteen verses, with the gusto that comes from pride in a hard battle well fought and won. The Apaches must have been truly astonished. Many others with pale faces would soon be coming down the road the Battalion was hacking out of the mesquite thickets along the river, but I doubt that any of them ever created as much astonishment among the Apaches as The Mormon Battalion did the night they sang their hymn to victory in the only battle they would ever fight in the Mexican War—the Battle of the Bulls.

7

T he afternoon is subtly transforming itself into early evening, but only the mountains at a distance know it yet. Ribs of the Dragoons are becoming a little more starkly outlined; their blue is a little bluer and their pink is a little brighter. Sunlight comes through the cottonwoods at a lower angle, and suddenly the heat along the river seems more intense. The breeze is dying down. But it's hard to pull a desert rat like me away from running water and shade. I don't have too many miles to go before I sleep—only about thirty-five to Bisbee, but I do have one promise to keep. Dinner at the Copper Queen with a lady named Ida, and you don't keep ladies like Ida waiting. I get up from where I've been sitting, a little stiff, and start wading downstream past the cliff-like banks where Babocomari Creek empties into the San Pedro.

I climb the bank, negotiate the flimsy barbed-wire fence without breaking it down, and there is Blue Boy, waiting. He always seems to perk up when I return after leaving him parked beside the road in the middle of nowhere, whether I've been gone a few minutes or a few days. As soon as I get dressed, we move out across the bridge, up over a railroad overpass, and drop down in the middle of what was once Fairbank. Highway 82 passes almost directly over the location of the old Montezuma Hotel. As we drive slowly through where the lobby probably stood, I think I can see two elderly ghosts half asleep in their favorite chairs. I nod to them.

"There goes the stage for Bisbee," one of them says with a yawn.

"Sandy Bob's late today," the other one answers. "Never make it to Bisbee. Have to stay the night in Tombstone. Play hell if he tries that pass after dark."

"What time's it gettin' to be?"

After some digging around, the other pulls a large gold watch with no chain out of his trouser pocket, consults it, and says, "He'll never make it over the pass before dark. It's too late."

And it is too late for Fairbank and its citizens. They are all gone—the shiftless and the steady, the drunken, the beautiful, the consumptive and the healthy, the laborers, clerks, card sharks, mule skinners, and cowboys. All gone. And the town is gone, although a few of the buildings remain. Whatever portion of the human spirit put down roots here and made it a town is gone, dead, and very nearly forgotten. The same is true of the other towns that grew up along the San Pedro after silver was discovered in the Tombstone Mountains in 1877, towns which owed their existence to silver, and when it could no longer be dug out of the earth, they died. Contention City, Emory City, Millville, Charleston. All gone.

Fairbank was different from the others along the river, and it lasted much longer. Its active life spanned twenty-three years, although it lingered on in a kind of half-life for another six decades. None of the other towns lasted more than ten years. And unlike the others, Fairbank was not a processing center for ore. It was a railroad and stage terminus. Until 1903, when a spur railroad was built from here into Tombstone, anybody traveling to Tombstone by train got off at Fairbank and finished the journey by stage, about thirteen miles over a terrible road made worse by the dangers of Apaches and bandits. By the time Fairbank was established in 1882, Tombstone was already one of the largest cities in the West, with a population of about fifteen thousand—bigger than San Francisco—and Fairbank became its closest railroad connection for both freight and passengers. Fairbank never had a large population, but the characters who passed through it on their way to or from Tombstone were the same ones whose activities, when properly ballyhooed in recent times, have made Tombstone the number one Wild West tourist trap in America.

In 1881, officials of the Atchison, Topeka, and Santa Fe Railroad began construction of their line from Benson to Nogales, incorporated as the New Mexico and Arizona Railroad. At Nogales it would connect with their Sonoran line and run to Guaymas and the sea, a cross-continental dream previously thwarted by Huntington and his consortium who owned the Southern Pacific. After following the San Pedro River south out of Benson for about eighteen miles, the New Mexico and Arizona line turned sharply westward, crossed the river, and followed Babocomari Creek to a low divide, after which it followed Sonoita Creek southwest toward Nogales. At the point where the railroad turned west and crossed the San Pedro, a "Y" was constructed for turning locomotives. It was the point at which the New Mexico and Arizona line would most closely approach Tombstone, and the people of Tombstone were quick to recognize the location's potential.

In the spring of 1882, as soon as the tracks were laid as far as the "Y," two enterprising developers claimed a homestead site and began selling lots. As it turned out, they never owned the land, but they thought they did. They named the town Fairbank after N. K. Fairbank, the merchant who organized the Grand Central Mining Company in Tombstone and was a shareholder in the New Mexico and Arizona Railroad. Buildings, some of adobe and some frame, began to go up immediately, and one of the earliest is still here. It is a large adobe structure with a tin roof, which was added later. It has three sets of double doors across the front, and its exterior walls have been covered, over the years, with layers of white plaster, now about three inches thick. Still visible in the plaster across the front is the sign "FAIRBANK COMMERCIAL CO." The building is a late nineteenth-century version of a shopping mall. It housed a general mercantile, a bar, the post office, and different stores at different times, possibly including stores operated by such pioneer Arizona merchants as Albert Steinfeld and Joseph Goldwater, both of whom had businesses in Fairbank.

Part of the back wall of the building has collapsed. What remains, as well as the front wall, has been shored up with wooden braces by the BLM, and stacks of adobe blocks nearby suggest that they plan to repair it. The Commercial Company and the three other remaining buildings, two houses and a schoolhouse, are all north of the present highway. In front of them, in a clearing, is the double-wide trailer the BLM uses as its headquarters for administering the Conservation Area, and beyond it to the north are three more trailers used as residences by some members of the BLM staff. The existing ruins would suggest that all the town was north of the present highway, which was built in the 1930s, and that the town was quite small, but neither is true. The hotel stood south of the Commercial Company building, which would have placed it about in the middle of the present highway, and most of the commercial buildings as well as the sizable depot were south of the highway along the railroad tracks in an area that is now hidden by mesquite.

In 1888 Fairbank had four stores, five saloons, three restaurants, a Wells Fargo office, several livery stables and smaller businesses, a depot, and many houses. The Montezuma Hotel, or Montezuma House, was built the following year, and the town continued to grow, with lots selling at between fifty and one hundred dollars.

Fairbank didn't die a sudden death as the silver-mill towns up and down the river did. It suffered a series of what might be called misfortunes. Some were "acts of God," to whom we always attribute such disasters. The town was damaged by the earthquake of 1887, and even more by floods during the monsoon seasons of 1890 and 1894, the last of which brought four feet of water into the Montezuma Hotel and crushed some of the houses. The San Pedro was a larger river then than it is now, and the beaver dams, which could have helped check the river, were gone.

When the spur railroad line to Tombstone was built in 1903, it removed much of Fairbank's reason for being, but the town lived on. The real blow came in 1905 when the Boquillas Land and Cattle Company evicted all the residents of Fairbank because it owned the land the town had been built on. Since the town's founding, the San Juan de las Boquillas y Nogales land grant had been confirmed by the U.S. Court of Private Land Claims, and the heirs of George Hearst had sold it to the Boquillas Land and Cattle Company. The town was located about dead center of the grant. Residents of Fairbank had purchased their lots years earlier in good faith and had built their homes and businesses, but it made no difference. Many of the buildings were probably torn down at that time, either by the previous "owners" or by the Cattle Company, which then leased most of the remaining buildings to the Heney family. Members of that family remained in Fairbank until the early 1970s, keeping the post office open through a long twilight of semi-ghost existence until Fairbank was completely abandoned.

Now it is part of the San Pedro Conservation Area, and as Stewart Udall said, "You own it. We own it." And yet, as far as Fairbank goes, I'm not sure I want it. It gives me an uneasy feeling. There is something uncomfortable about stepping out of the BLM office, with its air conditioning and the bustle of professional activity, and into the Fairbank Commercial Company, which still smells like the flood of 1894. The other ghost towns along the river died quickly and cleanly, but Fairbank lingered too long in a moribund condition. Something is not quite right here, and I can't put my finger on what it is, but the brightest spring day brings no warmth to the interior of the Fairbank Commercial Company, in spite of the huge gaps in the adobe walls. Stewart Udall is a very smart lawyer, but he can't determine who owns the ghosts of Fairbank, if they exist. Can anybody own a ghost? "Too late," they keep saying. "It's too late."

It is even later for the stamp-mill towns along the upper San Pedro. They were built to process ore which came out of the silver mines in the Tombstone Mountains, and when those mines began to flood in 1886, it was the beginning of the end for the stamp mills and the towns that had grown up around them. None of them lasted more than ten years. They were built on the terraces just above the river, close enough to obtain the water they needed for processing the ore but, unlike Fairbank, high enough to avoid being flooded by the San Pedro. Some of the same terraces had once been the sites of prehistoric Hohokam villages. The stamp-mill towns didn't last nearly as long as the Hohokam villages had, but they must have been a great deal noisier. Their function was to stamp rocks into ever smaller rocks, pulverizing them so thoroughly that when water from the river was added, the result was a kind of thick paste from which silver could be obtained by adding mercury. The silver adhered to the mercury, and when the silver and mercury amalgam was subjected to intense heat from a furnace, the mercury vaporized and was siphoned off to be used again, leaving a large lump of silver that usually contained some gold. This went on twenty-four hours a day.

The stamps which pulverized the ore were upright iron rods, each shod with iron and steel and linked so they would rise and fall one after the other in a frenzied dance that literally stamped the ore into powder. A typical stamp on the San Pedro had between ten and fifteen iron rods which dropped at the rate of one hundred times per minute. The entire valley must have trembled with the noise. Even from a great distance it could be heard as a dull roar. Not since the Mormon Battalion sang its victory hymn after its battle with the bulls had such a ruckus been heard on the San Pedro River.

There were three stamp-mill communities north of Fairbank and three south of it. Those to the north—Sunset (also called Bullion City), Contention City, and Grand Central—were all within four miles of Fairbank, each about a mile distant from the next. Those to the south were Emory City (also called Boston City), Millville, and Charleston. There was, however, no stamp mill at Charleston. It was a housing community across the river from Millville, but it was the largest of the stamp-mill towns.

Contention City, about three miles north of Fairbank, spread out on both sides of the river, although specialists like John Herron, the BLM historian, make a distinction between New Contention on the west bank and Old Contention on the east bank. Old Contention was the site of the stamp mill—all the stamp mills were on the east bank—and John says that New Contention was a railroad community built to house the railroad workers and engineers when the New Mexico and Arizona Railroad began building south from Benson to Nogales. This would have meant that Old Contention was about three years older than New Contention and that otherwise they existed contemporaneously. Neither was particularly contentious, certainly not in the same league with Tombstone and Bisbee. The name came about because the stamp mill processed ore from the Contention Mine in the Tombstone Mountains, and the mine got its name because its ownership was in contention for awhile.

One of the contenders was Ed Schieffelin, the prospector whose discoveries made Tombstone and all its satellite communities possible. As a lone prospector of the old school, with a pickax, a mule, and very little else, Ed was already out-of-date when he arrived in Arizona. He lacked both the scientific knowledge to evaluate his discoveries and the financial backing to develop them. He was long on determination, dreams, and hunches, and short on everything else. His breed was rapidly dying out even before Ed developed his monomaniacal idea that there were rich veins of silver in the Tombstone Mountains. But he had persistent dreams.

He had outfitted himself in California, drifted into the Grand Canyon area, and was prospecting there in 1877 when he joined a group of Hualapai Indian scouts who were sent by the military to the newly established Camp Huachuca, probably still called Camp Detachment. Ed used the struggling little military outpost as a base of operations while he prospected in the mountains on the other side of the river. He was a strange, tatterdemalion figure with long, tangled, greasy hair and the dark, glittering eyes of a fanatic. The soldiers at Camp Huachuca made fun of him. Some accounts say that they were the ones who told him that all he would find in the Apache-ridden mountains across the river would be his tombstone.

Ed's first big discovery, the one he thought would make him rich, produced ore samples that turned out to be almost worthless, but it was, in the long run, extremely valuable to Ed, since the samples showed enough promise to attract the partner he needed, someone with a real knowledge of both geology and metallurgy. Richard Gird was an assayer and mining engineer, and was thought to be one of the most knowledgeable men in Arizona when it came to mineral wealth. On the basis of the promise shown by Ed's first ore samples, Gird entered into a partnership with Ed and Ed's brother Al, and went with them to the Tombstone Mountains. The combination of Ed's determination and hunches and Dick Gird's scientific knowledge was exactly what was required to find silver, and find silver they did. Of the three richest strikes which eventually made Tombstone the most famous mining camp in the Southwest, Ed found two; but without Gird's expertise, he would probably not have been able to determine the value of what he had found nor to locate his claims effectively. He named those mines the "Lucky Cuss" and the "Tough Nut."

Word of his discoveries soon spread, and a pair of newcomers, Hank Williams and John Oliver, made the third major strike in the Tombstone Mountains, but not before they had made an agreement with Dick Gird to split anything they found with him and his partners in return for his assaying their ore. After they made their strike, they tried to forget about the agreement until Gird and the Schieffelin brothers forced them to acknowledge it. Ultimately, Williams and Oliver named their share of the mine the Grand Central and set up a stamp mill with that name on the San Pedro. The man who organized the financing for the Grand Central was N. K. Fairbank, after whom the town of Fairbank was later named. But Gird and the Schieffelin brothers, because of their prolonged struggle for ownership, named their share of the mine the "Contention," and its stamp-mill community became Contention City.

During its brief but noisy existence between 1879 and 1888, Contention City probably had a peak population of no more than two hundred, but for a couple of years until the depot was built at Fairbank, it was the railhead for Tombstone, handling all passengers and freight that came and went from that booming mining camp. It was a commercial center for the three stamp mills in the area, providing residents and those who passed through on their way to Tombstone with several stores and saloons, two stage lines, a livery stable, meat market, blacksmith shop, Chinese laundry, and a hotel—Mason's Western Hotel—which survives in a photograph of about 1880 and appears to have been a one-story adobe structure with a dirt roof.

Today, Contention City has reached the ultimate distinction that all ghost towns strive for. It has become so ghostly that it isn't even mentioned in the latest book on ghost towns of Arizona. This oversight might be caused by the fact that although there are still ruins to be seen at Contention City, finding them can prove hazardous and painful. Thick groves of mesquite have grown up around them, as if nature were throwing up a protective barrier, not to preserve the site of a dead community but to let it settle into the earth in dignity and peace.

What interests me most at Contention City isn't the ruins of adobe buildings. It's something much more monumental and beautiful, something difficult to see unless you know where to look—the stone foundations of the stamp mill itself. Maybe you have to be a stone-wall nut to be interested in such things, but massive stone walls fascinate me, and I'm sure that part of my preoccupation with Bisbee results from the fact that the town is built up the sides of steep hills, and many of its buildings are supported by magnificent stone retaining walls.

The stamp mills along the San Pedro were also built up the sides of steep hills, and sometimes cliffs, into which narrow terraces had been blasted. This was necessary for two reasons. The ore was dumped in at the top, and gravity provided most of the power that moved it along as it was being processed. The other reason was even more important. In order to obtain power for the turbines which drove the stamps in their destructive dance, water had to be dropped a vertical distance of about forty feet, the height of a four-story building. Consequently, most of the stamp mills were a series of tall buildings constructed almost like cliff dwellings up the vertical faces of cliffs and hills. They were usually nondescript frame structures covered with tin, but they rested on an intricate series of massive stone retaining walls, and these, for the most part, are all that is left of them, but it is enough. They rank with the most beautiful stone retaining walls I have ever seen anywhere.

The stones are often huge, with flat surfaces, and range from tan to gold to amber. They are fitted together, usually without mortar, and form a series of smooth perpendicular surfaces, some of which are thirty feet high. The stamp mills along the San Pedro may be gone now, but the stone retaining walls remain, glowing in the sun like natural cliffs. They are in such harmony with the surrounding landscape that it would be easy to hike through the area and never notice them.

Emory City, site of the Boston Stamp Mill, was a few miles south of Fairbank, where the river makes a big, lazy bend and the mill was set back in a kind of bay, surrounded with hills and cliffs on three sides. Even when it was literally booming, it must have had the feeling of isolation. Only the ruins of two fairly extensive stone buildings are left, and the stone retaining walls for the mill, which are still more impressive than the stone walls at Contention City. Tier after tier of golden walls rises above the river, and the view from the top is superlative, with the river curving below and the Huachuca Mountains like great blue ships in the west. Vandals have been at work on some sections of the walls, but most of the stones are so enormous and tightly fitted together that even determined vandals couldn't budge them without a bulldozer.

Last May, about noon on our second day of exploration of the river, Mike Hoffman and I were sitting on the stones which formed the highest layer of the Boston Mill retaining wall, dangling our feet into space where five turkey vultures were slowly circling on the thermals with motionless wings. Once in a while one of the vultures would skim low above us, peering down as if to question what we were and how soon we were going to lie down and turn into dinner. For two days Mike had been watching me pick up beer cans and shotgun shells as if it were my life's work, and I had been watching Mike react with anger to cut fences and ATV tracks in the riverbed. He knew that I thought it was a mistake to open up this magnificent riparian area with its ruins, which represented so many past cultures, to the great American public. And I knew that he had no control over BLM policy. He was in charge of recreation in the Conservation Area . . . and me, but we had gotten to know and like each other.

"I've got some paperwork to do in the office this afternoon," Mike said rather wistfully, "and I wondered if you would like to explore Charleston and Millville by yourself. I can draw you a map to get you to Charleston, and Millville is just across the river."

So he turned me loose on the most beautiful part of the San Pedro, and on some of its most fragile ruins. It was a gesture, I think, to show me that he felt the public could be trusted, since I was the public. But first we returned to Fairbank where we said goodbye and he went, rather grimly, to his paperwork. Then I drove Blue Boy into Tombstone and had lunch at the Lucky Cuss Cafe, named after Ed Schieffelin's first silver strike. It was fitting, since the ore from that mine was processed at Millville, and I was on my way to Millville. Then I drove out the old Charleston Road, parked Blue Boy on a bluff overlooking the river, and set off in search of Charleston first, then Millville.

The retaining walls of one of Millville's stamp mills were in plain sight from where I parked, but I didn't see them until later. They blended into the skyline along the edge of the Charleston Hills so perfectly that I looked right at them but, from a distance, didn't realize what I was seeing. I hiked down a long, hot arroyo, following Mike's directions, waded across the river, and began searching for Charleston. It took me almost an hour to find the first ruins, although I was within a quarter of a mile of them. But it wouldn't have been a disaster if I hadn't found them because what I found was a stretch of river more beautiful than I could have imagined and a golden afternoon I will never forget.

Charleston and Millville are on opposite sides of the river, and there was once a bridge between them, but it washed away many years ago.

Together they formed the largest community on the upper San Pedro. Charleston, particularly, has fascinated historians to such an extent that we know more about it than we do about most ghost towns in Arizona. We know, for instance, that between 1880 and 1886 the citizens of Charleston represented sixty-two professions, not counting the oldest profession of all, which was also amply represented. We have a list of Charleston's 173 registered voters for the year 1882, all male of course, with their occupations and the countries of their birth. Eleven of them were born in either Prussia or Germany, 7 in Ireland, and 4 in Scotland. And although the second major source of income in Charleston was its lucrative and often illegal trade across the nearby Mexican Border, there are only two Hispanic names on the list of registered voters— George Estrada, a miner, and Francisco Valenzuela, a teamster—and both were born in the United States. In spite of this, there was a sizable population of both American Hispanics and Mexican Nationals in and around Charleston, and when the town was abandoned by the Anglos, they moved into the empty dwellings and stayed at least a year.

I had read that there were almost no ruins left at Charleston and had seen an aerial photograph of the site that showed little but a dense thicket of mesquite and other growth. I had also read that the ruins of Charleston had pretty much been obliterated when the land on which they stood had been leased to the United States Army during World War II and used by the recruits at Ft. Huachuca to practice war games, often using live explosives. So I didn't expect much, but I was startled and shaken by what I found.

After about an hour of searching along the flat ground west of the river, I had almost given up and was about to go on in search of Millville. Then I decided to do what I sometimes decide to do when all else fails—use my head. I sat down, took a drink from my canteen, thought about the problem, and reviewed Mike's directions. It occurred to me that the land I was searching was probably low enough to flood when the river rose and was therefore not a very good site for Charleston. But the higher ground was covered with an impenetrable mesquite thicket. I had tried to enter the thicket at several points but had failed. Then I remembered that Mike had said something about a very tall cottonwood. But there were enormous cottonwoods all along the river. So I got up and went in search of the tallest cottonwood I could find, and sure enough, near it I found the merest suggestion of a trail leading up to the next terrace where the mesquite was thickest. After only a few hundred feet, the trail suddenly broadened and turned into something that might once have been a road or street running roughly parallel to the river. It was lined on both sides with thick stands of tall mesquite.

I wandered along, peering into the mesquite from time to time. It seemed thicker and darker than any mesquite grove I had ever encountered. With a sudden shock I realized that I wasn't looking at just a mesquite thicket, but I was standing no more than two feet away from an adobe wall about seven feet high that was so effectively screened by mesquite as to be almost invisible. I was close enough to touch the building before I knew it was there, and there were many others on both sides of the open space, like a street, down which I had been walking. I had passed several without seeing them. The adobe structures were darker than most adobe structures I had seen, almost the color of the trunks and branches of the mesquite, and they were very well camouflaged. To have them loom up that way was startling, as if I had suddenly discovered someone standing next to me when I thought I was alone.

The houses were all roofless, but many of them had three and sometimes four walls intact. After having seen the low adobe ruins at Terrenate and Contention City, I was amazed at how tall these were. Adobe quality varies from place to place, but these walls must have been built of very high quality adobe. And possibly the mesquite has protected them from some amount of exposure. They stood side by side along what was once a broad street, and had the feeling of a community. And they were so silent, so watchful. I was an intruder. I had penetrated another world where every step I took shouted my presence, and I was being observed by silent, dark beings all around me. I was ashamed of being frightened, but I was frightened, and I retreated quickly back to the river and the world I knew.

Shaken, I sat down beside the river in the sunlight filtered by the branches of cottonwoods and thought about it. I had just gained a whole new perspective on ghost towns. At Fairbank, the old Commercial Building had seemed to suggest the echo or tone of some vanished human presence, and it was a slightly unpleasant sensation; but this was different and much more powerful. There was no suggestion of the human at all—it was the buildings themselves. They had eroded into something natural, like trees or stones, but something sentient. The buildings themselves were the ghosts, and they were aware of my presence, aware of me.

Perhaps it was only that I had been standing next to them for some time before I saw them, or perhaps it was their dark, windowless solidity and height. Whatever it was, I suddenly realized that a haunted house doesn't have to be haunted by something or someone. The house itself may be the presence we feel, and it can be a presence as foreign as something from another planet. All talk about preserving the ruins became meaningless in the light of what I had just seen and felt. Preserve the ruins—my God! They weren't ruins. They were created from earth and the elements. They were something that has no connection with humans and never did have. They had evolved. And having become aware of them, as I just had, who would dare to destroy them? We should just leave them alone and try, if we can, to forget them. I won't ever be able to.

I wasn't ready to go off in search of Millville yet, and even less ready to go back up the slope to Charleston. I needed to stay by the river for awhile. It was the most beautiful stretch of the river I had encountered, and the water's gurgling voice was comforting. The banks were soft with grass and reeds, and the stones at the water's edge were mossy. I took off my shoes and waded downstream through undulating patches of water plants I couldn't identify. At one place I found dozens of small toads along the bank, scurrying in all directions. Ahead of me the river bottom narrowed dramatically, and low hills pressed in on both sides. I saw cow droppings along the bank, and it occurred to me that I must be very near where the Mormon Battalion encountered the bulls. A big blue heron rose from the water ahead of me, flapped its long wings as if they needed oiling, and sailed a couple of hundred feet farther downstream. Time to turn back. I was over my jitters and ready to find Millville. But I hated to leave the river. I always do.

I got out on the east bank, put my shoes and socks on, and climbed a steep, cindery bank to the railroad track which runs very close to the river on a high embankment. From the embankment I could see the stonework which had supported the two stamp mills at Millville, and for the first time I realized what I was seeing. The ruins of the Tombstone Milling and Mining Company, Dick Gird's operation, are tucked back in a kind of large indentation where the terraces of the hills make a deep jog and then return to the river. The mill must have faced almost northwest. South and a little to the east I could see the complicated stone terraces of the Corbin Mill and Mining Company. Much of the sloping land between was at one time covered with buildings, either mining company buildings or residences, but in most cases only the building sites remain, and some are almost impossible to identify. Between the railroad and the slope of the hills was an area of low ground completely covered with mesquite, which I negotiated slowly and carefully. As soon as I got away from the river, the sun got hot, and it got hotter as I climbed the hill toward the ruins of the Tombstone Mill.

The Tombstone Mining District was formed by the Schieffelin brothers and Dick Gird in April of 1878, and its ten-stamp mill processed the ore from the Tough Nut, Goodenough, Westside, and Defense mines. In order to obtain the finances they needed to develop their other mines, Gird and the Schieffelin brothers sold their first strike, the Lucky Cuss, to a group headed by George Corbin, a hardware magnate from Connecticut. It seemed at the time to be the only thing to do, but it proved to be a mistake in the long run because the Lucky Cuss turned out to be the richest producer of all the mines. Corbin's group constructed a fifteen-stamp mill south of Gird's and processed ore from the Lucky Cuss, Owl's Nest, Owl's Last Toot, Eastside, and Tribute mines. The two mills were basically different because the Corbin mill was powered by steam while Gird's mill was powered by water, and that resulted in a difference in the physical layout of the two mills which can be seen in the stonework remaining today. The stonework remaining from Gird's mill is much higher and more perpendicular, while that of the Corbin Mill is a series of long and fairly low walls running around the brow of the hill. Gird's mill was basically perpendicular, while the Corbin Mill was more nearly horizontal. And the Corbin Mill must have been more expensive to operate since it required large amounts of fuel, timber which had to be hauled all the way from the Huachuca Mountains. It was also more expensive to construct. The site was solid stone, and the terraces had to be excavated at a cost of twenty thousand dollars.

Dick Gird was undoubtedly a clever man and would have been considered energy conscious by today's standards. As compared to the Corbin Mill and many other stamp mills of the day, his was a relatively "clean" operation. He constructed a dam across the San Pedro River about a mile upstream from his mill and conducted water through a ditch and wooden flume to the mill, which stood high above the river. But the dam was far enough upstream that the ditch and flume had a drop of one-four-hundredth of an inch in one hundred feet, enough but barely enough. The force of gravity brought the water to the mill, and no pumps were required. At the mill, the water fell forty vertical feet toward the river, powering the turbine, and the water was then returned to the river in much the same condition as when it had been removed. Some fuel was required for the drying furnace and the final stage of the reduction process in which the mercury was vaporized, but it was slight as compared to that used in steam-driven mills, like the Corbin Mill.

The stone retaining walls at the site of Gird's mill are impressive and very tall but not so beautifully crafted as those at Emory City, although equally massive. The only other remains of his mill and the community which surrounded it are the rapidly disintegrating adobe walls of his residence and headquarters, which was called "Gird's Big House." It was a commodious, even luxurious structure by the standards of the day and place, and it had an inspiring view across the San Pedro Valley, but only a few low walls remain and they have been the playground of vandals. I had read about Gird's house, which was the scene of one unsolved and unexplained murder and of extravagant social functions, but its ruins gave no clue to its original grandeur.

So I began picking my way obliquely down and around the hill toward the site of the Corbin Mill. As I approached it, I began to have a feeling of déjà vu, although I would have sworn I had never been there before. The stone retaining walls seemed familiar. The way the hill sloped and even the heat radiating up from the valley seemed familiar. Perhaps I had gotten too much sun, I thought, or the experience at Charleston had left my mind a little tilted. I walked along the stone walls for awhile and then went down the hill a little way so I could look up at the walls from below. The view from below triggered a memory, and I knew I had been there before but it had been a long time ago and I hadn't known exactly where I was or what I was seeing.

It must have been about 1961 or 1962. I was teaching at the University of Arizona but also taking classes toward an advanced degree, and I had fallen under the dynamic influence of one of the most remarkable faculty members and personalities at the University, the folklorist Byrd Granger. Byrd was working on an edition of Will Barnes' *Arizona Place Names*, and was later to bring out her own definitive and exhausting work on that subject, *Arizona Names*. She had a huge following among the graduate students and younger faculty, whom she often entertained on weekends at the house she had built with her own hands east of Tucson. That she had been a pilot with the WASPS during World War II and that she claimed to be a witch didn't hurt her popularity with the students one bit. Byrd and I hit it off very well. She was one of my favorite teachers, certainly the one I got to know best, and I suspect I was one of her favorite students. I still have the descendants of plants she gave us when we built our house in the Tucson Mountains.

I don't remember why, but Byrd wanted to find Charleston, and she asked me to go with her. We set off from Tucson early one morning in my car. As it turned out, Byrd had only a general notion of where Charleston was, and I had no notion at all. I don't remember the route we took, but I remember driving down dirt roads and stopping at ranch houses to ask for directions and information. We never found Charleston, but we found something, and I didn't know until last May what it was. It was the ruins of the Corbin Mill. We saw no adobe ruins, but I remember climbing over steep hills and seeing long, low retaining walls. We also found some pieces of rusty metal equipment.

The thing I remember most about the whole trip was Byrd. She had a bad leg, although I didn't know it and she never mentioned it. In later years she began to use a cane, which made her even more impressive. But I remember coming down a steep hill and looking back to see the illustrious Byrd Granger sliding down the hill on her bottom. She said that with her gimp leg it was the only way she could get down a hill. And so we went on for the rest of the day. Each time we had to go down a hill, I walked and she slid. And she never complained or suggested a different route. It's no wonder I had forgotten where we were going or where we were. The most vivid memory I have of the whole day is of Byrd sliding on her bottom. But seeing the stonework at the site of the Corbin Mill after more than twenty-five years, I realized which hills she had been sliding down and what we had found. Memory, at least my memory, is a sieve with holes of varying sizes. There's no justification for what it chooses to retain and what it chooses to let go. For years I had thought I dreamed the whole thing.

Still thinking about Byrd Granger's singular method of locomotion, I managed to get my bones, which I realize are now a good deal older than hers were when she slid down the Charleston Hills, back to the deep wash and up to the road where Blue Boy was waiting, not too patiently as usual. I had one more stop to make that afternoon, one more ruin to see. It wasn't on BLM land, but it was the most legendary and, according to all that has been written about it, the most haunted ruin in the whole San Pedro area—swarming with ghosts and more than twenty years older than the mill towns along the river.

The Brunckow cabin is within sight of the Charleston Road between Tombstone and Sierra Vista, but I doubt that many people driving down that road have noticed it, since its crumbling gray adobe walls blend in so well with the surrounding terrain. It sits on a knoll about two hundred yards from the highway and about a half mile up from the river. All that is left is one adobe room with a small corner fireplace, no roof, and holes for doors and windows. Farther to the southwest is a tall, conical peak which is identified on maps as Brunckow Hill. The surrounding area is pockmarked with abandoned vertical mine shafts and constitutes the Brunckow Mine, which was never successful after its initial promise but is famous in a grisly kind of way. Estimates of how many men were murdered at the Brunckow Mine over the years vary from twenty to forty-six. Twenty is probably a fairly accurate figure. And those who have lived in the area, even as late as the mid-1960s, maintain that the ghosts of all of them are still there, singing in the night.

It wasn't night when I visited Brunckow cabin, just late afternoon, but I must admit I heard something. One of the sounds I heard, which could have passed for singing, I finally decided was coming from the high tension electric line that runs along the highway. But there was another sound, a kind of irregular boom or thud. The cabin sits in a fairly narrow defile winding sharply down to the river. Perhaps the sound I heard was made by the wind rushing through that pass and encountering caves or loose stones. But knowing the history of the place and listening to that sound, I was glad I didn't have to spend the night there.

Frederick Brunckow was a German mining engineer who emigrated to the United States and arrived in Southern Arizona in 1856 as one of the engineers of the Sonora Silver Mining Company, probably the first official mining expedition to explore the area now called the Tombstone Mountains. Brunckow's original discoveries showed some promise, but like Ed Schieffelin's first finds in the area, did not materialize. And as Schieffelin was to do about twenty years later, Brunckow persisted. He and his crew of Mexican laborers from across the border put down shaft after shaft, most of which are still there and uncovered, making hiking through the area dangerous. But Brunckow never lived to strike it rich and maybe he wouldn't have struck it rich anyway since the later strikes were considerably east of his mine. On July 23, 1860, the eleven Mexican laborers employed by Brunckow murdered him, his cousin who was also a mining engineer, and a chemist who was staying at the mine. The laborers loaded their mules with all the booty they could carry from Brunckow's extensive supplies, took his German cook hostage, and with their families fled into Mexico. They later released the German cook because, as they said, he was a good Catholic and had lived in Sonora. At first the cook was suspected of the crimes, but he was later exonerated when the murderers were seen with some of the stolen goods in Cananea and Hermosillo, and heard to brag about the murders. They were never apprehended.

Some histories of the Southwest, even some which are current, have mistakenly attributed this massacre to the Apaches, and there were plenty of Apaches in the area, but this is one crime which cannot be laid at their door. It was only the first of a long series of unrelated murders that were to occur at or near the Brunckow cabin. The second owner of the property, Major Milton Duffield, was killed there by a man named Joseph Holmes, who confessed to the crime and was sentenced to the Yuma Territorial Prison. But there were bloodless intervals, although they were usually brief. During one of them,

Ed Schieffelin, his brother Al, and Dick Gird moved into the deserted cabin while Ed hunted for silver and Dick assayed the samples he brought back. The original samples of ore from the Lucky Cuss Mine were probably smelted in the little corner fireplace of the Brunckow cabin. After that the murders resumed, for one reason or another, and always in or near the cabin. Ed Schieffelin was a lucky cuss, as he often called himself, in more ways than one.

Several reasons could probably be given to explain why the Brunckow Mine was the scene of so many murders. It was an isolated piece of property thought to contain a fortune in silver, and its ownership was often in dispute. The general level of lawlessness in the area was formidable, and the mine was near the border, across which murderers could easily escape. But even with all that taken into account, the Brunckow cabin did seem to come in for more than its share of violence. By 1881 it was already known as a jinxed building and was avoided by nearly everyone. It had become a legend in the mining community, and the legend spread.

After my experience at Charleston, I found the adobe ruins of the Brunckow cabin quite innocuous, although the setting and particularly the booming noise gave me a slightly uneasy feeling. I noticed how the cabin was located on a knoll with deep washes all the way around it. It would have been so easy to sneak up on. And before Charleston and Millville came into existence, it was incredibly isolated.

But the real danger, as far as I was concerned, was the open, vertical mine shafts. They were everywhere, and some of them were more than twenty feet deep. I wondered how many of them had been dug by the men who murdered Frederick Brunckow and his companions. In one of them I saw a large barn owl clinging to a timber which shored up the shaft about halfway down. The owl peered up at me for several seconds. I had forgotten how large barn owls could be. And what a wonderful round white face! Then I noticed that it was gripping something in its talons, and I leaned farther over the shaft to see what it was. Suddenly the owl released its grip and a large dead rabbit plummeted headfirst down the shaft with its legs outstretched just as the owl flew up in my face, causing me to lose my balance and lurch forward. As I grabbed for something, anything, to stop my fall, and caught onto a piece of desert broom with blessedly strong roots, I decided that it had been a spectacular afternoon but the sun was setting and my nerves were a little frayed. It was time to go home. Blue Boy thought it was a good idea too.

I haven't been back to any of the ruins since last May, and I haven't seen Mike Hoffman since then, although I have been in touch with him. But in a sense I'm on my way to more ruins now. Not in a physical sense—just the past. Something about the past and Bisbee. And I'm getting close. I'm approaching the point where Highway 82 intersects Highway 80 about three miles north of Tombstone. And now the past hits me in the face as if I had fallen down a mine shaft. I hate this section of the highway. I shouldn't have come this way. I should have gone around through St. David. Too many ghosts, too many memories.

It was a Saturday night in October 1957. I was stationed at Ft. Huachuca and living in the barracks. Two of my buddies and I had taken the post bus into Fry, which was officially Sierra Vista but nobody paid any attention to the name change. In one of Fry's three bars, where we were drinking beer and feeling bored, we ran into another young soldier whom my friends knew but I didn't. He had just bought a car. I don't remember the make, but it was a red convertible and very snazzy. Since there seemed to be nothing to do in Fry but sit in the bar and drink beer, the young man with the red convertible suggested that we all go to Tombstone. Heldorado Days, Tombstone's annual binge, was in full swing, and there would be plenty of excitement over there. It was only about eleven o'clock. The night's still young. Let's go!

We finished our beers and went out to get in the red convertible. Then something strange happened. I said no. I said I had changed my mind and was going to take the bus back to the barracks and turn in early. To this day I don't know exactly why I did that. I wanted to go to Heldorado, and I didn't have to get up early the next morning. But I said no. The other three got into the snazzy convertible and headed for Tombstone. The car rolled on a slight curve as it approached the intersection I am now approaching. The driver and one of my friends were killed. My other friend was crippled for life.

I have thought about that night many times, and I relive it every time I drive down this section of highway, trying to figure out why I was not in that red convertible when it rolled. To get in that car would have been the most natural thing in the world for me. Certainly I had gotten into many others under similar circumstances. To be drunk and speeding down the highway in a convertible was the epitome of what it meant to be young in the 1950s. It was the form of excitement our innocence chose, and we were innocent. Why, that time, did I say no and then kick myself all the way back to the barracks because of the fun I thought I was missing? I remember standing in the parking lot with my hand on the red convertible, and then some perverse impulse made me say no. I have felt that impulse a few times since and have obeyed it. Now I'm a grandfather, a survivor, but I don't understand the impulse much better than I did when I was twenty.

Thinking about all this, especially the accident in the red convertible, I am suddenly shocked to see a huge white tombstone straight ahead. It's a horribly gruesome piece of bad taste, about ten feet high, brilliantly white, and it says:

1879

TOMBSTONE

The Town Too Tough To Die

History

Health

Hospitality

I look alongside the road, but there are no small white crosses to mark where two young men died in 1957. The motor homes are speeding past, their drivers intent on getting to Tombstone to see the O.K. Corral. I guess they want to get a little history, health, and hospitality as quickly as possible without wasting too much time before they head on to the next tourist attraction—Bisbee. Or maybe they will skip Bisbee. It's not even a ghost town anyway. They are interested in history up to a point, but history has a way of being disappointing. Everybody dies in the end, although some deaths are much more interesting than others.

I turn onto Highway 80 and pass the sign advertising Boot Hill, remembering that the graveyard was moved from its original location to a spot beside the highway where it would be more convenient for the tourists. But I have been told that they didn't move the remains, just the more interesting and picturesque grave markers. I wonder what it would feel like to know that you are making your living from a fake graveyard. Probably about like being a poet. So onward and upward to Goose Flats. The town too tough to die is dead ahead.

8

I get a little cynical about Tombstone and its Wild West hype, and have to remind myself that Americans love ballyhoo. We always have and we always will. It takes different forms at different periods, but it's one of our national predilections. We love to be swindled, even when it's done clumsily and without finesse. We choose to believe in the dream even though we know, somehow, it's a lie. We cherish and reward our flimflam artists, those dream peddlers who can convince us of almost anything. By combining ballyhoo with history and emphasizing bloody violence—another of our national predilections—modern Tombstone has created an irresistible attraction.

In recent years our best flimflam artists seem to have come in the form of drawling evangelists whose dishonesty and greed know no bounds. And while religious swindles are probably almost as old as religion itself, this particular rash of flimflam, because of its enormous scale and its reliance on television, is a modern phenomenon. But the lure of the West has been creating suckers for many generations. In the mid-nineteenth century, starting in 1849, charlatans were quick to see the possibilities resulting from the discovery of gold in California. They organized companies and advertised that they would take men to the gold fields of California by one of the easy southern routes across Mexico, although no easy route to California existed. Thousands and thousands of eager, would-be gold miners signed up and paid large sums of money for what they were told would be a pleasant, safe trip to a land where they could pick up gold nuggets the size of hens' eggs with their bare hands.

The men were loaded onto often unseaworthy vessels that were chartered in New York or some other eastern seaport, and when the ships were too far out to sea to turn back, the men discovered that their leader and organizer had somehow neglected to get on board. When the travelers landed in some godforsaken little coastal frontier town on the Texas or Mexican Gulf Coast, or Vera Cruz, which was a pesthole of cholera and malaria, many of them, if they could afford it, had no alternative but to book passage on another unseaworthy vessel and return home. By then they realized that they could not stand up to the terribly difficult and dangerous overland journey to Mazatlán or San Blas, and even if they could, would not be able to afford the long sea voyage up the Pacific Coast to California and the gold fields. Others, who have come to be called Argonauts by historians, formed their own smaller companies, hired mules and *arrieros* or mule skinners, and set out for the dream. But between hostile Indians, Mexican bandits or *ladrones*, disease, and the rigors of the wild, mountainous country they had to cross, many were killed or died along the way.

The legend of the American West, the last frontier, still has its drawing power, but in spite of the hype and flimflam, which keeps a fake graveyard like Boot Hill crowded with tourists, there are some good things in Tombstone. Like ninety-three-year-old Nettie Fernley who plays piano six nights a week in the Lucky Cuss Bar. She really is ninety-three years old, and she really does play the piano. No flimflam there, although she is billed as "America's Oldest Professional Pianist." She is also Tombstone's Poet Laureate, but I don't know how official that title is.

There is another good thing about Tombstone in addition to its elderly piano player—its courthouse, which has been restored and serves as a historical museum run by the State Parks Board. I don't plan to stop in Tombstone, but I think I will swing over two blocks and drive down Toughnut Street just to get a good view of the courthouse, although I've seen it many times and spent some pleasant hours browsing through the museum. The highway runs down Fremont Street, fittingly named after the "great pathfinder," John C. Fremont, who was a pretty good flimflam artist himself. After he was found guilty of mutiny and was thrown out of the United States Army, he became Arizona's do-nothing and generally nonresident territorial governor.

Fremont Street was originally planned to be the main drag, but it didn't work out that way. The main drag is one block to the south, Allen Street, and even this late in the afternoon it is congested with motor homes, campers, and tourists hell-bent to see the O.K. Corral, the Crystal Palace Saloon, and the Bird Cage Theatre. In spite of local advertising, neither Lillian Russell, Lotta Crabtree, nor Jenny Lind ever appeared on the stage in Tombstone. But one entertainer who did appear there, Eddy Foy, said the Bird Cage Theatre should have been called the Coffin, which is what it resembles on the inside.

Toughnut Street, where the courthouse sits on a shady corner, is fairly quiet and navigable. The courthouse is a tall, two-story red brick charmer, with natural sandstone and white gingerbread trim, a tin roof, and a tiny widow's walk on top. It was completed in 1883, which means it is only thirteen years older than Nettie Fernley, although it has suffered far more from time, neglect, and the elements than she has. At least Nettie, as far as I can tell, has never had to be restored, and she looks far younger than her ninety-three years would suggest. But the courthouse has been brought back almost from the dead since the mid-1950s when the Tombstone Restoration Commission began to try to save it from destruction.

Although the Tombstone mines began to flood at the end of the 1880s and Tombstone began its long decline, it remained the County Seat of Cochise County until 1929, when the county seat was moved to Bisbee. The Tombstone courthouse was generally neglected until 1946 when somebody attempted to remodel it as a hotel. That venture quickly failed, and the building was deserted, a sad old beauty victimized by vandals and literally falling apart, until the Tombstone Restoration Commission took it in hand in 1955. In the meantime, Tombstone was becoming a tourist attraction of the first rank. In 1959, the courthouse was elevated to the status of a state park, and it was placed on the National Register of Historic Places in 1972. It seems to be out of danger now, spruced up and with its trim freshly painted, but it still needs work. Its eaves are badly water damaged, and some of the wood seems beyond repair.

Years ago I noticed a most curious thing about the outside of the building, which I never thought to ask anybody about until recently. It has little black lines painted all over the brickwork, as if someone had attempted to outline each of the bricks with a thin black line. But the placement of the lines doesn't correspond with that of the bricks. The horizontal lines follow the mortar lines, but the vertical lines usually divide the bricks in half. The effect is truly crazy. I had always assumed that this was the creative work of vandals, but recently I asked one of the state park employees about it. She told me what had happened, and with a perfectly straight face, although my perverted sense of humor caused me to laugh, and I found out that it is not a good idea to laugh when official employees of the state park bureau are explaining historical facts. But if we can't laugh at history from time to time, how could we bear it.

It seems that shortly after the courthouse was built, it proved to be too small for the legal needs of the burgeoning community, and the legal needs of Tombstone must have been considerable since one whole section of town, called Rotten Row, was devoted to nothing but lawyers' offices. The courthouse lacked space for a big enough jail, and the courtroom wasn't large enough to hold the crowds. So, in 1904, the citizens of Tombstone built an addition onto the rear of the courthouse, with space for a new courtroom upstairs and a jail below it. They tried hard to make the addition match the original building, and they succeeded. Only an architect would notice that the rear portion of the building was an addition.

As soon as it was finished, however, somebody noticed that the bricks in the addition didn't quite align with the bricks in the original structure, and this was a serious matter. The citizens of Tombstone wanted their courthouse to be correct and proper, like public buildings in the big cities in the East, and this small discrepancy bothered them. So somebody hit upon the idea of painting lines on the surface of the original part of the building to make it look as if the bricks aligned with those in the addition. Why they chose to paint lines on the original part of the building instead of the addition in the rear, and why they chose to use black paint when the mortar between the bricks was light gray, is anybody's guess. The result makes the major portion of the building look as if it had been assigned to a group of grade-school children as an art project. And the labor involved in painting all those thousands of little lines must have been staggering. But while the gamblers were gambling and the whores were whoring and the cowboys were shooting up everything in sight on Allen Street, one block away, somebody with a paint bucket and tiny brush was painting little black lines all over the outside of the beautiful Victorian courthouse. It was a result of the same principle that caused the good women of Tombstone to walk only on one side of Allen Street, studiously ignoring the fact that the other side of the street existed, since the whores walked on that side of the street.

Inside, the courthouse has been restored to a good semblance of its original dignity, with high ceilings, rich woodwork, and a graceful, circular staircase. There are touches of tourist-trap bad taste from time to time, like the gallows of obviously recent vintage which has been set up in the courtyard, but in general the building is a pleasant place to spend some time, and it isn't crowded. I've always enjoyed the museum, especially the photographs. Colonel Greene stares down from the wall—portly, jowly, and looking dreadfully rich and proper. In the extensive printed material beneath the photograph, there is no mention of the fact that he was once tried for the murder of James Burnett, nor that the trial took place in the next room, about ten feet away. There are photographs of several other cattle barons, including Colin Cameron, who was found guilty in 1887 of fencing public lands and had his ranch in the San Rafael Valley reduced from 170,243 acres to 17,353 acres. He must have been fencing quite a bit of public land. He sold what was left to Colonel Greene in 1905. There is also a photograph of Henry Clay Hooker, who got his start by herding five hundred turkeys to the gold fields of Nevada in 1872. That alone, it seems to me, is enough of an accomplishment to merit having his picture in the museum.

As I drive slowly past the courthouse, a man in a state park uniform is taking down the flag in front of the building. It's closing time. I nod to the building, and the man nods back. "Sleep well tonight, old girl," I think to myself, "beneath the black lines of your makeup. You knew what went on on both sides of Allen Street. You have earned your rest. And may tomorrow's tourists treat you with the respect you deserve."

A couple of blocks past the courthouse, on my right, is a low building that sits by itself with a ravine behind it. It is closed up, and looks as if it has been that way for several years. The sign says "1880 SILVER MINE TOURS." I have to stop and take a look, although it's not very interesting looking. I get out of the van and go around the building to the back. There it is—a large, metal gate, well chained and padlocked, and beyond it a hole in the side of the hill that looks like it might be the black hole of Calcutta. Just as I remember it, only now overgrown with weeds. It's the scene of a family joke, a two-family joke—one of those incidents which was unpleasant at the time but has provided hours of pleasure with the retelling. Ah, Mrs. Strong and Dewey and Gob, we remember you well.

It was 1965. Dr. Harry Robins had joined the English Department faculty of the University of Arizona the previous year, and he had brought with him from Illinois his remarkably bright and artistic family, his wife, Mary Louise, and their three children, Hal, Martha, and Jeff. My wife and I and our son Brad quickly became friends with the Robins family. We spent a great deal of time together and later were to spend a part of a summer together on the beach at Mazatlán. In 1965 we decided to spend a day in Tombstone. I guess we thought it would be an educational experience, and it turned out to be even more educational than we expected.

Somebody had recently begun running underground tours through the Goodenough Mine, which honeycombs the mesa directly below the town of Tombstone. Harry and I and the children decided to take the tour while the ladies prowled through the tourist shops. We didn't stop to think what confinement in an underground mine might do to two rambunctious little boys like Brad and Jeff, age seven and five, but we were soon to find out. At the hour for the next tour, we waited outside a large metal gate—the gate I am looking at now after twenty-five years—and our tour guide met us. The underground tours hadn't caught on very well, and we were the only members of our tour. That should have told us something, but it didn't.

Our tour guide introduced herself as Mrs. Strong and informed us that she and her husband were the proprietors of the operation and served as its guides. She unlocked the gate, escorted us through it, and then carefully locked it again. Mrs. Strong seemed to know everything there was to know concerning the mine and its history, mining operations in general, and the early history of Tombstone, and she intended to tell us all of it. She had a stentorian voice, which she used to great effect in the echoing tunnels and caverns, punctuating key phrases with increased volume, and often repeating things to make sure we would remember them. We did. During the next hour-and-a-half—which seemed like a week—while the two youngest of our children became restless at first, then troublesome, and then downright suicidal with boredom, Mrs. Strong enlightened us. She enjoyed her work.

I have since heard Harry, who can do a comic imitation of anyone, render parts of Mrs. Strong's spiel dozens of times. She told us about the mule "whose name was Dewey, that's D-E-W-E-Y, Dewey," who was pulling a wagon down the street in front of the firehouse one day when the ground suddenly collapsed and Dewey, wagon and all, plunged into one of the mine tunnels below. But Dewey, plucky mule that he was, survived. She explained in minute detail how the mining operation worked, and that the ore was called "gob, that's G-O-B, gob. Now remember so you can tell your friends that the ore was called G-O-B, gob." Harry whispered to me something about one of Dante's circles of Purgatory, but I was too busy trying to control Brad to pay much attention.

Although it had been provided with a few lights, the abandoned mine was a frightening labyrinth and a very dangerous place for children. Sometimes we inched along a narrow ledge with a sheer drop on one side, and we passed vertical shafts that were dark invitations to disaster. I had a firm grip on Brad's sweaty little hand, although at our frequent stops during which Mrs. Strong went on and on with her ear-splitting voice, he kept trying to get away. But Jeff was the biggest problem. Hal had him by the hand, but it was almost impossible to keep hold of the squirming, impatient five-year-old. At one point, Mrs. Strong led us onto a rickety wooden bridge suspended above a huge cavern, which seemed to extend about one hundred feet below. There she stopped and began one of her harangues. I tightened my grip on Brad's hand and watched Jeff inching toward the edge of the bridge while Hal tried desperately to hold onto him. I was suffering from vertigo. Mrs. Strong blasted on, repeating key phrases for effect, completely unaware of our growing apprehension and discomfort. She was having a wonderful time. Harry was making a heroic effort to look interested in what she was saying, but Hal and I had our hands too full to worry about being polite. Suddenly Jeff wrenched loose from Hal's grip and in a flash was dangling far over the cavern below. Harry grabbed him just in time. Mrs. Strong continued, oblivious and rapt in her performance.

Constrained again, Jeff began to vent his annoyance, with loud complaints and repeated pleadings to get out of the mine. Brad joined him. Mrs. Strong simply raised her volume a few decibels and continued above the caterwauling of the children. We were so far into the miles and miles of crisscrossing shafts and chambers that we knew we couldn't find our way out without Mrs. Strong's help, and she had no intention of giving up on a captive audience until she had finished what she had to say, and she had lots more to say. Harry's polite attempt to show an interest in what she was saying had turned into a frozen, glassy stare. His face twitched convulsively. He shouted threats of punishment at Jeffrey. It did no good. I had the same luck with Brad.

Finally, we got off the bridge and wound our way through more tunnels, past more cavernous rooms and vertical shafts. We had no idea which direction we were going, but up above somewhere were the streets of Tombstone and the blessed sunshine. Up above somewhere the birds were probably singing, but all we could hear was the whining of the children and Mrs. Strong's voice, which was driving us crazy. At last we could tell that we were nearing the end of the labyrinth. We could see sunlight ahead at the entrance of the tunnel, and beyond it was the metal gate through which we had been escorted into hell. Hal could hold Jeff no longer. The child pulled loose and lunged for freedom, with Brad right behind him. When we emerged from the tunnel, Jeff was banging on the metal gate and screaming, "Let me out! Let me out!" He was expressing our combined sentiments. But Mrs. Strong was not about to unlock the gate until she had finished her parting remarks, which were extensive, and which she delivered over Jeff's and Brad's complaints and repeated demands for freedom. When she unlocked the gate, I bolted with Hal and the children, but Harry, gentleman to the core, paused to thank her for a lovely and very thorough tour. There must have been more than a little irony in his voice, but as I looked back I could see that she was delighted. We were in a semi-hysterical state when we found the ladies waiting for us and wondering why the tour had taken so long. I decided that if tourists had to work that hard, I didn't want to be one.

Today, Tombstone survives by exploiting certain dramatic and often bloody elements of its past, while much of its present goes on all but unnoticed, at least by most tourists. The Contention Mine, which was abandoned for decades, was revived in the 1970s and is now operated by PBR Minerals, Inc. And there are many other active silver or gold mines in the area. Several of them can be seen from the Charleston Road just west of town. Last year I stopped to read the sign on a locked gate that blocked the road to one of them, evidently a gold mine. The sign said: ANANCO LTD. METALLURGICAL FACILITY. Nearby was another sign which said: SECURITY SYSTEMS EMPLOYED HERE ARE POTENTIALLY LETHAL. I didn't ask to whom? And I didn't try to go in.

About a week ago I noticed an article in the Tucson paper concerning Tombstone's water supply. Tombstone has two wells that supply it with drinking water. One, which supplies about 25 percent of the town's water, has just been discovered to be polluted with mercury. Mercury is used in the process of extracting silver from ore. The well is near the Contention Mine, and the water contains twice the amount of mercury permitted by federal standards. Mercury accumulates in all parts of the human body, causing nervous-system and kidney damage and resulting in, as the paper said, "bizarre" health problems, including mental disorders, depression, and breathing problems. It is a very real threat to the population of Tombstone, now just under two thousand, and it makes me wonder about the strange behavior of some of the people who lived in the stamp-mill towns along the San Pedro in the 1880s, long before such danger was recognized. Maybe some of those ornery characters, like James Burnett, were just sick and depressed because mercury had accumulated in their bodies.

During the earliest days of the Tombstone mining camp, water was brought in by wagons. Then, for a few years, it was piped in from Sycamore Springs in the Dragoon Mountains, seven miles away. The danger of fire was so great in the hastily built boomtown that barrels of water were kept on the ridgepoles of many of the buildings. In case of fire, the residents shot holes in the barrels, but it didn't prove to be a very effective method of controlling fires. The lack of a good water supply was a factor in both of Tombstone's disastrous fires. The first, in June of 1881, destroyed four blocks of the business district, which was quickly rebuilt—one visitor said it was rebuilt in two weeks—but not much improved. Less than a year later, in May, another fire burned down the same area. After that fire, the citizens of Tombstone rebuilt with more durable construction materials and took steps to obtain a better and more reliable water supply.

They contracted with a New York piano manufacturer named Haley, who was then living in Tombstone, to construct a pipeline to Tombstone from the Huachuca Mountains, twenty-three miles away and fifteen hundred feet higher on the other side of the San Pedro River. Soldiers from Ft. Huachuca guarded the materials and construction crews from the Apaches while the pipeline was being built. That basic system, using the force of gravity, is still in use, but over the years it has been augmented by two wells in the Tombstone Mountains, one of which is now polluted with mercury.

Unlike most of the mining towns of the Southwest, which simply grew up where the mines were no matter how unsuitable for a town the terrain happened to be, the site of Tombstone was deliberately chosen and laid out with broad, straight streets, although there was much confusion over property ownership for many years. With the exception of the lack of a water supply, it was a good choice. The mining community was first located at Watervale, near the Lucky Cuss Mine, about two miles from its present site. But the people knew there was enough silver under the Tombstone Mountains to last for a long time, and they didn't anticipate that the mines would flood from underground. They wanted a permanent town which they felt would grow into one of the major cities of the West—as it did for a brief period— and they needed room for expansion. About the only level ground in the area was at Goose Flats, a mesa above the Goodenough Mine, and so they moved the community there. From the aesthetic standpoint it was a smart move. Tombstone has a spacious, airy feeling, and it is high enough to provide a remarkable view to the north and east, where the Dragoon Mountains form a long phalanx of ever-changing colors.

Highway 80 leads southeast out of town and down the slopes of the Tombstones, which are actually a lower extension of the Mule Mountains. The saddle connecting the two ranges is a particularly bleak and barren stretch of country, supporting little but widely spaced grease-wood, cholla, and an occasional mesquite. The soil is pale and bare between clumps of greasewood, even after the recent rains, and in strong contrast with a narrow strip along either side of the road which is rank with grass about two feet high and vivid with wildflowers. At the fences on either side of the road the vegetation stops abruptly, and barren, desiccated land begins. The cows live on the other side of the fences, although I can't see any at the moment. It's hard to imagine what they can find to live on, unless they can eat greasewood. They've already eaten everything else. Or perhaps they have learned to live on the view, of which there is more than enough to spare.

This landscape was created by violence on a seismic scale, and re-cently enough that the results of violence are still everywhere appar-ent. Brunckow Hill off to the west, which is often mistakenly identified on maps as Bronco Hill but was named after a man and not a horse, is a beautifully symmetrical example of the top of a volcano, as are the Charleston Hills, mostly buried in their own debris and in soil washed down by erosion. Like icebergs, only their tips are visible. And all around me is evidence of block faulting on an enormous scale, great chunks of land tilted at severe angles with their strata, once layers of sediment at the bottom of an inland sea, running uphill. Sustained vio-lence and cataclysm created this landscape, and off to the west runs the San Pedro River with its broad, serene valley looking as peaceful this afternoon as anything I can imagine. For aeons the river has been doing the best it can to erase and cover all scars, but above it the land still shows dramatic evidence of slow, steady pressures and sudden explosions that have left it with hills which are volcanic cones and mountains that have buckled, fallen, and twisted.

Rolling down the slope that connects the Tombstone Mountains with the Mule Mountains, I come over a rise and suddenly there is the view which has always thrown me into a crazy, inexplicable state of euphoria. Here it is, the point at which I know, I really know, I am going back to Bisbee. Or perhaps to Bisbee and beyond. Perhaps I will just keep going southward across the border, just a few miles away, and into another world, another life, where I can be the person I have always wanted to be. Even now, after all these years, the temptation is strong. I can see up the broad basin of the San Pedro far into Mexico, with range after range of blue mountains outlined against one another along the valley corridor. It's no wonder, I think, that Coronado chose to come down this valley in search of the Seven Cities of Gold. The valley seems to stretch on forever, and in the hazy distances anything is possible.

This is the point at which I feel the pull of Mexico, when I am looking south down a broad valley lined with mountains on either side, more mountains than I could ever get to know in a lifetime. I can see the stretch of green ribbon that was once the San Rafael del Valle land grant, and beyond it, south of Hereford which doesn't exist anymore, the basin called Miracle Valley. Although I know that Miracle Valley was named by a modern religious sect whose members believe they can perform miracles, the valley itself looks like a miracle from here. East of the river, beyond the Mule Mountains and south of the border are the San Josés and Los Ajos—the Garlic Mountains. How can one help but be attracted to a culture so attuned to the sensory that it named mountain ranges after cinnamon, like the Canelos, and garlic, like the Ajos.

Far in the distance on the other side of the border, the San Pedro comes into being, where it collects the waters of its intermittent tributaries, creeks with names like El Sauz and La Coja (The Cripple). The corridor broadens out into low hills completely surrounded with mountains. South of the Huachucas are the Mariquitas, and south of them the Elenitas, where Colonel Greene developed his copper mine at Cananea. From where I am, the distances are staggering, romantic, deceptive. I feel the need to lose myself in those distances, in that baked land of chaotic hills and valleys, of tiny villages and sprawling collections of tin, wood, and adobe shacks which make up widely separated collective farms called *ejidos*. But I know I couldn't survive there for any long period of time. My delicate Anglo body is too much accustomed to pure water, conditioned air, and the comforts of suburbia. I couldn't survive the unmitigated heat, the dust, the distances. I know it's too late for me . . . and yet . . . maybe someday. Maybe I will give in to the dream that has haunted me for more than thirty years. A long time ago I wrote about it, and the dream hasn't changed. Only my ability to live it has lessened. In the poem "Mexico," I said:

something hits me like a shovel
and I am stunned into believing
anything is possible

. . . .

and suddenly I know
everything I need is waiting for me
south of here in another country
and I have been walking through empty
rooms and talking to furniture

I've lived in several Mexican cities for limited periods but never out in the country or in a very small town, which is what I've always wanted to do, where I probably couldn't survive without creating around me the comforts I am accustomed to. What is the attraction? I'm not sure. But I think it has more to do with the culture and the people than with the landscape.

The poem "Mexico" begins with my seeing Scorpio on the southern horizon, holding in one claw "the top / of a mountain in Mexico." It ends with this:

I never find what I am looking for
and each time I return older
with my ugliness intact
but with the knowledge that if it isn't there
in the darkness under Scorpio
it isn't anywhere

I guess what I am looking for is some quality of soul that is foreign to an Anglo culture. And I guess that I know, deep down somewhere, the only way to find it is to forgo my Anglo culture entirely, and I can't do that. To do without my own culture for long periods of time sends me into cultural shock. I would not make a very good exile or expatriate. I always retreat home "with my ugliness intact." But the dream remains. I know which direction I must go if I am ever to find it—south into Mexico—but it wouldn't be into urban Mexico, which has allowed itself to adopt a veneer of the worst elements of Anglo culture. It would be some very small, remote place where life goes on more slowly and deliberately, without the confusion or the comforts of the city. It's a romantic, impractical dream for a gringo, but at least it's not a dream based on greed, not a dream of great wealth or power. It would be presumptuous of me to dream of saving my soul. I would be satisfied just to find out for sure that I had one. And this view up the San Pedro Valley, which seems to go on forever, makes me suddenly aware of what a terrible thing it is not to be sure.

Off to the west, under white-and-silver cumulus clouds like floating cathedrals, are the Huachucas, rising abruptly from the valley floor and so magnificent that I can think of nothing but clichés. Closer, about two-thirds of the way across the valley and a little to the south, is a patch of walking rain, a thin purple veil not quite touching the ground. If I look hard at the base of the Huachucas toward their northern end, I can just make out some indication of Ft. Huachuca and Sierra Vista. From here they seem tiny and nonthreatening, but I know that the water pumped up over there is destroying the river below and the band of green that runs along it. Highway 90 comes almost straight across the valley from Sierra Vista, a thin, fragile thread lost in all this distance. It joins the highway I am on just before I curve to the east and start the long climb up to Mule Mountain Pass, entrance to Bisbee and the Sulphur Springs Valley beyond it.

The road follows Banning Creek, often dry but running a sizable stream now after the rains. It's a small mountain stream, wild and gurgling, hurrying toward its death in the desert. If any of the water makes it to the San Pedro, it has a good chance this time of year of making it to the Gila, but the Gila disappears into a series of irrigation canals less than thirty miles below where the San Pedro empties into it. There's no way any of the water from Banning Creek is going to make it to the Colorado River, and even if it did, it would be diverted for irrigation long before it reached the Gulf of California. The channel through which steamboats once chugged from the Gulf of California to Yuma or Ehrenberg or beyond is dry and has been for many years.

The road has a steeper grade now, heading up toward Mule Mountain Pass, and Blue Boy leans into it. Soon we will pass the site of the old Banning Toll Station, a private enterprise that was the source of much resentment on the part of early travelers going to and from Bisbee. This must have been quite a road in those days. Even in the late 1950s it was a fairly wild, narrow, twisting mountain highway leading over the pass, but it has been tamed since then to a broad, steady climb, with easy curves and no dips. And it doesn't go all the way over the pass anymore. While we were living in Bisbee in 1958, Mule Mountain Tunnel was completed, going straight through the mountain and making it possible to avoid the last few miles of steep grades and sharp curves. But I'm not going through the tunnel. I know where the old road cuts off from this highway, and it's still maintained, more or less, because of the few houses near the top of the mountain. I'm going over the pass, the way I first entered Bisbee thirty-three years ago, and if Blue Boy doesn't like it, that's just too bad. When he finds out I am serious, he will gear down and do just fine.

I still love this mountain road, although it isn't half the road it used to be. I've driven it in all kinds of weather, but each time is the first time, and it never ceases to excite me. One winter night before the tunnel was completed, my wife and I and our son, then about eight months old, were returning home from Benson when we found out that this road was closed because of ice and a blizzard. I called the Highway Patrol in Benson and explained that I was a schoolteacher from Bisbee and I had to get back in time for school the next morning. In those days, schoolteachers in the small communities of Southern Arizona had a certain amount of local status—I don't know if they still do or not. The man at the Highway Patrol headquarters asked me if I had tire chains. Of course I didn't have tire chains, I lived in Southern Arizona. But the man was very accommodating, since I was a schoolteacher and all. He arranged to have a patrol car meet us at the base of the mountain and lead us over the pass.

It was an exciting ride at five to ten miles an hour on solid ice, and it was snowing so hard I could barely make out the red glow of the taillights on the patrol car a few feet ahead of us. Automobile seat belts were not yet in use, and infant restraints were unheard of. My wife sat beside me, pale but silent, clutching our tiny son in her arms. From time to time, when we slid dangerously close to the drop on the right-hand side of the road, the passenger side, she gripped the baby so hard he would let out a wail. But we made it over the pass, and the baby didn't seem any the worse for the wear.

Now the drive up Banning Creek shows me its summer face. The stream is running and the flowers beside the road are shouting, "Look at me! Look at me!" Baileya, the bright desert marigold that seems to bloom when all else fails, has been providing color along the road since I left Tombstone and so have the soft white prickle poppies and tall sunflowers. At lower elevations most of the late summer wildflowers bloom yellow or gold, in big splashes, but as I climb, many of the flowers show softer shades of pink and lavender, also in large, dramatic patches. Big stands of lavender many-flowered gilia lean over the guard rail along the highway, each plant alive with bees. On the bank just above, gatuño is at the peak of its airy elegance. Gatuño is a low-bush relative of the mimosa and a member of the pea family. It has spikes like brushes, each about three inches long and covered with lavender-pink feathery filaments, which are the long stamens of otherwise inconspicuous blossoms, lavish and delicate at the same time. As the blossoms age, the stamens turn white, beginning at the far end of the brush. Many of the ones I am seeing are half lavender and half white. They look good enough to eat.

Here and there on the steep bank that comes down on my left are vivid spots of orange or bright red where both skyrocket and Indian paintbrush put in their bids as the showiest things around. This is the late summer or after-the-monsoons display. The early spring crop of annuals is even more spectacular but less dependable, since a dry winter, which is not uncommon, can mean almost no wildflowers in the spring, while the monsoons can usually be depended on, even in dry years, for enough rain to trigger the late-summer flowers. Many of the spring wildflowers, like baileya, bloom right on through until November.

I am climbing a mountain island which rises above the desert. It isn't one of the more spectacular desert islands in terms of its height, like the Catalina or Chiricahua mountains provide, but it is a distinct island nonetheless. The elevation of Mule Mountain Pass is only slightly more than 6,000 feet, but that is between 3,000 and 4,000 feet above the desert floor, and every thousand-foot rise in elevation is the equivalent of moving three hundred miles toward the north pole, with equivalent changes in flora and fauna. When we drive into the Catalina Mountains from Tucson to Mt. Lemmon, a trip of about forty miles, we pass through five distinct habitats—desert, grassland, chaparral, woodland, and forest. If Mt. Lemmon were 2,000 feet higher, it would have a zone of tundra at its summit. One day last summer I drove to Mt. Lemmon when it was 106 degrees warm in Tucson. The temperature at the ski resort on Mt. Lemmon was a blessed 65 degrees.

The Mule Mountains are not nearly as high as the Catalinas, but they are an island to the extent that the desert floor around them forms a barrier to the plants and creatures that live only in cooler temperatures and require slightly more water, just as the sea is a barrier to many of the plants and creatures which live on islands. I left the desert floor a few miles out of Tucson and have been driving mostly through grassland. Now the ascent to Mule Mountain Pass will take me out of grassland, through chaparral, and into the lower edge of an oak-pine woodland at about the elevation where the lower Sonoran life zone meets the upper Sonoran life zone, where the two overlap and the plant and animal life is a complex mixture of both.

As I began to climb, the predominant growth was the ubiquitous greasewood and some cacti, especially cholla and prickly pear. Now, beside the creek, I see the first patch of sycamores with their ghostly white trunks and big, rattling leaves. Arizona sycamores signal that I am entering a desert-mountain canyon and make me think of all the beautiful canyons in Southern Arizona where they thrive, often leaning out over a stream and providing dense shade—Sabino, Peppersauce, Arivaipa, Madera, and many more. For us, the desert rats, these canyons are enchanted, inviting places since they provide water and shade, the two things we crave.

Arizona sycamores don't usually stray far from the bed of a stream, and they are sociable trees, often growing close to one another, at least within earshot; and they always talk to one another, either quietly or with great excitement and animation, as the wind moves through their leaves. And they lean toward one another, reaching out with their pale arms as if to make sure that others of their kind are near. They are great trees for climbing and seem to invite tree houses. There is a large, old sycamore in the picnic area at Madera Canyon that is so eminently climbable it often looks as if it had sprouted children. I have seen it supporting as many as fifteen clambering urchins at the same time, one of which was usually my son, as if it were infested with the juvenile form of Homo sapiens. Fortunately, they don't eat it, or at least enough of it to do much damage.

Now the oaks begin to appear on the sides of the hills and rapidly become the predominant growth, along with some mesquite and palo-verde. The oaks, with their comfortable round contours, soften the harshness of the rocky outcrops and steep inclines of the hills. But the oaks are only part of the picture at this transition elevation where grassland vegetation shades into chaparral. And this is, after all, Southern Arizona, a land that does not like soft, rounded contours, a land which prefers jagged peaks and sharp, spiky plants with thorns or spines or leaves that can sever an artery. Various examples in my personal system of plant taxonomy, things-that-stick-straight-up, are well represented here, not only by yucca and agave, but by sotol, which seems to be everywhere, marching up the sides of the hills like flag-poles without flags, or fighting for space beside the road and down near the creek.

Sotol, or *dasylirion wheeleri*, is one of the most common plants of this region at this elevation. From a rosette of sharp, slender leaves about three feet long, it sends up a single stalk sometimes as high as seventeen feet. The stalk grows fat with thousands of tiny greenish-white blossoms that turn to the color of ripe wheat when past their prime, and the stalk remains stiffly erect for months. There is nothing soft, shrinking, or subtle about the sotol in bloom, but it has considerable dignity and a stark beauty that makes it a fit companion of the yucca and agave, with which it is often confused. Sotol is actually more closely related to the yucca than to agave, since it is a member of the lily family. The toothed leaves at the base of the stalk are often used to make "desert spoons," stiff contraptions used in exceedingly ugly floral displays. The fibers in those same leaves were, and still sometimes are, used by natives of the area to weave handsome mats and baskets. Like agave, the heart of the sotol has traditionally been used as a food or as the source of a powerful alcoholic drink.

It's a good time of day to see the canyon, with the low-slanting sun on the stone cliffs along one side of the road where the mountain has been cut back. The stones range from tan to gold to ocher, with patches of pink and terracotta and blue-green where various minerals have been leached out by rainwater. The stones glow, and the hazy light in the canyon is golden, softening the silhouettes of sotol and agave. Along the creek is a thick green screen of walnut, desert willow, mesquite, and desert broom. On the other side of it I can see an occasional house half hidden in the foliage. This side of the creek is a solid patch of lavender gilia to the edge of the road.

About two-thirds of the way up to the summit, I begin to see thick clumps of yet another small tree between the road and the creek, very green and tropical looking. At first I think it's sumac, but it's too green, too lush. Then I remember. I'm almost to Bisbee and this must be ailanthus, even here. It must have escaped from Bisbee and climbed over the pass somehow, and it is now spreading down Banning Creek on its way to who knows where. If there is one thing Bisbee has plenty of besides steep hills, it's ailanthus. I asked three long-time residents of Bisbee to identify it, and they all gave me the same name. "Oh, that's what we call 'cancer tree' because it spreads like cancer." If I had pointed out to any of them that in its native China ailanthus is called "the tree of heaven," it would probably have produced a grim laugh. It is clear that those who live in Bisbee today do not care much for the ailanthus. Bisbee, for the most part, was built on almost solid rock. It's water, sewer, and gas lines have been laid close to the surface, sometimes on the surface, and the roots of the ailanthus play hell with them. But ailanthus has given Bisbee what it desperately needed, or at least what those from less arid regions thought it needed—lush, green shade and heavy foliage.

It's amazing to compare photographs of Bisbee taken at about the turn of the century with photographs taken recently. In the older photos, everything is bare, stark, and bleak looking. There are no softening shadows of trees or thick foliage. The miners' houses range up the sides of the hills on narrow terraces so that, as an old Bisbee saying goes, "you can stand on your front porch and spit down your neighbor's chimney." The native growth of oak and mesquite had been destroyed for firewood, fenceposts, and building materials. Nothing shielded one house from the next, and nothing gave relief from the barren, sun-blasted, dusty look of the landscape. But that was before cancer trees. Now there are parts of Bisbee that are almost like a jungle.

Over the years, inhabitants of Bisbee have introduced many non-indigenous plants to their mile-high desert island, like the morning glory, which has spread to such an extent that I think it is now all that is holding some of the houses onto their hillside sites. Introducing any nonindigenous plant or creature into an island habitat is potentially dangerous. In the case of ailanthus it was about like dropping a live coal into a keg of dynamite. Ailanthus loves rocky soil and tight, con-stricted places, and it grows with amazing speed. It has been known to grow out of cracks in city sidewalks or concrete building founda-tions. It spreads by sending out suckers. Bisbee, with its rocky hills and outcroppings, stone retaining walls, and mild climate was just the place for ailanthus; and like the people of its native China, it has been defeated in places but never conquered. The tree of heaven has truly blessed Bisbee with green shade, and the residents of Bisbee, almost universally, curse it and call it "cancer tree." It is to Bisbee what the wildly spreading tamarisk is to Tucson, a tree introduced because it grew fast and provided shade.

Because it comes from China, the ever-spreading ailanthus tree in Bisbee makes me think of a curious aspect of Bisbee's history. After the Civil War, when the rich mineral deposits in the Western Territories were beginning to be systematically exploited, Chinese immigrants were coming to the West in great numbers. Some came as part of the labor pool that built the railroads. Others simply came, usually walk-ing cross-country with their possessions on their backs. The impact of so much "pauper" labor on western mining communities was seen as a threat to Anglo-American miners and was met with swift, defensive measures. Starting in the California gold fields and spreading through-out all Western states, mining communities passed statutes forbidding the use of foreign and particularly Chinese labor. This attitude was re-flected in a federal statute which stated that mineral lands were open to location only by citizens of the United States or those who were about to become citizens.

Bisbee has always been a town of extremes, and it took an extreme stand on this issue. Although the industrious Chinese had settled in

Tombstone where they ran laundries and bath houses, and a good many were quite successful just across the Mexican border where they grew vegetable gardens, no Chinese were allowed to settle in Bisbee. In fact, tradition has it that there was a law stating that no one of Chinese ancestry could spend the night in Bisbee, and none did until 1934 when a Chinese member of a visiting baseball team stayed the night. The Chinese truck-garden farmers from across the border were allowed to peddle their produce in Bisbee during the day but had to be out of town before the sun set. It has been said that this law, which was probably unwritten, was designed to protect the laundresses of Bisbee from competition with the Chinese. Laundresses in Bisbee were often the wives or widows of miners who had been disabled or killed in mine accidents, and the mining community felt some responsibility for their welfare.

But the economic protection of the Bisbee laundresses, after whom a hill in Bisbee is still called Laundry Hill, was only a small facet of an attitude endemic to the Western mining regions. Mexicans, for instance, were not allowed to work underground in the Bisbee mines, and when they were hired to work above ground, they were paid far less than were the Anglos who did the same work. This rule was based on ethnicity rather than citizenship. Bisbee was "a White Man's mining camp," and the mines gave precedence to workers from the British Isles, especially from Wales or the county of Cornwall. Chinese, at the bottom of the pecking order, were not even allowed to spend the night in town.

I doubt that ailanthus was imported by any of the Chinese who passed hastily through Bisbee, although it might have been introduced into their gardens across the border and then brought into Bisbee. But somebody introduced it, and something Chinese took root in Bisbee and stayed, even on Laundry Hill. It is now one of the major elements of Bisbee's plant population. I can imagine an upper-class Bisbee matron of about 1915 saying, "You know how it is with those Chinese trees—they spread so." In fact the Chinese tree of heaven is so widespread and common in Bisbee today that many Bisbeeites consider it indigenous.

As I climb, the growth continues to change. I am beginning to see more and more high-country plants with which I have little familiarity in recent years, but these are mixed with old friends from lower elevations, particularly the juniper and alligator juniper, which always looks old no matter how old it is. And there is the first large stand of manzanita, indicative of the chaparral community of plants. It grows in impenetrable thickets almost as tall as a human, but it does wonders for a landscape of jagged stone outcroppings and stiff plants that stick straight up. It has lovely, rounded green contours, and it stays green all year long.

Chaparral, as a community of plants, is much more common along the West Coast from Baja to Northern California, where there are more than forty species of manzanita and they are sometimes called bearberry or kinnikinnick. There is a strange relationship between chaparral and fire. Chaparral is a term for a large group of associated shrubs that grow fairly low and bushy, forming a dense canopy which is explosively flammable, although the manzanita is said to be highly fire-resistant, and many other plants in a chaparral community are particularly adapted to survive a fire. In fact, the seeds of some chaparral plants cannot germinate until they have been scorched by fire or unless they have been exposed on barren soil with no shade. Botanists say that without a fire most chaparral growth begins to die out after a period of about fifty years.

In Arizona we have only three species of manzanita and the most common, which I am seeing here, is greenleaf. It's a truly beautiful plant, with nearly round, small, rubbery leaves, and it is very green indeed, especially in contrast with its glowing, dark red branches, which look as if they had been polished to a high luster. It usually grows to about four feet high and forms a canopy something like an umbrella. In the spring it produces small reddish bell-shaped blossoms hanging in clusters. They turn into dark red fruit that resemble tiny apples, and hence the name of the plant, which means "little apple" in Spanish. I always associate manzanita with Black Oak Cemetery in the Canelo Hills south of Sonoita, where it forms a magnificent backdrop for the natural stones and boulders used as tombstones.

There's my turnoff, unmarked, on the left, but the road is paved, although in bad shape. It goes over the summit while the new highway continues lower down and goes through the tunnel. The growth is thicker up here, and the desert plants are rapidly giving way to chaparral and even larger woodland trees. At the summit I am directly above the tunnel, and the view to the west is incredible. All the way down to the San Pedro Valley and beyond. At the summit, I pull off the road at a little viewpoint strewn with litter. Next to a small Apache pine, which indicates what the growth would be like if the Mule Mountains were a little higher, I see a concrete marker I have never noticed before. It says:

CONTINENTAL DIVIDE

ELEVATION 6,030

Road Constructed by Prison Labor A.D. 1913–14

George W. R. Hunt, Gov.

The elevation is about right, I would guess, but this can't possibly be the Continental Divide unless they have moved it recently without telling anyone. Government bureaus can be very high-handed, but I can't believe they would just up and move the Continental Divide without informing the public, and when last heard of it was about fifty miles east of here on the other side of the New Mexico state line. An error of fifty miles, even in the wide open spaces of Arizona, is difficult to overlook. I'll bet there's a good story behind that one, but I don't know what it is.

The rest of the information on the marker is probably accurate enough. George W. R. Hunt, a fat, bald liberal Democrat with several chins and a great, shaggy moustache, was elected governor of the State of Arizona two months before there was a State of Arizona. He was called "a socialist" and "very illiterate" by his political opponents. He took office on Valentine's Day, 1912, the day Arizona officially became a state with the signing of a proclamation by President Taft. The signing had been scheduled for the previous day, but it was delayed one day because of the superstitious significance of the number thirteen.

Hunt was a self-made businessman who had started as a waiter, and he was politically astute. On the day he was to be sworn in as governor, he made his highly touted "Economy Walk," a matter of strolling a few blocks from his hotel in Phoenix to the Capitol, accompanied, of course, by members of the press and several political associates. It signaled that he was a simple man of the people and that he was

203 ❖

frugal, and it was written up in the *New York Times* as a walk of "two miles." From then on Hunt was chauffeured in an automobile that cost the taxpayers the scandalous sum of three thousand dollars plus three hundred dollars a month to operate, but his reputation for simplicity and frugality was already established.

Hunt's two major campaign promises had been that he would clean out the Corporation Commission, making it answerable to the public, and that he would build highways throughout the state. If he kept the first promise, it wasn't too noticeable, but he did improve the roads in Arizona, mostly by using convict labor, which was not unusual in those days. Getting from one place to another had always been a major problem in the Arizona Territory, even after the automobile came into use, and before that it had been pure misery by any means but the railroad.

From here, looking west toward the San Pedro Valley, I can see two roads and the remains of two others that make their way up the steep draw. Directly below me, Highway 80, which I turned off of to come over Mule Mountain Pass, disappears into the tunnel. Winding along the hills on the north side of the draw is the road I have come up, now called the old road. Below it and somewhat parallel to it I can see the intermittent remnants of a still older road, very narrow but paved. I suspect that was the road first constructed by convict labor in 1913–14, since it would have crossed what somebody thought was the Continental Divide at about where I am standing, near the concrete marker. But plummeting down the south side of the draw is a section of an unpaved road which loses itself in rock slides and chaparral. This, I think, must have been the original road that linked Bisbee, in its earliest days, with Tombstone and the railhead at Fairbank. My God! What a trip that must have been. The road doesn't seem to have bothered much with switchbacks; it just plunged down the mountain at a steep angle. I wonder how many teams careened over the edge of that one and wound up in the gulch hundreds of feet below in a tangle of harness, dead animals, and human bodies.

Between the establishment of the first smelter in Bisbee in 1880 and the arrival of the railroad in Bisbee in 1889, a hundred tons of copper and supplies were moved over that road daily in huge freight wagons drawn by teams of twenty mules. I can imagine one of the wagons as it hurtled down the hill, brakes screaming, driver cursing, and the wagon threatening at every moment to run over the mules or careen off into space. The skill and daring of those muleskinners and their intelligent little animals, all of whom risked their lives every day on that road, is beyond calculation. But freighting was as important to the mine operation as digging the ore out of the mountain, and it was expensive. It cost seven dollars a ton to haul the copper ingots, called "pigs," over that dreadful road to Fairbank, and it was the cost of such freighting that eventually turned the Phelps Dodge Corporation into a builder of railroads on a grand scale.

In fact, in the earliest infancy of the yet-to-be-developed Copper Queen Mine, it was Louis Zeckendorf, a Tucson merchant and freighter, who provided capital for the mine's future because he saw the potential for a large profit from freighting copper and supplies. In return, Zeckendorf and Company obtained a two-year contract to haul all ore and bullion out of the mining camp and over Mule Mountain Pass to the railhead. But the amount of copper produced in Bisbee outstripped the ability of the doughty little animals to haul it out. At one point, the company imported a steam-driven tractor from England to haul copper to Fairbank and the railroad. The weird-looking contraption with its metal wheels—larger in back—was named Geronimo, but it never proved totally satisfactory. It had the power to do the job, but it mired down in sand or mud, and there was a lot of sand or mud in the San Pedro River Valley, depending on the season.

Fuel also had to be hauled in to feed the smelter furnaces, which were kept going night and day. At first, charcoal was used. Mexican woodcutters denuded the Mule Mountains of oak, mesquite, and even manzanita in their quest for wood that could be converted into charcoal. But soon, when the wood was all gone, the mines turned to the use of coke, a product of coal, which was hauled by railroad to Fairbank or Benson and freighted the rest of the way in wagons.

Hundreds of sturdy mules were necessary to every phase of the mining operation in its early days, and they never went on strike or demanded a raise. As shafts were angled far into the mountains, mules were used to haul the ore to the surface. They lived in the darkness of the mine and were never permitted to go out of it since it proved too difficult to get them back in again. The Mule Mountains were not named after the mules who made the copper mines possible. They had already been named, probably because of an old mule trail that went through the pass, long before copper was discovered under what was later to become Bisbee. But I like to think they were named after those mules who lived and died underground and never saw the light, or for the ones who hauled the copper down that ghastly road, listening to the crack of the muleskinner's long whip and to his curses. The muleskinners elevated cursing to a fine art, and it was always directed at their mules, without which there could have been no mining operation in the Mule Mountains before the railroad came into Bisbee.

I get back in the van and start winding around to the southeastern side of the mountain toward Tombstone Canyon, which will be the major thoroughfare through Bisbee. Around one curve and there it is—my first view of Bisbee, which has got to be one of the most unusual-looking towns in the United States. From up here, it looks like a toy town, straggling down the canyon and up the hills on both sides. There's not nearly as much of it as there was when I lived here in the late fifties, but what is left looks good to me. I try to think of a word to describe it and can't. How can a town be beautiful and ridiculous looking at the same time? Incongruous, I suppose, is the word I am looking for. Tiny patches of exquisite beauty as well as patches of shocking, ratty ugliness, and all thrown together without pattern or control. Unplanned town built of fierce craftsmanship and total neglect.

I don't know why, but the first sight of Bisbee from up here always makes me feel happy, foolishly happy. Those silly Italian cypresses sticking up everywhere are about as out of place in this landscape as is the Art Deco courthouse. The cypresses look fake, as if they were part of the set of a bad Italian opera. There are elaborate stone foundations everywhere, and many of them now support nothing but a jungle of morning glory vines, while some of the houses look as if they had no foundations at all. Crowded, cluttered, unkempt, amazing, magnificent Bisbee, still living on borrowed time as it always has, but living in the present, always in the present, because tomorrow brings only fresh disasters.

Tombstone may be the town too tough to die, but Bisbee has died a hundred times and never noticed it. It was built where no town should ever have been built, where it was sure to be destroyed by flood and fire. And its entire economy was based on one company that left it to its fate in 1975. But Bisbee never knows what tomorrow may bring, and it doesn't seem to care. It is a town that never grew up, just got older and older, a town that has survived because it has always steadfastly refused to face reality, a toy town where real people live and suffer, but always in the present. Live today because tomorrow the copper may be gone. Live today because tomorrow the canyon may flood and everything will be swept away. Live today because tomorrow the town may burn down again. That's Bisbee, and it hasn't changed really, although it's no longer a mining town and it now scrapes its meager living from whatever comes to hand. It hasn't changed its attitude or its heart. Live today, for tomorrow . . . well, forget about tomorrow.

Maybe Bisbee was born this way because it was built in a canyon through which tremendous flash floods swept periodically during the monsoon rains that washed down from the mountains all around it. Over the years, measures have been taken to prevent floods, but most of those measures seem to have been taken by the company or by the state government or by the WPA but not by the people of Bisbee. I was reminded of this the last time I went to the Bisbee Historical Museum to talk to its curator, Tom Vaughan. In the course of our conversation, one of us mentioned the check dams, small dams of stone and concrete that were built, one above the other, up most of the major draws leading into the canyon. The check dams were constructed by the WPA in the 1930s to prevent flooding, and they have been very effective. When the dams were mentioned, I saw a shadow of what looked like fear flit momentarily across Tom's face, and he looked out the window of his office and up toward the side of the hill. "They're all filled up now," he said. He passed his hand quickly across his youthful, bearded face, and then he was as cheerful as ever. The conversation moved on to other things, and it wasn't until I was out of his office that it hit me, what he had said. They're all filled up now and cannot be effective against floods anymore. Dirt and stones have washed down into them until they are level with the slopes of the hills. We don't clean them out; we wait for the next flood.

That's Bisbee, a town built directly in the path of disaster, a town which has survived so many disasters it has lost track, a town where everything breaks down and goes wrong and everybody laughs, picks up the pieces and tries to patch them back together again. That's Bisbee, cheerfully making do as best it can amid the wreckage of its disasters. And as I start the long slide down Tombstone Canyon, Bisbee's twisting Main Street, I say, "Damn, I love this town!"

9

As I drive down Tombstone Canyon, I am trying to remember the first time I saw Bisbee, but the memory is hazy, almost nonexistent. It must have been shortly after I was stationed at Ft. Huachuca, in the late fall or early winter of 1956. I had two army buddies who were brothers, and one of them had a car. We traveled around the area a good deal in that car on weekends, and one of those jaunts was to Bisbee. I barely remember walking along Main Street and thinking what a strange little town Bisbee was, the strangest I had ever seen, all piled on top of itself as if some child had poured toy houses down the sides of the mountains. It was interesting in a bizarre way, and that was that. I had no connection with it and it had no connection with me. I assumed that I would probably never see it again. Now I wonder what my life would have been like if I had never seen this funny little town again. I know it would have been a completely different life. I can see now that my decision to move to Bisbee less than two years later was, in terms of my subsequent life, one of the most important decisions I have ever made, a decision from which all else followed as surely as summer follows spring, but the decision was made hastily and with little thought. By then I was a married man with an infant son and my time in the army was coming to an end. I needed a job, and I needed one quickly.

I was due for a discharge at the end of September of 1958, and all I had to recommend me for employment was a bachelor's degree in English from a small Texas college. The degree qualified me for teaching in the Texas public schools, and I assumed that it qualified me for teaching in the Arizona public schools as well. I don't remember how I found out about available jobs. I must have used a placement service or job list from somewhere, but I have forgotten all about it, although I remember considering three possible jobs—two in high schools in small Texas towns and the third in a junior high school in Bisbee. From the depths of my inexperience, I thought it would somehow be better to teach in a high school than a junior high school, but I had decided that I wanted to stay in Southern Arizona, in the desert or high desert country. It was an attraction I did not understand and could not have explained, but it was strong. And on that basis, I applied for the job in Bisbee, the only available job I knew about in the area.

Almost immediately I received a reply from the Cochise County superintendent of public schools asking me to come to Bisbee for an interview. I didn't question the speed of the reply. Perhaps I thought I was an attractive candidate, although that seems incredible since I had a degree from a small college nobody in Arizona had ever heard of and no public school experience. I had put myself through school working at a series of temporary jobs, mostly selling shoes, and hadn't been inside a junior high school since I attended one. But I was young and willing to learn, and I had a degree, good grades, and some letters of recommendation.

It didn't occur to me that the Cochise County superintendent might be desperate, and that he might not have been exactly deluged with applications for his teaching job in Bisbee. Most young teachers wanted to locate in the larger cities of Arizona, and a ratty little mining town in the mountains near the Mexican Border was not their idea of a place to put down roots. Months later, I learned how desperate the superintendent had been. His junior-high-school English teacher had found herself pregnant and quit suddenly at the end of the school year, leaving him with the prospect of a school with no English teacher come early September. He was beginning to sweat when he got my application, and he didn't waste any time answering it. So I made my second trip from Ft. Huachuca to Bisbee in response to his request, and I remember it quite well.

The Signal Corp battalion of which I was a reluctant and low-ranking member was in the midst of field maneuvers lasting most of the summer. We were operating out of tents set up in the desert near Ft. Huachuca's North Gate, and under simulated battle conditions. I was running the battalion personnel office from a large tent, which made it look like the circus it was. Everything was covered with dust, the heat was terrible, and we had only battery operated field telephones and field radios with which to communicate with the rest of the base. We were a Signal Corps unit, but communication was always our biggest problem since nobody could get the radios to work properly and the phones had limited range and were unpredictable. I remember cranking those phones for what seemed like hours and often hearing a very faint voice at the other end, although I was talking to someone at base headquarters less than four miles away. We did a lot of sweating, cussing, and cranking. Dust got into our typewriters and made some of them inoperable. We had a couple of monsoons that knocked down some of the tents and turned the floors of all of them into clay bogs.

But I was a short-timer, sailing down the home stretch toward freedom, and I had developed a short-timer's detachment from the chaos around me. I had already had my mandatory interview with the re-enlistment officer, who worked, I think, on a commission basis. It was hard sell. He had offered me easy duty in Paris, Hawaii, or just about anywhere I might want to go if I would enlist when my time as a draftee expired; but I wouldn't have been tempted even if I thought he could keep his promises. I don't remember exactly what I told him, but I remember his interview with the man just ahead of me in line. I will never forget that one.

The draftee was a young private, and the reenlistment officer asked him if he would like to enlist at the end of his tour of duty. The private, very quiet and uncomfortable, said, "No." The officer asked him "Why?" Something seemed to click in the private's head. He began to speak very rapidly in a monotone, but his voice rose hysterically as he continued. By the time he finished, he was screaming.

"Yesterday I was on a detail moving rocks and it was very hot and I got a headache. I had some aspirin with me and decided to take a couple of them for my headache, but when I asked the sergeant in charge of the detail if I could go in the barracks next to where we were working and get some water to take the aspirins with, he said, 'No.' Have you ever taken two fucking aspirins without any fucking water to wash them down with? THAT'S WHY I'M NOT STAYING IN THE FUCKING ARMY!"

My experience with the army had been somewhat better than the private's, although I was never comfortable and suffered from the knowledge that I could be given orders at any time from officers or noncommissioned officers who were often stupid, drunk, or incompetent, and for whom I had no respect. But my rank as a specialist and my position in the office had helped me avoid some of the worst of the harassment many of the draftees endured. The fact that, as a draftee, I had been placed in charge of a battalion personnel office suggested there were no career men available who had even the modicum of intelligence required to do such a job. As far as I could see, the assumption was correct. Draftees and civilians seemed to be providing the necessary oil that kept the post running. The draftees were slaves, but without their energy and intelligence, Ft. Huachuca would have ground to a halt.

I forged officers' signatures on documents daily, but if I had not, allotments would not have been paid, discharges would not have been granted, and men would not have been shipped to their assignments. I filled the overseas roster each month, which meant that I decided which men in the battalion would go to which overseas assignments. The officers whose signatures I forged or whose signature stamps I used were delighted to have somebody else do the work. They trusted me to do it, and I knew that as long as I did it they would stay out of my way. So I had been lucky. I was allowed to come and go pretty much as I pleased in carrying out my duties, and was usually left alone with the fifteen or so clerks who processed paperwork in the office, most of whom were also draftees.

I ran the office very casually when there were no officers in sight, and it paid off in higher morale and better work. Each man kept a water pistol in his desk, and late in the afternoon when no officers were around, we would have wild water pistol fights that raged up and down the office, after which we would quickly clean up the mess and go back to work, somewhat the better for having been able to vent our aggressiveness and tension. One afternoon, during one of our more spectacular water-pistol wars, one of the men hit upon the idea of filling a condom with water, which made a huge water balloon he could barely carry in both arms. He threw the balloon up in the air above somebody and it hit the ceiling and burst, drenching his target and most of the rest of the office.

Just then I received a phone call which was part of our carefully worked out warning system. The battalion commander was on his way for a surprise inspection. We had five minutes to get ready. Everybody knew exactly what to do, and we did it like lightning. When the commander's aide strode into the room and shouted " 'Ten-Shun!" the office was gleaming as if it had just been scrubbed, which it had. The floor had been freshly mopped, and fifteen somewhat breathless soldiers leaped to their feet from behind their desks, where they had been busily typing. Each man had on a freshly laundered shirt—we always kept spares for just such an emergency—and my bottom desk drawer was stuffed with wet laundry.

The battalion commander was pleased. He walked around the room, running his finger over a few desk tops and finding them amazingly clean. Then he stopped near my desk to ask me a few questions about some paperwork we were processing. While we talked, I noticed the one thing my crew and I had overlooked. The ceiling beam above the officer's head was heavily beaded with water, drops of which were about to begin to fall directly onto him. Several of the men had also noticed the water and were getting visibly nervous. At that moment, as if in answer to my prayer, one of the phones on my desk rang. As I turned to answer it, the officer walked on and a big glob of water fell on the floor behind him, exactly on the spot where he had been standing. By then the officer was on his way out the door. Every member of my crew let out a long breath of relief. It was the closest we ever came to getting caught. I don't think I could have talked fast enough to explain why the ceiling was covered with water, but after that I never had to warn the men about limiting condoms to the use for which they were intended.

In July of 1958 the personnel office was in a tent with its sides rolled up to give us the benefit of whatever breeze was available, and our shirts were often soaked, but not with water from water pistols. We were in full view of everybody, so we behaved accordingly. My appointment with the county superintendent of public schools was for late in the afternoon, so I simply slipped out of the office a little early.

Dark clouds were gathering as I drove across the San Pedro Valley, and when I started down Tombstone Canyon it began to rain in a serious, biblical fashion.

The superintendent's office was in what has come to be known as the "old" high-school building, and the high school itself had just moved to its new quarters on some semi-flat land south of Warren. The "old" high school sits on the steep slope of Clawson Hill, and according to local folklore, it is the only four-story school in the world that has a ground floor entrance on each level. As I came down Main Street in a downpour, I could see the building on the hill above, but I couldn't find a road that led up to it, and I was running out of time. Finally, I decided to park in the lot behind the Phelps Dodge Mercantile and make a dash for the high school, about the equivalent of two blocks up the hill. With the rain pounding, I ran through a maze of little alleyways, which I later found out were streets, and up several flights of concrete steps, which in Bisbee serve the function of sidewalks. I don't know what the superintendent was expecting, but what he got was a young redheaded soldier in uniform and with a crew cut, drenched and dripping and out of breath from having just run two blocks straight up.

The superintendent was a pale, cheerful, mild-mannered man. I guessed that he had spent a good many years in the classroom, and he had the slightly befuddled look that male teachers often get. We chatted briefly, mostly about the rain, but I think he had made up his mind before I ever stopped dripping; before my hands were dry, he had a contract in front of me, which I signed. It was all over in about fifteen minutes, and I walked out to take my first real look at Bisbee, which was going to become home to me and my family.

The rain had stopped and the late afternoon sun was coming out, making everything glisten and shine. Directly in front of me I saw a stone retaining wall about twelve feet high. The rain had brought out the rich, deep color of each stone. I thought it was the most beautiful stone wall I had ever seen. I was lifted on a great wave of euphoria which I will always associate with that wall. The euphoria was probably caused by relief, by the knowledge that I had a teaching job, that I would be able to feed my family and keep a roof over our heads, but suddenly I felt that Bisbee was a very beautiful place, an exotic place, with stairways instead of sidewalks, and little water channels that ran down the hills, now filled with gurgling water. The quality of light after a late afternoon storm in Bisbee is enchanting. It reflects off the tawny hills on all sides and illuminates everything with an amber glow. The wet tin roofs become mirrors flashing on the sides of the hills. The silly Italian cypresses become mysterious, glowing columns, and the cancer trees take on a soft luminescence. It is magical, and I fell in love with Bisbee that afternoon while standing in front of a wet stone wall. I was about to enter a new life.

About four months earlier, when I had first seen our son in the makeshift barracks hospital in which he was born, I had taken a giant step toward maturity. There was a moment when I knew that I was irrevocably on the doorstep of a new and different life, an adult life I had always wanted. But as long as I was in the army, in bondage, I couldn't enter that life fully. I entered it that afternoon in Bisbee when I realized that I had a job, that I was going to be free, that I was going to take my place in this little community as a person with a function and a purpose. Never mind that I was going to be making barely enough money to live on, or that I was burying myself and my family in a remote little mountain mining town without television or the cultural advantages of the cities. I was going to be my own man. I would never have to salute another officer, regardless of whether or not he deserved it, as long as I lived. I was going to earn my way in a community in which I would be an important and integral part—a teacher. And I swore to myself that in spite of my inexperience I would work so hard the community would accept me and let me be part of it.

The feeling of euphoria lasted as I went down a narrow flight of steps toward Main Street, looking at more stone walls and stairways leading off at interesting angles. The town was a delightful maze, a puzzle I must solve. It didn't occur to me that I had no knowledge of what it was I was so determined to become a part of and fit into—this strange little town and the lives of the people in it. I heard a loud sirenlike whistle and couldn't tell where it was coming from, but I knew it was a five o'clock signal and thought, in my complete ignorance, "How odd. In most towns they use bells." Later I would learn that the whistle ruled the lives of most of the people in town. When it sounded each afternoon, hundreds of weary, grime-covered men would get into cages

215 ❖

to be hauled to the surface from deep underground. But that whistle, which sounded four times a day and was loud enough to be heard all over town, would never rule my life because I was not one of those men nor a member of one of their families. And because I was not, I would live on the surface of Bisbee in more ways than one.

I would never be permitted to go into the underground mines, nor even into Lavender Pit, then about seven hundred feet deep and almost a half-mile across, from which I could hear the sound of blasting every afternoon at four o'clock. Nor would I be permitted anything but a surface view of the lives of the majority of citizens in Bisbee. I was stepping into a professional role as if I had been born into a caste, and that role would make it impossible for me to penetrate the lives of the miners and their families.

I would soon find out that Bisbee was two separate worlds, and while each world had its own social strata and divisions, the two worlds were basically distinct from one another. One Bisbee, the larger of the two worlds in terms of numbers, was made up of the miners and their families. The entire town depended on the labor of the miners, and yet I seldom met a miner, although I taught their children. The other Bisbee, the one in which I was permitted and even encouraged to circulate, was a world of professional people, business people, and bureaucrats, all of whom depended on the miners in one way or another. That world floated on the surface and was supported by the world of the miners, and yet it studiously ignored the miners' darker world, as if that world did not exist. As a teacher, I came into contact with the miners' world through their children, but that was a tangential, professional contact, although it proved to be deeply moving and terrible at times. I could never live in the miners' world nor really come to know what it was like. Everything about Bisbee was structured in such a way as to make that impossible.

The dividing line between the two worlds was not economic. As a beginning teacher in Bisbee, I made less money than most of the miners. The dividing line was one of class. I entered Bisbee as a member of the professional class, although a new and very lowly member of that class, and it would have been unthinkable for the citizens of Bisbee to allow me to forget, even for a moment, which class I belonged to. Many doors were opened to me and my family in Bisbee, but they were never the doors of the miners' homes. I met insurance salesmen, doctors, engineers, county employees, librarians, and other teachers. I met the mayor's wife, the undertaker, and the local madam. But never, except in my official capacity as the teacher of one of their children, did I ever meet a miner or a miner's wife.

The children of the miners, unlike the children of my colleagues or the children of the scientists who lived in Bisbee and commuted to Ft. Huachuca, treated me with marked respect, and not because I had earned their respect, but because such behavior had been drummed into them by their parents. It was a formal, automatic respect that one class grants to all members of what it considers to be a higher class. It made my work easier and somewhat more pleasant than it might have been, but it gave me the feeling that I had stepped through some kind of time warp and that I was living in nineteenth-century Europe. And I was experiencing the remnants of a nineteenth-century European class structure. Again Faulkner's line comes back to me—"The past is not dead; it is not even past."

Well before the Phelps Dodge Company gained control of the Copper Queen Mine in 1885, Bisbee's class system was in place, and it functioned to some degree until Phelps Dodge closed the mines in the mid 1970s. It has also affected the history of Bisbee since the closing of the mines because many of the retired miners remained, as did some of those who belonged to Bisbee's other world. That class system, in some residual way, must still affect life in Bisbee today, although its effect is probably much weakened by the influx of "new" people who have dramatically altered Bisbee's social fabric.

Before Phelps Dodge, then a mercantile company, showed any interest in the copper under the Mule Mountains, the management of the Copper Queen Mine had been successfully mining it. Underground mining on a large scale was hideously difficult and dangerous work in the 1880s, but there was one group of experienced and highly trained men who knew how to do it and do it well. Mining was their life, and they were proud of their ability and their courage. They passed their skill down from generation to generation and with it the acceptance that they must risk their lives each day to do what few others could do as effectively. They were the skilled miners of Cornwall, products of England's industrial revolution, who supplied coal and metals to

England's factories. The owners of the Copper Queen Mine had imported Cornish miners, called "Cousin Jacks," in large numbers to work the mine, and when Phelps Dodge bought the Copper Queen in 1885, it gladly acquired the Cousin Jacks and their families.

Cornish miners seem to have had uncanny, intuitive abilities when it came to working with stone. Merely by looking at and touching a stone, a Cousin Jack seemed to have been able to tell many things about it, things like density, weight, stability, dimensions, and interior texture, which were not revealed to the average person. Consequently, they were not as prone to accidents in the mines as others were, accidents often caused by loose stones or the miscalculation of a wall or ceiling's ability to bear weight. And when it came to building stone walls on the surface, Cousin Jacks were masters with few peers. I have come to believe that many of the earliest stone walls still standing in Bisbee, and probably some of those at the sites of the mill towns along the San Pedro River, were built by Cousin Jacks.

The oldest retaining walls still standing in Bisbee are marvels of formal design, precision, and elegance, and have proved to be more durable than many of the walls built later. I used to think the older walls were built by Mexican stone masons, and that seemed logical since Hispanics were not allowed to work in the mines until the 1920s. I assumed that they must have been employed building the stone retaining walls that have prevented Bisbee from becoming a heap of rubble at the bottoms of two canyons. But history is seldom logical; it is too much determined by human actions. With more observation and the help of two experts—Tom Vaughan of the Bisbee Mining and Historical Museum and Lee Adcock, probably the best stone mason in Cochise County—I have changed my mind. I now think those magnificent early walls were built by Cousin Jacks. No other explanation can account for the skill and formality with which they were constructed.

Just now I can see a tall retaining wall high on the south side of Tombstone Canyon. It must have supported a house at one time, although the house is long since gone. The wall is about one hundred years old, completely intact, and has become a pale gray-lavender with age. It does not look, at this distance, like a man-made thing. It looks like something that grew there. It forms a right-angle corner, and the vertical line of the corner is still sharp and well defined—better defined, in fact, than the corners of most of the walls built in more recent times. Lee Adcock says that compared to the formality of such a wall, most of the later walls built in Bisbee are rather shoddy affairs, although I consider the later walls very beautiful. Tom Vaughan, who has studied the stone walls of Bisbee with considerable care, says that he has seen such remarkable early stone work in only one other place in the world, the County of Cornwall in the mining district of Central England.

It would seem that the Cousin Jacks not only set the standards for stone walls in Bisbee, but they made their influence felt in other ways. They were a large, very clannish minority—they all seemed to be cousins—and were generally uneducated and noted for feats of strength and endurance. A fictionalized portrait of one of them got into Conrad Richter's fine novel, *Tacey Cromwell*, which is set in Bisbee. She is Mrs. Odell, a Cornishwoman of giant proportions and strength who says, "I'm no the woman I once was. Not since I spaded forty acres."

In the mines, the Cousin Jacks with their great strength, stamina, and uncanny ability to work with stone, were at the top of the pecking order. Until the 1920s, only Anglo-Saxons, usually Cornishmen and Welshmen, were allowed to do the most important underground work in the mines. They operated single- and double-jack drills, from which they got the other half of the name "Cousin Jack." It was work requiring great stamina, strength, and precision with a hammer. They also worked as timbermen, measuring and buttressing the underground excavations and tunnels, the highest-paid work in the mines. Below them on the mining scale were Finns, Italians, Serbs, Croations, and Montenegrins, who usually did the work of loading and hauling the ore, and were called "muckers" or "trammers."

In the two decades between 1890 and 1910, the boom years of Bisbee's development, poverty and wars in Europe supplied the mines throughout the Western United States with constant fresh supplies of immigrant labor, most of which came from Europe's peasant classes. The social stratification that developed in Bisbee and which was encouraged by the mining company, was not unusual among Western mining towns, but it was perhaps more extreme in Bisbee than in some. The Cousin Jacks and other English and Welsh mining families fought to maintain their position at the top of the heap of what was basically a peasant-class immigrant society, but they were very much aware of the great social gulf which separated them from the professional and entrepreneurial class, and few of them attempted to bridge that gulf. To a large extent, that gulf still existed in 1958, although several generations of miners had come and gone. There were still the miners with their rather rigid pecking order, and the others with their more fluid social conventions, but few crossed the line between those two basic strata in Bisbee in 1958.

The stratification had long since become formalized in terms of housing communities. In general, most of the mine foremen had lived in a small community called "Jiggerville." The bulk of the miners had lived in "Old" Bisbee, Lowell, or Bakerville. The mine managers, executives, and engineers lived in Warren. Most of the successful merchants, doctors, and lawyers lived on Quality Hill. The civilian scientists who commuted to Ft. Huachuca lived in a recent development called "Huachuca Terrace," south of Lavender Pit and near the older community of Don Luis. Many of the Hispanics lived in Tintown, a shanty community built largely of rusty tin and scrap lumber. By then, Hispanics were permitted to work underground in the mines or in Lavender Pit, but the Hispanics, many of whom came across the border in search of work, formed their own enclave and were not readily acceptable in the non-Hispanic social life of Bisbee at any level.

Of course, the day I signed my contract in the county superintendent's office, I didn't know anything about all this. I would find out about it in the next two years, but first, before I could take my place in Bisbee—whatever it was—I had to be tested. I had to lose my precious job in order to gain it. About a week after my interview with the county superintendent, I received another summons from him, this one by telephone and rather frantic. I drove back to Bisbee to learn that I didn't have the job after all. My application for an Arizona teaching certificate had been denied, and without it I couldn't enter the classroom. I had, in effect, been caught in the act of trying to enter a foreign country without a passport. My degree in English, with a minor in education, had qualified me to teach in the public schools of Texas, but the laws of Arizona required something called "student teaching," an additional semester of work as an apprentice teacher under close supervision. I had not done any student teaching, and therefore I could not teach in the State of Arizona.

The superintendent told me all this in a fatherly way. He was disappointed. I was devastated. But he added that there might still be a remote chance, an end run if I were willing to make it. It was only a possibility, but there were more ways to skin a cat . . . etc. He asked me detailed questions about my background: Had I ever done any kind of teaching? Had I ever taught anybody while I was a student? Had my army duties involved any teaching? I quickly got the drift, and we ascertained that I had taught Sunday School, that I had once tutored one of my friends in college, and that my army duties routinely involved my training of the men who worked under me in the personnel office. The superintendent then suggested that I could go to Phoenix with the information we had accumulated and plead my case before the state superintendent of public instruction in the hope of obtaining a temporary, emergency teaching certificate. It was a long shot, but he trusted me to do the best I could, and it was the only chance. I agreed to do it. He called Phoenix and made an appointment for me with the state superintendent of public instruction. The rest, he said, was up to me.

Two days later I got up at 3:00 A.M., dressed in civies, downed a bowl of cereal and a cup of coffee, and went AWOL. I knew that if I requested leave to go to Phoenix for the day, my request would be denied because the battalion was on maneuvers in the field, under simulated battle conditions. But I also knew that I was often gone from my desk for several hours at a time on legitimate business, while I tracked down documents at one of the offices on the widely decentralized base. I had weighed the danger and decided that stealth was my only alternative. I had thought about explaining my situation to one of the other men in the office and asking him to cover for me if I were missed, but I had rejected that option because I would, in effect, be asking him to lie for me. I would simply have to count on speed, and hope that my absence would not be seriously questioned. The night before, I had left my desk in such a condition that it looked as if I had just stepped out for a few minutes.

In the meantime, I was driving much too fast through the predawn darkness toward Phoenix to keep my appointment with the state superintendent of public instruction at 8:00 A.M. It was a long drive from Ft. Huachuca to Phoenix in those pre-freeway days. I had to go north to Highway 82, east to a point a few miles above Tombstone— passing the dreaded curve where my friends had rolled in a red convertible less than a year before—north to Benson, where I picked up the main highway that went right through Tucson, with at least twenty stop lights, then northwest through Eloy, Casa Grande, Chandler, Mesa, Tempe, and finally Phoenix. It was a round trip of well over four hundred miles, and slow going through the towns. The sun came up as I crested the ridge at the base of Picacho Peak at seventy-five miles an hour. I remember the ghostly, pale beauty of that thick stand of saguaros as the first rays of sun struck them. I knew when I saw them that I wasn't just fighting for a job; I was fighting to stay in the desert, their desert, which I wanted someday to be able to think of as my desert as well. And I was also fighting sleep, but I didn't dare take the time to stop for coffee.

I arrived at the office of the state department of public instruction at ten minutes before eight, and it wasn't open yet. It was housed in a dilapidated old Southern mansion on a side street near the Capitol Building. The house had a deep verandah across the front and had at one time been quite elegant. I sat down in one of the chairs on the verandah to wait. Soon the front door opened and an elderly gentleman with a push broom came out to sweep the front porch. I liked him on sight. Remembering him now, I would say that he looked like Colonel Sanders of fried chicken fame, but I'm not sure if Colonel Sanders had yet been heard of in 1958. He had about the whitest hair I had ever seen, dazzlingly white and worn rather long, although his beard was short and pointed. He was wearing felt house slippers, baggy trousers, and a white shirt with suspenders. His face was ruddy, and he had little pale blue eyes which seemed to be laughing all the time. He looked so absolutely right in his setting that I decided he must have come with the house. I thought he must have been the old family retainer, and when the state took over the decaying Southern mansion, he must have stayed on.

He said good morning, I answered, and we began to chat as strangers often do, about the weather and this and that. I told him I was waiting for the office to open, and he said that a secretary would be opening it in a few minutes. I helped him move the chairs on the porch so he could sweep under them. He seemed to be in no hurry to get his sweeping done and stopped to lean on his broom while making observations about what a shame it was the house had been allowed to go to wrack and ruin. Eventually, he went in, and in a few more minutes a secretary opened the front door and I went in to the reception room, where I verified my appointment and sat down to wait.

In about five more minutes the secretary ushered me into a large room that had once been the parlor of the house and was still furnished with velvet drapes and antique furniture. Seated behind an expansive desk was the state superintendent of public instruction, Colonel Sanders himself, beaming at me with his little blue eyes laughing harder than ever. He had changed his house slippers for shoes and put on a rumpled coat and tie, and he thought it was a wonderful joke that I had mistaken him for the janitor. Of course he had known I was waiting to see him when we chatted on the porch, and I wondered how many others he had played his little joke on. But he never laughed out loud, only with his eyes, and somehow, in spite of my embarrassment, he put me at ease.

I outlined my problem as quickly as possible and told him about my alternative teaching experience. He seemed quite interested in the fact that I had once taught Sunday School and nodded eagerly when I got to that part. He took a few notes, smiled at me, and said he didn't see why I couldn't be granted a temporary teaching certificate to tide me over until I had a year's teaching under my belt, at which time the state's requirement would be satisfied by the teaching I had done and I would be granted a regular certificate. He pressed a button and a secretary came in. He instructed her to draw up a temporary teaching certificate for me, which he would sign and mail to Bisbee that afternoon.

He reminded me that I would be required to take a course in Arizona State Constitution and one in United States Constitution during the coming year but pointed out that both were offered by extension at Douglas and that I could take them at night. He said he hoped I would be happy with my teaching in Bisbee, "what a . . . ahem . . . interesting little town. The county super down there seems quite . . . ahem . . . eager to hire you." The laughing eyes told me he thought this

223 ❖

was a great joke, too, and now the "county super down there" owed him one. It crossed my mind that every county superintendent in the state probably owed him quite a few, and he loved it. We shook hands, and as I was leaving I noticed the push broom leaning against the wall near the door. I suppose he had to keep it handy in case he wanted to check out some other eager supplicant waiting on the porch. I thought I had learned to play fox and goose in the army, but I could see from watching an old professional operate that I had much to learn. After I left, it occurred to me that I should have told him I was AWOL from the army. That would have given him a chuckle. Then it dawned on me that he had probably already figured that out, and that gave me a chuckle.

I stopped before I left Phoenix to drain two cups of coffee quickly, and streaked for Ft. Huachuca. By 12:30 P.M. I was behind my desk and immersed in paperwork when my crew came back from lunch. Their eyebrows were raised and their eyes were full of questions, but they didn't say a word. One of the officers had noticed my absence, and the draftee he asked about it had lied and said I had just gone over to base headquarters to get some papers signed. It was the code of the army. I was a short-timer, and they were all pulling for me. Instead of going to the brig, I was able to get an "early out," which meant that I was discharged one month early in order to take the job at Bisbee. I was discharged on August 31. The next morning I was at Lowell School in Bisbee attending meetings preliminary to my first day of classes. I was going to be a teacher at last.

10

Twisting down Tombstone Canyon, I see the cream-colored house on the right where Molly Bendixon used to live. Dear, good Molly. How fierce you were, and how fiercely I have missed you for thirty years. They tell me you are old now and in a rest home in Phoenix, but that can't be. You will never be old as long as I can remember you. You will always be a tall, gaunt, rawboned woman, ramrod straight, with dark hair and eyes, a grown-up hellion tomboy with a Black Irish heart as tough and tender as was ever produced in an Irish mining family, all boys but you, and you held your own with your huge, rough brothers as you held your own with the world. Watching you make those sudden transitions from cursing wildcat to genteel spinster schoolteacher taught me about women and more. Molly, my nemesis, my protector, my companion in crime and trusted confidante. Molly, my dear friend, I miss you still.

I encountered her during the morning of my first day on the job at Lowell School when I ducked into the tiny teacher's lounge just across the hall from my classroom to have a quick cup of coffee and a smoke. We were supposed to devote that first day to attending orientation meetings and getting our classrooms and textbooks in order. The onslaught of students would arrive the following day. But I don't remember seeing Molly at the first meeting that morning. I guess she didn't need any orientation; she knew which direction she was going and she had no intention changing it.

Later they told me she had taught math in the same classroom for twenty years, and she thought she owned the building. She didn't own it, but there was soon no doubt in my mind who ran it. The principal, Paul Rose, was an excellent but generally hands-off administrator who had given up trying to do anything about Molly Bendixon years before I arrived. He preferred to keep her from shouting obscenities at the other teachers in front of the students, but he usually settled for staying out of earshot and letting the other teachers protect themselves as best they could. From time to time, when somebody complained to him, he would "have a talk" with Molly, but he knew such talks were exercises in futility. And in spite of her sometimes less-than-professional outbursts, he admired her. Molly hated and loved with a deep, passionate energy. If she found that some teacher in the building was slacking off or mistreating the students, she turned into a virago. She could drive a bad or lazy teacher out of the building, and even out of the profession, with the same fierceness that she lavished love on the students, who feared her and adored her at the same time.

Molly hated carelessness, indolence, and indecision. There was no room in her professional life for foul-ups. She must have learned her attitudes from her father and brothers, all miners who worked underground where one careless or foolish act could cost many lives. The school was her mine. She expected her colleagues to act responsibly and with full knowledge of the damage they could do to the children in their care. She was a strict teacher of the old school, but she loved the children so much that I sometimes wondered why she hadn't married and had a family of her own. Even in her mid-fifties she was a darned attractive woman. She liked men and wasn't above telling them so, although she was incapable of flirting. I guess she never wanted to give up any of her freedom and settle into marriage, or else she had never found a man with enough courage to ask her.

Of course I didn't know any of this when I encountered Molly Bendixon in the teachers' lounge that first morning after a long orientation meeting in the library. She was sitting at the table with her coffee and her cigarette, looking glum. I said "Good morning," got my coffee, and lit a cigarette, aware that she was staring at me all the time with an expression somewhere between irritation and amusement in her bright black eyes.

"You a Mormon?" she asked with apparent disgust.

What an incredibly rude and unobservant woman, I thought, to ask such a thing while I'm drinking coffee and smoking. And what business is it of hers anyway! "No," I said, bridling. "What makes you ask?"

"You look so damned clean," she said, throwing her head back and exhaling a long breath of smoke as if to say, "Wanna make something of it?"

Suddenly I realized that I was dealing with a woman of unusual dignity. In her tough way, she was almost regal. And I must have looked "damned clean" to her, with my scrubbed youth, fair skin with freckles, and my almost bald GI crewcut. Compared to the men in her family who came up from the mine each night looking like chimney sweeps, I must have looked very clean to her. On the other hand, she wasn't exactly what I had expected to find in the teachers' lounge on my first day at Lowell School, sitting there as if she owned the place and blowing smoke out of her nose like a dragon. I finished my coffee and got up to leave, making a mental note to avoid her if I could. I wasn't very old or experienced, but I could recognize trouble when I saw it, and she was it. I could feel those dark eyes burning two holes in my back as I left the room.

But I didn't have time to worry about Molly Bendixon, and in the excitement of my first day on the job, I forgot all about her, at least for a little while. My classroom was a delight. It was just old-fashioned enough to have character and charm, and I liked everything about it, even the way it smelled—like old, polished wood and the cleaning compound, a reddish substance the texture of sand, which school janitors always used when sweeping the floors. It was a large, high-ceilinged room with pale walls, dark oak woodwork, and blackboards along two sides. What I liked best was the bank of tall windows that ran the full length of the room, beneath which was a low wooden bookcase forming a deep window seat or shelf. The windows actually opened, and when the venetian blinds were raised, let in a flood of Arizona light with motes of dust dancing like magical things. Such a room could never be dreary, I thought, and I was determined never to let it be.

The first thing I did after opening the windows as far as they would go and raising the blinds to the ceiling, was to begin cleaning and counting my textbooks, which I found in a big metal cabinet at the rear of the room. There were hundreds and hundreds of them in sets of about thirty-five for each class I would teach. Texts for seventh-grade reading (literature) and eighth-grade reading. Texts for seventh-grade English (grammar) and eighth-grade English. And several sets of supplementary texts which I didn't know exactly what I was supposed to do with. But at least I wouldn't have to worry about a lack of text-books. I took them all out of the cabinet and ranged them along the shelf under the windows. Then I began cleaning and counting them. They needed an accurate count in the office.

About the middle of the afternoon, when I was almost finished with my chores, a bell rang signaling another teachers' meeting, and I dashed off for the library. During the next hour, while I sat in the library listening to the principal and some of the other teachers discuss whatever it is they discuss at such meetings—and I can't remember what it was—the Sonoran Desert played a terrible trick on me, a trick so devastating that it determined the general thrust of my work for the next two years and caused me to have to work at least twice as hard as I would have otherwise.

It was early September. While we attended the meeting in the library, a sudden monsoon storm came up, a real gully-washer. I was so en-grossed in the excitement of my first day on the job as a teacher, so intent on playing my new role, trying to look intelligent and interested in the meeting, that I actually enjoyed watching the lightning and rain outside without thinking about what might be happening in my class-room in another wing of the building. By the time the meeting was over, the downpour had stopped. I sauntered back to my classroom and found the floor covered with water and all my textbooks, which I had left on the long shelf under the open windows, soaked and ruined, turned to swollen lumps of wet pulp.

I stared into my beautiful classroom as if into a black hole of despair. I had destroyed all my textbooks even before the students arrived. My mind began to race, and I thought of the probable results of my stupidity and carelessness. At the very least, I would be fired, and I might also be required to pay for the destroyed books, which I could not do. I would become the laughingstock of the whole school, probably the whole district. I thought about Molly Bendixon and her accusing eyes and voice . . . Oh, my God!

We never know what kinds of disasters we are prepared to handle or how we will handle them until they occur. Looking back from the safe vantage point of thirty years later, I can see that most of my previous life had prepared me to handle that crisis, and handle it in my own peculiar fashion. My childhood, itself, had been a disaster during which I faced crisis after crisis, and I had learned to cope. I had learned to depend on my own ingenuity and a certain creative flair. At the moment, I felt completely overwhelmed and helpless, but within seconds my adrenalin and my instincts for survival took over.

First, I closed the door so that nobody who happened to be passing down the hall could look in and see my ruined books. Then I took a deep breath, told myself not to panic, and sat down to think of ways to get myself out of the mess I was in. My mind was working at triple speed, and it seemed that I sat there a long time, but it was probably only a few minutes, concentrating on the problem with every ounce of energy I had.

There is a poem by Longfellow which was probably in some of those textbooks I had ruined that day, and it comes to mind when I remember myself sitting there, staring into disaster and trying to think. Longfellow was a pretty dreadful poet by just about any standards one wants to apply, but about 80 percent of the poetry in my ruined textbooks, and in most junior high school textbooks of that time, was written by him. I don't know how Longfellow's bad poetry managed to take over the textbooks of America, but it had done so by the time I was in grade school, and it was still doing considerable damage to the minds of young people when I began teaching. Evidently, those who compiled textbooks thought it would appeal to the young, but it didn't. The young were bored silly with "by the shores of Gitche Gumee" and they had been for many years. But the poem that comes to mind now was one of Longfellow's better, and blessedly shorter, efforts. It was probably better because so much of it was stolen from an earlier work by somebody else.

Its title is lugubrious—"My Lost Youth." But even that fits the situation, because whatever shreds of my youth the army had not managed to knock out of me were rapidly disappearing as I sat and looked at the wreckage I had created on my first day of my first professional job. Longfellow based his poem on an old Lapland song, and the refrain line (probably stolen) which comes to mind in connection with that terrible afternoon is: "And the thoughts of youth are long, long thoughts."

I sat there thinking "long, long thoughts," but thinking them quickly, with a speed imposed by desperation. Gradually the outlines of a plan began to form in my mind. It was wild and outrageous, but it was the only plan I could come up with which might possibly cover the situation—and my tail. If it didn't work, I told myself, I might just as well go out and find myself a job selling shoes.

While the plan was still forming, I got up, took off my coat, rolled up my sleeves and began shoving the soggy, dripping books back into the metal storage cabinet, which I locked. I would have to find time later, when nobody was around, to get them out a few at a time and let them dry so they wouldn't mildew and begin to smell so badly that someone might get curious about what I had hidden in the cabinet. Then I went down the hall to the janitor's closet and got a mop, bucket, and some rags. Soon I had the room looking much as it had looked when I arrived that morning, although the floor was cleaner. There was no need to close the windows—the storm was over—but I closed them anyway. Then I went to the faculty men's room and rinsed my sweating face in cold water, put my coat on, and headed for the principal's office, with my plan still developing in my head.

As I went down the hall, distracted, I nearly ran into Molly Bendixon coming in the opposite direction. I must have looked like a guilty schoolboy. Her eyes were inquisitive and mocking, almost accusatory. It occurred to me, sickeningly, that she might know my secret. If she had gone to the teachers' lounge before I got back from the meeting, she might have looked into my classroom and seen the disaster. She might even now be coming from the principal's office where she had blabbed the whole story. "Maybe she knows," I said to myself, "but it's a chance I'll have to take. Maybe she'll just blackmail me for the rest of my life, threatening to expose me. I'll worry about that when the time comes. Right now I've got bigger problems, and they can't wait."

I tried to look nonchalant as I went into the principal's office and asked the secretary if I could see Mr. Rose. His door was open, and he called me in as soon as he saw me.

"How's it going on your first day in the salt mines?" he asked, and I could tell that Molly hadn't blabbed, even if she knew about my ruined books. "Fine," I said, "just fine. Everybody's been very helpful. I can find my way to the men's room and the teachers' lounge, so I guess I'm all set. But I wanted to talk to you about my textbooks."

"Fine," he said, and his face relaxed. Textbooks were something he could handle. (It occurred to me months later that he might have thought I had come in to complain about Molly. Maybe he thought she had worked me over already, although usually she waited until a new teacher had been there a couple of weeks, but she hadn't been feeling very well lately and maybe she had jumped the gun. He would much prefer to talk about textbooks.) "Those texts," he continued, "are the ones your predecessor used." (I thought about his use of the word "predecessor," meaning "pre-deceased," but I didn't dwell on it.) "She seemed to like them, but I thought you might want to make some changes. However, it takes about three months for the district to process new book orders, so I was hoping you could limp along with what you've got until you could pick out some new ones and we could get them ordered for you. Maybe we could get them in by the beginning of next semester."

"Thank you," I said, "but it's not that. The books are O.K. Not great, but O.K." (And as I told this monstrous lie, I had a vision of them—soaked, pulpy masses which, if they continued to swell up, would probably burst the metal storage cabinet into which I had crammed them.)

"It's just that I had an idea I wanted to run by you. If it meets with your approval, it would save us having to order new texts right away. It's a system used in the English classes in some of the progressive schools in the East lately, and it's had great results." (Nobody, to my knowledge, had ever heard of the system I was about to propose, since I had been making it up for the last hour, although some of its elements were known. And as for the "progressive schools in the East," I was prepared to pull the names of some Eastern cities out of thin air if I had to and hope he didn't know anything about their school systems. But he didn't ask.)

Paul Rose looked mildly interested. One eyebrow had gone up above his glasses, and he leaned back, prepared to listen. He probably liked the idea that he might not have to order new books. School budgets were always tight. "O.K.," he said, "Let's hear it."

"Well," I said, launching into it, "you know how bored students usually are by the textbooks in English classes. I was at that age, and you probably were too. It isn't that the texts lack good material, but it's so hard to get the students interested. The material doesn't seem relevant to them, and that's partly because they have no say in choosing it. The material in the grammar texts is purely functional and dry; and as for the literature texts, somebody assumes the students will like it, and so it is simply forced on them from outer space. They don't know where it came from, and they don't care anything about it. The system I am talking about is one in which each student produces his own text. They end up with much the same material, but since they have put it together themselves, it has relevance to them and each one takes pride in his own copy of the text. (In those days, before somebody invented "sexist" language and jerked our consciences up, we all talked that way.)

Mr. Rose looked skeptical but still interested. "How does it work? Do the books have to be printed?"

"No, no," I said quickly. "Each of the students produces his own handwritten copy of the text. By producing the text themselves, they learn what it contains, and it is supplemented by mimeographed material provided by the teacher. The students can even illustrate the texts themselves, if they want to. Or the art class can make it a project. (I had attended enough meetings already to learn that the word "project" was very big with educators. I hadn't yet picked up on "unit," but that would come.)

"We don't have an art class at the junior-high level," he said a little defensively, "but some of the teachers do work in that area."

"Well, whatever . . ." I was momentarily thrown off the track, but I got back on. "It works differently in the grammar classes than in the literature classes, but it works in both. In the grammar classes, I would dictate to them the concepts and rules of usage, along with examples, and they would copy them down in their personal texts. They learn a lot of spelling along the way. I would check their copies of the texts each day to make sure they were getting things right. Then, based on the material in their individual texts, which they could refer to, we would do exercises and diagram sentences at the blackboard. I believe in doing a lot of work at the blackboard where the teacher can monitor it constantly. (He seemed to like that, especially the part about diagramming sentences.)

"You know," he broke in, "I've noticed that most English teachers don't seem to believe in diagramming sentences anymore."

"Well I do," I said. "It's the only way to learn what makes a sentence work. Of course you have to know the parts of speech and build from the beginning, but that would be the first section of the texts the students produced. It seems to me that one of the reasons students have so much trouble with grammar is that we never start them at the beginning. We assume that by the time they get to the seventh grade they know the parts of speech, but most of them don't. With this kind of approach I could start at the beginning, with the parts of speech, and build from there. I could tailor the texts to the exact needs of the individual student, and they wouldn't all have to be the same."

"Hmmm . . ." he said. "We have a broad range of students here. Come from very different backgrounds. Some of the kids whose parents are scientists over at Ft. Huachuca are sharp as tacks, way ahead of themselves. And some of the ones from Tintown are almost illiterate. And the farmers' kids from out near Elfrida, they have different problems than the miners' kids. Terrible range. We've been talking about some way to divide them up and put them on different tracks according to ability, but we haven't figured out a way to do it. Hmmm . . . What you're suggesting might work. So the texts wouldn't all have to be the same . . ."

"No," I answered, modifying my plan as I went along. "They could work in small groups within one classroom but at different levels, producing different texts depending on their needs. But that's just for the grammar classes. For the reading classes, it's even better. I would teach them to read and enjoy literature by not teaching literature at all. I would teach performance—literature as an oral art. Have you ever heard a choral speaking group?" (I was now getting into an area I knew a little about, but not much.)

His face lit up. "Is that like a verse-speaking choir?"

"Exactly," I said. "Only a choral speaking group performs all kinds of literature, not just poetry."

"I heard one of them once," he said, "when I was in college. I'll never forget how good they were, or how much I enjoyed it. Just like a choir, only they spoke instead of singing."

"We wouldn't need a text," I rushed on. "I would bring in the literature on mimeographed sheets and let them read it and vote on what they wanted to perform. That way, I would have control over everything they read and could make sure it was suitable." (That was another word I had already learned at the meetings. "Suitable" meant no sex and no naughty words.) "They would have to read a lot of things in order to make their final choices, and we would always be adding new material to the show. I would divide them into sections according to their voices, like baritone, tenor, alto, and soprano. Everything would be geared toward performance. After we chose the material, the classes would be rehearsals. When they started rehearsing for performance, they would really learn the material, probably memorize most of it."

Now Mr. Rose was very interested. He was leaning forward across his desk and almost frowning with concentration. "But I didn't think English teachers believed in making students memorize poems anymore."

"Well," I said, "generally they don't believe in forcing students to memorize poems, but there is more than one way to skin a cat. When students are in a choral speaking group, they work so long and hard with individual pieces that most of them memorize the stuff without realizing what they are doing. Then they have it for the rest of their lives. And they love to perform; it makes them feel important. They could perform for the rest of the students or for the P.T.A. or something."

"Well I'll be damned!" said Mr. Paul Rose, who stared at me through his glasses like an owl. "Have you seen our auditorium?"

"No, not from the inside."

"Come with me, Mr. Shelton," he said, getting up from his desk and herding me out of the office. "I've got something very special to show you. Best damned auditorium south of Tucson. Seats five hundred. Full balcony. They tell me the acoustics are almost perfect. We never get to use it except for assemblies once in awhile. Don't have any regular drama classes. The Little Theater group in town uses the auditorium over at Greenway School because this one is too big for them. They don't do much anyway."

By this time he had me down the hall and was opening the doors to the auditorium. It was black inside. He found a light switch, and there it was, a dream of a theater, all leather seats and velvet and gold trim. It had a huge proscenium stage with pale blue velvet curtains, and a fortune in velvet draping the tall, formal windows that ran along both sides. It was gorgeous, tasteful, and everything a theater should be, and it was huge.

"My God!" I thought. "What am I getting into? He doesn't want an English teacher. What he wants is a choir director and drama coach." But I was as excited about the auditorium as he was.

Then he was showing me the public address system, and he opened the light box and switched on the footlights, then the full complement of spotlights rigged across the ceiling. I could tell the acoustics were good. There might be a few dead spots in an auditorium this big, but the acoustics were basically excellent. The auditorium had been built in 1931, the same year the school had been built, in a time when they knew how to build auditoriums, and it had been built for the ages. But I could see why it got little use. It was just too big, frighteningly big when you stood on the stage and imagined all those seats filled with people.

"We could use music," I said, "lots of music, and special effects with the lights. We could do antiphonal pieces with two spotlights. Have you got any risers?"

"Plenty of risers. They're folded up backstage."

"Choir robes," I said. "We'd have to have choir robes."

"Borrow them from the high school. The principal's a friend of mine."

We had the auditorium blazing with lights and were standing in the middle of it talking excitedly when I saw somebody in the doorway, peering in. It was Molly Bendixon. Something was going on she hadn't been told about, something big. Neither of us volunteered any information. She turned and marched down the hall, her head high, her back ramrod stiff, but for me there was no turning back now.

"Mr. Rose," I said, "let me turn my reading classes into a choral speaking group and we'll perform in your auditorium. We'll use it a lot. We'll put on shows everybody will remember for a long time."

"It's a deal," he said smiling, and started turning off the lights.

That was the beginning, the easy part. Then all I had to do was convince the students, whom I hadn't seen yet, that they wanted to get up on that stage in front of all those people and perform. And I had to provide them with something to perform and teach them how to do it. And I had to make damned sure that nobody, especially Molly Bendixon, found out what was hidden in my metal storage cabinet.

When I arrived at Lowell School the next morning, big yellow buses were already lined up in front of the building, disgorging students of all shapes and sizes, most of them berserk with excitement at the beginning of a new school year, and I was as excited as they were. For them, school was about to start again after a long, dull summer, but for me it was the beginning of a teaching career, year number one. In a few minutes I would be facing my first class ever, adrenalin pumping, wavering between eagerness and terror.

I would be teaching five classes of seventh and eighth graders each day, without any textbooks, in addition to conducting a homeroom and a study hall. I would have lunchroom duty, playground duty, and hall duty, and I would somehow have to find time to prepare for my classes. But I was young and determined, and I knew I could do it, even without any previous experience, if the students would only give me a chance. Just a little chance. As for the other teachers, the principal, and the county superintendent who had said he would be dropping in from time to time to observe my classes, they were adults and I was used to working with adults. I wasn't afraid of them. (A brief vision of Molly Bendixon's disapproving face crossed my mind, but I shrugged it off.) Compared with some of the people I had worked with in the army, they couldn't be so bad. But everything depended on whether or not the students accepted me. What if they just took one look and decided not to cooperate?

I watched them pouring off the buses, shouting and running for the playground. They were everywhere, but their shouting stopped the moment they saw me. Three of them rushed to the front door and began to push each other in their eagerness to open the door for me, while several just stood on the sidewalk, staring at the new teacher as if at a creature from Mars. Some had on new clothes, while others wore faded and ill-fitting hand-me-downs from older brothers and sisters. Most of them looked fairly well scrubbed for the first day of school, but that would change as the year wore on and their clothes wore out. I tried to look older than I was, stern and authoritarian, but their excitement was catching, and I was grinning wildly as I went into the building, which they were not allowed to enter until the bell rang, although a couple of small boys sneaked in behind me and ran to hide before Miss Bendixon caught them.

Only one floor of one wing of the building was a junior high. The rest was a grade school including a kindergarten, and as the students plunged off the buses they included everything from tiny, terrified five-year-olds to nearly full-grown eighth graders trying to look sophisticated and hide their excitement from "the children" around them. Some of the eighth-grade boys had begun to experiment with shaving, and some of the eighth-grade girls had begun to experiment with wearing their sweaters backward to enhance the effect of their breasts, which were as yet mostly promises of future glory. To what extent the boys and girls had begun to experiment with one another, I had no way of knowing, but the more mature ones had obviously fallen under the influence of certain hormones and were beginning to behave in weird ways that marked them as pubertal.

Lowell School is a handsome two-story brick structure in the shape of an E with its auditorium forming the middle wing. In 1958 it had no gymnasium, only a large asphalt-covered playground on the south and west sides, with areas for basketball and softball. The school stands between Evergreen Cemetery and the traffic circle on Highway 80, and not far from the geographical center of what was then the Warren Mining District, one of the richest copper-producing areas in the world.

Just to the northwest of the school, on the other side of the traffic circle, was all that was left of the little town of Lowell—one narrow, crowded street lined with shops and bars, a restaurant, post office, and movie theater. The street, really only one long block, ended abruptly at a chain-link fence, as if it had been cut off there. And it had been cut off there, in 1951 when Phelps Dodge began to exploit the low-grade copper ore which lay directly beneath Lowell's residential district. The houses, most of them company houses, had been moved to the out-lying communities of Saginaw, Galena, and Briggs, but Lowell's one long block of commercial buildings remained, trapped between the traffic circle on Highway 80 and a huge hole in the ground. That hole in the ground, which remains today as a regular stop on the tourist route through Southeastern Arizona, is lavender, a soft shade between gray, pink, and purple, although it was not named because of its color, as I then thought, but for Harrison M. Lavender, who had been general manager of Phelps Dodge's mining operations and was instrumental in the evaluation of the Bisbee East ore body, which was to become Lavender Pit. Phelps Dodge had been gouging and blasting away at the Bisbee East ore body for only seven years when I arrived, but already it was the biggest man-made hole in the ground I had ever seen, and it was to become much bigger before they stopped working on it in 1974.

On the morning of my first day of classes at Lowell School I had pulled off the highway on my way to work, got out of the car and stood on the edge of Lavender Pit, looking down into it as if into a vast amphitheater a half mile across. It had symmetrical terraces all the way around it, and at the bottom, power shovels were scooping up great chunks of stone and dropping them into huge dump trucks, which looked like toy trucks from my vantage point, and which raced madly around the terraces and up the switchback road to deposit their loads at a building near the surface. That building housed the crusher, and crushed stones emerged in a steady stream from the other end of the building on a conveyor belt that took them up and over High-way 80 to the processing plant on the hill above. The processing plant didn't look too impressive to me as I stood beside the pit, but much of it was hidden on the far slope of the hill. The frenzied activity in the pit went on day and night, and every afternoon at four o'clock, workmen stopped all traffic on Highway 80 for about fifteen minutes while somebody down below detonated dozens of dynamite charges.

What amazed me was the vastness, the scale of everything, and the fact that there was so little noise except when the miners were blast-ing. That, I would soon learn, could be heard for miles, and it rattled the windows in Lowell School. But standing on the edge of the pit, I could only faintly hear what must have been the deafening racket made by the huge shovels below. It was all so far away, as if in a dream, and none of it seemed real. I had come to teach in a school near the edge of a man-made excavation that I could have used as an illustration of Dante's circles of Hell, but Hell would surely have been much smaller, something within my ability to grasp. At its bottom, toy machines dug frantically to make it even deeper, and around its circles toy trucks careened wildly. By day it was sun-drenched and lavender, and at night it was full of moving lights and shadows. We would have a slight earthquake every afternoon at four o'clock. Otherwise, the pit was almost silent and dreamlike. By the time I got to school that morning and saw the yellow buses arriving, I had decided I must have dreamed it the night before.

And the buses kept coming, as they would five mornings a week for the next nine months. All three of the major roads in the area converge at the traffic circle beside Lowell School, and the buses came from all directions. One of them came from the south, where the Mule Mountains fade into the majestic slope of the Espinal Plain. It came over the Naco Road which leads from Naco, Mexico, and Naco, Arizona, about six miles south of Bisbee. When it got to where the Naco Road joins Highway 92, it picked up a mob of children from an old community called San Jose.

One of the buses came from the southwest along Highway 92, skirting the southern end of the Mule Mountains. It picked up children from two subdivisions, one fairly modest and one rather posh, inhabited mostly by civilian employees at Ft. Huachuca, scientists and technocrats. That bus continued on to Tintown, a shantytown whose Hispanic population lived in shelters built of scrap lumber, sheets of tin, flattened metal containers, cardboard, and old car bodies.

I never knew how many of the people who lived in Tintown were citizens of the United States and how many were illegal aliens—probably nobody did. But it was not uncommon for Mexican citizens living in Naco or farther south to send their children to live with relatives in Tintown in order for the children to attend school in the United States, improve their English, and get what they considered to be a superior education. Tintown was a compact, tightly knit ghetto community, and none of the other students at Lowell School messed with a student from Tintown. To fight one of them was to fight all of them, and everybody in school knew it. During the school year I collected an amazing number of weapons from boys in the seventh and eighth grades, including some impressive switchblades, but I don't think any of the weapons were from boys who came from Tintown. They never flashed knives unless they were willing to use them, and they were much too clever to let me confiscate their most prized possessions.

Just past Tintown and on the other side of the highway the bus stopped for the students from South Bisbee, but I don't think the bus actually went into South Bisbee because the tunnel was too small. South Bisbee is a community which once had its own school, church, and store. Over the years it has become completely surrounded with tailings from several nearby mines, man-made walls of stone debris as tall as four-story buildings. The community can be entered only through two metal culverts, each a one-way tunnel barely large enough for a car to pass through. South Bisbee looks like a community built inside the cone of a volcano. The only view is straight up, and it's not a good place for the claustrophobic.

In 1958, South Bisbee was an extreme example of a general trend that determined housing patterns in the entire Warren Mining District—a tendency for each community to be isolated from all other communities in spite of the fact that the distance separating them might be very slight. That tendency had historical roots that went deep, roots which even the coming of the automobile and the general fluidity of modern society had been unable to overcome completely. In the Bisbee of today, the post-mining Bisbee, one has the feeling that everybody knows everybody else. But in the Bisbee of 1958, I had the feeling that hardly anybody knew anybody else, at least not well. The Warren Mining District had evolved into a series of discrete communities which seemed to be isolated from one another in many ways—geographically, culturally, and socially.

Even when the area was first settled, the natural geographical barriers were awesome. The miners built their houses up the sides of steep hills that would challenge a goat, and each hill was separated from the next by a deep ravine that became a torrent during the summer rains. In the three decades after 1877, when rich ore was being discovered in the mountainous area and each strike was worked by a different mining company, small communities grew up around each shaft. The largest concentration of housing and commercial buildings clustered around the Copper Queen Mine near the confluence of Tombstone Canyon and what came to be known as Brewery Gulch, and even though the miners who located in that area built their houses almost literally on top of one another, they were mostly immigrants and tended to group themselves in ethnic communities. The ravines often marked barriers that were more than topographical.

As time passed, pocket communities developed for reasons that were sometimes ethnic and cultural and sometimes economic and social. Many place names in Bisbee still reflect those pocket communities. The laundresses and their families, mostly Irish, lived on Laundry Hill. The mine foremen, mostly Anglo and northern European, lived in Jiggerville. The bankers, lawyers, and more successful merchants lived on Quality Hill. Most of the bartenders and gamblers lived and worked near the southern end of Brewery Gulch, while the prostitutes lived and worked near the northern end of that same colorful but extremely muddy thoroughfare. The Mexicans lived on Chihuahua Hill, and the Chinese were not allowed to live in Bisbee at all. Society in Bisbee was divided and stratified along many complex lines, creating a multitude of small, tightly knit housing communities.

As new mines were developed, new little towns grew up around them. Lowell came into being in 1900, made up originally of two saloons and a livery stable. San Jose was the inflated dream of a real estate entrepreneur in 1903, a developer who included in his plans an electric railroad system to minimize the town's isolation but went bankrupt before he could get the system built. The Calumet and Arizona Mining Company, which was for many years Phelps Dodge's chief local competitor, planned the town of Warren from scratch and built it between 1905 and 1915 on a fairly flat alluvial plain south and east of most of the mines. Warren is one of the few communities in the mining district with wide enough streets, and it became an elite community for upper-echelon mine management and engineers.

Even the pleasant community of Warren, with its planned spaciousness and tree-lined streets, suffered great disfigurement and increased isolation when the second round of surface mining began in 1951 with the removal of forty-six million tons of overburden above what was to become Lavender Pit, which was eventually to produce another seventy million tons of waste material. Something had to be done with all that stone debris, and it was. Phelps Dodge dumped it, thousands of tons of it, in the form of tailings, north of Bakerville and Warren, isolating those communities from Saginaw and Galena to the north and encroaching on the northern end of Warren where the most elegant mansions in the area had been built. Today, those mansions appear to have been built at the foot of a vertical mountain of stone debris. Digging Lavender Pit required the removal of the residential area of Lowell and relegated its business district to an isolation from which it never recovered. South Bisbee was surrounded with tailings. Several other small communities ceased to exist entirely.

Over the years, the Warren Mining District developed into a series of little towns and communities separated from one another by many seen and unseen barriers. One could live in the district all one's life and never enter South Bisbee or Tintown. After living there for two years, I was not sure where Saginaw was, although I thought it was very near where I lived in Bakerville but on the other side of a mountain-high wall of tailings.

At Lowell School in 1958, however, thanks to the buses, everybody's children got all mixed up with everybody else's, tailings or no tailings. The mixture of students from various communities was further complicated by the fact that one of the buses came from the northeast, down Highway 80 from the Sulphur Springs Valley beyond the Mule Mountains, and it came loaded with an amazingly diverse assortment of students, the sons and daughters of ranchers, orchard growers, and small farmers who had nothing to do with mining at all. It brought children from the Double Adobe area and from the tiny community of Elfrida and its surroundings, where some of the farmers raised their families in conditions of poverty even more desperate and probably far less pleasant than those in Tintown. In contrast, one of the students who rode that bus in from the Sulphur Springs Valley lived on a cattle ranch so large that I could never figure out exactly how large it was, but I came to find out that the ranch hands used jeeps instead of horses to herd the cattle, and that I could go there on weekends and ride a horse in a straight line all day without ever leaving the ranch.

There they were, getting off the buses that brought them from all directions, the seventh- and eighth-grade students at Lowell School, and I was seeing them for the first time: the ones I was going to turn into a choral speaking group and teach grammar to by having them create their own textbooks, the ones Molly Bendixon was going to try to protect from my harebrained notions if she could, the ones I was going to work among for the next two years and remember for the rest of my life.

When the bell rang for the first period of the day, which was homeroom, nearly every desk in my large classroom was filled with a seventh grader, some trying to control their excitement in order to impress the new teacher, others trying to test him by behaving at their worst. I still have the class photograph of that homeroom group. At the bottom it says, "Lowell School—Grade 7—1958–59." The students look out at me like a raggle-taggle crew of orphans, angels, and miscreants perched on the brink of the rest of their lives. But they were much better behaved than I had expected, certainly much better behaved than I and my peers had been at that age. Looking at them that morning, I remembered suddenly, and with horror, that I and my friends at the same age had deliberately and systematically driven a female teacher into a mental institution. And I remembered how shocked we had been when we finally succeeded, when they carted her off, and how, little hypocrites that we were, we had taken up a collection and sent her a nice plant for her room in the loony bin, where she may still be for all I know.

But most of the students at Lowell School treated their teachers with marked respect. The exceptions were notable, but they were exceptions. It was part of the miners' culture, which still held on to many traditions of immigrant European parents and grandparents, to be respectful to people with "an education," and to teachers especially. Courtesy to teachers was endemic in the Hispanic culture, and it was also an element in the culture of the farmers and ranchers in the Sulphur Springs Valley. And so, whatever they did on their own time, most of the students behaved well while they were in the classroom, and were eager to please the teacher.

After thirty years I still remember those students vividly, even many of their names. I remember Melva, freckle-faced and big for her age. She was the extremely bright daughter of scientists who worked at Ft. Huachuca. She called me years later to tell me that she had just got a Ph.D. in French. I remember Jane, the motherless child of a drunken miner who beat her regularly. She sat in the front row and cowered every time I raised the cane that I used as a blackboard pointer. I sent her to the school nurse who examined her and found bruises all over her thin body. Eventually they removed Jane from her father's house and placed her in a foster home. I don't know what became of her, but I can guess.

And Bobby, the son of another teacher in the Bisbee system. His tough attitude and constant defiance marked him as different from the others. He would have died of mortification if he had known it, but he was probably my favorite among the seventh graders. Where there was trouble, there was Bobby, but he never lied to get out of a scrape. His life at school was a constant round of sin and almost immediate punishment, but even while he was being punished, his look was direct and defiant, like a young bull confronting his tormentors. There was also a look in his eyes which said that he was trying hard to accomplish something, something important, and he didn't know exactly what it was. Molly Bendixon adored him, and I think he responded better to her than to any teacher in the building.

And I remember Pablo, so different from Bobby that he seemed to have come from a different planet. Pablo was one of the sweetest children I have ever known, and one of the most beautiful physically. I could not bear the soft velvet and vulnerability of his magnificent eyes. He was semi-retarded and tried desperately, again and again, to learn the things I taught him, but he always forgot them in a few hours. He was an orphan who had fallen into the hands of two uncles who owned a chili farm in the valley. For lunch each day, he brought a sack of green chilies, and nothing else. I convinced him that I loved chilies, in order to get him to trade me some of them for part of my sack lunch. It would have been easier for me simply to bring two lunches and give him one of them, but Pablo was proud and would not accept charity. It had to be a trade. It got so that I dreaded the lunch hour because the chilies were so hot, and I hated to have the students watch me while the tears ran down my face.

Once, after school, Pablo missed the bus. He came to me in tears and panic. If he didn't get home to go to work in the fields at the usual time, his uncles would do terrible things to him. He didn't have to spell out to me what those terrible things were. I drove him home, down the long slope of the Mule Mountains and into the Sulphur Springs Valley, with him urging me in Spanish and English to go faster. We almost caught up with the bus. When we got to the chili farm, he showed me, with a kind of shy pride, "his room," where he slept. It was a little wooden shed outside, about the size of a doghouse and with a dirt floor. I wondered if they chained him there at night, but I could see no chain. Yes, I remember Pablo.

And Frank, with his freckles and one front tooth missing. Small for his age and very pale. Fourteen years later, when I entered the State Prison at Florence to begin teaching the Writers' Workshop there, Frank was one of the first inmates to greet me. He was almost bald by then, but he still had his freckles.

And I remember Rosa and Yolanda, cousins. Both their mothers were prostitutes in the red-light district just south of Naco and had sent the girls to live with relatives in Tintown in order to get an "American" education and learn good English, which would help them when they entered their mothers' profession as soon as they graduated from the eighth grade. They were quiet, dutiful students who accepted the "C" and "D" grades they received without complaint. They seldom asked for help or ventured an opinion, and they had almost nothing to do with the other students. They had each other, and it seemed to be all they needed. After a couple of months, I became aware of what lay ahead for them, and I also became aware that there was nothing I could do about it. They were citizens of another country, in more ways than one, and it was a country over which I had no control. They were so quiet I didn't realize they were genuinely fond of me, or that they cherished their two years in an "American" school, learning English from their crew-cut teacher, before the adult world closed in on them.

But I got some indication of how they felt later, after they graduated. My mother had come to visit us in Bisbee, and my wife and I were showing her around the area. We drove across the border to Naco so she could see a little of Mexico, and on through the red-light district, which fascinated and repelled my very proper mother who, if she had lived in Tombstone in the 1880s would have marched resolutely down one side of Allen Street without ever glancing to the other side of the street, where the painted ladies could be seen. It was a Saturday afternoon, warm and sunny, and many of the prostitutes were sitting on benches in front of the brothels, enjoying the sun, and done up in all their finery in case any "window shoppers" should be driving by. When we stopped for a stop sign, two of the women suddenly jumped up and ran to the car excitedly, calling my name. I would not have recognized them in their working clothes and makeup, but it was Rosa and Yolanda, looking ten years older. They were beside themselves with excitement at seeing me again. I was afraid they were going to kiss my hand when I got out of the car and shook hands with them.

From the back seat of the car, where my mother held our son in her lap, I heard a great intake of breath, but she didn't faint, which I thought was a real possibility. After we drove away and I stopped laughing at Mother's reaction, I tried to explain to her that the girls had been my students at Lowell School. "Students!" she hissed through clenched teeth. "Students! They didn't look like students to me!" And so how could I forget Rosa and Yolanda, who never distinguished themselves in their teacher's eyes until after they had graduated.

And I remember Maria, sweet Maria, whose father was a miner and whose mother made tortillas so thin I could see through them. In the class picture she looks somehow younger than the others, tiny and fragile. She was neither ugly nor particularly pretty, neither brilliant nor stupid, just a good little girl. She was never the first nor the last at anything, and she seemed to take up almost no space in the class-room—just two enormous eyes in a small face. It was, in fact, her mother who brought Maria to the forefront of my attention. One day when the bell rang for lunch and I opened the classroom door, a very short Hispanic woman was standing in the hall holding a foil-covered plate. She spoke broken English, but there was great pride in her face as she identified herself as Maria's mother and held the plate out to me. She had cooked me a Mexican dinner and brought it to school while it was still hot. She was a superb cook, and it meant that I would have an excuse not to eat Pablo's chilies that day, and I wouldn't suffer from heartburn later. From then on, she appeared outside my class-room several times a month at the lunch hour, and always with a hot plate of food.

Maria was not an exceptional student in any way, but she was deter-mined, and I could tell by her mother that her parents were behind her 100 percent. Her one claim to distinction was that she had never been absent from school a day in her life. She had a perfect attendance record. Both she and her mother were very proud of that. But one Friday morning, in the spring of my second year, when Maria was in the eighth grade, I noticed while I was taking roll that she looked very ill. She was somewhere between gray and green, and her eyes were dull with fever. She held onto her desk as if the room were spinning around her.

"Maria," I said, "you're sick. There's been a lot of intestinal flu going around and I suspect you have it. You will have to go home."

Great tears appeared in Maria's fever-stricken eyes. "Please, pleeease don't make me go home. I will have to be absent. I will lose my perfect attendance record. It's only two months to graduation. I'm O.K. I'm not really sick. Pleeeeeeease."

It was a hard decision for me, with those huge dark eyes pleading from that tiny sick face, but she was probably contagious and I had to get her out of the classroom. I thought hard and said, "The nurse isn't here today, so I guess you could go to the nurse's room and lie down for awhile." Then, in response to her wildly questioning eyes, I added, "And that way I won't have to mark you absent."

I watched her wobble down the hall, but before she was out of sight, she began to vomit in great projectile arcs. She looked back over her shoulder at me like a whipped puppy, but I waved her on. When I sent for the janitor, he was madder than hell. "Damned little brats ought to stay home when they're sick," he muttered as he began the unpleasant job of cleaning up the hall, long sections of which Maria had messed up thoroughly.

All day Maria stayed in the nurse's room, lying on a cot, alternating between chills and fever. As soon as I could leave the classroom, I went to the office, past the janitor who was still mopping and muttering, and put in a surreptitious call to the lady who brought me delicious Mexican dinners. She came to school at once and sat with Maria the rest of the day, holding her hand and putting wet towels on her forehead. And although Maria didn't attend any of her classes that day, she wasn't exactly absent either. By the following Monday, she had recovered.

Two months later Maria graduated almost exactly in the middle of her class in terms of grades, and with no special achievements to mark her eight years in school except that when she stepped forward to

247 ❖

receive her diploma, the principal pinned a small gold medal on her and announced that she was the only student in the entire district to graduate with a perfect attendance record. As Maria walked across the stage in her first pair of semi-high heels and her fancy graduation dress, with a white ribbon in her hair and her eyes shining, suddenly she looked almost grown up, and very beautiful.

I also remember Tony and Juan, the leading athletes in the eighth grade. Although they were not particularly large, they seemed more mature than the other boys. They had a quiet self-assurance and the kind of good looks that caused many of the girls to sigh and stare at them during class. Girls were interesting to Tony and Juan, but they were much more comfortable with a basketball or baseball, and they were excellent students. They already seemed to know who they were and had a good notion of where they were going. They had exquisite Latin manners, and so I was surprised one day in class when they both suddenly but quietly left their seats near the back of the room and walked out of class.

"Getting too big for their britches," I said to myself. Normally a student would ask permission to leave the class and needed a pass from me to go down the hall, even to the toilet. But I was in the middle of a lesson and simply made a mental note to speak to the boys later. In about twenty minutes they returned as quietly as they had left and took their seats. At the end of the class they stopped by my desk.

"O.K., do you want to tell me what that was all about?"

"Well," Tony said with a grin that was going to break many hearts in the next few years, "the auditorium was on fire and we had to go put it out. We didn't want anybody to get shook up about it."

From their seats they had a good view of the next wing of the building, the big auditorium, and one of them had seen flames through one of the auditorium windows. Evidently, somebody had been sneaking a smoke in the auditorium and had discarded a cigarette in a wastebasket full of trash. The trash had ignited one of the curtains. A few minutes more and the entire auditorium would have been blazing. Without alarming anyone, Tony and Juan had gone into the auditorium, found the fire extinguisher, and put out the fire. Then, without telling anyone in the office, they had returned to class.

Tony and Juan became the school heroes, of course, but most of the other students were disappointed at having missed the excitement and the chance to have a fire drill, something everybody enjoyed. Fire drills were exciting, a welcome break from the routine, and in a large two-story building, they were important. We had unannounced drills throughout the year, and they always got our adrenalin pumping. We practiced for them rigorously, and all the students knew which exit route to take from whatever classroom they happened to be in. The principal recorded the number of seconds it took us to evacuate the building, and we were always trying to beat our previous record.

I remember one of the drills particularly, not only because it was a near disaster, but because of its aftermath. It must have been in late November of my first year. The students were supposed to evacuate from my classroom by walking rapidly, two abreast, the length of the east wing hallway, taking a sharp right, and going down a short flight of stairs to a landing and out the double doors. I was supposed to follow them after I had closed all the windows. (Since I had destroyed all my textbooks by leaving the windows open during a sudden storm, I never again forgot to close the windows when I left the room, fire drill or no fire drill.) But there was another door opening onto the landing at the foot of the stairs, and it led into a large all-purpose room that was temporarily being used as a kindergarten. However, that door was not supposed to be used during fire drills because the room had another exit door which led directly outside.

During the fire drill I remember best, for some reason the kindergarten teacher had trouble getting the outside door open. She panicked and sent thirty kindergarten children out the door which led onto the landing, directly in the path of my thirty eighth graders, who were plunging single-mindedly down the stairs. Unable to overcome their momentum, my students knocked the smaller children down and trampled them quite thoroughly. By the time I got there, the entire landing was a wild melee of screaming kindergarten children in various stages of panic and injury, a teacher almost in shock, and the last of my eighth-graders trying to pick up the tots and carry them bodily out, bruised and battered though they were. It was one of the more memorable scenes I still carry with me from Lowell School.

Fortunately, none of the smaller students was seriously injured, which was some kind of miracle, although many of them were bruised, scratched, scraped, and badly shaken up. As soon as I got my class back in the room and settled down a little, I went to see how bad the damage was downstairs. Also, I knew I was going to get a dressing down from Molly Bendixon, since it had been my class that did the damage, and I didn't want the tirade to be within earshot of my students. But Molly had already reconstructed the entire affair and had made up her mind who was to blame. I could hear her clearly as I started down the hall. She was standing at the top of the short flight of stairs, and the unfortunate young woman who taught kindergarten was cowering on the landing below. Molly tended to shout when she got angry, and she was livid then. It was exactly the kind of dangerous, unnecessary foul-up she hated most.

"You stupid son-of-a-bitch!" she was yelling at the kindergarten teacher. (Molly wasn't always too accurate with her epithets when she got angry, but they were effective nonetheless.) "Damn you! You could have got those kids killed. You don't have brains God gave a goose. Why didn't you take them out the door you were supposed to?"

"I, I couldn't," the teacher stammered, "get the door . . ."

"There's nothing wrong with that door," Molly cut in. "You just have to push hard on it. You didn't even try. You just panicked. Jesus Christ! What is the district coming to when they hire screw-ups like you? I feel sorry for those poor little kids if all they've got is you."

Still in a rage, Molly had turned and started back to her classroom when she saw me, with my mouth open, in the hallway. "Oh-oh," I thought, "it's my turn now."

But instead of laying into me, she shook her head and made a gesture of disgust toward the teacher on the landing below. "I should have known that would happen," she said. "You and me have got to keep our eyes open. Some of these sonsabitches don't know what they're doing." With that, she strode off down the hall with the dignity of an avenging angel who had accomplished her mission.

At that moment I realized Molly's attitude toward me had changed and that I was one of the chosen people, one of the lucky ones whom she accepted as a professional and a peer, for better or for worse. I would have nothing to fear from her in the future, but I never knew exactly why or when she had changed her mind about me. Perhaps it hadn't been any one thing, but a combination of things, an accumulation of impressions. Who knew what would make a good impression on Molly Bendixon? And I had been much too busy keeping my head above water to think about it. I had been working my tail off, and she must have known it, although she had expressed misgivings about my methods. I cared deeply about the students, and they seemed to like me. I'm sure Molly knew that, too, since she was a master at extracting information from the students, and she could do it so cleverly that they were seldom aware of the information they were giving her. Or perhaps her change in attitude was partly the result of our first and only serious confrontation, although I couldn't have imagined at the time that such a negative encounter could have anything but negative results.

It happened about a month before the disastrous fire drill. Since our first meeting in the teachers' lounge I had expected a battle sooner or later, but I had no way of knowing when or in what form it would come. As it was, she caught me first thing in the morning when I was at my worst and least tolerant, and I reacted accordingly. Each morning in homeroom, the first thing I was supposed to do after the Pledge of Allegiance was take roll and send a student to the office with my absence report. The school secretary would then start making phone calls to find out if the missing students were at home or playing hooky.

One morning, however, something distracted me. I don't remember what it was, but it might well have been a brawl in the back of the room with Bobby in the middle of it, or it might have been the time Pablo came in without bathing or changing his clothes after tangling with a skunk, and I had to send him out in the hall while the other students stood along the wall of the classroom with their heads out the windows. Whatever it was, it caused me to be late getting the roll taken, and I had just turned to that task when the door opened and Molly Bendixon walked in abruptly.

"Where's your absence report?" she demanded. "They're waiting for it in the office. It's holding everybody up. Haven't you been told that you're supposed to take the roll first thing and get it down there?" Her tone was sarcastic and patronizing.

"I'm just taking it now," I said. "I'll have it down there right away." I was furious but determined not to show it in front of the students. Molly turned and marched out, and I followed her, closing the door behind us. I hadn't had my morning coffee yet, and my anger was getting the upper hand. "Miss Bendixon," I said, "let me explain something." She sighed and turned, evidently expecting an excuse. "My classroom is off limits to you. You are never again to enter it unless I invite you. And if you ever humiliate me in front of my students again, I will knock you on your ass. You can tell that to the principal if you want to, and if you don't believe me, try me."

I went back into my classroom and slammed the door, hard. Several of the students had slipped up to the door and had been straining to hear what I was saying to Molly, but they scuttled back to their seats when I came in, and everybody was very quiet. I took the roll, as leisurely as possible, and sent my absence report to the office. Within minutes of my outburst, I realized that I had overreacted. I had never spoken like that to a woman in my life, but then I had never known a woman like Molly Bendixon. All day I expected fireworks, some kind of retaliation, but nothing unusual happened, and I didn't see Molly again that day. During the rest of the week, we nodded curtly to each other when we passed in the hall or met in the teachers' lounge. I felt wretched about the whole thing.

And I felt even worse the following Monday when Paul Rose told me that Molly was in the hospital and had undergone surgery. I don't remember exactly what the surgery was, but I think it was a gall bladder operation. (In those days, when a woman had surgery, a man didn't ask questions.) By that time my classes were working out fairly well, and I wasn't so worried about somebody finding out that I had accidentally destroyed all my textbooks, and I had smuggled the ruined books out of the building, a few at a time in my briefcase, and put them in the trash at home. I had decided that Molly didn't know about it anyway. Surely she wouldn't have passed up an opportunity like that to get me in trouble. I could see no indication that she had told Paul Rose about it, or about our confrontation in the hall. But I had gone much too far in my anger, and I knew it. You didn't go around threatening to hit spinster schoolteachers, at least not in Bisbee.

I wasn't quite prepared to apologize, but on the other hand, I had to make some gesture to let her know I was sorry, and to test the water. After worrying about it all day Monday, I decided to go see her that night in the hospital. The Phelps Dodge Company Hospital, the only hospital in the area, was next door to the Phelps Dodge headquarters, both in old brick buildings in the center of Bisbee and only two blocks from where my family and I were living on O.K. Street. While I walked those two blocks that evening, I thought of a dozen excuses not to enter the hospital, but I entered it anyway, and once I had inquired what room she was in, there was no turning back.

She looked sallow and weak. I had forgotten how big and dark her eyes were in that thin, square-jawed face. She was obviously very surprised to see me, but she seemed pleased. We chatted about nothing much for a few minutes, and I asked her if there was anything I could bring her. She said no. She was fumbling around on the table beside her bed for a cigarette, and I noticed that her hand was trembling. I got the cigarette out of the package and lit it for her. We chatted a few more minutes and that was that. Neither of us referred to the scene in the hall.

As I recall, I visited her one more time before she was discharged from the hospital, and about a week later she was back at school, a little more gaunt than she had been, but basically the same, and complaining about the nitwit who had substituted for her and created nothing but confusion in her classes. But she told a wonderfully funny dirty joke in the teachers' lounge, and it relieved the tension. I was beginning to find out that women often tell better dirty jokes than men— truly funny rather than merely crude.

Until the disastrous fire drill, there had been only one other indication of Molly's attitude toward me, and it was one I couldn't interpret. Late one afternoon when the last class was dismissed and all the students had gone, I was so exhausted that all I could do was put my head down on my desk and go to sleep. I had been walking to and from school, not a great distance, but on that afternoon I was too drained to face even a short walk without first taking a short nap. My door was open, and as Molly left the teachers' lounge, she saw me asleep at my desk. She went to the office, phoned my wife, and asked her (my wife said it sounded more like an order) to drive to school and pick me up because I was too exhausted to walk home. And my wife did, right away. At the time, I couldn't tell if Molly did it out of concern or contempt.

But after the fire drill episode, as our acquaintance grew into a friendship, I realized she had made that phone call out of concern, and that she used her gruff ways to mask the concern that gripped her heart. Sometimes she would phone me at night, never late, and she never talked very long. Usually she called to discuss the problems of some student who was having trouble, since we both dealt with the same students. She taught them math and I taught them English, but it wasn't their ability to learn math or English that concerned her most. It was just them. Their lives, their welfare, their problems, whether or not they had enough to eat, and what kind of problems at home we were seeing the results of in class. All of them were her children, and I think she sensed that I knew it and I was willing to share the burdens with her. It occurred to me that maybe she was lonely, and I was pleased that when she wanted someone to talk to, she chose me.

It was a strange friendship, perhaps—a middle-aged spinster school-teacher and a young novice who was flying by the seat of his pants. It took me a while to realize it, and we never discussed it, but we were reaching out to one another because of something each of us sensed about the other, something important. We had both been damaged when we were young—I guess everybody is but we had been damaged in similar ways, and that damage had made us fierce and tender in the heart. We both cared desperately about the children who were growing up in front of us and all around us. We cared about each individual one. More often than not we couldn't help them very much, but we wanted to, and we were willing to try. We became partisans in a struggle we could seldom win, and we knew that, but the struggle drew us closer to one another.

Somebody else lives in Molly's cream-colored house now, and I have been teaching in a university for thirty years. It doesn't seem possible. Surely, if I stop and get out of the van, Molly will come to the door with her braying laugh and it will be 1958 and everything will be the same. The trees are taller and thicker, but the house looks much as it did. I slow down, but I don't stop. There is nothing in that house for me to stop for now. There is no way I can make Molly understand how much she meant to me, and I don't even know how to describe our relationship. One word comes to mind, although it is a badly abused word. Colleagues. We were colleagues.

In the years that I have taught at the university, I have heard that word used often. Whether our English Department faculty meetings are long and boring or long and stormy, that word will come up, and it is often used with an irony bordering on contempt. Somebody will say, "I must disagree with my esteemed colleague," and the fight is on. It has occurred to me that the people who use that word the most have the least knowledge of what it means and the least right to use it. In their battles for turf they sometimes forget that it means they are leagued together, and not for their own benefit, but in order to supply the needs of their students.

Molly and I were colleagues. We leagued together in the face of our students' overwhelming problems, and we knew we would fight for those students, side by side and with our bodies if we had to. We had other colleagues at Lowell School, good people who cared deeply about the students. But there were others. Molly taught me that they weren't all worthy to be thought of as our colleagues.

Molly and I functioned on a professional level, but beneath it was another level. We were devious if we had to be, and downright subversive at times, but always for the students. We failed much of the time, but even then we had each other. I can still hear her saying, "Watch out for the sonsabitches, Dick, just watch out for the sonsabitches!"

11

Bisbee's narrow Main Street, winding down Tombstone Canyon, isn't exactly bustling this late afternoon. It's all in shadow, like a cavern, but the setting sun is lighting the surrounding mountains brilliantly, and the town is filled with an amber, reflected light, the way I remember it best. Three tourists are ambling along, looking in the windows of curio shops and art galleries. A German shepherd bitch trots down the sidewalk with her sideways gait, checking the doorway of each shop and moving on in search of the one particular smell she associates with all she knows of human kindness and love. At a glance, everything seems to be about the same as I remember it, although much quieter, and yet it is a facade, like the set of a turn-of-the-century movie but more convincing. Nothing is really the same as I remember it, except maybe Castle Rock, an imposing limestone formation that juts out from the north side of the canyon, causing Main Street to veer sharply around it.

I guess people like me can live in the past if we want to, but towns can't. Towns can pretend for the benefit of tourists, who love illusion because they have plenty of reality back home, but towns can't really live in the past. It's natural for me to want to sustain the illusion that I'm driving down Main Street in 1958 because that's one way to pretend that I'm still young, that I don't show or feel the ravages of the last thirty years and more. And for a moment, at least, I can believe it, until I pass the big white Baptist church on the right, built flush with the street like everything else in this narrow part of the canyon. It's empty now and has a forlorn look and big "For Sale" sign.

I wonder what happened to the Baptists who used to worship there. Maybe a few of them stayed on and found a smaller building somewhere else, or maybe they all just packed up their Bibles and got the hell out, like most of the rest of Bisbee's residents did, with or without Bibles, when Phelps Dodge shut down operations on June 13, 1975. It's a shock to think that even churches can't live in the past, at least Protestant churches. It gives me renewed respect for the Catholic church, which has managed to live in the past for centuries, and whose supreme commander shows little inclination to change that policy in recent times. Surely, if he can ignore so many centuries, I can ignore the last thirty-plus years and pretend that I'm still young and driving down Bisbee's Main Street for the first time.

Perhaps it isn't so strange that when the end came for the Warren Mining District, many of the people of Bisbee had trouble believing it. Considering the history of the district, where generation after generation had ridden the copper roller coaster as it climbed and plunged from good times to bad times, through shut-downs and prolonged strikes, booms and busts, it isn't so strange that when the Phelps Dodge officials said, "This is it, this is absolutely the end," many citizens of Bisbee did not believe them, could not believe them. They had lived under the shadow of disaster all their lives, and predictions of doom didn't mean much to them. Bisbee had burned down three times, but it had risen again, stronger each time. And as for devastating floods, they had been too common to keep an accurate count of.

Lynn R. Bailey, in his 1983 history, *Bisbee: Queen of the Copper Camps*, takes the residents of Bisbee to task for the way they reacted, or didn't react, to the news that Phelps Dodge was closing down operations. He says the Bisbeeites had become so dependent on Phelps Dodge that they were helpless when the end came. "Paternalism had sapped the town's initiative." And maybe he's right. I'm no historian, and I lived in Bisbee for only two years, but I think that many of the people of Bisbee reacted with a kind of faith, perhaps blind faith, that no matter how bad things got, no matter what disaster occurred—flood, fire, depressed copper prices, the closing of the mines—things would get better if they were only able to tough it out, to hang on a little longer. That faith had been handed down to them by their parents and grandparents. They couldn't give up hope just because the company had given up. History is full of examples of people who continued to believe in their gods long after it was obvious that their gods had abandoned them.

The German shepherd bitch now decides to try the other side of the street, and I brake sharply as she crosses in front of the van. I wonder if she has been dumped and what will happen to her if she doesn't find that one smell, that hope she lives for. She keeps trying each doorway and moving quickly on to the next. She has on a collar, but she doesn't look particularly well fed. I wonder how long she has been searching up one side of Main Street and down the other.

The miners who had put down roots in Bisbee were tough, but when the end came, and it was a long time coming, they couldn't live and support their families on hope alone. Even in Bisbee, with its blessed climate, it gets very cold on winter nights. They couldn't pay rent or mortgages and buy groceries when there was nothing for them to do but watch television and play checkers. Phelps Dodge offered six hundred of them jobs in its other mines in Arizona and New Mexico. Most of the rest of them eventually drifted on in search of work. Some went to Tucson to try to hire on at the mines just south of town. Others went to Colorado or Nevada. Some headed for California and completed the transcontinental journey their immigrant ancestors had begun when they landed at Ellis Island almost a century earlier. Some settled for work in coal mines at lower wages, where their highly developed skills were often wasted; but mining was all they knew, and they had to mine something or starve.

Most of the miners who had already retired stayed on in Bisbee, where their property values plummeted as the bottom dropped out of the real-estate market. Many of the houses were simply abandoned. Miners' cottages were selling for one thousand dollars, although few of them sold even at that price. Some nonretired miners, merchants, and professional people held on, scrambling to make a living in whatever way they could until things picked up. Surely, they thought, things would pick up because things always had picked up in the past. After all, Bisbee was still the county seat. After 1975, Cochise County became the largest employer, almost the only employer, in Bisbee.

There's an expression often heard on the streets or in the shops and homes of Bisbee today. It reflects many years of history and has probably been current for more than a century. When something goes wrong, people respond with a particular kind of shrug and grin and say, "That's Bisbee." Those two words carry a world of meaning to Bisbee residents and bond them together into a psychological community which outsiders often do not understand. When you live in Bisbee, those words suggest, anything that can go wrong will go wrong because it always has. It's the Bisbee attitude. And although most of the present residents of Bisbee form a new society grafted onto the roots of the old Bisbee mining society, they have been here long enough and have had sufficient experience with the old society, the retired miners, to have picked up the Bisbee attitude. "That's Bisbee," they say when a wall collapses or the ancient water or gas lines fall apart.

I remember how it worked when I lived in Bisbee in the late fifties. One morning as I was driving down Tombstone Canyon, I noticed that a house, which had been in good shape the previous day, had suddenly sunk about ten feet into a forgotten mine shaft over which it had been built years before. A small crowd had gathered to stare at the house. Only the roof was still visible. When I joined the crowd and asked what had happened, one of them grinned, shrugged, and said, "That's Bisbee." It was the only explanation I got, the only one which seemed to them adequate to explain the rather bizarre circumstances.

Whatever else disappeared when Phelps Dodge pulled out in 1975, the Bisbee attitude lived on. Robert Houston, a friend who wrote the novel *Bisbee 17* and now has a house in Bisbee, is full of stories that reflect the Bisbee attitude in recent times. It must have been in 1977 or 1978, after Bob had bought one of the small Bisbee houses to use as a studio, that he went to the Bisbee Fire Department to get a building permit in order to renovate the house. The fire chief didn't look too chipper, and Bob asked him what was the matter.

"Well," the chief said, "We've been working for a long time on a big fire-prevention exhibit to take to the state fair in Phoenix. We finally finished it, and yesterday we loaded it on a flatbed truck and started out for Phoenix. Damned exhibit caught fire and burned up before we got halfway there." Then, with a shrug and that ironic grin that always accompanies the Bisbee attitude, he added, "That's Bisbee," as if he had expected all along that such a thing would happen.

It's a kind of fatalism, of course, but it isn't entirely a negative attitude because, as soon as they say, "That's Bisbee," residents go to work to clear away the debris and try to repair the damage, even if it means simply propping things up until the next disaster. I think it is unfair to say the fatalism with which Bisbeeites viewed the pull-out of Phelps Dodge was caused by the fact they had become so dependent on one huge, paternalistic corporation that they had lost all initiative. Their dogged fatalism in the face of imminent disaster is the result of the history of Bisbee, since the history of Bisbee is the history of disasters, one after the other, and repeated disaster can become a way of life and foster attitudes which are handed down for generations. Perhaps the attitude goes well beyond the history of Bisbee. Perhaps it is endemic among underground miners, who face the strong possibility of death or severe injury each time they go down into the mine.

After Phelps Dodge shut down everything but a tiny leaching operation, those who remained knew the history of Bisbee. It was in their bones, in their genes, and they had been raised on it. They told and retold the old stories about Bisbee in its earliest days, stories which would suggest that the mining camp had overcome problems as severe as those they were facing. The young Copper Queen Mine had run out of ore as early as 1884, and the mine manager had declared that all operations would cease immediately. But a small group of determined Cornish miners kept on blasting and digging, in the face of direct orders to stop. They said they could smell copper ore, and they ran an exploratory shaft in the direction their instincts told them to go. In a few days they hit a rich plume of ore that kept the mine going for years.

Bisbee had burned down three times, twice before it could find a decent water supply with which to fight fires. By 1885, at least five hundred people lived in flimsy wooden structures packed closely together and hemmed in by the steep hills that formed Tombstone Canyon and Brewery Gulch. In February of that year, the first major fire destroyed the entire business district and many of the houses, while residents formed a bucket brigade and tried to save the Copper Queen smelter. And when the first big fire had burned itself out, I know what they did. They looked at the smoking ruins of what had been their little town and said, "That's Bisbee." But there is no record that an appreciable number of them left, or even considered leaving.

They rebuilt in the same places and with the same flammable materials, but they organized themselves into a volunteer fire-fighting brigade, and purchased some crude fire-fighting equipment. In 1894 they reorganized the volunteer fire fighters into a real fire department, with a two-wheel pump cart and hose, three hundred feet of it, which could be supplied with water from the spring at the base of Castle Rock. The speed with which the firemen could race down Bisbee's tortuous streets pulling the pump cart was a source of great pride to Bisbee's residents.

But the handsome young firemen, with their handlebar mustaches and their dark, underwearlike uniform, which made each of them look like the man on the flying trapeze, were not enough to prevent another conflagration on a June morning in 1907. It broke out at the lower end of O.K. Street, which follows the base of Chihuahua Hill up Brewery Gulch. Swept by strong winds, the fire moved up the east side of Brewery Gulch to the newly constructed Pythian Hall, one of Bisbee's most impressive brick structures, which was saved by the fire fighters, but barely. The miners were brought up from the mines to help fight the fire, and they dynamited dozens of houses in its path and cleared away the debris to form a firebreak, but the fire roared up Chihuahua Hill, which was densely covered with the frame dwellings of most of the town's Hispanic population. Everything on Chihuahua Hill was destroyed, and about one-fourth of the town was gone.

Even that wasn't the worst. The worst came a little more than a year later on the evening of October 14 when a fire broke out in or near the Grand Hotel on Main Street about six o'clock. It spread through the heart of the business district in two directions and on both sides of Main Street all the way to Castle Rock, sparing only a cluster of buildings at the confluence of Main Street and Brewery Gulch. It destroyed every house on Clawson Hill except two, and left three-quarters of the city—by then Bisbee was a city—in ruins.

The Arizona Historical Society has a photograph of that inferno, taken during the night, evidently from the roof of a building near Main Street, and it captures the most dramatic version of a fiery hell that I have ever seen. The photographer used the light of the flames to expose his plate, and I can't imagine how he got close enough to do it. It is an amazing work of art, and totally horrifying. The same museum has another photograph, taken the next morning, looking east along Main Street from somewhere near Castle Rock, probably at about the spot I am now passing. The street has become a pathway between high mounds of smoking rubble. Down this pathway, which winds toward what had been the center of Bisbee, a number of people are promenading. They all seem to be dressed up for the occasion. One couple has just passed the camera. The man is wearing a dark suit and hat, the woman a white shirtwaist with mutton-leg sleeves, a long stylish skirt, and one of those enormous, overdecorated hats that women of that period somehow managed to balance on their heads. They appear to be out for a stroll down a narrow pathway through the center of hell, with smoke erupting from the black cinder piles on either side of them. That photograph is a dramatic visual representation of the Bisbee attitude, and it was taken on the morning of October 15, 1908. Not one of Bisbee's better mornings, but life in Bisbee goes on.

Later that day, the residents of Bisbee began to clear away the rubble in order to rebuild. This time, they built the business district of more fire-resistant materials. Most of the handsome masonry buildings along Main Street now, with their facades of intricately patterned brick, are the result of that rebuilding. But the miners rebuilt their houses of wood, and so close together that privacy has always been a scarce commodity in what has come to be known as "Old Bisbee," a recent and trendy name for the Tombstone Canyon–Brewery Gulch community to distinguish it from the outlying communities, although all of them are part of the City of Bisbee. They built their houses where their houses had been before the fire, up the sides of the hills, and they provided access to the roads below by means of long, steep flights of concrete stairs, up which all furniture, groceries, and sometimes water had to be carried by hand. And although the houses were usually simple and unremarkable, their locations created a singular kind of architectural beauty, which I can see now as I look to the left and right of the road. Few architectural structures are more beautiful to me than a long, unbroken flight of exterior stairs leading up and out of sight to . . . who knows what?

That building pattern, which has altered none at all since the turn of the century, determined that Bisbee would never have door-to-door mail delivery. Only a mountain goat could climb those interminable stairs to deliver the mail. And it also determined that Bisbee would always be particularly susceptible to the danger of fire, and particularly difficult to protect from that danger.

In 1909, the year after the worst fire in Bisbee's history, the people adopted measures to prevent such a calamity in the future. They raised 2.5 million dollars through bond issues, an incredible sum in those days, for a new fire department housed in the city hall, near the junction of Tombstone Canyon and Brewery Gulch. They spent some of that money on a magnificent pair of black horses, said to be "the handsomest fire horses in the Southwest," to pull the fire wagon and its three thousand feet of hose. In 1913 they built a second fire station at the junction of Moon Canyon and Tombstone Canyon, and by 1917 they had replaced all the horse-drawn wagons with fire trucks. I just passed the station at the bottom of Moon Canyon, and it's still in use. Its major piece of equipment was visible through the open doors as I passed, a 1941 fire truck, which has proven, because of Bisbee's narrow, twisting streets, to be more practical than wider, more recent models.

In addition to the constant threat of fire, early Bisbee had devastating flash floods each year during the monsoon season. With almost no warning, walls of water crashed down the ravines leading into Tombstone Canyon and Brewery Gulch, often sweeping houses, outhouses, horses, mules, and residents with them. One lucky miner who lived at the upper end of Brewery Gulch happened to be taking his weekly— or possibly monthly—bath when a flash flood struck and his house was washed away. He rode his bathtub all the way down the gulch, and when the flood abated, found himself on Main Street in the center of town completely naked. But he was alive and soon to become a legend.

Although Bisbee experienced flooding every year, the worst floods recorded were in 1890, 1896, 1902, and 1908, at six-year intervals. Considering the Bisbee attitude, I suppose the residents considered themselves lucky that the town didn't usually wash out and burn down in the same year. At least they probably felt that way until 1908, the year the town flooded out one month and burned down the next. The 1890 flood killed two miners, but the volume of water and debris hurtling down Tombstone Canyon was so great that the citizens were able to find only one body. The 1902 flood hit Brewery Gulch hardest, and it was probably that flood which brought the naked miner down the gulch in his bathtub and taught him the value of cleanliness. By 1908, the floods seemed to be made up more of mud than water. That year, thousands of tons of mud and debris flowed down Main Street and into the post office, filling it to a depth of five feet.

The rainy seasons were warm and damp, good breeding seasons for insects and disease. Rains flooded the shallow privies, washing their contents down the hills and into the center of town. In the early days of Bisbee, dysentery was a problem all year long, largely because many of the residents built their privies close to or uphill from their sources of water. Early photographs show privies in some of the most unaccountable places. Some were in front of the houses and right on the edge of Main Street, on the sidewalk, so to speak, if there had been a sidewalk. On Chihuahua Hill, most of the houses and boarding houses had no privies at all. Occupants simply dumped the contents of their chamber pots off the porch onto the side of the hill, along with their garbage and trash. During the rainy seasons, everything washed down to Brewery Gulch, where anyone crossing the street on foot was forced to wade through it.

Starting in 1883 with the first typhoid epidemic and continuing for nearly thirty years, the monsoon season was known as "plague season." Between 1888 and 1900, hundreds of Bisbee residents died of typhoid, smallpox, and diphtheria. The sick and dying lay on pallets lining the streets, where it was cooler than in the houses. And although a long series of company doctors led heroic struggles against unsanitary conditions, the diseases were never brought under control until the floods were brought under control.

After the 1890 flood, the citizens of Bisbee built large wooden floodgates in upper Tombstone Canyon to divert the floodwaters from the central part of town, but the gates were not effective, as shown by the subsequent floods. In later years they built a wooden flume which led through town, and when this also failed, they built a series of concrete flumes leading down some of the ravines and into a central concrete canal that channeled the water through town. I have been seeing that large canal, sometimes on one side of the road and sometimes on the other, most of the way down Tombstone Canyon. Garages and even houses have been built over it in places, and finally it disappears underground and runs, appropriately enough, under Subway Avenue. Without that system of canals, the downtown section of Bisbee would be a disaster area during the rainy seasons, like right now.

So the Bisbee attitude developed. If the flood doesn't get you, the fire will. And there were always typhoid, smallpox, and diphtheria. That's Bisbee. In the early days of the community, every descent into a mine shaft was a flirtation with death, and Bisbee has always had more than its share of widows and orphans. Life was very hard. Some of the residents couldn't take it and went mad or committed suicide, like the mail-order bride of the miner who lived at 147 Brewery Gulch. She poisoned herself by soaking Japanese sulfur matches in water and drinking the water. The men most often turned to alcohol, gambling, or the solace of the brothels and opium dens at the north end of the gulch, and that muddy thoroughfare quickly became the most wide-open, rip-roaring center for sin in the Southwest, far surpassing anything Tombstone had been able to provide along the same lines. Everything in Brewery Gulch was open twenty-four hours a day to accommodate miners as they came off the various shifts.

Gradually a terrible tension developed between life as it was actually lived in Bisbee and the deeply felt moral, spiritual, and religious impulses of the day. Starting just before the last decade of the nineteenth century and lasting until well after World War I, most of the non-Hispanic residents of Bisbee were trapped between the hardships of life in a small Western mining community, including the horrors of mining itself, and the pressures of an uncompromising Calvinist God. It is no wonder that those two pressures, one from below and one from above, created a society that was basically fatalistic and often hypocritical. The wonder is that the society survived at all.

Before Phelps Dodge placed its imprint on the little mining camp by purchasing the Atlanta Mine in 1881 and the Copper Queen Mine four years later, the people of Bisbee suffered primarily from frontier life

265 ❖

and the requirements of a primitive mining industry, with its grinding labor, danger, health hazards, and uncertainty about the future. And if, after a twelve-hour shift of hideously exhausting and dangerous work in the underground darkness with only a candle for light, a miner chose to get drunk or visit a brothel, or both, he could usually do so without qualms of conscience or much fear of social disapproval. But the family behind Phelps Dodge brought more than capital to the rowdy mining camp at the confluence of Tombstone Canyon and Brewery Gulch. They brought God, a stern, uncompromising Puritan God. And in His name they brought "civilizing" influences and pressures that steadily increased until they were translated into law as city ordinances. Those city ordinances resulted in the public, moral sanitizing of Bisbee, which took place between midnight of March 31, 1910, when all brothels in Brewery Gulch were closed, and midnight of December 31, 1914, years in advance of national prohibition, when a city ordinance shut down every saloon in Bisbee.

In Robert Cleland's *A History of Phelps Dodge*, there is a reproduction of a portrait that sends cold chills down my spine, although I feel a little guilty about my reaction to it because the man in the portrait was considered to be a very good man, a deeply religious man, and he overcame many hardships and obstacles during his childhood and youth. But it could be a portrait of one of the more sinister characters in a Charles Dickens novel. I want to believe that the qualities of that face which are so repellent were given to it by the artist and were not really the qualities of the man. I want to believe, in other words, that the painting lies; but I have some difficulty believing it, since portraits of the wealthy of that period were usually as flattering as possible. The mouth is hard, thin, and slightly twisted, the eyes cruel, and the face reflects icy contempt, repressed sensuality, a disdainful sneer. It is the portrait of Anson Greene Phelps, founder of the Phelps Dodge family, and must have been painted in the early 1840s when he was about sixty years old.

Anson Greene Phelps was raised in Connecticut in extreme poverty, and both his parents died by the time he was eleven. A minister adopted him and he was, as he said, "fed and clothed from place to place," until he was apprenticed to his older brother, a saddler. Eventually he, too, became a saddler and established a small shop in Hartford, where he made and sold saddles, harness, and trunks. He moved to a larger shop and expanded his business to include groceries, crockery, and stoneware, and moved again to New York City where he made the leap into trade on a larger scale. He shipped cotton from South Carolina to New York, sold it to the textile mills in England, and received from England the products of those mills as well as iron, copper, and tin products so much in demand in the United States. He became a mercantile shipping agent with his own small fleet.

The mercantile history of the first forty years of the Phelps Dodge family is in many ways a microcosm of trade patterns in the United States between 1820 and the Civil War. Anson Phelps recognized that the United States produced a raw material, cotton, which was much in demand in Europe. He also recognized that Europe produced manufactured articles, particularly metal articles, and raw materials such as tin, iron, and copper, much needed in the United States. By exporting the former and importing the latter on the return trip, he made a fortune.

It is curious, but it was not particularly unusual at the time, that Anson Phelps, as a deeply religious and upright New Englander, was strongly opposed to slavery, but that his trading empire and his fortune were built on cotton produced by Southern slaves. I don't know how he felt about that or how he justified it, but it might have been a compromise which helped give his face the look that frightens me. Somehow he managed to function successfully at the intersection where economic needs collide with moral principles. Later, the Civil War would be fought at exactly that intersection, but by then the traffic on both roads would have grown much heavier.

In 1821, Anson Phelps went into partnership with another New England merchant named Elisha Peck, and the firm expanded its trade, exporting cotton and importing metals, with an office in Liverpool, which Peck managed, and an office and large warehouse in New York, managed by Phelps. On May 4, 1832, the overloaded Phelps-Peck warehouse in New York suddenly collapsed, burying many of Phelps' employees under bales of cotton. Seven died and several others were seriously injured. Among the dead was a young man, Josiah Stokes, who had been engaged to Caroline, one of Anson Phelps's three daughters, and whom Phelps had been grooming as a future business partner. At the time of the accident, Phelps himself had been in another part of the city attending a meeting of one of the charitable organizations in which he was very active. Six years later, Charles Dickens would publish *Oliver Twist*, which has nothing whatever to do with Anson Phelps except in my mind, where he will always be a character out of Dickens.

After the debacle at the warehouse, Phelps bought Elisha Peck's interest in the firm and established the husbands of his other two daughters as his partners. They were William E. Dodge and Daniel James, both merchants and, like their father-in-law, devout Presbyterians. Caroline, rather dutifully it would seem, married the younger brother of her dead fiancé, and he too became a partner in the firm, although not a dominant one. The other partner was Phelps's only son, who seems never to have taken a major interest in the firm, devoted his life to travel, music, literature, and philanthropy, and died of smallpox while still young, ending the Phelps male lineage.

Anson Phelps died in 1853 at the age of seventy-two, a multimillionaire. By then, the family's business interests, and they were many, were firmly in the hands of William E. Dodge and Daniel James, the sons-in-law, and each would pass his share of the partnership to his son. Under the leadership of Dodge and James, the family vastly expanded its interests and activities. Dodge, the primary force toward expansion, was interested in railroads and involved himself with several of them, but the family business was still primarily a trading and manufacturing concern, dealing in iron, tin, copper, and lumber.

The merger of the Phelps, Dodge, and James families, from which was to grow the leviathan of the American mining industry later known as Phelps Dodge, with all its subsidiaries, adjuncts, and entanglements, was a merger by marriage of three New England families with almost identical views and aims. They were all Calvinists of the deepest stripe, practicing Presbyterians; and it is just another of history's ironies that America entered its Gilded Age—the age of almost limitless exploitation and chicanery, the age of corrupt politicians leagued with unscrupulous, greedy developers and entrepreneurs—with one of its largest and most successful industrial and mercantile empires controlled by a family of devout Presbyterians who espoused the rigorous Puritan principles of their religion, including large doses of thrift, faith, righteousness, denial of the flesh, and charity to the poor, although to the modern viewer that dogma might seem to have been a little short on human understanding and even love.

To contrast the lives of the Phelps-Dodge-James family in 1881 with the lives of the miners in the little mining camp that had just adopted the name Bisbee, and over which that New England family was soon to wield enormous power, simply boggles the imagination. And even now, almost 110 years after that morally upright family began to apply much of its wealth as well as its stern religious principles to the unwashed and often ungodly little camp in the Mule Mountains of the Southwest, even now as I turn off Main Street and begin the steep climb up Howell Avenue, the evidence of a lasting but uneasy truce between the two opposite forces is all around me.

On my left is the stately brick Bisbee Historical and Mining Museum, previously the Phelps Dodge headquarters, and higher up, on the other side of Howell Avenue, which is no wider at this point than a self-respecting alley, the impressive Copper Queen Hotel, and close beside it the prim, somewhat dour Presbyterian church, with its steeple visible from all over town. Then the YWCA building, and farther up the hill the towering YMCA—all tributes to the power and principles of the Phelps-Dodge-James family. But just around the corner, and in marked contrast to all this faded properness and tasteful prosperity, lurks the ghost of Brewery Gulch. To enter the gulch, when I lived in Bisbee between 1958 and 1960, was to enter another world, a world that always seemed more real to me, even in its moribund condition, than the world just around the corner. The cribs of the prostitutes at the north end of the gulch were gone then, but the series of steep concrete steps which led up to them were still there, and they still are, although in recent years they have become tourist attractions and up and down them the children of tourists play while their parents grin and smirk knowingly.

In 1958 the gulch had not exactly revived from the sanitizing actions which killed it between 1910 and 1914, but there were echoes, and respectable people did not go "up the gulch" unless they went after dark, hoping nobody would recognize them. The spirit of the gulch had returned only to the extent of one small brothel, housed, as I recall, in a ramshackle old hotel and patronized mostly by soldiers from Ft. Huachuca, and two bars across the street, one smelling so badly of ancient beer, bad drains, and male urine that I found it hard to believe it had ever been shut down in 1914.

The clash between Presbyterian principles and the natural inclinations of the miners of Bisbee began about 1881, and I wouldn't describe it as a struggle between the forces of good and evil, at least not exactly, although I'm sure the representatives of the Phelps-Dodge-James family saw it in that light much of the time, as they attempted to institute a modicum of sanitation, hygiene, moral behavior, education, and law and order in the mining camp. But the struggle was much too complex to be described merely in terms of good and evil. Although the quality of life in Bisbee, both physically and morally, improved over the long haul, I don't think there was ever a clear victory for either side, in spite of the city ordinances of 1910 and 1914 that would seem to have signaled defeat for the powers of . . . I hate to say "darkness." It seems an inappropriate term to apply to Brewery Gulch, where the bright lights burned all night long and were never dimmed until they were extinguished by the city fathers—or perhaps, more accurately, mothers.

It was just one long series of battles, with some gradual gains for the forces of "decency and order," fought against a background of constant backsliding, as individuals, like the sides of the denuded, eroding hills, slid from time to time into the muddy bottom of Brewery Gulch under the weight of exhaustion and despair. To me, those beautiful stone retaining walls which range up the sides of the hills are symbols of the struggle to prop the town up and keep it elevated, in more ways than one. But gravity is a powerful force, and even well-built stone walls can't always withstand it, especially when the rains come and the thin layer of soil on the hills turns to clay.

While New England Calvinism was able to influence the people of Bisbee, the results were never definitive. Moral convictions that were quite at home in a tasteful New York mansion did not always suit the raw Western landscape of Southern Arizona, and the devastating physical scars left by the destruction of Sacramento Hill, and by the tailings, and by Lavender Pit were not the only kinds of scars produced by the simultaneous exposure of Bisbee to Eastern exploitation and uplift.

With all its mining operations under the direction of Dr. James Douglas, who had come within inches of being ordained a Presbyterian minister before he discovered that his true calling was metallurgy, Phelps Dodge struggled to bring cleanliness, godliness, and sobriety—especially sobriety—to the little mining town. Dr. Douglas was aware that the consumption of alcohol was responsible for the loss of thousands of man-hours in the mines each year, and that many of the accidents in the mines were related to alcohol. Before Phelps Dodge took over the Copper Queen Mine, the mining company had employed many hard-drinking "tramp" miners, bachelors who drifted from mine to mine and did little to help build a stable community, although they often did a great deal to add to its local color and tough reputation. Many of the "tramp" miners had drifted into Bisbee from Tombstone, as the silver mines there were gradually closed because of flooding. Dr. Douglas adopted strong measures to discourage "tramp" miners from coming to Bisbee. He gave precedence, when hiring, to married men with families, and to men with reputations for sobriety. And he tried to provide the men with wholesome alternative forms of recreation in order to keep them out of the saloons and brothels in Brewery Gulch.

Almost immediately upon taking over the Phelps Dodge operation in Bisbee, Douglas established the Copper Queen Library, which he nursed from a small collection of books into a large and excellent library that has been housed over the years in a series of large, prominent buildings, all provided at company expense. When my wife and I lived in Bisbee, television had not yet come to the Mule Mountains, and there were only two movie theaters, one in Bisbee and one in Lowell. Both of the theaters were closed for many months during a prolonged strike, but we had the excellent Copper Queen Library, and we devoured it.

We went to the library every Monday night and left with twenty or thirty books. We got acquainted with the charming librarian, and when new books came in that she thought we might want to read, she hid them for us under the counter and brought them out for us on Monday nights, shyly and with great pleasure, like the treasures they were. The library didn't seem to be used very much in those days, and I think the librarian got a little lonely. The huge reading room on the second floor was usually empty, and up on the third floor we romped through the deserted stacks like children in a candy store. One night the librarian produced a large ring of keys and led me to a storage room, which she unlocked. Inside were dozens and dozens of boxes of books, older books not in demand which had been removed from the shelves to make room for more recent acquisitions. A couple of hours later, I came out of that storage room covered with dust and loaded with books, knowing I had just struck a rich vein of ore. Some of those older books, with their ornate Victorian bindings and marbled end-papers, were probably part of the original collection that James Douglas provided as a start for the library—whole sets of Trollope, Thackeray, and Jane Austen. They were in remarkably good condition. Evidently the learned Dr. Douglas didn't have too much success getting the miners to read Trollope, Thackeray, and Jane Austen, especially since many of the miners couldn't read at all, but I have to admire his attempt, which paid off for us three-quarters of a century later. His Copper Queen Library was, on the whole, a success. As the years passed, it became a social nexus for a large segment of the community and a decided force in the movement toward educational, social, and moral betterment. A few of the miners and their families read the books, and many of them sat in the reading room, laboriously deciphering the newspapers which came from all over and were attached to wooden spines and hung on racks.

Just past the Copper Queen Hotel and the Presbyterian church, Howell Avenue curves to the right to avoid the YWCA building, which still seems to be functioning as a YWCA. Up the hill on my right is the tall, narrow YMCA building, which has been converted into apartments and displays a big sign saying that it is now renting, although it looks totally deserted. The three leading mining companies in the Warren District, with Dr. Douglas and Phelps Dodge taking the lead, provided the YMCA building and its equipment, and for the same reasons that Douglas started the library. But I suspect that the smaller building on my left, the YWCA, is more significant in terms of the taming of Bisbee. The miners could play basketball and swim in the YMCA, but their wives met at the YWCA, and they had more important things to do than play basketball and go swimming.

Long before the Phelps Dodge family donated the YWCA building, the ladies of Bisbee had involved themselves with the important issues of the day, issues like women's suffrage, the fledgling prohibition movement, and what to do about those women with bobbed hair who lived at the north end of Brewery Gulch and rode their mules down through town every afternoon, right in front of the children and everybody. Those dreadful, scandalous, painted hussies! Something had to be done about them, and something had to be done about the saloons, which were open around-the-clock, even on the Sabbath. Eventually something was done about all those things. The respectable women of Bisbee, operating almost always behind the scenes, pressuring their husbands and the town's leading political figures, formed a social and political bloc that could be temporarily resisted but never totally withstood. And they had the support of Dr. James Douglas and the Phelps Dodge family, even though that family was far away in the East. They were determined to elevate Bisbee by its own bootstraps, and they did; but sometimes they had trouble holding it up, and the strain on both them and the community was, at times, dreadful, though not as dreadful as the alternatives.

From the time of Bisbee's beginnings and extending through the first two decades of the twentieth century, the women of Bisbee were part of a nationwide struggle on the part of women in the United States to get at least partial control of their lives. Living in a rough, isolated Western mining camp as they did, however, their struggle seems somehow more desperate and more immediate than that of women in some other parts of the country. At least it was desperate and immediate enough. The Prohibition Movement and the Women's Suffrage Movement, which resulted in the eighteenth and nineteenth amendments to the Constitution, were inextricably bound; but my guess is that, of the two, the Prohibition Movement was more important to the women of Bisbee.

We have no reliable figures concerning alcoholism among the male population of Bisbee between 1880 and 1914, when Arizona went dry, but accounts written at the time suggest that it was rampant and created untold suffering for the miners' wives and children, whose lives were often defined by three things: poverty, alcoholism, and brutality. In that cycle, which fed upon itself, many of the wives were trapped. Divorce was seldom a real option for them, not only because of the stigma attached to it, but because of economic realities. They could not support themselves and their children, and neither the government nor the social structure provided them with any real help. Suicide was an option, but it violated all social and religious principles, and it only made things worse for the children.

As portrayed in *Tacey Cromwell*, Conrad Richter's fictional account of life in Bisbee during the first decade of the twentieth century, the ladies of Bisbee seem very hypocritical and unattractive, especially when they take Tacey's children away from her because she was once a prostitute. But that view, although it probably includes elements of the truth in some instances, was a view from the underside. A broader historical view would show the respectable women of Bisbee as soldiers on the front line of a war, and the stakes were high for the entire community. Like all of us, they made mistakes. Sometimes their struggle degenerated into mere silliness, but in the end, insofar as prohibition and the right to vote were their goals, they won.

The genteel ladies of Bisbee! How few of their names have been recorded in the history books as compared to the names of the more colorful women who lived up the gulch and never claimed to be ladies, like Black Fanny and Irish Mag. But it was the respectable ladies, rather than the painted ones, who shaped Bisbee's future while somehow making its present bearable. They reflected the narrow attitudes of their time and place, and some of their social pretensions seem laughable today—although no more laughable than today's social pretensions—but they fought their battles out of sheer desperation and against incredible odds. The number of battles they won, using the only means available to them, is truly impressive.

My all-time favorite story about Bisbee involves them and one of their attempts to bring a little bit of class and culture to the benighted community they found themselves in. I don't know exactly when it happened, but it happened, and it could serve as a blueprint for the entire social history of Bisbee during the many years that history was influenced by the Phelps Dodge family and their representatives, the Douglas family.

According to the story, the respectable women of Bisbee had decided to produce an evening of high-class musical entertainment, a cultivated cultural event that would rival anything of its kind available in larger, more sophisticated Eastern communities. They rented a hall and spent months making costumes and sets, rehearsing, and advertising the gala event. The finale of the evening's entertainment was to be spectacular, stunning. One of Bisbee's social leaders, a mezzo-soprano with a trained operatic voice, was to sing the closing number, beautifully gowned and seated on a large copper crescent moon, which would rise majestically as she sang and would float across the stage.

The program went well until the closing number, and even that began well. The copper moon was rigged with ropes and pulleys, but when the men backstage began to pull on the ropes that would hoist it above the stage, they discovered that the matronly mezzo-soprano was somewhat heavier than they had anticipated. They couldn't control the moon once they got it into the air. It began to swing and buck wildly. As they pulled harder and harder, trying to stabilize it, one of the ropes broke, causing the moon to tilt at a dangerous angle as it was jerked higher and higher. Through it all, the terrified singer never missed a note, although she threw both arms around one horn of the moon and hung on with all her strength. She was singing "Nearer My God to Thee."

During this truly riveting performance, while the audience was holding its collective breath with all eyes on the singer as the moon careened crazily above the stage, a drunken miner from Brewery Gulch wandered in, probably expecting a girlie show or some kind of burlesque. Astonished and mesmerized by the performance, he staggered down the aisle until he was directly in front of the stage. There he stopped, shook his head, and said with profound sincerity, "Well, Old Girl, I hope to hell you make it."

And that's Bisbee, the place where, if anything can go wrong it will, and where all pretentious balloons eventually get punctured. Bisbee, riding its bucking copper moon across the sky, in danger of collapse at any moment, but singing as it climbs and plunges. "Nearer My God to Thee." That's Bisbee. But on June 13, 1975, the copper moon fell out of the sky for Bisbee, and the music stopped. At least it stopped for awhile. Or maybe it didn't stop. Maybe it was just that nobody was listening hard enough.

As I pull into the parking lot, or what is used as a parking lot for the Copper Queen Hotel, a series of terraces where a miner's boarding house once stood, I can hear music, but it's faint and sounds like somebody playing blues on a guitar up in the old Central School building beyond the YMCA. I'm running late. Just time to check into the hotel and call my date for the evening. Ida Power will know, if anybody does, whether or not Bisbee is still singing, and how much survived when the copper moon fell out of the sky.

I grab my bag out of the van and turn to go back down the hill to the hotel, but I stop for a second, looking down toward the center of town which is backlit by late afternoon light reflected from the hills above. Not a bad view of this little toy town where real people lived and suffered, and some of them still do. "Well, Old Girl," I say, addressing all of Bisbee I can see from here and all I can't, "I hope to hell you make it."

❖ ❖ 12

W hile I'm checking in at the desk of the Copper Queen Hotel, I ask the clerk how late the dining room is open. I'd like to have time to shower and change clothes before I pick up Ida and bring her back to the hotel for dinner.

"Sorry, the dining room is closed," the clerk says with a finality that makes me look up from the registration form quickly, remembering the many excellent meals I've had in that elegant room.

"For good?" I ask. In today's Bisbee, where the few restaurants come and go like mayflies, it's a serious and alarming possibility.

"Oh, no," she says. "The gas is off. We can't cook. The gas is off all over town. Nobody is going to be able to cook tonight."

I finish filling out the form and then ask her, "How come the whole town ran out of gas?"

"Well, we didn't exactly run out of gas," she replies, "but it amounts to the same thing. The power company was working on the electric lines over on the other side of the pit in Lowell and they dug up the gas line by mistake. I think they've almost got it fixed by now, but somehow or other nobody can turn the gas on. I guess they're afraid of explosions or fires. They're sending a big crew down from Tucson to go around to every building and turn the gas back on, but it will take all night and most of tomorrow. They have to do something to the gas meters or pilots or something. I don't understand it exactly, but they said the hotel would probably have gas by morning, although lots of people won't get any until tomorrow afternoon. If you want a shower, you'd better take it right away while there's still some hot water in the tanks. There won't be any later."

"That's Bisbee!" I say with a grin and a shrug. I don't know if I have the tone exactly right, but I must be close because she breaks into a big smile and says, "Oh, you've been here before, haven't you?"

"I used to live here," I say, "but it was about a hundred years ago, and I've lost track of things. Do you know anywhere I can get dinner?"

"There's nothing open on this side of the pit, but there's a little Mexican restaurant over in Warren, actually in Bakerville between here and Warren. I hear it's open, and it's about the only place that is. It's not elegant, but the food's good if you like Mexican. It's called El Chaparral, right next door to the Hitching Post Bar on the road to Warren."

She's remarkably cheerful, considering that she must have an entire hotel full of irate customers—no food and no hot water. I can see the evening I had planned going down the drain very quickly, but as soon as I drove over the pass the Bisbee air must have infected me with the Bisbee attitude, and I can't seem to work up any irritation. It won't be the evening I had hoped for, but things will work out. Anyway, it's not the hotel desk clerk's fault that the power company dug up the gas line. It's probably not anybody's fault; it's just Bisbee. And if there's anybody I know who can take things in stride and roll with the punches, it's my date for the evening, Ida Power. Some people require comforts and conveniences for their well-being, but others carry their well-being inside themselves. That's how Ida is. She's terrific. Whatever it is she's got—and I've never been able to define exactly what it is—she carries it with her wherever she goes. She won't require a fancy meal or, for that matter, any meal at all, and her presence is all the elegance any room needs.

The clerk directs me to the elevator, but I take the stairs. It's only two flights up to my room, and as I climb toward the second floor parlor-lobby, I remember how fond I am of this building, and how it came close to death a few years ago. Now it seems to be back on its feet again, like a grande dame under layers and layers of makeup, but sturdy after almost ninety years, and still charming. She was born in 1902, the same year Bisbee was incorporated, and she's held up remarkably well, as might be expected, considering that she was built by Phelps Dodge and is a pure product of that family's sturdy value system. She is reinforced from her foundation to her tile roof with steel beams, and her brick exterior walls are a foot and a half thick. She has withstood earthquakes, floods and fires.

Even when Phelps Dodge abandoned her and placed her on the auction block, she survived, although suffering terribly from neglect. She has changed some over the years, but never lost her dignity. She was born to dignity, and she made the most of it, since real beauty was denied her. Her exterior is basically "Romanesque," an architectural style which covered a multitude of aesthetic sins at the turn of the century. In her case, the result was merely a heaviness and lack of grace. She is stolid and somewhat plain, but her bulk and mass and the dignity of her bearing are impressive. In the Bisbee of 1902, which still consisted mostly of flimsy frame structures just waiting for the fires of 1907 and 1908, she must have been impressive indeed.

I've probably spent the night at the Copper Queen seven or eight times since my wife and I left Bisbee about thirty years ago, and nearly every one of those nights turned into some kind of unexpected adventure, not always amusing except in retrospect. I remember one of those earlier visits very well, although I don't remember exactly what year it was. It must have been in the late seventies. My wife and I arrived at the Copper Queen in the early evening, about this time of day, I would guess. It might have been a Saturday, but I'm not sure. My wife lingered in the lobby to look at the turquoise on display there, and I started up the stairs with our luggage. When I got near the top of the stairs, approaching the second floor parlor-lobby, I saw a purely naked woman standing above me, a statuesque blond. She had a bottle of whiskey in one hand and was shaking a finger at me sternly.

"You can't come up here!" she said.

I stopped in confusion. The only thing I could think of to explain the situation was that the entire hotel had been rented to a group of nudists, but that didn't seem very likely.

"Why?" I stammered, overcoming the impulse to turn and run headlong back down into the lobby.

The blond made a sweeping gesture with her whiskey bottle, indicating the air all around us, and said in a loud whisper, "Ghosts!" Then she giggled and fled, laughing and shrieking as she careened down the hall. I never saw her again, but I knew there was only one explanation for the ghosts. She must have been referring to the ghosts of the ladies of early Bisbee. When the hotel was built, it had a separate ladies parlor on the ground floor, with its own outside entrance so that ladies would not have to pass by any drummers or mining engineers who might be sitting beside the potted palms in the main lobby, smoking their cigars. *The Bisbee Review* described that ladies parlor as "exceptionally fine and tastefully arranged in mahogany with rich green silk plush and satins." As near as I can figure out, that parlor was the room presently occupied by the bar. Desecration! No wonder ghosts of the ladies of early Bisbee march through the halls like Carry Nation, objecting to the use of their sacrosanct space. What the ghosts thought of the purely naked blond with her whiskey bottle in the second floor parlor-lobby is beyond my ability to imagine, because girls from the wrong end of Brewery Gulch were definitely never allowed in the Copper Queen Hotel under any circumstances.

The ghosts of the ladies of early Bisbee must have had their hands full after Phelps Dodge pulled out in 1975, and so did the contemporary women of Bisbee and everybody else who was trying to keep the town alive and maintain some semblance of conventional order. Things went downhill fast, but the decline of Bisbee had been taking place, at a slower pace, for decades before 1975.

The economic welfare of the people who put down roots in the Warren Mining District was always based on two factors over which they had no control: the current price of copper and the availability of ore. Like all such mining communities, Bisbee lived on its capital from the beginning, since its economy at any time depended upon its using up the one resource which would make its future economy possible. The seeds of the community's ultimate collapse were present from the beginning. Bisbee, as a mining town, was born into its own death; and scores of ghost towns scattered around Arizona, like Jerome, Lochiel, and Washington Camp, are testimonials to the same principle. But Bisbee was better endowed with ore than were most of the other mining communities, and its dominant managing organization over the years, Phelps Dodge, had enormous economic resources upon which to rely in hard times. By expanding and contracting, as the giant saguaro does during wet and dry seasons, the Warren Mining District had been able to survive fluctuations in the price of copper, the booms and busts which had always been a major element of its economy. But as the richest ore bodies were depleted, each year brought the community closer to ultimate collapse.

In spite of the various forces directed toward social and economic stability and growth, forces which included Bisbee's city government, its local businesses, its social, religious, and civic organizations, and certainly the women of Bisbee, the total synergy of the community was moving it always toward destruction, and sometimes rapidly. One has only to look at Lavender Pit or at the huge hole where Sacramento Hill once stood or at the tailings, which have degraded and divided the various housing areas, to see that Bisbee was eating itself up, living and thriving on its own destruction.

The fact that it was able to stay alive for almost a century as a viable mining community, unlike most similar communities in the West, says something about the vastness of the ore body underlying the district; but it also says something about Phelps Dodge's long-range strategy of developing and ultimately using new technology which made it possible, as the years passed, to mine and process, at a profit, ore of an increasingly lower grade. As the available ore decreased in quality, more and more earth had to be moved in order to mine it, creating more and more destruction to the physical community. But the technology which was developed specifically to do this depended on enormous machines, and the process required fewer and fewer miners than had been needed previously. And so, as the pace of the physical destruction of the district increased, its population shrank.

In Bisbee's earliest days as a mining camp, several small companies worked various claims, all struggling for capital to stay afloat. Most of these, like the companies that developed the original Atlanta Mine and the original Copper Queen, were short-lived. Phelps Dodge, a larger and more solidly funded corporation, arrived on the scene in 1881, although its initial activities were so unsuccessful that it nearly pulled out in 1884 because the mining operation had required larger and larger amounts of investment and had brought little in the way of return. But Phelps Dodge was a creature with many arms involved in many enterprises. These provided it with a reserve capital sufficient to absorb its initial mining losses and survive.

Phelps Dodge was the only large mining company operating in the

Warren District from 1884 until the turn of the century. Then other substantial companies began to work the adjacent ore bodies. The Michigan-based Calumet and Arizona Mining Company was Phelps Dodge's greatest rival in the area until the Great Depression forced it to merge with the more powerful and better-financed Phelps Dodge. The other chief competitor was the Shattuck-Denn Mining Corporation, which mined fabulously rich ore from 1906 until after World War I, when low copper prices and the exhaustion of its best ore wiped it out. Eventually Phelps Dodge gained control of its holdings also.

Over the years, as the richest ore was increasingly exhausted, leaving only lower grade ore which was more costly to mine and process, the pattern was that of consolidation from several companies to one giant corporation—Phelps Dodge. This centrifugal impulse resulted in a pooling of financial resources, which helped minimize the effect of the wildly fluctuating price of copper. When the price of copper dropped, Phelps Dodge could shrink its operation, sometimes almost ceasing to operate entirely, and depend on its cash reserve to see it through hard times. When the price went up, it would expand again.

This constant expansion and contraction of production was, of course, hard on the Bisbee miners and their families. At times, it was necessary for the company to lay off as many as five hundred workers, most of whom were forced to leave Bisbee in search of employment elsewhere. When the price of copper rose and the company began hiring on a large scale, many of them returned. Often the company reduced production by simply cutting down on the number of hours the miners were allowed to work each week. During the worst of the Depression, in the 1930s, Phelps Dodge kept some of the mines operating, but barely. It laid off hundreds of miners, deported most of its above-ground Mexican labor force back to Mexico, and curtailed operations to twelve working days a month, barely subsistence for the miners. The miners suffered, but the company somehow survived. Old Bisbee, as a town, would probably not have survived the Depression years if it had not been for the Sacramento Pit strip-mining operation, which began to produce ore in 1921, and for the fact that the county seat was moved from Tombstone to Bisbee in 1929.

Starting as early as 1910, the gradual population movement had been away from Old Bisbee and into the outlying communities. By 1940, Old

Bisbee was a dilapidated community with a population of 5,853. Many of its commercial buildings were closed and many of its houses were vacant. With the outbreak of World War II, the community revived dramatically but began to fade again in 1945 when a glut of copper hit the market and the price dropped correspondingly. Between 1945 and 1950, only the production of subsidiary metals, especially lead and zinc, kept Bisbee alive, if barely, but by 1950, advancing technology and the price of copper cooperated to make exploitation of low grade ore in the enormous east ore body feasible. The following year Phelps Dodge began a stripping procedure that resulted in Lavender Pit. Bisbee had a slight resurgence, although the creation of Lavender Pit was a death blow for Lowell and South Bisbee, and it severely damaged Warren and other communities as residential locations.

Strip mining depends on huge earth-moving machines and requires relatively fewer workers than underground mining. While the Warren Mining District survived, it did not grow. When we moved to Bisbee in 1958, it was already well into its final slow decline, which would culminate in the Phelps Dodge pull-out of 1975. Many of the businesses, especially on Brewery Gulch, were already closed, and Main Street was not a thriving affair. No other industry had developed, and there was no tourism to speak of. Even then there was a general feeling of abandonment, of dying, and a lack of energy in the air.

In Bisbee, in 1958, it seemed as though the same few people did everything, and if they didn't do it, it didn't get done. That's probably true in Bisbee today. Perhaps it's true everywhere, but it's more apparent in small communities, especially in those with a distinct division between professional and blue-collar classes. Ida Power was one of the small group of people who was doing everything. That's how we came to meet her, and she was one of the first residents of Bisbee we met.

Ida is eighty now, which would put her in her very late fifties when we first met her, although I guessed at the time that she was about forty, and today I would guess by her appearance and activities that she is a very snappy sixty-five. In terms of the American Era of history in Arizona, Ida's family arrived on the Mayflower. (I suspect that her great-grandmother rowed most of the way.) Ida's family background contains exactly what the tourists who overrun Tombstone are looking for, and it's authentic, but they wouldn't expect to find the real

Wild West lurking in the family tree of a lovely, retired schoolteacher in Bisbee. Even if they managed to track Ida down, she wouldn't satisfy their blood lust. She would talk to them about the art movement in today's Bisbee, or Bisbee's contemporary problems, all of which she is involved in up to her eyebrows and above.

Ida's great-grandmother, whose husband was killed in one of territorial Arizona's earliest land wars called "The War on the Gila," lived in several settlements in the raw territory which was, many years later, to become the State of Arizona. For awhile she lived in Charleston, one of the stamp-mill towns on the San Pedro and now the ghost town from which I fled somewhat precipitously last May. She also lived in Tombstone, and finally established a boarding house for miners in Bisbee. All of this suggests a family associated with Arizona mining since the early 1880s. Ida was born in Bisbee. Her grandfather, Dayton Graham, was the infant town's first city marshal and the first man chosen to be a sergeant of the famed (sometimes infamous) Arizona Rangers, established by the territorial legislature in 1901.

During the time that Dayton Graham was a member, the Arizona Rangers was a fourteen-man force—one captain, one sergeant, and twelve privates—of gunslingers whose courage and expert ability with several kinds of firearms had previously been established beyond any doubt. The territorial legislature hired them to apprehend rustlers, train and bank robbers, and any other desperado types who happened to be troubling the territory. Later, as the force grew, it was used extensively to put down and control violence connected with labor unrest and strikes in various Arizona mines. Ranchers and mine owners were much in favor of the Arizona Rangers, but many other residents of the territory feared them as a freewheeling, para-military force whose members could, and sometimes did, take the law into their own hands, a kind of standing posse hired by the government to serve the rich and powerful. Most of the rangers, like Dayton Graham, were considered to be trustworthy men of very high character, although tough; but there were exceptions, and there were times when the ranks of the Arizona Rangers included notorious outlaws, presumably for the "inside" help such men could give the forces of law and order.

In 1901, when the territorial legislature passed the bill creating the Arizona Rangers, the governor of the territory named Burt Mossman its first captain. Mossman had been superintendent of the famous Hash Knife Ranch, a two-million acre range owned by the Aztec Land and Cattle Company. The bill creating the Arizona Rangers stated that the captain should choose "as his base the most unprotected and exposed settlement of the frontier." Mossman chose Bisbee, and he knew Bisbee well because he had once owned and operated a meat-packing business there. The second captain of the rangers moved the headquarters to Douglas a year later, saying that Douglas, named after Dr. James Douglas, who had almost become a Presbyterian minister and later ran the Phelps Dodge mining operations, was "the toughest proposition on the whole American Border." He was probably right. As soon as Phelps Dodge announced that it would build a smelter near the border in the Sulphur Springs Valley and establish a town to house the workers, a boom town grew up there, containing mostly gamblers, saloon keepers, and prostitutes. Outlaws from both sides of the border found Douglas an ideal location, and cattle rustlers scuttled back and forth across the border between Douglas and Agua Prieta, as drug dealers do today.

Burt Mossman waited almost a year to appoint a sergeant for the rangers because he felt there was only one man in the territory who could handle the job, and that man was already employed as the marshal of Bisbee. He was Dayton Graham, Ida's grandfather, and finally, in 1902, he accepted the position with the rangers. Dayton Graham's exploits are documented in *The Arizona Rangers* by Bill O'Neal, and in several other histories. He was obviously a gunslinger of unquestioned ability and nerve, famous in his day, and he chose to use his considerable talent with a gun on the side of the law. In fact, for a long time in Southeastern Arizona his gun was the law. Presumably, he resigned from the rangers in order to become constable of Douglas, but there is conflicting testimony about his resignation. Burt Mossman said that Graham did not resign from the rangers, which leads to the possibility that he served as constable of Douglas while actually an undercover agent for the Arizona Rangers.

As constable of Douglas, Graham was involved in a famous gunfight in a saloon there. An unidentified assailant wounded him and killed his assistant. The first day Graham was back on his feet after a two-month recuperation from his wounds, he went into a different saloon and shot and killed a man named Ephraim Schmidt, whom he believed to have been the assailant, although Schmidt had never been formally accused or tried. "I went there to kill him and did so," Graham said, obviously not a man given to long speeches. A jury quickly acquitted him of murder. It was a time when Western juries had little difficulty determining which were the good guys and which were the bad guys, and Date Graham was definitely a good guy. The *Bisbee Review* said he was "without a peer in the Southwest as a man of rapid action in tight places."

I keep running across photographs of Ida's illustrious grandfather, and I think Ida resembles him remarkably, especially the eyes. Each time I see Ida's dark, incredibly alert eyes, I think of that other pair of eyes I have seen staring out of the pages of several books. Those eyes must have been the last thing quite a few people ever saw, just before everything was obscured by a haze of gun smoke. Ida doesn't carry a gun, at least I don't think so; but I don't want to get her riled, and I don't want to keep a lady with such handsome eyes waiting for dinner, even if the gas is off all over town.

With a little difficulty I get the door to my hotel room open—both the key and the lock are genuine antiques—and go straight to the phone. After about eight rings, Ida answers. She has recently moved from Old Bisbee to one of the more spacious houses in Warren, once the home of a mining engineer, and she was out in the yard encouraging the flowers to grow. She already knows about the gas problem. The little Mexican restaurant in Bakerville will be fine. I tell her I'll pick her up in thirty minutes. While I'm taking a quick shower in tepid water, I think about the last thing she said before I hung up. "I'll be ready when you get here." She was ready when my wife and I got here in 1958. And she was ready when Phelps Dodge pulled out in 1975. In that case, she was one of the few residents of Bisbee who was ready.

When we met Ida Power in 1958, she was teaching at Central School, but we met her in one of her many subsidiary roles. She was chairperson of the Hospitality Committee whose function it was to help new teachers in the Bisbee School District find a place to live, and she did, Lord knows she did. She drove us around to the various communities that make up Bisbee, and we poked through an assortment of rentals which ranged from grotesque-but-interesting to elegant. Finally we settled on grotesque-but-interesting. Elegant was beyond our means.

I never could understand what caused us to choose the apartment we first rented in Bisbee. Maybe it was the view. Maybe it was the only thing we could afford. Or maybe, in some bizarre way, it reminded my wife of a ratty loft in New York City where she had lived while studying voice. I had lived in some strange places but never anywhere quite that strange. It was upstairs above an Armenian grocery store at #5 O.K. Street, and from the windows of its two bedrooms, which were across the front, it had a fantastic view looking west down Bisbee's Main Street, with the center of town in the foreground and the hills beyond, each covered with turn-of-the-century houses. But the long, narrow living room–dining room had only a very old and dirty skylight, and the kitchen windows faced the almost perpendicular side of Chihuahua Hill, about eight feet away.

The apartment had been the home of the Armenian family who owned the grocery store, and it had been rather posh at one time, although that time had been about fifty years earlier. In a dark, heavy kind of way, it was flamboyant, large, and probably haunted. Most of it had red wall-to-wall carpeting with the same pattern of huge flowers, each about as big around as a bushel basket. There was really no getting away from those flowers except to stay in the kitchen. After awhile my wife claimed that the carpeting and the flowers ran up the walls as well, but by then I think the apartment had caused her to start hallucinating because she spent much more time in it than I did. The cockroaches took their meals downstairs in the grocery store but actually lived in our apartment. The first thing we did was hire a woman to help us scrub the walls. By the time we got all the walls scrubbed and realized what color they really were, we had decided to move.

In spite of its many drawbacks, the apartment had considerable charm. Most of its charm and its drawbacks were caused by the same thing—its location. It was one very short block from where Brewery Gulch converged on Main Street, near the absolute center of Old Bisbee. And it was next door to Bisbee's ancient jail, a tall, narrow stone and brick structure that had not been in use for years. The passageway between the apartment and the jail, which led to a stairway that went up Chihuahua Hill, was a favorite hangout and dormitory for nearly every wino in town. Our trash cans were in that passageway, and it was a convenient arrangement. We could open a door in our hallway, a door which had no outside stairway, and simply drop our trash and garbage into the cans about five feet below. Once, in the night, I accidentally dropped a large bag of trash and garbage directly onto a sleeping drunk who roused only enough to mutter in confusion and then went back to sleep.

The windows of both bedrooms were directly above a stretch of Main Street between O.K. Street and Brewery Gulch, where the hookers paraded in front of the Lyric Theater and the mortuary. When our windows were open, we could not only see but hear them haggling with potential customers. It was fascinating for awhile, but after the newness wore off, it became merely sordid. Our address was not a fashionable address in 1958, and I remember that Ida could not quite hide her surprise when we chose the apartment, although she said nothing and remained nonjudgmental, merely commenting on how close it was to "everything."

As soon as we moved in, we found out just how close it was to some things, one thing in particular, that we wished it had been farther away from. Around the corner from the apartment was the city hall and fire station, built in about 1906–1907 just in time for the fire of 1908, which destroyed most of Bisbee's business district. Although that building faced on a different street, it and the apartment were almost adjacent to each other in the rear. On top of the city hall—fire station was an innocuous-looking cupola, a kind of roofed but open gazebo, not unusual on structures of about that period, especially in Southern Arizona. After we had moved into the apartment, we found out that the cupola contained the town whistle, an earsplitting siren which went off four times a day. The neighbors told me that it was the signal for shift changes in the underground mines, and I didn't doubt that it could be heard thousands of feet underground. In the apartment, it made the dishes and windows rattle, and its first blast each day was at 8:00 A.M.

At breakfast each morning, we would watch the clock carefully. As eight o'clock approached, one of us would hold the baby and the other one would get a good grip on the table. We braced ourselves. Ready!

Set! WHEEEEEEEEEE! Then it was over, although it continued to reverberate in our heads, and we had until noon before it would erupt again. Then at 1:00 and 5:00 P.M. We never got used to it and I don't think we ever could have, although the baby seemed to adjust to it without difficulty.

We lived in that apartment for only a few months, but I remember it better than I do other places we lived in for longer periods. One of the things I remember happened during our first few days in that apartment. Now, it makes me laugh, but at the time it was a social calamity. Such things can happen anywhere, but I think they happen more frequently in Bisbee.

We had just moved into the apartment and our telephone had not yet been connected. One of our young friends from Sierra Vista was a painter named Paula, who worked as a librarian at Ft. Huachuca. As soon as we told her about the view of picturesque Bisbee from our bedroom windows, she was wild to come over and do a painting. She drove from Sierra Vista early the morning of our first Saturday in the apartment and set up her easel. A little later that morning, my wife had to drive to Sierra Vista to sing for a funeral, leaving me to care for the baby while Paula painted. I was still in my bathrobe, holding the baby in my arms, when the doorbell rang about ten o'clock. It was Paul Rose, my new boss, the principal of Lowell School. Someone in another state was trying to reach me by telephone and had called the school, where Mr. Rose happened to be that Saturday morning. Since he knew our phone had not yet been installed, he decided to drive over and deliver the message himself. While he was delivering it, Paula walked out of the bedroom in her artist's smock, which looked like a maternity blouse. Just at that moment, the baby began to scream, and I couldn't get him to stop. Over his wails, I introduced Paula to Mr. Rose, and Mr. Rose left immediately. As he was going down the stairs, he called back, "It was very good to meet you, Mrs. Shelton," and he was gone.

Paula and I looked at each other in consternation. It was a natural assumption for Mr. Rose to make, but what was I going to do? Paula was petite and had short, dark hair. My wife was a tall, willowy blond. Somehow, I knew that Mr. Rose would be able to tell the difference when he finally met my wife. Things looked so bad already that I decided any attempt at an explanation would only make matters worse. When my wife got home and we told her what had happened, she agreed.

The following night, Mr. and Mrs. Paul Rose hosted their annual reception and party for all the teachers at Lowell School. I watched Paul's face carefully when I introduced my wife, my real wife. His eyes widened for a second and his smile froze but remained in place. He was very gracious to both of us and made sure we met everyone at the party. I don't know exactly what he was thinking, but he wasn't saying anything and he wasn't about to ask any questions. Later in the evening I saw him looking at me from across the room with a strange, puzzled expression on his face, a look of wonderment. By then he must have come to the conclusion that his new English teacher lived openly with two wives, and when the school board found out about it, things were going to get wilder around Lowell School than he liked them to be.

Paul Rose was a gentleman, and it was none of his business whom I lived with unless someone else forced the issue. During my entire two years at Lowell School, we never discussed it. But from time to time, as I passed him in the hall, I would catch him staring at me from a distance with that look of wonderment, almost envy. *Two wives, and both of them so young and good looking.* Later, it occurred to me that he might have discussed the matter, as a professional problem, of course, with Molly Bendixon, whose advice he sometimes sought. That would help explain what Molly said to me when I first encountered her in the teacher's lounge. It was a question, but it sounded more like an accusation. "You a Mormon?"

Molly and Ida were good friends and almost exact contemporaries— they both began teaching in 1929—although in appearance, temperament, and style they were worlds apart. Ida was small, perky, and vivacious. She had a kind of steady, unflagging good humor and energy. Molly was tall and gaunt, and the flame of her energy flared from time to time. Between outbursts, she was relaxed and laconic. Ida had married and raised three sons. Molly had remained Miss Bendixon, and had satisfied her motherly impulses by taking under her wing nearly every troubled student at Lowell School, and there were plenty of them. Both women were well-known and respected in Bisbee in 1958, but Ida was one of the most active people in town. As well-known as she was, she was not as well-known as she is today.

I guess nobody could have foreseen what lay in store for Ida Power, a small, middle-aged schoolteacher with alert brown eyes and a gunslinger grandfather. We couldn't have known then that she was equipped, almost tailor-made, to be a pivotal and decisive factor in the future of the entire town. But I think that in some way Ida knew. I think she must have had some prescience about her role in Bisbee's future. There are early indications that she knew what was going to happen to Bisbee and what she was going to do about it, indications that she was quietly preparing herself and the town for what was to come. She was laying foundations for the new Bisbee, the post–Phelps Dodge Bisbee, although few people in town understood how important those foundations would be.

As early as 1966, when Phelps Dodge was giving out signals that there was less than ten years' worth of ore left in the east ore body, Ida was instrumental in founding both the Cochise Fine Arts Gallery and the Bisbee Mining and Historical Museum. Through the sixties and early seventies she kept on hammering, organizing and promoting the artistic and cultural life of the dying town. Many of those around her must have thought she was cracked. Why organize artists and demand gallery space when the whole town was going down the drain? Why collect photographs and artifacts for a museum when there would be nobody around to look at them?

Ida made some of the more farsighted members of the community understand. It was their only hope, the only way they had to go, and she wasn't going to sit around and watch Bisbee die in front of her.

In 1974, the year Phelps Dodge made its final preparations for pulling out, Ida retired, after thirty-five years of teaching school, and immediately devoted herself, full-time, to her real life's work—Bisbee. And it has been more than a full-time job since then, but now that the people of Bisbee are beginning to see the light at the end of a long, dark, and painful tunnel, now that Bisbee is getting to be a stable community, although an unusual one, and no longer faces death every morning and civil war every night, the citizens of Bisbee honor her and a few others like her who planted the seeds for the future and nurtured them. In addition to all her other qualifications to take on the job—her intelligence, energy, courage—Ida had the one other quality required for the struggle she engaged herself in. Ida is an artist, a painter with training and considerable talent. She is unassuming and modest about her ability, but it makes her comfortable with other artists and wins her their respect. And Ida is no closet artist, no Sunday painter. I'm not sure exactly when she did it, but at some point in the mid 1970s, Ida put on her uniform as a soldier puts on a uniform when going into battle. Hers is an artist's beret—she has them in several colors—worn at a cocky and provocative angle. And more than any historic landmark in town, Ida's beret has become a symbol of Bisbee's survival.

The late 1970s in Bisbee were disaster years, frightening enough to make me think of a line from the poet Yeats, a time when "The best lack all conviction, while the worst / Are full of passionate intensity." But in Bisbee, as it went through the darkest time of its existence, not all of the best lacked conviction. Ida and a few others had conviction, and with it they faced the economic and social struggle that was to damage Bisbee worse than any fire or flood ever had, worse even than the Great Depression of the thirties. "Bisbee has been a fun place to live in," Ida told me recently, and she didn't exclude any of the years. I'll just bet it was during the late seventies. Her grandfather would have been right at home in Bisbee then, and the town would have kept him almost as busy as it kept her.

Well before Phelps Dodge closed down all its activities in Bisbee except the tiny leaching operation it still maintains, it was evident that the town was up for grabs if anybody should happen to want it. Even I, pauper that I am, was offered the Copper Queen Hotel and the Pythian Castle, two of Bisbee's most impressive and substantial large buildings, in a package for fifty thousand dollars. The price went down after that. Ultimately, the Pythian Castle sold for one thousand dollars at auction. And the people who might happen to want the town were not always those who deserved it or should have it. As Bisbee slid into a moribund condition approaching true ghost-town status, it became a community fragmented into warring camps. Factions fought for survival while the town as a whole was neglected and apparently in its death throes, directing its last remaining energy against itself.

Bisbee could never die quickly and cleanly as so many other Arizona mining towns had. Ida had foreseen that. While it was at its weakest point, unable to defend itself, it would suffer repeated invasions often worse than neglect. Ida knew that, too, and she knew that if it were going to survive, it had to have new blood and new energy. Where was that new blood and energy to come from? Ida knew, but she hardly dared whisper it to any of the retired miners who made up the bulk of the original population that remained. The new energy, the new direction, had to come from one of the invading groups, of course. There was no other way. Bisbee had to choose from among its would-be conquerors, viewed as destroyers by most of the original residents, and it had to choose wisely. Then it had to accept and absorb before it could be reborn as a new social culture, a combination of the new and the old.

That process is not yet complete, but it is far enough along to predict success, and I hope Ida will live long enough to see that success completed. She and her cadre of friends never struggled to maintain the status quo. That way led straight to the graveyard. What they had to do was determine which of the invaders could help them save the town, and how. But it was a tough proposition, and before it was resolved, things got very ugly in Bisbee.

Various Bisbee residents have different explanations as to why members of the counter-culture, known locally at the time as "the dirty hippies," descended on Bisbee in the late 1970s. Some say they were lured to Bisbee by two developers, entrepreneurs who began buying up, at the lowest possible prices, large amounts of Old Bisbee's downtown property in order to develop the community as a tourist attraction and retirement settlement, another Sausalito, another Aspen, in spite of the fact that Bisbee has no bay and no skiing. If this is true, it isn't clear what the motives of those developers might have been. Did they want members of the counter-culture to invade Bisbee in order to make it more arty and picturesque to attract tourists and retirees? Or did they attract the influx in order to further depress property values so they could take advantage of them, which was the end result?

There may be some truth to the bitter charges which old-time residents threw at the would-be developers when the influx of "hippies" arrived. But it was only a small part of the truth. I think most of the counter-culturists came because they heard through the grapevine, their own legitimate grapevine, what Bisbee had to offer them: a good climate, plenty of cheap—even free—housing, and a remote location well off the beaten track, isolated from the mainstream of America's rampantly consumerist and conservative middle-class society. At any rate, they came. They came on foot with their thumbs out. They came in converted school buses with nearly empty gas tanks. They came in old vans painted with psychedelic colors and designs that boggled the imagination. They came with their guitars, their beads, and their outlandish costumes, often little more than rags. Some came on bicycles. Some came with large plastic garbage bags full of marijuana or small plastic sandwich bags full of drugs; but they came without the one thing Bisbee needed most—money.

Most of the old-time residents of Bisbee reacted to them as might be expected, with horror. It was positively the last straw for the residents. Their commercial ventures had failed, their property values had plummeted, and about all they had left was a place to live quietly, if very simply. Now even the quality of that quiet life was being threatened by drugs, loud music, sexual promiscuity, and general mayhem. Most of the old-time residents of Bisbee could not see the newcomers as individuals, but only as a single army of bizarre and ragged invaders opposed to their values and bent upon the destruction of what little they had left to call their own.

But a few of the old-time residents, mostly Ida and her cadre of friends who were interested in artistic and cultural matters, could see that the newcomers, as they continued to arrive through the late seventies, were not a unified group but were individuals with varying degrees of drive and ability, and even quite different philosophies. Some were sincere in their deeply felt opposition to their country's involvement in war, and to the industrial-military complex which they felt encouraged war. Part of that complex was, of course, Phelps Dodge and the retired miners who had worked for Phelps Dodge. So the pacifists and the retired miners squared off, philosophically and sometimes physically.

Some of the newcomers were talented artists—painters, sculptors, musicians—and some were skilled artisans in wood, glass, or metal. Others, if they weren't in a drugged stupor, could string beads on a better than average day. In spite of their uniformly nonconventional

dress and disgust with middle-class values, the counter-culturists included an entire spectrum of human types. At one end of the spectrum were the serious artists and artisans with brains and drive. But
those at the other end, and there were many of them, were sad and
frightening. I thought of them at the time as "flower children" after the
flower had gone to seed, the decadent and exhausted remnants of a
counter-culture movement that had lost its vitality and purpose. Many
of them were very young, often runaway or cast-off teenagers. Some
moved into the abandoned houses of the miners and lived in communal squalor and wretchedness. They were often helpless, destructive,
and dependent on others.

It must have been in about 1976, in the winter, that I spent a day and
night in Bisbee, and I could see that things had about hit bottom. The
night, particularly, was distressing. It was cold and had snowed some
during the early evening, but I saw several young people, little more
than children, sleeping in nothing but their rags and beads along the
sidewalk on Brewery Gulch and around the corner on Howell Avenue.
A few were huddled around a fire in a large open space on Brewery
Gulch where one of the commercial buildings had recently burned,
leaving only debris and two charred walls. In St. Elmo's Bar, the only
bar then open on the gulch, I saw a young "flower child"—she looked
to be about fifteen or sixteen—attempting to sell her body to any man
in the bar in return for enough money to buy drugs. She was in a
drugged haze and appeared to be seriously undernourished. As I was
going back to the Copper Queen Hotel, bitterly depressed, I nearly
stumbled over another very young girl, stoned out of her mind and
raving, stretched out on the sidewalk. Behind her, shapeless human
bundles lay in the space between two buildings.

The invading counter-culturists had a powerful effect upon Bisbee,
but they were never truly a unified force, and they were only one fac-
tion in the struggle which threatened to tear Bisbee to pieces, although
the physical destruction they sometimes caused in an attempt to "improve" their surroundings was more readily apparent than the warfare
that swirled around them. The struggle was many-sided, as factions
regrouped and realigned from time to time. In addition to the broad
range of counter-culturists and the old-time residents, who opposed
one another in almost every way, there were the two early developers,

Steve Hutchinson and Ed Smart, who came to Bisbee and bought up many of the downtown buildings at unbelievably low prices, creating rumors of future art schools and condominiums on a vast scale, none of which materialized.

Hutchinson had become interested in the prominent historic buildings in Old Bisbee as early as 1971, and during the next six years he bought ten of them, including the Copper Queen Hotel, the Mulheim Building (Old Brewery Building), and the Pythian Castle. Ed Smart bought the old city jail at auction, and also several of the more important commercial and residential buildings. As rumor spread that the developers were responsible for the invasion of the counter-culturists and had somehow attracted the "dirty hippies" to Bisbee, most of the old-time residents declared war. It consisted mostly of rotten eggs, violent rhetoric, and an attempted boycott of Hutchinson's Copper Queen Hotel restaurant, then the best and almost the only restaurant in town. In the hysteria, the city council introduced an ordinance prohibiting communal living and tried to deny Hutchinson a liquor license for the restaurant he was opening in the Old Brewery Building.

But there was another loosely federated group, not so easily defined since it cut across many lines, including the line between new and old residents, and it involved itself in activities under many names and organizations using various acronyms. It tried to remain aloof from the warfare while providing solutions rather than exacerbating the problems, and its thrust was the artistic and cultural development of Bisbee, an attempt to make the town a home for real artists of all kinds and to create a community that would attract both tourists and retirees. Much of the impetus for this group's activities came from the Bisbee Council on the Arts and Humanities, of which Ida Power was an extremely visible and active member. Another focal point of this group was the Bisbee Women's Club, which through all the hubbub and warfare continued to meet in its handsome building on Quality Hill and pursue its cultural goals. Shades of the ladies of early Bisbee. Probably the most active member of that group, who had also been its president, was Ida Power.

I have at home a newspaper reproduction of a photograph of Ida Power and her mother, Emma Loan (nee Graham), taken in 1911 when Ida was between two and three years old. Ida is standing on a wicker chair, leaning against her mother, who has one arm around her, supporting her. Ida is wearing a frilly white dress with a heavily starched short skirt, long white stockings, black Mary Janes, and has a big white ribbon perched on top of her head. She is looking slightly up and away from the camera and smiling like the good, bright little girl she was. But what interests me most about the photograph is Ida's mother. She is young, slim, and beautifully erect, with a waistline which could have been achieved only by means of the most stringent of corsets. She is wearing a long white dress, elegantly simple, and a huge dark hat with a round brim richly covered with feathers. She is an extremely attractive woman, and she looks into the camera with a cool, direct gaze. She is not smiling. Everything about her tells me who she was. She was one of the respectable ladies of Bisbee. When she posed for this photograph, she obviously intended to leave no doubt, and the little girl standing beside her was going to become one of the ladies of Bisbee, too, but she would choose to wear a different kind of hat.

I'm thinking about that photograph and the beautiful Emma Loan as I hurry downstairs and out the front door of the hotel on my way to pick up Ida. A group of tourists are milling around on the steps outside, hungry and trying to find out from anybody available where they can get something to eat. It's been a long, hot day, and some of them look a little frayed around the edges. Howell Avenue is still glistening from the brief afternoon rain, and even the silly Italian cypresses look fresh and inviting. Bisbee's mountain air is exhilarating, the temperature almost perfect. As I start down the steps of the hotel, somebody calls my name, and I look up to see Dick Bakken on the hotel terrace. It's good to see a smiling, friendly face amongst the grumpy tourists, but I'm not going to be able to linger.

Dick Bakken is one of the poets who live in Bisbee, and I've known him for years. Like nearly everybody else in town who isn't retired, Dick scrambles to make a living. He publishes, does poetry readings, teaches, and works for the Arizona Commission on the Arts in a program that sends him into the public schools throughout the state as an artist in residence. After we shake hands, Dick asks if I know about the gas situation, which leads to the inevitable "That's Bisbee" and a laugh. Dick settled in Bisbee in 1980, and by then the worst of the intramural battles were over, although several aftershocks and even a few major eruptions were still to come, acrimonious and damaging. I suppose such things were inevitable, considering that an avant-garde society, made up mostly of artists, was attempting to graft itself onto a society whose base was retired miners, one of the most conservative cultures in America, while at the same time several aggressive developers were attempting to turn the community into exactly the kind of place the artists didn't want.

By the time Dick arrived, Cochise Fine Arts, which Ida had worked hard to help establish in 1966, had become far more than a gallery providing space for artists to show their work. It had become a focal point and visible symbol of the entire community, a unifying force which attracted artists in many fields. Operating out of a ratty but spacious old storefront building on Subway Avenue, it provided gallery space, a film series, dramatic performances, poetry readings, monthly gallery openings, and an arts newsletter. It functioned as both the social center and the arts center of Bisbee at a time when Bisbee was in danger of being pulled apart at the seams, and the seams were already badly ripped in places, exposing large expanses of Bisbee's bruised social anatomy.

In 1979, members of Cochise Fine Arts inaugurated a poetry festival which Dick Bakken was later to become a co-director of, and which was to become a national arts event of considerable significance. It brought to Bisbee some of America's leading poets to read their work and conduct informal workshops with hundreds of apprentice poets who flocked from all over the country. In spite of the fact that the poetry festival ran afoul of the more conservative members of the community in 1980, it lasted about five years, was very successful, and died quietly; but in 1984, its parent organization, Cochise Fine Arts, went out with a bang rather than a whimper.

In the meantime, the first wave of would-be developers, Hutchinson and Smart, had sold their buildings and left town, and a new wave had arrived and begun buying up buildings while a whole new set of rumors concerning condominiums and high-rise hotels swept down Main Street and up Brewery Gulch. This time it was Garth Collier, an architect, and Greg Craft, an entrepreneur from California. They incorporated under the name Collier-Craft, a name which can still strike sparks in Bisbee, but eventually Collier-Craft either went bankrupt or sold out, depending on whom you talk to, and most of its holdings are now in the hands of a shadowy figure who lives in Texas and whose name invariably makes me smile—O. T. Pitts. When I first heard of Mr. Pitts, I thought perhaps he had bought the pits, both Lavender and Sacramento, and was going to dump the tailings back into them, or at least do something creative with them, like fashioning a quarry garden whose terraces would far surpass those of the Hanging Gardens of Babylon. But no such luck. The pits are not for sale, and Mr. Pitts has bought only buildings. What he intends to do with them, nobody seems to know.

In the early eighties, Collier-Craft bought the building on Subway Avenue that served as headquarters and gallery for Cochise Fine Arts, and the new owners immediately raised the rent from about $110 a month to about $1,400 a month. It seemed a deliberate attempt to drive the artists out, and it succeeded in doing even more than that. What ensued might have happened in other places, but I doubt it. The whole thing strikes me as one of those "only in Bisbee" events, and I'm sorry I missed it. It was a party of sorts.

During the afternoon of May 29, 1984, when it had become apparent that Cochise Fine Arts must vacate the building, word quietly spread through the artistic and counter-culture community that there was going to be a "paint in" that evening. I don't know who organized it or spread the word. Many people in Bisbee today blame it on one of the previous directors of Cochise Fine Arts, but others, who were members of the organization, say he had nothing to do with it. About dusk, a sizable group had gathered on the sidewalk outside the building which had been the home of the arts organization. A small hard-rock band began playing very loud, very strident music. People drifted into the gallery where somebody was handing out paint brushes, mostly large, and buckets of paint, mostly black. Painting the interior walls of the gallery became a kind of community effort, and everybody had a good time. Some painted grotesque figures, some painted blasphemous graffiti, and some merely doodled on a large scale. It was understood that the walls would have to be repainted anyway, as was customary, for the new renter, and it seemed like a wonderful opportunity for self-expression, a way of venting frustration and signifying disapproval of all that developers stood for. No windows were broken, and the walls were not physically damaged, merely decorated. Somebody, however, did empty a large receptacle of trash in the middle of the floor, and it got scattered around a bit. A crowd stood outside and watched through the storefront windows. A police car came by. The policemen looked at the party, shook their heads, and drove away. The party ended shortly after dark, but it should have lasted longer since it was actually a wake for Cochise Fine Arts.

The next day, newspapers carried startling photographs of the newly "decorated" interior of the gallery, which had been "vandalized," and newspaper accounts implied serious property damage. Like many parties viewed in retrospect on the morning after, it seemed childish and destructive. Cochise Fine Arts had lost its home, and the bad publicity made it impossible to find another one. That was the end of one of Ida's dreams, and she didn't even attend the party.

In spite of constant rumors that Bisbee is about to pop, about to "be discovered," its road to survival has been long and slow, although to many of the residents it must have seemed that the road led through a mine field. The town has been spared, thus far, the worst horrors of fashionable development, and has been allowed to grow in its own way, to find its own new and distinctive personality, a funky and fascinating mixture of the new and the old, the artistic, historical, and commercial.

"Have you heard that we're going to start the poetry festival up again?" Dick Bakken asks, grinning all over his face with pride. "I just got a Marshall Foundation Grant for six thousand dollars. All I have to do is get it matched locally, and I think I can."

Bisbee is still a town in which a six-thousand-dollar grant is very big news. I like that, and I like the fact that Dick got one. In fact, I'm very glad to have run into him, even though I am in a hurry; and he seems pleased to see me too. He's probably a lonely person. Most artists are, I think. It helps keep them in touch with themselves and provides them with an interior energy they need. And Bisbee isn't exactly the social capital of the world, especially for the artists since they've lost Cochise Fine Arts, which gave them a place to hang out and be sociable.

I tell Dick that I have a dinner date with Ida Power and that I'm running late. His face lights up with something like wistful respect.

"Did you know Ida when you lived here in the fifties?" he asks.

"Yes," I say, "and loved her."

"Everybody loves her now," he says.

As I leave Dick and start up the hill to where Blue Boy is waiting in the terraced parking lot, I think about that and the fact that it comes from a representative of the artist culture which now dominates much of the life in Bisbee. Ida is one of the "others," one of the old-time retired residents. And yet she has not only bridged the gap herself, she has formed a bridge for nearly everybody else. She has one foot in each camp, but she wears her artist's beret with pride.

I think about her as a little girl in the photograph, and about her very attractive mother who managed to look lovely and comfortable in spite of her corset, in spite of her life in a small, rough mining town, in spite of the alcoholism, prostitution, and squalor of Brewery Gulch just around the corner, in spite of the mud and filth through which she had to drag her long white skirt, and could never raise it for fear a man might see her ankle. She was one of the ladies of Bisbee, and she maintained her position, her cool, long look of elegance and gentility, because to fall from that position was a plunge beyond our ability to comprehend—although not beyond hers—a plunge all the way around the corner. She had only two choices, and that calm, un-smiling face tells me she had made hers, and it was irrevocable because the alternative was . . . not impossible . . . but inconceivable.

Everywhere I go in Bisbee, it's nostalgia time. Every street I turn down reminds me of something that happened there when I was a Bisbee resident—can it have been thirty years ago? I wrote a poem once which had to do with what it is like to go back to one's hometown after many years, and although Bisbee isn't my hometown, the effect is much the same. "Every street drives a nail in my foot / and each corner says this is where . . ."

As I pass Lavender Pit, approaching all that is left of Lowell, one long block of mostly deserted commercial buildings erected during the first decade of the century, I see the spot where Molly Bendixon, one Saturday morning, ran her car off the road in amazement when she saw me riding along on a mule. I will never forget the look on her face as her big—I think it was a Buick—car careened wildly into the weeds beside the road and came to a lurching stop. What I remember most about the entire experience was that the mule was wearing, instead of a conventional saddle, a pack saddle with a wooden frame, and how painfully that saddle dug into my skinny rear end. The mule was slightly balky, but the saddle was pure hell, and I rode all the way from the northernmost end of Brewery Gulch to the astonished extremities of Warren. I was sore for weeks.

It's strange how the big things, the issues, the reasons and motivations, have faded from my memory, and I am left with only details and impressions. I remember the name of the family from which I rented the mule at the extreme northern end of Brewery Gulch—it was Encinas—and I remember the look of incredulity on Molly's face when she saw me, and the pain of that long ride, but I don't remember precisely why I was doing it. It was a fund-raising stunt and I remember that there were banners on each side of the mule advertising something (which might explain the pack saddle), but I don't remember what I was raising funds for or why it was necessary for me to ride a mule, with my long legs hanging down almost to the ground, all one hot Saturday morning.

The Encinas family, who raised mules up Brewery Gulch, was a truly extended family with many, many children, probably cousins rather than brothers and sisters, since there were at least fifteen of them watching me in round-eyed amazement as I mounted the mule in their front yard, obviously puzzled as to why the gringo schoolteacher was going to ride away on a mule with a packsaddle when he had arrived in a perfectly good car. I don't think any of them understood that the gringo schoolteacher was going to sell his ass, one layer of skin at a time, for some good, or questionable cause. It was probably for the Boy Scouts of America. Most of the more ridiculous and painful things I did in Bisbee between 1958 and 1960 had something to do with Boy Scouts, the little monsters for whom I labored and who managed to grow up in spite of everything I could do.

I had been teaching at Lowell School only a few weeks when the principal, Paul Rose, approached me on behalf of the Bisbee Elks Club. The Elks Club sponsored two Boy Scout troops, one of which was older boys in their teens, called Sea Scouts, but there was currently no member of the Elks Club who was willing to take on the responsibility of scoutmaster. That should have told me something, but I was young and stupid, although I had been a boy and even a Boy Scout once myself, and should have known what I was getting into. The Elks Club owned one of the largest and most elaborate of the buildings on Main Street, and there they provided a room for the boys to meet in each week, a large cubbyhole in the attic and as far away from the bar as possible. I found out later that the bar, with its slot machines, was where all the action was at the Elks Club and that nobody but members were welcome there, least of all the scoutmaster or any of his waifs. Just keeping the boys out of that alluring den of iniquity turned out to be one of my most difficult functions.

I wasn't a very good scoutmaster, but I was the only one available. Most of the hocus-pocus came back to me easily. I memorized the pledge, the oath, the salute, and brushed up on merit badges and how to tie knots. Some of my recent army training came in handy, although if I had tried to teach the boys what I *really* learned in the army, I would have been run out of town. Paul Rose had made me feel obligated to take on the two troops because he said most of the boys were "underprivileged," a buzz-word which could be interpreted in many ways. I guess some of them were underprivileged, probably most of them, because I remember teaching two of them, brothers about ten and twelve years old, how to use a toothbrush, an implement that was totally foreign to their experience. But one of the boys was the mayor's son, and he certainly wasn't underprivileged, just a typical hellion. Another was the son of the madam who ran the only brothel in Brewery Gulch. He lived with his mother in the brothel, and when he told stories around the campfire, they were always the most interesting, and the other boys listened to them with great attention. They were truly educational stories, even for the scoutmaster. Especially for the scoutmaster.

One member of the Elks Club, an engineer with Phelps Dodge, made available an ancient flatbed truck so that I could transport the boys across the San Pedro Valley when we wanted to hike or camp in the Huachuca Mountains. I was never quite sure to whom the truck actually belonged—probably Phelps Dodge—but it was a mixed blessing. It overheated badly and there was something wrong with its fuel system. We never got more than fifteen miles without its breaking down, and we spent much time beside the road while I tinkered with its rusty motor and while the boys engaged in mayhem and mutual destruction. I didn't want to act like a top sergeant, but it was very difficult to control a large number of boys between the ages of nine and fifteen while bent over the fender of an old truck and examining the mystery of its rusty innards, about which I knew next to nothing.

At such times I realized that the boys needed exactly what I had needed and hadn't had—a father who would teach them how to deal with the intricacies of an automobile motor rather than a scoutmaster who would teach them to tie intricate knots, which simply made it easier for them to torture one another in intricate ways. My father had taught me three skills: how to chop kindling without cutting my fingers off, how to pour a glass of beer so it didn't have too much head, and how to open his cigarette packages neatly. Beyond that, I had learned many things from him—attitudes, prejudices, funny songs and witty stories—but no skills. Those I have had to pick up along the way as best I could, and they are few. I am constantly aware of the enormous gaps, which is probably why I was willing to take on the two Boy Scout troops in the first place. While I was poorly equipped to teach the boys the things they needed to know, I was vitally concerned that they learn them. The result was a long series of frustrations with a few minor successes in between.

Although many of the boys were underprivileged, and I think I had some idea from my own childhood of what that word meant, they turned out to be more knowledgeable in certain areas than I had anticipated. Once, when we were hiking up the side of one of the Huachuca Mountains to a campsite, several of the boys gave out under the weight of their packs. I sent them on without their packs and made several trips up the side of the mountain lugging two packs at a time. When I had finally gotten all our gear to the campsite, it occurred to me that the packs were inordinantly heavy. When I opened them, I found that they contained many bottles of beer. It gave me great pleasure to throw each bottle of beer off the side of the mountain and hear it break on the rocks below. The next day I made the guilty members of the group pick up all the shards of glass and carry them two miles to the nearest trash can.

Annoying as it was to be made a fool of by helping them carry their beer up the mountain, it was just between me and the boys, and not the worst humiliation they caused me. The worst was more public, much more public. We were coming back in the flatbed truck from one of our outings. As I drove up Main Street, between the post office and the bank, through Bisbee's busiest intersection, I noticed that people along the street were reacting strangely, much as Molly Bendixon had reacted when she saw me riding the mule, but some of them were laughing. I looked back through the tiny window of the cab and saw that all the boys were standing up on the flatbed of the truck, which was strictly forbidden when the truck was moving. Not only were they standing up, but they had all dropped their pants and were proudly exhibiting whatever they had of genitalia to anyone who happened to be walking or driving along Main Street at four o'clock in the afternoon. There was really nothing in *The Boy Scout Manual* which applied to the situation, but after it happened, none of the boys got any merit badges for a long time.

Our major ongoing activity was raising money to buy uniforms for the boys, which they had been brainwashed into believing they needed. I guess they needed something to sew their merit badges on, although I was happy with them in raggedy shirts and jeans, anything, as long as they kept their pants on in public. But they wanted Boy Scout uniforms, and I decided that uniforms they would have. Looking back, I have mixed feelings about the Boy Scouts of America as an organization. It seems like its major function was to get thousands of small boys to raise money in order to buy uniforms and equipment, most of which they had to purchase from, of course, the Boy Scouts of America. Several of the boys in my troops could not even afford their dues, which were ten cents a week. And my view of the Bisbee Elks Club isn't too rosy either. In hindsight it looks to me like a male organization whose major function was to provide its members with a place to drink and gamble—and I once saw a young prostitute in the building, although they got her out of the way quickly when I passed down the hall—while masquerading as a service organization which sponsored such things as Boy Scout troops, although no member of the Bisbee Elks Club was willing to serve as scoutmaster.

But the Boy Scouts of Bisbee and their insane, masochistic leader lurched onward, generally sober and with their pants on. Our first big drive to raise money came as Christmas approached and we decided to sell mistletoe. Who could resist, I thought, a small waif standing on the corner of Bisbee's picturesque Main Street selling clumps of mistletoe, preferably while it was snowing, which it seldom does in Bisbee, but I was sure God would be on our side in this economic venture. So we all went out into the desert south and west of Bisbee to gather mistletoe, a parasitic plant that grows in large clumps on paloverde and mesquite trees in the Sonoran Desert, and which can eventually kill the host tree. I figured that we would not only make some money for uniforms, but rid the trees of a parasite that was slowly killing them.

We had been gathering mistletoe for less than an hour when a highway patrolman came along and arrested all of us. We were, without knowing it, on United States government land, and it was illegal to remove any growth, even mistletoe, although overgrazing was obviously not illegal since the area had been grazed to the point where there was almost nothing left but a few trees. I had a long discussion with the highway patrolman while the boys stood around looking as pitiful and innocent as possible, and they could look innocent, although none of them were. I mentioned that one of the boys was the mayor's son and that we were a kind of extension of the Bisbee Elks Club, which was probably the most powerful and prestigious fraternity in town. Finally the highway patrolman let us off with a severe reprimand, after taking away all our mistletoe.

On weekends, when we weren't raising money for uniforms or nursing the ancient flatbed truck across the valley to the Huachucas, we sometimes hiked in the Mule Mountains. We had only to take off up any of the canyons leading generally north and we were well away from town in minutes. The Mule Mountains are much smaller and less spectacular than the Huachucas, but we always had plenty of adventures when we hiked there, like the time a wasp flew up the scoutmaster's pant leg, which the boys found wildly amusing. Once we stumbled into the midst of a large herd of javelina who were sleeping through the heat of the afternoon. I had never had any experience with the wild boar of the Sonoran Desert and didn't know how dangerous they could be.

Although often called "pigs," javelinas are actually peccaries, in this case collared peccaries, and are not closely related to domestic pigs. I have read somewhere that they are closely related to the hippopotamus but couldn't vouch for it. Nor do they resemble domestic pigs except for the fact that they have hooves and a snout. They don't resemble any other creature I have ever seen. They measure about three-and-a-half feet from their snouts to their tails, which are so small as to be almost invisible, and about two feet in height. Their bodies are covered with long, bristly hair, which they can erect when they are angry or frightened. At those times they have the look of huge porcupines. Their bodies are narrow, as if they had been flattened from side to side, and their large heads and powerful shoulders are out of all proportion to the rest of them, especially their small, delicate legs and hooves. Their hair is a grizzled brown-gray except for a buff "collar," a narrow band of light buff around their shoulders. They run with a peculiar stiff-legged trot like no other creature I know of, except perhaps a hippopotamus.

Fortunately for my Boy Scouts and their ignorantly fearless leader, javelina are not one of the Sonoran Desert's major threats to humans, although they can be very dangerous under certain circumstances. They have long and extremely sharp canine teeth, like fangs, extending downward from their upper jaws, with which they can rip open a leg with astonishing speed. Normally they do not attack, but if they feel particularly threatened or if the herd includes babies, the boar and sometimes the sows will charge, teeth flashing, and rip up whatever or whomever they come in contact with. But they have very poor eyesight and usually rely on their keen sense of smell. When charged by one of them, the thing to do is sidestep quickly. The angry animal will usually hurtle right on past, unless, of course, it swerves toward you. Then, the thing to do is run as if you were carrying the ball and dodging through scattered opposition. It's amazing how fast and well one can run with a javelina boar close behind.

When we encountered the herd in the Mule Mountains, however, I didn't know anything about javelina, not even enough to be frightened. I associated them with domestic pigs, with which I had had plenty of experience as a child. But the boys were mostly natives of Southern Arizona, and they knew better. While I stood in the middle of a herd of wildly milling javelinas, the boys took off in all directions. I had no idea my Boy Scouts could run so fast. Some tried to climb the closest mesquite, while others plunged down arroyos and through stands of cactus, screaming as they went. Within a minute the javelinas were all gone, but it took me a half hour to find all of my troops, and some of them were in a sorry state, scratched by mesquite thorns and bristling with cactus spines.

I was proud of myself for having stood my ground and merely stepped aside when the boar charged me, but none of the boys had stayed around long enough to witness my act of heroism. And the fact that I hadn't run like hell when we encountered the javelinas was just one more proof of what they suspected anyway. The scoutmaster was crazy. First, he carried their beer all the way up the mountain, only to throw it off the edge of a cliff. Then he stood around in the middle of a herd of javelinas. The boys looked at one another, grinned, and made the sign with the index finger revolving at the temple. *Loco* in the *cabeza.*

I drive past Lowell School in the growing dusk, and it's almost dark when I pull up in front of Ida's house in Warren. While I'm parking the van, she comes out on the front porch to greet me. Each time I see her again I am reminded by the way she dresses that she is an artist with an eye for color and texture. During the day she often wears bright, true purples and magentas. Tonight it's lustrous black with a subtle pattern of deep orange and gold, dark and rich like the feathers on her mother's hat in the photo. She stands there as if perched on one foot, her head to the side, carriage jaunty, and eyes laughing, happy to see me. The years have been much kinder to her than they have been to me. What a privilege it is to walk up on the porch and put my arms around this good and beautiful woman. For a moment I am holding Bisbee in my arms, and it has survived. But the bones are light and fragile like the bones of a bird. A couple of lines by E. E. Cummings pop into my head and make me sad and happy all at once: "the power of your intense fragility; whose texture / compels me with the colour of its countries."

Suddenly I realize that Bisbee was always fragile, even while I lived here, while Lavender Pit was a maelstrom of activity and the whistle blew every day, and while on my way to work I could watch long lines of grim-looking men filing onto open elevator platforms which dropped them hundreds of feet into the earth. Bisbee has always been fragile, and never more so than now. I wonder if the people who live here realize how fragile it is, a kind of Shangri-La in the Mule Mountains, a timeless space attacked from without and within, an attitude threatened by the forces of greed. Bisbee was born of greed, but it has outlived its parents. For many, Bisbee has become an idea, a way to live simply, even in poverty according to some standards, but well. Such an idea will always be a threat to the forces of greed, which assume that everyone is as greedy as they are and can't bear it when they find that some are not.

But I can't stand here on Ida's front porch thinking about all this while Ida hops around me, talking in her rapid-fire way. She's all energy, bottled up and ready to take on the world. I feel old by comparison, and I sense that Bisbee is young again and that Ida's energy reflects the town's energy. It is much younger than it was when I lived here. Young and fresh and eager, although the buildings are old. I was wrong to refer to Bisbee as "old girl" this afternoon. Bisbee has grown younger while I have grown older. And all at once I know why I had to come back. I had to touch youth again, my own past youth and the renewed youth of a town where I lived in ignorance and audacity, as only the young can live. I thought towns had to grow old, but Bisbee has grown young, and seeing this eighty-year-old woman with her laughing eyes and young spirit has finally made me understand it.

"Come in and see my new digs," Ida says with a little mock curtsy, like a ballerina. She always seems to be dancing, even when she's standing still. It must be the way she carries her body and the way expressions flash across her face. She leads me through the living room of the spacious old home she has recently moved to after spending most of her life in Old Bisbee's cramped and crowded Tombstone Canyon. "It cost too much," she says, biting her lip in a momentary gesture of annoyance, "terribly expensive, but I wanted it so much and I just decided to do it." Her face lights up again.

It's a beautiful house on Warren's most attractive street, which is actually two streets with a narrow park between them. The house must have been built shortly after 1906, when the Calumet and Arizona Mining Company began construction of Warren as a housing community for upper-echelon employees. "It was owned by a mining engineer," Ida says as she takes me between the dark, wooden pillars and built-in bookcases that separate the living room and the dining room, a standard arrangement in houses of the period. The floor plan is typical of the one-story "cottage" houses built in the Warren Mining District at the time, with a long expanse of living room and dining room, kitchen and sun porch in the rear, and bedrooms and bath to one side. But the house is larger and more spacious than most of the others built on the same plan. It has been well maintained and never remodeled or "restored," a fate which has destroyed the beauty of all too many houses in the district, some of which have been improved to the point of destruction by what appears to have been do-it-yourself enthusiasts.

But with the exception of wall-to-wall carpeting, Ida's house is much as it has always been. It has both dignity and charm.

As we wander through the house, I notice several of Ida's paintings and collages on the walls. They are honest, unpretentious, rich, and vibrant. What comes through most immediately is an intense feeling for place and a wonderful sense of texture. Her collages, done with tissue paper and sometimes watercolors, are stunning. One is a panorama view of the basin and range country she knows so well. By gluing several layers of cut or torn tissue paper on canvas, she has achieved the visual effect of seeing several mountain ranges superimposed on one another. "I just experiment and try this and that and see what comes out," Ida says.

Her oils and water colors, at least the ones I can see, seem to be mostly scenes of Bisbee, lively and attractive. One is a view of the tall Presbyterian church from above and behind, with part of the Copper Queen Hotel to one side. Another is a Bisbee hillside with the funky little houses covered with snow and a long stairway wandering upward. But the trolley collage is my favorite. The Bisbee Street Car was inaugurated the year Ida was born, 1908, with a citywide celebration that included upwards of six thousand people. Ida rode the streetcar during much of her youth, and the noisy but delightful contraption affected the spread of Bisbee's communities, making it convenient for the miners to live a greater distance from their work. Ida's collage catches the excitement of a child seeing the streetcar for the first time. The trolley is rounding a curve on Main Street between the post office/library and the Bank of Bisbee, heading toward the intersection of Main Street and Brewery Gulch, at exactly the spot where my Boy Scouts, many years later, decided to expose themselves to the world from the back of an old flatbed truck. I want to tell Ida that story, but I'm sure she has already heard it several times.

Ida is quiet while I'm looking at her art work, but restless. Maybe she's just hungry, as I am, but I suspect that she's shy about having me see her work. I understand that feeling. I feel the same way whenever I have to stand around while somebody reads one of my poems, wondering if the person will say, "It's interesting," which means "I can't make heads nor tails of it and wouldn't like it if I could." But I like Ida's work, and I tell her so. I don't tell her that I used to paint, too, when I lived in Bisbee. Lord, I would almost die if she ever saw one of those astonishingly awful things I did with house paint and laundry detergent.

But as soon as we get in the van and start for the cafe, Ida is talking rapidly in response to my questions. I want to know what she's been up to lately and how things are going for her and the town, and I know that her story is the town's story, and she won't be able to tell me about one without telling me about the other. She begins to throw acronyms and the names of local organizations around like confetti, and I can't make much sense of it, but I'm listening so hard I run a stop sign and we nearly get hit by a fast-moving car, which swerves around us with its horn blaring. After a moment's pause Ida picks up her account where she left off, somewhere between CSP (whatever that is), the Revitalization Council, the Main Street Project, and a wine festival, which seems to be imminent.

When we get to the cafe, it's jammed as I expected because it is the only one open in the entire area thanks to the power company's accidental tearing up of the gas line to Old Bisbee. Three booths are taken up by men who have been sent down from Tucson by the gas company to turn the pilot lights back on. The clerk at the hotel said they were going to work through the night, so they must be taking their dinner break. They are very noisy and several of them appear to be drunk. Gas, alcohol, and pilot lights—what a combination. I hope they don't blow up the entire town. Wouldn't that be the limit, after all Bisbee has been through and just as it is getting back on its feet, to be destroyed by a bunch of drunken gas company employees imported from Tucson. But knowing Bisbee, it's not beyond the realm of possibility.

After a long wait, we get a booth, but it's covered with dirty dishes. Ida shows no sign that any of the inconvenience bothers her. She seems to know everybody in the restaurant except the gas crew from Tucson. By the time the waitress has cleared the table and come back to take our orders, I'm beginning to sort out the various acronyms and organizations Ida is talking about. But just in spots. The difficulty is how they all fit together and which is the child or subsidiary of which. I suppose I'll never get that straightened out.

The Bisbee Council on the Arts and Humanities is probably one of the seminal organizations which has made Bisbee what it is today. Ida helped found the Arts Council in the late sixties and serves on its board, which was the founder of the Bisbee Mining and Historical Museum. Somehow, the board of the Arts Council convinced the management of Phelps Dodge to donate the handsome Phelps Dodge headquarters, Old Bisbee's architectural centerpiece, to house the museum, and it also got Phelps Dodge to provide the first six years salary for a director in order to get the museum started and in good operating condition. Hundreds of Bisbee and ex-Bisbee families, as well as Phelps Dodge, donated items of historical interest. The old photographs and samples of mining equipment alone make the museum a real charmer, crammed with bits of surprising information.

Out in front are several pieces of old mining equipment, including some ore cars which were pulled on tracks by mules through miles of underground tunnels. I wonder how many tourists notice that one of the ore cars is different from the others. It is shaped like the other ore cars, but unlike them, it is covered and the metal cover has two round holes that are fitted with metal lids on hinges. It's a portable two-hole privy without privacy, and the man who was in charge of transporting it to wherever it was most urgently needed in the mine was called a "shit nipper." I don't know where that job fell in the carefully regulated echelon of jobs in the mines. Although it was a very important job, I doubt that it had much prestige.

The Central School Project, which Ida speaks about with marked enthusiasm, may also be a product of the Bisbee Council on the Arts and Humanities, but I'm not sure about that. It sounds like a great project. Central School, where Ida taught for twenty-five years, is a large, handsome old structure on Howell Avenue just up the hill from the YMCA Building, whose purchase and "development" has been the source of so much animosity in Bisbee. The Central School Project involved leasing the old building from the school district and turning it into studio space for artists and performers of all kinds, as well as work space for some scientists. The original idea was to provide the much-needed studios free, but now a small fee is charged to help with the maintenance of the building. In return for the studios, those who use them conduct workshops for the school children of Bisbee, greatly enriching the schools' offerings for the students. The whole scheme is something very dear to Ida's heart, since it involves artists, school children, and the building she worked in for so many years. It sounds to me like a system which should be adopted in many cities and towns where old and outmoded school buildings are not uncommon.

Other civic and arts organizations in which Ida is involved seem to be legion. She talks about the Main Street Project, which hires Bisbee's handicapped; she is a founder of the local chapter of the National Society of Arts and Letters and has served as its president; and she is involved with the Cochise College Performing Arts Series. Referring to the artists in Bisbee, Ida was once quoted in the newspaper as saying, "Because of them, we have been able to keep the town alive." I believe it, but how does she keep all those organizations straight?

While we are eating our Mexican dinner and trying to talk above the general din in the restaurant, much of which is coming from the gas company workers who seem to consider their sudden trip to Bisbee a wild vacation spree, I notice that Ida has a remarkably robust appetite for a woman of her age and diminutive size. All that energy, I think, must have fuel. As birdlike as she is, she must burn up food at a great rate. I envy everything about her, including her metabolism, but most of all her quick, bright mind, as she leaps from one subject to another like a trapeze artist. I feel slow-witted and dull trying to follow her.

"We are pushing for tourists through little celebrations," she says, referring to both a wine festival and the upcoming poetry festival. I don't ask her who the "we" is because I think I know. "We" must include anybody who is willing to help, anybody who is not trying to make large amounts of money but is concerned about the town's survival, attempting to provide a steady flow of customers for the merchants and artists. It is obvious from the kinds of "little celebrations" they are involved in that Ida and those she includes as "we" are not trying to turn Bisbee into another Tombstone, mecca of the Winnebago and history-on-the-run tourist. I sense a big difference in scale and thrust, as well as quality. Ida doesn't speak of it—it's too obvious to mention—but those tourists interested in shoot-em-ups in Tombstone will not be interested in wine or poetry festivals in Bisbee. And it is also obvious that Ida and the organizations that take up her time and energy would view large-scale development leading to "another Sausalito, another Aspen" with unrestrained horror.

I am suddenly reminded of another Bisbeeite, Don Fry, who sits in his office behind his dark glasses and represents large-scale development and the Bisbee Convention Center, a center that suffers from a great dearth of conventions since it was unable to build the convention hotel which Don badly wanted. I don't think Don Fry is a sinister person, as he is sometimes portrayed by the artists of Bisbee. He is neither particularly greedy nor callous, but he has a dream, a dream he wants to superimpose on Bisbee. He has offered his dream of development to Bisbee, and the people of Bisbee have, for the most part, rejected it.

Emperors and beggars have been broken because their dreams were rejected. I fear for Don Fry. It is a matter of opposing dreams. Ida dreams on a much smaller scale, but she dreams of important things, like survival, and the people of Bisbee adore her. I think I know what Ida represents, and I like it; but I don't know all that Don Fry represents. On the surface of things, he represents a millionaire named O. T. Pitts who lives somewhere in Texas and owns large chunks of Bisbee, which he may or may not "develop" into something commercially rewarding on a big scale, and nobody except O. T. Pitts seems to know what that development will include, if indeed it takes place. Other developers have come and gone and the town has not changed appreciably, although each wave of would-be development has left behind a growing residue of conflict and bad feelings, and even Don Fry, who represents development with a big D, is somewhat ambiguous around the edges.

Recently, with some prodding, Don Fry admitted to me that he dreamed of the future Bisbee as "a mining town with culture." I didn't point out to him that that is exactly what it is now, and with considerable charm and charisma. I guess he was thinking of a different scale of things than I was. And I don't know exactly what he meant by "culture." It's an ambiguous term. Maybe he meant more of the same horror that development usually brings: the hills covered with asphalt and condominiums, shopping malls full of real trees and artificial people. But maybe he didn't. I had the feeling that if I could get him to take off those dark glasses for a minute, we could be friends;

315 ❖

but I didn't ask him to. Perhaps his eyes are sensitive to the light. It is clear that he represents big money, but it is not clear how that money will be used in Bisbee, or if it will be used at all.

But it's time to ask Ida the big question, the sixty-four-dollar question I've been wanting to ask her all evening. How does she feel about the news that Phelps Dodge might be coming back to Bisbee, just as the new Bisbee is beginning to show signs that it can make it on its own, and even grow? For several years Phelps Dodge has been drilling and testing on the hills immediately across the highway from Sacramento Pit between Old Bisbee and all that is left of Lowell. Recently, the company held meetings with the people of Bisbee to explain what its managers had in mind, although everything seems to depend on the future price of copper.

Phelps Dodge has never relinquished its ownership to most of the land in the Warren Mining District, nor its ownership to the mineral rights beneath the land it does not own outright. In a sense, the mining industry operates on the same principles that modern archaeologists do. When archaeologists have excavated the site of a center of prehistoric culture and learned all they can from it, they often backfill it and wait for the development of new technology that will make it possible for them to return to the site and learn even more. When it pulled out in the mid-1970s, Phelps Dodge did not fill in the enormous pits it had created nor clear away the tons of tailings that scar the landscape, but it has been waiting while new mining technology has developed, technology that will make it possible to process, at a profit, ore of a lower grade than was previously worthwhile. That technology has now been developed.

Phelps Dodge plans to strip-mine a new section of the Mule Mountains just across the highway from Sacramento Pit, creating a new pit, and to process the ore by means of a recently improved electrolytic method. They would then dump the waste material and tons of overburden into Lavender Pit. The company is not specific as to when this process will begin, but there is little doubt in the minds of most Bisbee residents that it will occur, and probably soon. Because it will be a highly technical operation depending on huge earth-moving machines and a very sophisticated processing plant, it will employ relatively few people, possibly as few as one hundred and no more than two hundred. Don Fry says that the addition of even one hundred workers and their families would revolutionize the Bisbee economy. "There isn't a merchant here that isn't hanging on by his fingernails," Fry says. The reactions of Bisbee residents to the Phelps Dodge plan range from wild enthusiasm to horror. The possibility of renewed paternalism, like a spectre, now walks the streets of Bisbee, feared by some and welcomed by others.

But what does Ida think about all this? She has had time to weigh the pros and cons and estimate the impact on the town and the landscape she loves. In answer to my question, she raises her head and gives me a long, cool look which reminds me of her mother's look in the photograph I so much admire. "I would be pleased," she says very quietly and very deliberately, "to see Phelps Dodge return."

Again I am reminded of what Don Fry said. "A mining town with culture." Maybe he and Ida are not so far apart in their dreams after all. But is it possible to have a town of Bisbee's size that includes both a high level of artistic culture and a large, active copper mine? It's possible, I suppose, but difficult to imagine, and so many questions pop up. Would the artists accept the miners and their families? Would the miners drive the artists out? Would the people who have worked so hard to make Bisbee a good town to live in slide back into the complacency that comes with paternalism? What would become of Bisbee's rapidly growing tourism? Would water seeping through thousands of tons of debris in Lavender Pit pollute the water supply as it does at abandoned mine sites in Colorado?

Ida seems satisfied that it will all work out for the best. "It's good to get these new people with new ideas in," she says, referring to all kinds of people. "My theory is that I like people and I don't get torn apart with arguments. I do what I can. Gradually, some of the newer people will take over." I think about what she says, remembering that it comes from a woman who has been walking through a social and political mine field for the last twenty years and has come through in excellent shape. Some good angel has been watching over her, and it isn't the angel of ignorance. Ida knows what she is doing, and she does it with care and precision.

As I am driving her home, we are both quiet, pensive. I don't know what Ida is thinking about, but I'm thinking about Sacramento Hill, which exists only in photographs, where it stands as the most prominent feature of the horizon southeast of Old Bisbee. I'm wondering how many of the neighboring hills will soon be gone as well, and how much of the Mule Mountains will be transformed into enormous pits? How do you put a dollar value on a mountain? How do you weigh a mountain's survival against the survival of a town? It's just landscape, I keep telling myself, and look at what has happened to the surrounding landscape. Gone, destroyed, ravaged. And it's only two or three more hills. What are two or three more hills as compared with what all that money will do for the town?

It's easy for me to say that I like Bisbee as it is and wouldn't want to change it. Easy because I live in Tucson and have a steady income. But how would I feel if I lived in Bisbee and had to scramble every day to make a rather meager living? So much for picturesque! Things look different when you have children to feed and no bank account. And yet . . . the hills . . . the tawny hills . . . the way they throw off amber light in the late afternoon, turning Bisbee into a magic place as seen in a sepia print. Why must the mountains be sacrificed for economic progress that will be temporary at best?

I don't know the answers to any of the questions. I am not as old or wise as Ida, but I don't think I agree with her on this matter, and it makes me sad. She has given her life and her labor for the people of Bisbee, and now she must sacrifice even the mountains she loves. I think of her beautiful collages of the mountains fading into blue distances. Somehow it isn't right, it isn't fair. Not for Ida or the other artists in Bisbee, and not for the mountains.

I say good-night to Ida on her front porch and tell her that I probably won't see her again on this trip. I'm going hiking tomorrow, and then I will probably drive back to Tucson tomorrow night or the next morning. But I will be back in a few months, and then we can have the elegant dinner I had planned, maybe at the Copper Queen or the Courtyard. I'll call her and warn her that I am coming.

"If you don't get me the first time," she says, "keep trying. I'm gone a lot during the day. Meetings and things."

"I'll catch you one way or the other," I say as I wave good-bye and get into Blue Boy. Yes, I'll catch her. I'll call city hall or the Arts Commission or Central School or the Women's Club or the county courthouse or the historical museum. I'll catch her in midflight somewhere. And I wonder where they will catch me when I'm eighty. Probably not on the wing.

Driving back to the Copper Queen Hotel, I come around the traffic circle and see Lowell School, all locked up and dark under a blazing full moon and a sky full of stars. The clouds have blown away until tomorrow afternoon, when they will probably reappear for the usual late afternoon storm. Arizona moon and Arizona stars, I think. Bigger and brighter than anywhere else. I will never get used to them or take them for granted. Maybe I will come back to Lowell School in the morning and poke around some. School won't be in session, but there will probably be a secretary or an assistant principal or somebody around to let me in. There won't be anybody who will remember me, but that's O.K. I was the youngest of the crew. Paul Rose is dead now. Molly Bendixon is in a rest home in Phoenix. Carol Mosely and Bill Taylor have retired. Marguerite Knowles lives somewhere in California, surrounded by grandchildren. But I want to see my classroom again, with its high ceilings, dark woodwork, and bank of tall windows. I want to see if it has been changed, and I want to look at the auditorium where my choral speaking groups performed, like the troopers they were, for wildly enthusiastic audiences. It's hard to imagine that those students are all in their mid forties now, the ones who have survived.

So maybe I'll come back in the morning and have a look around. Then I'll amble through Old Bisbee and hike up Brewery Gulch all the way to the top of the ridge of hills that circles the town like the arm of a sleeping giant. From up there, I will be able to get a better perspective on Bisbee and its current problems. I will see it below like a little toy town, with toy houses ranging up the hills and miniature church steeples and silly Italian cypresses sticking up in formal rows. I will not be able to hear any sounds from down there except a dog barking once in awhile or a particularly loud truck as it climbs the high road on the other side of Tombstone Canyon. Bisbee will look very peaceful from there, like a painting by some artist who paints only what is picturesque. I'll sit on the ridge and look down at it, as I have many times in the past.

I'll have a chance to think about the changes, and how the town has grown younger while I haven't. And I'll realize more fully, as I am be-

319 ❖

ginning to realize now, that my trip has been pure nostalgia-time and I can never really go back to Bisbee. My trips to Bisbee will always be visits, brief raids on the past that will retreat before me and remain just out of reach. Whatever I came here to find is part of the past and will have to remain part of the past—part of the old Bisbee that doesn't exist anymore. I'll come to realize, in spite of the old cliche, that home is the only place I *can* go back to if I plan to stay, and my home is in the Tucson Mountains, in a house that is getting old now, as I am. Bisbee and I have both been busy surviving for the past thirty years, and we've both been successful at it.

Then, when I've figured it all out, I'll come zigzagging and sliding down the steep hill behind the Copper Queen, get into Blue Boy, and drive the one hundred miles back to Tucson while monsoon clouds rise behind me and lightning dances through the darkening sky above the Mule Mountains. Going home.

11 RICHARD SHELTON. "The Upper Bajadas" from *Of All the Dirty Words*, University of Pittsburgh Press, 1972.

29 ARCHIBALD MACLEISH. *J.B.*, Houghton Mifflin Co., 1961.

30 ROBERT CREELEY. "I Know a Man" from *Selected Poems*. © 1991, the Regents of the University of California.

34 LEWIS CARROLL. "The Hunting of the Snark" from *Collected Verse of Lewis Carroll*, Macmillan and Co., 1932.

68 ROBERT BLY. *The Morning Glory*, Kayak Press, 1969.

93 EDNA ST. VINCENT MILLAY. "Dirge Without Music" from *The Buck in the Snow*, Harper & Brothers, 1928.

120 RICHARD SHELTON. "Glen Canyon on the Colorado" from *The Forgotten Language: Contemporary Poets and Nature*, Peregrine-Smith Books, 1991.

138 T. S. ELIOT. Excerpt from "Burnt Norton" in *The Four Quartets*, copyright 1943 by T. S. Eliot and renewed 1971 by Esme Valerie Eliot. Reprinted by permission of Harcourt Brace Jovanovich, Inc.

157 LEVI W. HANCOCK. "The Bull Fight on the San Pedro" from *A Concise History of the Mormon Battalion in the Mexican War, 1846–1848*, by Sgt. Daniel Tyler, the Rio Grande Press, Inc., 1964.

193 RICHARD SHELTON. "Mexico" and "Harry Orchard" from *Selected Poems, 1969–1981*, University of Pittsburgh Press, 1982.

292 WILLIAM BUTLER YEATS. "The Second Coming" from *The Selected Poems and Two Plays*, Macmillan Co., 1962.

302 RICHARD SHELTON. "Hometown" from *Chosen Place*, Best Cellar Press, 1975.

309 E. E. CUMMINGS. "somewhere I have never travelled, gladly beyond" from *Complete Poems, 1913–1962*, Harcourt Brace Javanovich, Inc., 1972.

❖ ❖ SUGGESTED READING

ARRINGTON, LEONARD J. *Brigham Young: American Moses.* New York: Knopf, 1986.

BAILEY, LYNN R. *Bisbee: Queen of the Copper Camps.* Tucson: Westernlore Press, 1983.

BANNON, JOHN FRANCIS. *The Spanish Borderlands Frontier, 1513–1821.* Albuquerque: University of New Mexico Press, 1974.

BARNES, WILL C. *Arizona Place Names.* (Revised and enlarged by Byrd Granger.) Tucson: University of Arizona Press, 1979.

BOROWIEC, MARGARET. *Bisbee's Pioneer Homes.* Bisbee: A Bicentennial Project, 1976.

BOURKE, JOHN G. *On the Border with Crook.* New York: Charles Scribner's Sons, 1891.

BRANDES, RAY. *Frontier Military Posts of Arizona.* Globe: Dale Stuart King, 1960.

BROWN, J. CABELL. *Calabazas: Amusing Recollections of an Arizona City.* Tucson: Arizona Silhouettes, 1961.

BROWNE, J. ROSS. *A Tour through Arizona, 1864 or Adventures in Apache Country.* Tucson: Arizona Silhouettes, 1950.

BRYANT, KEITH L., JR. *History of the Atchison, Topeka & Santa Fe Railway.* Lincoln: University of Nebraska Press, 1974.

BURGESS, OPIE R. *Bisbee Not So Long Ago.* San Antonio: The Naylor Co., 1964.

BYRKIT, JAMES W. *Forging the Copper Collar: Arizona's Labor-Management Wars, 1901–1921*. Tucson: University of Arizona Press, 1982.

CHISHOLM, JOE. *Brewery Gulch: Frontier Days of Old Arizona*. San Antonio: Naylor Publishers, 1949.

CLELAND, ROBERT GLASS. *History of Phelps Dodge, 1834–1950*. New York: Knopf, 1952.

COSULICH, BERNICE. *Tucson*. Tucson: Arizona Silhouettes, 1953.

COWLES, RAYMOND B., AND ELNA S. BAKKER. *Desert Journal*. Berkeley: University of California Press, 1977.

COX, A. M. "History of Bisbee, 1877–1937." Unpublished Master's thesis, Department of History, University of Arizona, 1938.

CREMONY, JOHN C. *Life among the Apaches*. Lincoln: University of Nebraska Press, 1983.

CURTIN, L.S.M. *By the Prophet of the Earth: Ethnobotany of the Pima*. Tucson: University of Arizona Press, 1984.

DAVIS, GOODE P. *Man and Wildlife in Arizona: The Pre-settlement Era, 1823–1864*. Master's thesis, University of Arizona, Tucson, 1973.

DEVOTO, BERNARD. *The Year of Decision, 1846*. Boston: Little Brown and Co., 1943.

DOBIE, J. FRANK. *The Voice of the Coyote*. Lincoln: University of Nebraska Press, 1961.

ECCLESTON, ROBERT. *Overland to California on the Southwestern Trail, 1849*. Berkeley: University of California Press, 1950.

EPLER, WILLIAM C. *Bisbee Vignettes*. Bisbee: Copper Queen Pub. Co., 1978.

EWING, RAY. *Souvenir of Bisbee by a Re-cycled Miner*. (Privately printed, n.d.)

FAULK, ODIE B. *Tombstone: Myth and Reality*. New York: Oxford University Press, 1972.

FIREMAN, BERT M. *Arizona: Historic Land*. New York: Knopf, 1982.

FRADKIN, PHILIP. *A River No More: The Colorado River and the West*. New York: Knopf, 1981.

FRANCAVIGLIA, RICHARD V. "Copper Mining and Landscape Evolution: A Century of Change in Arizona's Warren Mining District." *The Journal of Arizona History* (Autumn 1982).

FULTON, RICHARD. "Millville-Charleston, Cochise County, 1879–1889." *The Journal of Arizona History* (Spring 1966).

FULTON, RICHARD, AND CONRAD J. BAHRE. "Charleston Arizona: A Documentary Reconstruction." *Arizona and the West*, vol. 9, no. 1 (1967).

GOLDER, FRANK ALFRED. *The March of the Mormon Battalion from Council Bluffs to California.* (Taken from "The Journal of Henry Standage.") New York: The Century Co., 1928.

GRANGER, BYRD. *Arizona's Names.* Tucson: Falconer Pub. Co., 1983.

HARING, C. H. *The Spanish Empire in America.* New York: Oxford University Press, 1947.

HAURY, EMIL W. *The Hohokam: Desert Farmers and Craftsmen.* Tucson: University of Arizona Press, 1976.

HOLLON, WILLIAM EUGENE. *The Great American Desert Then and Now.* Lincoln: The University of Nebraska Press, 1975.

HOUSTON, ROBERT. *Bisbee 17.* New York: Pantheon Books, 1979.

HUGHES, A. DANIEL. *South from Tombstone.* London: Methuen Pub., 1938.

JAEGER, EDMUND C. *Desert Wildlife.* Stanford: Stanford University Press, 1961.

KRUTCH, JOSEPH WOOD. *The Desert Year.* New York: Viking Press, 1963.

————. *The Voice of the Desert.* New York: Wm. Sloan Assoc., 1969.

LECKIE, WILLIAM H. *The Buffalo Soldiers: A Narrative of the Negro Cavalry in the West.* Norman: University of Oklahoma Press, 1967.

LEYDET, FRANÇOIS. *The Coyote: Defiant Songdog of the West.* San Francisco: Chronicle Books, 1977.

LOCKWOOD, FRANK C., AND DONALD W. PAGE. *Tucson—the Old Pueblo.* The Manufacturing Stationers, 1930.

MCCLINTOCK, JAMES H. *Mormon Settlement in Arizona.* Tucson: University of Arizona Press, 1985.

MCGINNIES, WILLIAM G. *Discovering the Desert.* Tucson: University of Arizona Press, 1981.

MCPHEE, JOHN. *Basin and Range.* New York: Farrar, Straus, Giroux, 1980.

MARSHALL, JAMES L. *Santa Fe, the Railroad that Built an Empire*. New York: Random House, 1945.

MURBARGER, NELL. *Ghosts of the Adobe Walls*. Los Angeles: Westernlore Press, 1964.

MYERS, JOHN MYERS. *The Last Chance: Tombstone's Early Years*. New York: E.P. Dutton, 1950.

NABHAN, GARY. *Gathering the Desert*. Tucson: University of Arizona Press, 1985.

OFFICER, JAMES E. *Hispanic Arizona, 1536–1856*. Tucson: University of Arizona Press, 1987.

O'KANE, WALTER COLLINS. *The Intimate Desert*. Tucson: University of Arizona Press. 1969.

O'NEAL, BILL. *The Arizona Rangers*. Austin: Eakin Press, 1987.

PARKES, HENRY BAMFORD. *A History of Mexico*. Boston: Houghton-Mifflin Co., 1969.

Phelps Dodge: A Copper Centennial 1881–1981. A supplement to *Pay Dirt* (Summer 1981).

POWELL, JOHN WESLEY. *Report on the Lands of the Arid Region of the United States*. Harvard: Harvard Common Press, 1983.

POWELL, LAWRENCE CLARK. *Arizona: A History*. New York: W. W. Norton, 1976.

READY, ALMA. *Open Range and Hidden Silver: Arizona's Santa Cruz County*. Nogales: Alto Press, 1973.

REISNER, MARC. *Cadillac Desert, the American West and Its Disappearing Water*. New York: Viking Press, 1986.

RICHTER, CONRAD. *Tacey Cromwell*. Albuquerque: University of New Mexico Press, 1974.

RIEGEL, ROBERT EDGAR. *The Story of the Western Railroads from 1852 through the Reign of the Giants*. Lincoln: University of Nebraska Press, 1964.

RYDEN, HOPE. *God's Dog: A Celebration of the North American Coyote*. New York: Coward, McCann, 1975.

SHERMAN, JAMES E., AND BARBARA H. SHERMAN. *Ghost Towns of Arizona*. Norman: University of Oklahoma Press, 1969.

SMITH, HENRY NASH. *Virgin Land: The American West as Symbol & Myth.* Cambridge: Harvard University Press, 1976.

SONNICHSEN, C. L. *Colonel Greene and the Copper Skyrocket.* Tucson: University of Arizona Press, 1976.

SOWLS, LYLE K. *The Peccaries.* Tucson: University of Arizona Press, 1984.

SPOONER, JANE. *Tubac, Town of 9 Lives.* Tucson: Paragon Press, 1962.

STEGNER, WALLACE. *Beyond the Hundredth Meridian.* Lincoln: University of Nebraska Press, 1982.

————. *The Gathering of Zion: The Story of the Mormon Trail.* New York: McGraw-Hill, 1964.

TILLER, KERRY C.S. "Charleston Townsite Revisited." *Journal of Arizona History* (Autumn 1982).

TRAYWICK, BEN T. *Thunder Fort: the Story of Fort Huachuca.* Tombstone: 1972.

TREADWAY, WILLIAM E. *Cyrus K. Holliday: A Documentary Biography.* Topeka: Kansas State Historical Society, 1979.

TURNER, HENRY SMITH. *The Original Journals of Henry Smith Turner: With Stephen Watts Kearny to New Mexico and California, 1846–1847.* Norman: University of Oklahoma Press.

TYLER, DANIEL. *A Concise History of the Mormon Battalion in the Mexican War.* Glorieta: Rio Grande Press, 1969.

VARNEY, PHILIP. *Arizona's Best Ghost Towns.* Flagstaff: Northland Press, 1980.

VAUGHAN, TOM. "Bisbee's Transition Years: 1899–1918." *The Cochise Quarterly,* vol. 14, no. 4 (Winter 1984).

WAGONER, JAY J. *Arizona Territory 1863–1912: A Political History.* Tucson: University of Arizona Press, 1970.

————. *Early Arizona: Prehistory to the Civil War.* Tucson: University of Arizona Press, 1975.

WATERS, LAWRENCE LESLIE. *Steel Trails to Santa Fe.* Lawrence: University of Kansas Press, 1950.

WEBER, DAVID J. *The Mexican Frontier, 1821–1846: The American Southwest under Mexico.* Albuquerque: University of New Mexico Press, 1982.

WENTWORTH, FRANK. *Bisbee with a Big "B."* Iowa City: Mercer Printing Co., 1938.

WILEY, PETER, AND ROBERT GOTTLIEB. *Empires in the Sun: The Rise of the New American West.* Tucson: University of Arizona Press, 1982.

WORSTER, DONALD. *Rivers of Empire: Water, Aridity, and the Growth of the American West.* New York: Pantheon Books, 1985.

ZWINGER, ANN. *The Mysterious Lands.* New York: E.P. Dutton, 1989.

Richard Shelton is the author of nine books of poetry including *The Bus to Veracruz* (1978) and *Selected Poems: 1969–1981* (1982). His poems and prose pieces have appeared in more than two hundred magazines and journals including *The New Yorker, The Atlantic, The Paris Review,* and *The Antioch Review.* They have been translated into Spanish, French, Swedish, Polish, and Japanese.

In 1974, Shelton established, under the auspices of the Arizona Commission of the Arts, a Writer's Workshop at the Arizona State Prison. Eight books of poetry and prose by the men in that workshop have been published. Shelton is currently directing a Writer's Workshop in the Cimarron Unit of the Arizona State Prison near Tucson.

Shelton has lived in Southern Arizona since 1956 and is Regents Professor of English at the University of Arizona, Tucson. *Going Back to Bisbee* is his first major book of nonfiction.